THE RISE OF

THE CREATIVE CLASS

THE RISE OF
THE CREATIVE CLASS

And How It's Transforming

Work, Leisure, Community

and Everyday Life

RICHARD FLORIDA

BASIC
BOOKS

A Member of the Perseus Books Group

Published by Basic Books,
A Member of the Perseus Books Group

The performance piece "Perfect Pitch," © 2000 by Steve Tomlinson, is used by permission of the author.

Design by Jane Raese

A CIP catalog record for this book is available from the Library of Congress.
ISBN 0-465-02476-9

The paper used in this publication meets the requirements of the American National Standard for Permanence of Paper for Printed Library Materials Z39.48-1984.

DHSB   02 03 04 05   10 9 8 7 6 5 4

TO LOUIS AND ELEANOR FLORIDA

who provided the inspiration for this book
and the larger intellectual journey it reflects.
They taught me much more about the
importance of human creativity and community
than they might have imagined.

CONTENTS

PREFACE

This book describes the emergence of a new social class. If you are a scientist or engineer, an architect or designer, a writer, artist or musician, or if you use your creativity as a key factor in your work in business, education, health care, law or some other profession, you are a member. With 38 million members, more than 30 percent of the nation's workforce, the Creative Class has shaped and will continue to shape deep and profound shifts in the ways we work, in our values and desires, and in the very fabric of our everyday lives.

As with other classes, the defining basis of this new class is economic. Just as the feudal aristocracy derived its power and identity from its hereditary control of land and people, and the bourgeoisie from its members' roles as merchants and factory owners, the Creative Class derives its identity from its members' roles as purveyors of creativity. Because creativity is the driving force of economic growth, in terms of influence the Creative Class has become the dominant class in society. Only by understanding the rise of this new class and its values can we begin to understand the sweeping and seemingly disjointed changes in our society and begin to shape our future more intelligently.

Like most books, this one did not spring to life fully formed. Rather, my ideas evolved gradually from things I saw and heard that seemed to be at odds with conventional wisdom. In my work on regional economic development, I try to identify the factors that make some cities and regions grow and prosper, while others lag behind. One of the oldest pieces of conventional wisdom in this field says the key to economic growth is attracting and retaining companies—the bigger the company, the better—because companies create jobs and people go where the jobs are. During the 1980s and 1990s, many cities in the United States and around the world tried to turn themselves into the next "Silicon Somewhere" by building high-tech office parks or starting up venture capital funds. The game plan was to nourish high-tech startup companies or, in its cruder variants, to lure them from other cities. But it quickly became clear that this wasn't working.

I saw this firsthand in the mid-1990s with Lycos, a Carnegie Mellon spin-off company. The Lycos technology, which you have probably used to search the Internet, was developed in Pittsburgh. But the company eventually moved its operations to Boston to gain access to a deep pool of skilled managers, technologists and business people. These departures were happening repeatedly, in Pittsburgh and elsewhere. All too often the technologies, the companies and even the venture capital dollars flowed out of town to places that had a bigger and better stock of talented and creative people. In a curious reversal, instead of people moving to jobs, I was finding that companies were moving to or forming in places that had the skilled *people.*

Why was this happening? This was the basic puzzle that ultimately led to this book. Frustrated by the limits of the conventional wisdom and even more by how economic development was actually being practiced, I began asking people how they chose where to live and work. It quickly became clear to me that people were not slavishly following jobs to places. Their location choices were based to a large degree on their lifestyle interests and these, I found, went well beyond the standard quality-of-life amenities that most experts thought were important.

Then came the real stunner. In 1998 I met Gary Gates, then a doctoral student at Carnegie Mellon. While I had been studying the location decisions of high-tech industries and talented people, Gates had been exploring the location patterns of gay people. My list of the country's high-tech hotspots looked an awful lot like his list of the places with the highest concentrations of gay people. When we compared the two lists with greater statistical rigor, his Gay Index turned out to correlate very strongly with my measures of high-tech growth. Other measures I came up with, like the Bohemian Index—a measure of the density of artists, writers and performers in a region—produced similar results. My conclusion was that rather than being driven exclusively by companies, economic growth was occurring in places that were tolerant, diverse and open to creativity—because these were places where creative people of *all* types wanted to live. While some in academe were taken aback by my findings, I was amazed by how quickly city and regional leaders began to use my measures and indicators to shape their development strategies.

As I delved more deeply into the research, I came to realize that something even bigger was going on. Though most experts continued to point to technology as the driving force of broad social change, I became convinced that the truly fundamental changes of our time had to do with subtler alterations in the way we live and work—gradually accumulating shifts in our workplaces, leisure activities, communities and everyday lives. Everything from the kinds of lifestyles we seek to the ways in which we schedule our time and relate to others was changing. And yes, there was a common thread: The role of creativity as the fundamental source of economic growth and the rise of the new Creative Class.

Despite the giddy economic euphoria so prevalent in the late 1990s, it became increasingly evident to me that the emerging Creative Economy was a dynamic and turbulent system—exciting and liberating in some ways, divisive and stressful in others. My thinking was reinforced by earth-shaking events that occurred while I was writing this book. First came the bursting of the stock-market bubble, the rapid fall of technology stocks and the subsequent recession. This put an end to the naive optimism of the so-called New Economy and to the always unfounded notion that new technology is a magic elixir that will make us rich, eliminate our economic problems and cure pressing social ills. The NASDAQ's plummet was an early signal that it was time for people to get serious.

Then came the tragic events of September 11, 2001. For me and for many others, the stunning attack on the United States was a potent wake-up call. In addition to showing us how vulnerable we are, it brought home the message that too many of us, particularly the members of the Creative Class, had been living in a world of our own concerns—selfishly pursuing narrow goals with little regard for others or for broader social issues. We had grown complacent, even aimless, but also discontent at having become so.

Here I found myself confronting a great paradox. Even as I was chronicling their rise and impact, it struck me that the members of the Creative Class do not see themselves as a *class*—a coherent group of people with common traits and concerns. Emerging classes in previous times of great transition had pulled together to forge new social mechanisms and steer their societies. But not this group. We thus find ourselves in the puzzling situation of having the dominant class in America—whose members occupy the power centers of industry, media and government, as well as the arts and popular culture—virtually unaware of its own existence and thus unable to consciously influence the course of the society it largely leads.

The Creative Class has the power, talent and numbers to play a big role in reshaping our world. Its members—in fact all of society—now have the opportunity to turn their introspection and soul-searching into real energy for broader renewal and transformation. History shows that enduring social change occurs not during economic boom times, like the 1920s or 1990s, but in periods of crisis and questioning such as the 1930s—and today. The task before us is to build new forms of social cohesion appropriate to the new Creative Age—the old forms don't work, because they no longer fit the people we've become—and from there, to pursue a collective vision of a better and more prosperous future for all.

This is easier said than done. To build true social cohesion, the members of the Creative Class will need to offer those in other classes a tangible vision of ways to improve their own lives, either by becoming part of the Creative Economy or, at the very least, by reaping some of its rewards. If the Creative Class does not commit itself to this effort, the growing social and economic divides in our society will only worsen, and I fear that we will find ourselves living perpetually uneasy lives at the top of an unhappy heap.

It's time for the Creative Class to grow up and take responsibility. But first, we must understand who we are.

Richard Florida
Pittsburgh, Pennsylvania
February 2002

CHAPTER 1

The Transformation of Everyday Life

Something's happening here but
you don't know what it is, do you, Mr. Jones?
—*Bob Dylan*

H ere's a thought experiment. Take a typical man on the street from the year 1900 and drop him into the 1950s. Then take someone from the 1950s and move him Austin Powers-style into the present day. Who would experience the greater change?

At first glance the answer seems obvious. Thrust forward into the 1950s, a person from the turn of the twentieth century would be awestruck by a world filled with baffling technological wonders. In place of horse-drawn carriages, he would see streets and highways jammed with cars, trucks and buses. In the cities, immense skyscrapers would line the horizon, and mammoth bridges would span rivers and inlets where once only ferries could cross. Flying machines would soar overhead, carrying people across the continent or the oceans in a matter of hours rather than days. At home, our 1900-to-1950s time-traveler would grope his way through a strange new environment filled with appliances powered by electricity: radios and televisions emanating musical sounds and even human images, refrigerators to keep things cold, washing machines to clean his clothes automatically, and much more. A massive new super market would replace daily trips to the market with an array of technologically enhanced foods, such as instant coffee or frozen vegetables to put into the refrigerator. Life itself would be dramatically extended. Many once-fatal ailments could be prevented with an injection or cured with a pill. The newness of this time-traveler's physical surroundings—the speed and power of everyday machines—would be profoundly disorienting.

1

On the other hand, someone from the 1950s would have little trouble navigating the physical landscape of today. Although we like to think ours is the age of boundless technological wonders, our second time-traveler would find himself in a world not all that different from the one he left. He would still drive a car to work. If he took the train, it would likely be on the same line leaving from the same station. He could probably board an airplane at the same airport. He might still live in a suburban house, though a bigger one. Television would have more channels, but it would basically be the same, and he could still catch some of his favorite 1950s shows on reruns. He would know how, or quickly learn how, to operate most household appliances—even the personal computer, with its familiar QWERTY keyboard. In fact with just a few exceptions, such as the PC, the Internet, CD and DVD players, the cash machine and a wireless phone he could carry with him, he would be familiar with almost all current-day technology. Perhaps disappointed by the pace of progress, he might ask: "Why haven't we conquered outer space?" or "Where are all the robots?"

On the basis of big, obvious technological changes alone, surely the 1900-to-1950s traveler would experience the greater shift, while the other might easily conclude that we'd spent the second half of the twentieth century doing little more than tweaking the great waves of the first half.[1]

But the longer they stayed in their new homes, the more each time-traveler would become aware of subtler dimensions of change. Once the glare of technology had dimmed, each would begin to notice their respective society's changed norms and values, and the ways in which everyday people live and work. And here the tables would be turned. In terms of adjusting to the social structures and the rhythms and patterns of daily life, our second time-traveler would be much more disoriented.

Someone from the early 1900s would find the social world of the 1950s remarkably similar to his own. If he worked in a factory, he might find much the same divisions of labor, the same hierarchical systems of control. If he worked in an office, he would be immersed in the same bureaucracy, the same climb up the corporate ladder. He would come to work at 8 or 9 each morning and leave promptly at 5, his life neatly segmented into compartments of home and work. He would wear a suit and tie. Most of his business associates would be white and male. Their values and office politics would hardly have changed. He would seldom see women in the workplace, except as secretaries, and almost never interact professionally with someone of another race. He would marry young, have children quickly thereafter, stay married to the same person and probably work for the same company for the rest of his life. In his leisure time, he'd find that movies and TV had largely superseded live stage shows, but otherwise his recreational activities would be much the same as they were in 1900: taking in a baseball game or a boxing match, maybe playing a round of golf. He would join the clubs and civic groups befitting his socioeconomic class, observe the same social distinctions, and fully expect his children to do likewise. The tempo of his life would be structured by the values and norms of organizations. He would find himself living the life of the "company man" so aptly chronicled by writers from Sinclair Lewis and John Kenneth Galbraith to William Whyte and C. Wright Mills.[2]

Our second time-traveler, however, would be quite unnerved by the dizzying social and cultural changes that had accumulated between the 1950s and today. At work he would find a new dress code, a new schedule, and new rules. He would see office workers dressed like folks relaxing on the weekend, in jeans and open-necked shirts, and be shocked to learn they occupy positions of authority. People at the office would seemingly come and go as they pleased. The younger ones might sport bizarre piercings and tattoos. Women and even nonwhites would be managers. Individuality and self-expression would be valued over conformity to organizational norms—and yet these people would seem strangely puritanical to this time-traveler. His ethnic jokes would fall embarrassingly flat. His smoking would get him banished to the parking lot, and his two-martini lunches would raise genuine concern. Attitudes and expressions he had never thought about would cause repeated offense. He would continually suffer the painful feeling of not knowing how to behave.

Out on the street, this time-traveler would see different ethnic groups in greater numbers than he ever could have imagined—Asian-, Indian-, and Latin-Americans and others—all mingling in ways he found strange and perhaps inappropriate. There would be mixed-race couples, and same-sex couples carrying the upbeat-sounding moniker "gay." While some of these people would be acting in familiar ways—a woman shopping while pushing a stroller, an office worker having lunch at a counter—others, such as grown men clad in form-fitting gear whizzing by on high-tech bicycles, or women on strange new roller skates with their torsos covered only by "brassieres"—would appear to be engaged in alien activities.

People would seem to be always working and yet never working when they were supposed to. They would strike him as lazy and yet obsessed with exercise. They would seem career-conscious yet fickle—doesn't anybody stay with the company more than three years?—and caring yet anti-social: What happened to the ladies' clubs, Moose Lodges and bowling leagues? While the physical surroundings would be relatively familiar, the *feel* of the place would be bewilderingly different.

Thus, although the first time-traveler had to adjust to some drastic technological changes, it is the second who experiences the deeper, more pervasive transformation. It is the second who has been thrust into a time when lifestyles and worldviews are most assuredly changing—a time when the old order has broken down, when flux and uncertainty themselves seem to be part of the everyday norm.

The Force Behind the Shift

What caused this transformation? What happened between the 1950s and today that did not happen in the earlier period? Scholars and pundits have floated many theories, along with a range of opinions on whether the changes are good or bad. Some bemoan the passing of traditional social and cultural forms, while others point to a rosy future based largely on new technology. Yet on one point most of them agree. Most tend to see the transformation as something that's being done to us unwittingly. Some complain that certain factions of society have imposed their values on the rest of us; others say that our own inventions are turning around to re-shape us. They're wrong.

Society is changing in large measure because we want it to. Moreover it is changing neither in random chaotic ways nor in some mysterious collective-unconscious way, but in ways that are perfectly sensible and rational. The logic behind the transformation has been unclear to this point because the transformation is still in progress. But lately a number of diverse and seemingly unconnected threads are starting to come together. The deeper pattern, the force behind the shift, can now be discerned.

That driving force is the rise of human creativity as the key factor in our economy and society. Both at work and in other spheres of our lives, we value creativity more highly than ever, and cultivate it more intensely. The creative impulse—the attribute that distinguishes us, as humans, from other species—is now being let loose on an unprecedented scale. The purpose of this book is to examine how and why this is so, and to trace its effects as they ripple through our world.

Consider first the realm of economics. Many say that we now live in an "information" economy or a "knowledge" economy. But what's more fundamentally true is that we now have an economy powered by human creativity. Creativity—"the ability to create meaningful new forms," as Webster's dictionary puts it—is now the *decisive* source of competitive advantage. In virtually every industry, from automobiles to fashion, food products, and information technology itself, the winners in the long run are those who can create and keep creating. This has always been true, from the days of the Agricultural Revolution to the Industrial Revolution. But in the past few decades we've come to recognize it clearly and act upon it systematically.

Creativity is multidimensional and comes in many mutually reinforcing forms. It is a mistake to think, as many do, that creativity can be reduced to the creation of new blockbuster inventions, new products and new firms. In today's economy creativity is pervasive and ongoing: We constantly revise and enhance every product, process and activity imaginable, and fit them together in new ways. Moreover, technological and economic creativity are nurtured by and interact with artistic and cultural creativity. This kind of interplay is evident in the rise of whole new industries from computer graphics to digital music and animation. Creativity also requires a social and economic environment that can nurture its many forms. Max Weber said long ago that the Protestant ethic provided the underlying spirit of thrift, hard work and efficiency that motivated the rise of early capitalism. In similar fashion, the shared commitment to the creative spirit in its many, varied manifestations underpins the new creative ethos that powers our age.

Thus creativity has come to be the most highly prized commodity in our economy—and yet it is not a "commodity." Creativity comes from people. And while people can be hired and fired, their creative capacity cannot be bought and sold, or turned on and off at will. This is why, for instance, we see the emergence of a new order in the workplace. Hiring for diversity, once a matter of legal compliance, has become a matter of economic survival because creativity comes in all colors, genders and personal preferences. Schedules, rules and dress codes have become more flexible to cater to how the creative process works. Creativity must be motivated and nurtured in a multitude of ways, by employers, by people themselves and by the communities where they locate. Small wonder that we find the creative ethos bleeding out from the sphere of work to infuse every corner of our lives.

At the same time, entirely new forms of economic infrastructure, such as systematic spending on research and development, the high-tech startup company and an extensive system of venture finance, have evolved to support creativity and mobilize creative people around promising ideas and products. Capitalism has also expanded its reach to capture the talents of heretofore excluded groups of eccentrics and nonconformists. In doing so, it has pulled off yet another astonishing mutation: taking people who would once have been viewed as bizarre mavericks operating at the bohemian fringe and setting them at the very heart of the process of innovation and economic growth. These changes in the economy and in the workplace have in turn helped to propagate and legitimize similar changes in society at large. The creative individual is no longer viewed as an iconoclast. He—or she—is the new mainstream.

In tracing economic shifts, I often say that our economy is moving from an older corporate-centered system defined by large companies to a more people-driven one. This view should not be confused with the unfounded and silly notion that big companies are dying off. Nor do I buy the fantasy of an economy organized around small enterprises and independent "free agents."[3] Companies, including very big ones, obviously still exist, are still influential and probably always will be. I simply mean to stress that as the fundamental source of creativity, people are the critical resource of the new age. This has far-reaching effects—for instance, on our economic and social geography and the nature of our communities.

It's often been said that in this age of high technology, "geography is dead" and place doesn't matter any more.[4] Nothing could be further from the truth: Witness how high-tech firms themselves concentrate in specific places like the San Francisco Bay Area or Austin or Seattle. Place has become the central organizing unit of our time, taking on many of the functions that used to be played by firms and other organizations. Corporations have historically played a key economic role in matching people to jobs, particularly given the long-term employment system of the post–World War II era. But today corporations are far less committed to their employees and people change jobs frequently, making the employment contract more contingent. In this environment, it is geographic place rather than the corporation that provides the organizational matrix for matching people and jobs. Access to talented and creative people is to modern business what access to coal and iron ore was to steelmaking. It determines where companies will choose to locate and grow, and this in turn changes the ways cities must compete. As Hewlett-Packard CEO Carley Fiorina once told this nation's governors: "Keep your tax incentives and highway interchanges; we will go where the highly skilled people are."[5]

Creative people, in turn, don't just cluster where the jobs are. They cluster in places that are centers of creativity and also where they like to live. From classical Athens and Rome, to the Florence of the Medici and Elizabethan London, to Greenwich Village and the San Francisco Bay Area, creativity has always gravitated to specific locations. As the great urbanist Jane Jacobs pointed out long ago, successful places are multidimensional and diverse—they don't just cater to a single industry or a single demographic group; they are full of stimulation and creativity interplay.[6] In my consulting work, I often tell business and political leaders that places need a people climate—or a creativity climate—as well as a business climate. Cities like Seattle, Austin, Toronto and Dublin recognize the multidimensional nature of this transformation and are striving to become broadly creative communities, not just centers of technological innovation and high-tech industry. If places like Buffalo, Grand Rapids, Memphis and Louisville do not follow suit, they will be hard-pressed to survive.

Our fundamental social forms are shifting as well, driven by forces traceable to the creative ethos. In virtually every aspect of life, weak ties have replaced the stronger bonds that once gave structure to society. Rather than live in one town for decades, we now move about. Instead of communities defined by close associations and deep commitments to family, friends and organizations, we seek places where we can make friends and acquaintances easily and live quasi-anonymous lives. The decline in the strength of our ties to people and institutions is a product of the increasing number of ties we have. As a retired industrialist who was the head of a technology transfer center in Ottawa, Canada, told me: "My father grew up in a small town and worked for the same company. He knew the same fourteen people in his entire life. I meet more people than that in any given day."[7] Modern life is increasingly defined by contingent commitments. We progress from job to job with amazingly little concern or effort. Where people once found themselves bound together by social institutions and formed their identities in groups, a fundamental characteristic of life today is that we strive to create our own identities.[8] It is this creation and re-creation of the self, often in ways that reflect our creativity, that is a key feature of the creative ethos.

In this new world, it is no longer the organizations we work for, churches, neighborhoods or even family ties that define us. Instead, we do this ourselves, defining our identities along the varied dimensions of our creativity. Other aspects of our lives—what we consume, new forms of leisure and recreation, efforts at community-building—then organize themselves around this process of identity creation.

Furthermore, when we think about group identity in this new world, we must rethink our notions of class. We often tend to classify people on the basis of their consumption habits or lifestyle choices, or, more crudely, by their income level. For instance, we often equate middle income with middle class. Though I view these things as significant markers of class, they are not its primary determinants. A *class* is a cluster of people who have common interests and tend to think, feel and behave similarly, but these similarities are fundamentally determined by economic function—by the kind of work they do for a living. All the other distinctions follow from that. And a key fact of our age is that more of us than ever are doing creative work for a living.

The New Class

The economic need for creativity has registered itself in the rise of a new class, which I call the Creative Class. Some *38 million* Americans, 30 percent of all employed people, belong to this new class. I define the core of the Creative Class to include people in science and engineering, architecture and design, education, arts, music and entertainment, whose economic function is to create new ideas, new technology and/or new creative content. Around the core, the Creative Class also includes a broader group of *creative professionals* in business and finance, law, health care and related fields. These people engage in complex problem solving that involves a great deal of independent judgment and requires high levels of education or human capital. In addition, all members of the Creative Class— whether they are artists or engineers, musicians or computer scientists, writers or entrepreneurs—share a common creative ethos that values creativity, individuality, difference and merit. For the members of the Creative Class, every aspect and every manifestation of creativity—technological, cultural and economic—is interlinked and inseparable.

The key difference between the Creative Class and other classes lies in what they are primarily paid to do. Those in the Working Class and the Service Class are primarily paid to execute according to plan, while those in the Creative Class are primarily paid to create and have considerably more autonomy and flexibility than the other two classes to do so. There are gray areas and boundary issues in my scheme of things, to be sure. And while some may quibble with my definition of the Creative Class and the numerical estimates that are based on it, I believe it has a good deal more precision than existing, more amorphous definitions of knowledge workers, symbolic analysts or professional and technical workers.

The class structure of the United States and other advanced nations has been the subject of great debate for well over a century. For a host of writers in the 1800s and 1900s, the big story was the rise, and then the decline, of the Working Class.[9] For writers like Daniel Bell and others in the middle to later 1900s, a second big story was the rise of a postindustrial society in which many of us shifted from making goods to delivering services.[10] The big story unfolding now—one that has been unfolding for some time—is the rise of the Creative Class, the great emerging class of our time.

The reason modern society feels so different to our time-traveler is the staggering growth of this class. Over the twentieth century, the Creative Class grew from roughly 3 million workers to its current size, a tenfold-plus increase; since 1980 alone it has more than doubled. Roughly 15 million Americans, more than 12 percent of the workforce, compose the Super-Creative Core of this new class. The Creative Class in the United States today is larger than the traditional Working Class—for instance those who work in manufacturing, construction and transportation industries.

The long sweep of the twentieth century has seen the rise and fall of the Working Class, which peaked at roughly 40 percent of the U.S. workforce between 1920 and 1950 before beginning its long slide to roughly a quarter of the workforce today. The Service Class, which includes fields such as personal care, food service and clerical work, has grown steadily over the same period, doubling from roughly 16 to 30 percent of the workforce between 1900 and 1950 before climbing to more than 45 percent by 1980. With some 55 million members today it is the largest class in terms of sheer numbers.

Although the Creative Class remains somewhat smaller than the Service Class, its crucial economic role makes it the most influential. The Creative Class is also considerably larger than the class of "organization men" described in William Whyte's 1956 book. Like Whyte's managerial class, which "set the American temper" in the 1950s, the Creative Class is the norm-setting class of our time. But its norms are very different: Individuality, self-expression and openness to difference are favored over the homogeneity, conformity and "fitting in" that defined the organizational age. Furthermore, the Creative Class is dominant in terms of wealth and income, with its members earning nearly twice as much on average as members of the other two classes.

But the sacrifices we will make for money are very different from those once made by Whyte's organization men. Very few of us work for the same large company or organization for life, and we are far less likely to pin our identity or sense of self-worth on whom we work for. We balance financial considerations against the ability to be ourselves, set our own schedules, do challenging work and live in communities that reflect our values and priorities. According to one large-scale survey of people who work in information technology fields—a relatively conservative subgroup of the Creative Class—challenge and responsibility, the ability to work a flexible schedule and a secure and stable work environment all rank ahead of money as the key elements of what people value in their jobs. The upheaval in our private lives is epitomized by one well-publicized statistic: Fewer than one-quarter of all Americans (23.5 percent) accounted for by the 2000 Census lived in a "conventional" nuclear family, down from 45 percent in 1960.[11] These profound changes are not, as commonly portrayed, signs of the reckless self-indulgence of a spoiled people. They are undergirded by a simple economic rationality. We live by our creativity, so we try to take care of it and seek environments that allow it to flourish— much as the blacksmith once cared for his forge, and farmers took care of the oxen that drove their plows.

Creativity in the world of work is not limited to members of the Creative Class. Factory workers and even the lowest-end service workers always have been creative in certain valuable ways. Also, the creative content of many working-class and service-class jobs is growing—a prime example being the continuous-improvement programs on many factory floors, which call on line workers to contribute ideas as well as their physical labor. On the basis of these trends, I expect that the Creative Class, which is still emergent, will continue to grow in coming decades, as more traditional economic functions are transformed into Creative Class occupations. And, as the last chapter of this book will argue, I strongly believe that the key to improving the lot of underpaid, underemployed and disadvantaged people lies not in social welfare programs or low-end make-work jobs—nor in somehow bringing back the factory jobs of the past—but rather in tapping the creativity of these people, paying them appropriately for it and integrating them fully into the Creative Economy.

Not all is rosy in this emerging mainstream of the Creative Age. With no big company to provide security, we bear much more risk than the corporate and working classes of the organizational age did. We experience and often create high levels of mental and emotional stress, at work and at home. We crave flexibility but have less time to pursue the things we truly desire. The technologies that were supposed to liberate us from work have invaded our lives. And though the Creative Class does not have a monopoly on creativity, it certainly has cornered the lion's share of the market for it—while segmenting both the labor market and society in new ways. Significant fault lines are appearing as the values, attitudes and aspirations of the Creative Class inexorably clash with those of the other established classes. Our society may well be splitting into two or three separate types of economies, cultures and communities, with deepening divides of education, occupation and geographic location.

The nation's geographic center of gravity has shifted away from traditional industrial regions toward new axes of creativity and innovation. The Creative Class is strongly oriented to large cities and regions that offer a variety of economic opportunities, a stimulating environment and amenities for every possible lifestyle. The nation's leading creative centers include major East Coast regions like Washington, D.C., Boston and the greater New York region, and leading high-tech centers like the San Francisco Bay Area, Seattle and Austin. These places offer something for everyone— vibrant urban districts, abundant natural amenities and comfortable suburban "nerdistans" for techies so inclined.[12] But large regions do not have an exclusive hold on the members of this new class. Smaller places like Boulder, Colorado and Santa Fe, New Mexico boast significant concentrations of the Creative Class, as do less obvious places like Gainesville, Florida; Provo, Utah; and Huntsville, Alabama.

This remaking of our economic geography is intimately tied to class identity. Today's professionals see themselves as members of a broad creative force, not as corporate officers or organization men. Thus they gravitate to stimulating creative environments—to places that offer not only opportunities and amenities, but openness to diversity, where they feel they can express themselves and validate their identities. They are fleeing older working-class strongholds and in many cases avoiding newer but conservative Sunbelt cities—increasingly opting out of places where tradition is more valued and where the social norms of the organizational age still prevail. In fact, many of these places are being almost entirely abandoned by the Creative Class.

One of the most significant fault lines of our age is the growing geographic segregation of the Creative Class and the other classes. The geographic trends I will describe in this book do *not* favor the tightly knit old-style communities that are so often celebrated in our songs, stories and sentimental TV commercials. Moreover, a number of serious social commentators in recent years have urged us to recultivate and rebuild the old forms of "social capital" found in these communities. Such efforts are fruitless, since they fly in the face of today's economic realities. A central task ahead is developing new forms of social cohesion appropriate to the Creative Age.

The Transformation of Everyday Life

Economic shifts are thus altering the structure of everyday life. The rise and decline of the New Economy did not cause these changes, though it did help push them to the surface and make them more noticeable. In a deeper and more pervasive way, the September 11, 2001, tragedy and subsequent terrorist threats have caused Americans, particularly those in the Creative Class, to ask sobering questions about what really matters in our lives. What we are witnessing in America and across the world extends far beyond high-tech industry or any so-called New Economy: It is the emergence of a new society and a new culture—indeed a whole new way of life. It is these shifts that will prove to be the most enduring developments of our time. And they thrust hard questions upon us. For now that forces have been unleashed that allow us to pursue our desires, the question for each of us becomes: What do we really want?

I have spent the past several years conducting research on the changing attitudes and desires of the Creative Class and the other classes, as well as the key factors that have brought new attitudes to the fore. I have interviewed and conducted focus groups with people across the United States and elsewhere. I have visited companies and communities of all kinds in my attempts to determine what is going on. And with teams of colleagues and graduate students, I delved deeply into statistical correlations to develop more substantial evidence of the fundamental trends and patterns. Based on my research, I would describe several dimensions of the transformation that I see, corresponding to several basic categories of human existence: work, lifestyle, time and community. In each case, the changes reflect a society in which the creative ethos is on the rise.

The No-Collar Workplace

Artists, musicians, professors and scientists have always set their own hours, dressed in relaxed and casual clothes and worked in stimulating environments. They could never be forced to work, yet they were never truly not at work. With the rise of the Creative Class, this way of working has moved from the margins to the economic mainstream. While the no-collar workplace certainly appears more casual than the old, it replaces traditional hierarchical systems of control with new forms of self-management, peer recognition and pressure and intrinsic forms of motivation, which I call *soft control*. In this setting, we strive to work more independently and find it much harder to cope with incompetent managers and bullying bosses. We trade job security for autonomy. In addition to being fairly compensated for the work we do and the skills we bring, we want the ability to learn and grow, shape the content of our work, control our own schedules and express our identities through work. And companies of all types, including large established ones, are adapting to this change by striving to create new workplaces that are more amenable to creative work. In this, they have no choice: Either they will create these kinds of environments or they will wither and die.

The Experiential Lifestyle

Because we identify ourselves as creative people, we increasingly demand a lifestyle built around creative experiences. We are impatient with the strict separations that previously demarcated work, home and leisure. Whereas the lifestyle of the previous organizational age emphasized conformity, the new lifestyle favors individuality, self-statement, acceptance of difference and the desire for rich multidimensional experiences. David Brooks has argued in his clever book *Bobos in Paradise* that the new culture represents a blending of bourgeois and bohemian values.[13] But we have done more than blend these two categories; we have transcended them completely so that they no longer even apply. Spurred on by the creative ethos, we blend work and lifestyle to construct our identities as creative people. In the past, people often literally "identified" themselves through several basic social categories: occupation, employer and family status (husband, wife, father, mother). Today, the people in my interviews identify themselves through a tangle of connections to myriad creative activities. One person may be simultaneously a writer, researcher, consultant, cyclist, rock climber, electronic/world music/acid jazz lover, amateur gourmet cook, wine enthusiast or micro-brewer. The people in my interviews report that they have little trouble integrating such multiple interests and personae. This kind of synthesis is integral to establishing a unique creative identity.

It's almost impossible to be a nonconformist today because conformity is no longer an issue. But at the same time, this more open attitude toward lifestyle forms a deep and growing division between the Creative Class and the more traditional classes.

The Time Warp

Creative people always have experienced and even cultivated a blurring of time. Writers, artists, musicians, scientists and inventors often have erratic and irregular schedules, working from home and seemingly playing at work. Now more of us do as well. How we organize and use time is changing in ways that go far beyond simplistic notions of the "overworked American" or the 24/7 workday. The core issue is not when we work or the number of hours we put in, but that our use of time has intensified. We pack every second—whether at work or at leisure—full of creative stimuli and experiences. And as we do so, our conception of time has completely morphed. The old boundaries that told us when we should do certain things have faded into oblivion. We in fact work at times when we are supposed to be off and play when we are supposed to be working. This is because creativity cannot be switched on and off at predetermined times, and is itself an odd mixture of work and play. Writing a book, producing a work of art or developing new software requires long periods of intense concentration, punctuated by the need to relax, incubate ideas and recharge. So too does designing a new marketing campaign or investment strategy.

A whole new social construction of time is thus emerging—and not only in how we use our time from day to day, but in how we use it over the course of a life. Careers, for instance, now tend to be front-loaded. Rather than climb the corporate ladder as they grow older, people now often pack their most intense and productive creative work into their younger years, when their potential for advancement and sheer physical energy are at a peak. Meanwhile the time-consuming obligations of marriage and children are deferred: The average age of women at childbearing in the United States recently topped thirty for the first time in history. Not only have the midlife crisis and midlife career change become more prevalent, they are being augmented by the "quarter-life" and "three-quarter-life" changes as people of all ages continue to seek new outlets for their creative capacities.

The Creative Community

Creative people have always gravitated to certain kinds of communities, such as the Left Bank in Paris or New York's Greenwich Village. Such communities provide the stimulation, diversity and a richness of experiences that are the wellsprings of creativity. Now more of us are looking for the same thing. Even if the community we choose isn't quite the kind of place where Gertrude Stein would live, it tends to meet a lot of the same basic criteria: a place that enables us to reflect and reinforce our identities as creative people, pursuing the kind of work we choose and having ready access to a wide range of lifestyle amenities. In place of the tightly knit urban neighborhoods of the past or alienated and generic suburbs, we prefer communities that have a distinctive character. These communities are defined by the impermanent relationships and loose ties that let us live the quasi-anonymous lives we want rather than those that are imposed on us.

The key to understanding all of these shifts lies in seeing them as part of a more global change—as thickly interwoven strands of a single underlying transformation that is affecting every dimension of our lives. This transformation is the shift to an economic and social system based on human creativity. Most people would never suppose that changes in our tastes for work, lifestyle and community might be driven by such basic economic changes. I argue that they are.

Romanticizing the Future, Glorifying the Past

After reading scores of books and countless articles on today's social changes, I have come to the conclusion that much of the time we are locked in a misleading and fruitless debate. The two sides in this debate amount to little more than flip sides of the same coin, opposing mythologies steeped in outdated ideologies, equally short-sighted and misleading.

On one side is an eclectic group of commentators with a utopian faith in the power of technology to cure virtually all social and economic ills. According to techno-futurists like George Gilder and Kevin Kelly, the combination of new technology and unfettered market forces promises to deliver us from the mundanities of everyday work and life and lead us toward an ever more prosperous and liberated future.[14] Greater numbers of people are able to manage their careers as virtual "free agents," to use Dan Pink's phrase, moving from job to job or project to project at will, free from bureaucratic incompetence and the inanities of everyday office life.[15] More and more people will live "virtual" lives, coming together in on-line communities of like-minded individuals. There will be less and less need to shop or go to the movies when anything we desire can be delivered to our homes from a giant on-line mall. We can escape the constraints of geography; escape harsh, dirty and congested cities; and give up long commutes in favor of working from wherever we happen to be.[16]

Juxtaposed to this view are those who believe technology and unbridled market forces are making us work harder and faster, leaving us less time to enjoy each other and our interests, destroying human connections and damaging our neighborhoods and communities. If the techno-utopians romanticize the future, these techno-pessimists glorify the past. Unfettered hypercapitalism is leading to the end of work and the demise of high-paying, secure jobs, according to social critics like Jeremy Rifkin.[17] Worse yet, the elimination of such jobs destroys an important source of social stability, argues Richard Sennett, casting people adrift, corroding our collective character and damaging the very fiber of society.[18] The workplace is evolving into an increasingly stressful and dehumanizing "white-collar sweatshop" in Jill Fraser's view, beset by long hours and chronic overwork.[19] In the eyes of the cultural critic Tom Frank, business has become an all-powerful and hegemonic cultural force, as entities like MTV and The Gap turn alternative-culture symbols into moneymaking devices.[20] Neighborhoods, cities and society as a whole are losing the strong sense of community and civic-minded spirit that were the source of our prosperity, argues Robert Putnam.[21] In his nostalgia for a bygone era of VFW halls, bowling leagues, Cub Scout troops and Little League, Putnam contends that the demise of these repositories of "social capital" is the source of virtually all of our woes.

Despite their obvious ideological differences, all of these viewpoints suggest that forces beyond our control are exogenously reshaping our work, communities and lives. All, as a result, underestimate the extent and power of the ongoing social changes at work today. By insisting that these social changes are somehow imposed on us, all of these commentators avoid the real question of our age: Why are we *choosing* to live and work like this? Why do we want this life, or think that we do?

In an insightful essay, the economic historian Paul David points to the limits of this kind of thinking.[22] It is not technology per se that powers long-run economic growth. Technology is certainly important, but the sources of growth are more complicated and messy. Long-run growth requires a series of gradually accumulating changes in the organizational and institutional fabric of society, taking place over perhaps half a century. These changes are not dictated by technology; rather they are the result of incremental shifts in human behavior and social organization. We have been going through such a process of social adaptation, organizational readjustment and changing personal expectations. At first glance, these recent changes seem centered on new forms of information and biotechnology, much as the Industrial Revolution seemed to be powered by new machines and new forms of energy. But upon closer examination, the current transformation, like its predecessor, turns out to be broader.

The deep and enduring changes of our age are not technological but social and cultural. They are thus harder to see, for they result from the gradual accumulation of small, incremental changes in our day-to-day lives. These changes have been building for decades and are only now coming to the fore.

PART ONE

The Creative Age

CHAPTER 2

The Creative Ethos

Powering the great ongoing changes of our time is the rise of human creativity as the defining feature of economic life. Creativity has come to be valued—and systems have evolved to encourage and harness it—because new technologies, new industries, new wealth and all other good economic things flow from it. And as a result, our lives and society have begun to resonate with a creative ethos. An ethos is defined as "the fundamental spirit or character of a culture." It is our commitment to creativity in its varied dimensions that forms the underlying spirit of our age. To grasp the spirit and character of the emerging Creative Age, this chapter takes a closer look at creativity itself: what it is, and where it comes from. In order to structure the arguments that follow, I want to start with three basic points.

First, creativity is *essential* to the way we live and work today, and in many senses always has been. As the Stanford University economist Paul Romer likes to say, the big advances in standard of living—not to mention the big competitive advantages in the marketplace—always have come from "better recipes, not just more cooking."[1] One might argue that's not strictly true. One might point out, for instance, that during the long period from the early days of the Industrial Revolution to modern times, much of the growth in productivity and material wealth in the industrial nations came not just from creative inventions like the steam engine, but from the widespread application of hard-nosed, "cooking in quantity" business methods like massive division of labor, concentration of assets, vertical integration and economies of scale. But those methods themselves were creative developments. They were the new business models of their time, seldom used before and never in such forms or on such a scale. Factories with massive division of labor were a radical departure from the small-shop craftsmanship of the 1700s. In the late 1800s, when Andrew Carnegie built his highly integrated steel empire, he was hailed as one of the first to truly understand the power of such integration.[2] Since then creativity has grown even more important. Traditional economic factors such as land

21

and natural resources, physical labor and capital have become either less crucial or more readily obtainable. Moreover, as the next chapter will show, new structures for systematically eliciting and applying creativity— such as large-scale funding for basic research and an extensive system of venture capital, as well as a broad milieu for harnessing artistic and cultural creativity—have become ingrained features of our economic life.

Second, human creativity is multifaceted and multidimensional. It is not limited to technological innovation or new business models. It is not something that can be kept in a box and trotted out when one arrives at the office. Creativity involves distinct kinds of thinking and habits that must be cultivated both in the individual and in the surrounding society. Thus, the creative ethos pervades everything from our workplace culture to our values and communities, reshaping the way we see ourselves as economic and social actors—our very identities. It reflects norms and values that both nurture creativity and reinforce the role that it plays. Furthermore, creativity requires a supportive environment that provides a broad array of social and cultural as well as economic stimuli. It is thus associated with the rise of new work environments, lifestyles, associations and neighborhoods, which in turn are conducive to creative work. Such a broadly creative environment is critical for generating technological creativity and the commercial innovations and wealth that flow from it.

Third, perhaps the biggest issue at stake in this emerging age is the ongoing tension between creativity and organization. The creative process is social, not just individual, and thus forms of organization are necessary. But elements of organization can and frequently do stifle creativity. A defining feature of life in the early to mid-twentieth century—a period referred to as the organizational age—was the dominance of large-scale and highly specialized bureaucratic organizations. Writing in the 1940s, the great economist Joseph Schumpeter called attention to the chilling effect of large organizations on creativity. In his landmark book *Capitalism, Socialism and Democracy,* Schumpeter noted that capitalism's great strength had long been the "function of entrepreneurs" who "revolutionize the pattern of production." And then he gloomily predicted its demise:

This social function is already losing its importance. . . . Technological progress is increasingly becoming the business of teams of trained specialists who turn out what is required and make it work in predictable ways. . . . Bureau and committee work tends to replace individual action. . . . The perfectly bureaucratized giant industrial unit not only ousts the small or medium-sized firm and "expropriates" its owners, but in the end it also ousts the entrepreneur. [3]

In an interview that I conducted in 2000, a young woman described this same chilling effect in stark and memorable terms:

> Where I grew up, we were conditioned to play the roles that we were dealt. We were not encouraged to create and build our visions, but rather to fit into the visions of a select few. I like to say that we were "institutionalized" individuals—because institutions defined our lives.[4]

The rise of creativity as an economic force over the past few decades has brought new economic and social forms into existence that mitigate this tension to some degree, but they have not fully resolved it. Everything from the rise of the entrepreneurial startup company and the formal venture capital system to the loosening of traditional cultural norms regarding work and life reflects attempts to elude the strictures of organizational conformity. Of course large organizations still play dominant roles in our society, and are required to do many things. Whereas one person can write brilliant software, it takes large organizations to consistently upgrade, produce and distribute that software. And though many larger organizations have become more nimble and flexible, they remain large-scale bureaucracies. As a result, organizations are evolving too—developing new ways to foster creativity while providing a structure in which to produce and manage work.

This does not mean that creativity has won the day and now powers everything we do. Our new creative economic system is far from fully formed and continues to evolve. Furthermore, it is not a panacea for the myriad social and economic ills that confront modern society. It will not somehow magically alleviate poverty, eliminate unemployment, overcome the business cycle and lead to greater happiness and harmony for all. In some respects, left unchecked and without appropriate forms of human intervention, this creativity-based system may well make some of our problems worse.

Myths and Misconceptions

While many commentators have picked up on aspects of these themes, we still lack a good overall working model of the economic and social system that is carrying us into the Creative Age. One problem is that most public discourse about what's really new in our economy and society tends to polarize. Time and again, we are offered utopian prophecies versus prophecies of gloom and doom—those who believe technology will liberate us versus those who see it as a new oppressor; those who herald the rise of so-called New Economies and those who deplore them. What I'd like to do here is dispel a few of the more popular strains of happy talk. Some of these lines of thinking may easily be confused with what I am trying to say. Indeed, I occasionally agree with some of their premises. So by making it clear exactly where and why I get off the boat, perhaps I can also make it clear what I do think is happening. Herewith, then, a mild rant on four common happy-talk themes.

"Technology Will Liberate Us"

One of the most enduring myths of the modern age is that technology will liberate us from large, faceless organizations—be they large corporations or bureaucratic governments—as well as from other burdens and constraints, and somehow give us the lives we want. Techno-utopianism has been around for a long time. In the early 1900s, some claimed that the car would set us free from the constraints of geography and liberate us from dirty congested cities, and that the airplane would eliminate war by bringing the peoples of the earth closer together. In the 1950s, nuclear power was going to make electricity "too cheap to meter."

Techno-utopianism gathered steam again with the advent of computing and networks. Perhaps its most extreme contemporary spokesman is George Gilder, the former conservative social commentator turned technology guru. His 2000 book *Telecosm* is subtitled *How Infinite Bandwidth Will Revolutionize Our World.*[5] The savior this time is optical networking. Gilder declares that new advances in the use of optics to transmit data will give us almost "infinite bandwidth," such vast signal-carrying capacity that there will be virtually no limits on who can communicate how much to whom. It will all be lightning-fast and affordable; the true potential of the Internet and our other networks will be unlocked at last.

Telecosm evokes the great themes of computer-age techno-utopianism in florid, almost hallucinogenic prose. As Gilder describes it, the optical web will usher in a new age of wonders:

Imagine gazing at the web from far in space . . . the web appears as a global efflorescence, a resonant sphere of light. It is the physical expression of the converging telecosm, the radiant chrysalis from which will spring a new global economy.[6]

It will transform business from a dreary dog-eat-dog game to a Zen-like activity:

> The customers are the product and the product is the customer and both serve one another, in a rhythm of creativity between producers and users, a resonance of buyers and sellers in which the buyers also sell and the sellers also buy in widening webs of commerce. The resonance is the wealth and the light and there is no impedance in the middle.[7]

It will free us from the stinking oppression of governments everywhere:

> At the millennium, the incandescence is diffusing around the world, offering a promise of new freedom and prosperity. . . . Encircling the globe under oceans and beaming from satellites, the radiance is increasingly eroding the powers of despots and bureaucracies, powers and principalities.[8]

Because surely we can all agree that:

> Within the market space of the net, anyone anywhere can issue a petition or publication, utter a cry for help, broadcast a work of art. Anyone can create a product, launch a company, finance its growth, and spin it off into the web of trust.[9]

I would just warn that before you spin anything off into the web of trust, be sure your credit card number is properly encrypted. One of the great flaws of techno-utopianism is the notion that a new technology will give rein only to that which is good and positive in us, and not be used for deception, destruction—or, indeed, for oppression. I haven't seen a technology yet that cures the dark side of human nature.

But Gilder does not stop there. In his telecosmic wonder-world, the web will erase the limits of geography and even of physicality:

> Imagine that any worker could collaborate with any other worker at any time. . . . Imagine the mesh of lights—the radiance of sine waves—as an efflorescence of learning curves as people around the world launch projects and experiments without requiring the physical plant and equipment and

regimented workers in Adam Smith's factory. Without the overhead and entropy, noise and geographical friction, entrepreneurial creativity takes off.[10]

Best of all, time itself will be transcended:

> The entire [present-day] economy is riddled with time-wasting routines and regimes. . . . The message of the telecosm is that this era is over. . . . Liberated from hierarchies that often waste their time and talents, people will be able to discover their most productive roles. [11]

Techno-utopianism is a variant of the old great-man theory of history, in which leaders, generals and discoverers shape the course of human events. In this version—the killer app theory—it's the technology that does it. The Liberator is not Simón Bolívar; it's bandwidth.

Moreover, even if we resist the unbridled optimism of utopian thinking—even if we admit, for instance, that we've found plenty of ways to let computers and networks waste our time as well as save it—we can still fall prey to techno-utopianism's more sober and rational-sounding cousin, techno-determinism: the notion that technology is the key factor in social change. Of course, technology has impact. Economists from Adam Smith to Karl Marx to Joseph Schumpeter have acknowledged it. But each of them also knew that this is not the whole story. For technology to be effective, it requires a whole set of supportive organizational, social and economic adjustments. After all technology is a human creation. The great wonder of our times is not what technological artifacts can do or how quickly they have evolved and grown. The greater wonder is the tremendous outpouring of human creativity that has produced such things. The most fundamental changes are the social structures and mind-sets we are adopting, which feed and sustain this outpouring of creativity.

"The Dinosaurs Are Doomed"

A related myth is that the age of large corporations is over—that they have outlived their usefulness, their power has been broken, and they will eventually fade away along with other big organizational forms, like Big Government. The classic metaphor is the lumbering dinosaur made obsolete and usurped by small, nimble mammals—the usurpers in this case being small, nimble startup companies.[12]

The death-to-the-dinosaurs fallacy has been fed by diverse streams of thought: the small-is-beautiful movement of the 1960s, the culture of entrepreneurship that emerged in the wake of Silicon Valley and of course the great New Economy hype of the late 1990s, which promoted the notion that any twenty-six-year-old with a good idea could start a company, make a mint and retire by forty. This pipe dream is an old one with deep roots in American culture. From the outset, we have seen ourselves as a nation of entrepreneurs and self-created individuals. We are steeped in the myth of Horatio Alger. Note how the ideal of the self-made person toiling away in the "garage"—from the garage startup to the garage band—permeates our popular culture today. It is as important for a modern enterprise to have been born in a garage as it was for a nineteenth-century presidential candidate to have been born in a log cabin.

But big companies are by no means going away. Microsoft and Intel continue to control much of the so-called information economy, along with Oracle, Cisco, IBM and AOL Time Warner. Big industrial concerns, from General Motors to General Electric, General Dynamics and General Foods, still turn out most of the nation's goods. Our money is managed not by upstarts but by large financial institutions. The resources that power our economy are similarly managed and controlled by giant corporations. Mega-mergers among mega-corporations have if anything accelerated in recent years. A September 2000 cover story in *Business Week* raised the question: "Too Much Corporate Power?" The answer according to most Americans was a resounding yes. According to a *Business Week*/Harris Poll featured in the story, nearly three-quarters (72 percent) of Americans said "business had too much power over many aspects of American life."[13] Nor as far as I can tell, is government being replaced by some newer, smaller form of organization.

The economy, like nature, is a dynamic system. New companies form and help to propel it forward, with some dying out while others carry on to grow quite large themselves, like Microsoft and Intel. An economy composed only of small, short-lived entities would be no more sustainable than an ecosystem composed only of insects. And the mere fact that an organization has existed for a long time or is engaged in a long-standing business does not make it "Old Economy" and therefore obsolescent. The key point is that organizations of *all* sizes and types have distinct roles to play in a creative economy. Small firms, big firms, the federal government, and nonprofit research universities all come into play in interlocking ways to develop and refine ideas and bring them to market. To borrow a concept from my colleague Ashish Arora, it is this very "division of innovative labor" that has spurred so much of our recent creativity.[14]

"Power to the People"

A related myth is the "power to the people" fantasy. This too goes back a long time and achieved wide currency in the 1960s. An increasingly influential view, associated with Daniel Pink, is that of the so-called "free agent."[15] In this view, more and more workers are becoming independent agents, blissfully hopping from one short-term engagement to the next in pursuit of the top dollar and the hottest projects. Free agents, so the argument goes, are able to break free from the stranglehold of large organizations and take control of their lives. Companies are accepting and helping to promote this state of affairs, since they no longer have to carry as many long-term employees, the result being freedom and prosperity for all.

There is some truth in this view. Creative people are indeed the chief currency of the emerging economic age. And these people tend to be mobile and change jobs frequently. But the upshot is complex. First, it's certainly not true that all leverage and bargaining power devolves to the free-agent worker—more likely, the balance of power shifts back and forth with supply and demand for particular talents. The free agent assumes more risk and responsibility along with more freedom. While the system looks lovely during good times, these risks and their consequences can be quite dire when the economy turns down. Furthermore, people are complex. Their motivations are many and varied, and not all creative people want to be self-employed or job-hopping free agents. The one consistent quality I detect among creative people is that they seek opportunities to exercise their creativity. If they can find these opportunities by becoming free agents they will do so, and if they can find them by joining a firm and staying with it for a good while, they will do that.

"Going Hollywood"

In the view of many evangelists of the new world of work, much of the economy is coming to operate on the same principles as the Hollywood movie industry, with the fundamental shifts reflecting what has happened in Hollywood itself.[16] Hollywood once was ruled by big studios that employed actors and production crews under long-term contracts, and cranked out movies in assembly-line fashion, much like the factories of the old corporate world. Then in the 1950s the studio system broke down and Hollywood began to run on a more fluid model. Typically, a producer today will sell a group of investors on a script idea, then pull together an ad hoc team of actors, technicians and others to make the film. Once the project is done the team dissolves, and its members re-form in new combinations around other ideas.

Now, so the argument goes, the rest of our economy is emulating Hollywood. Entire business firms are often pulled together on an ad hoc basis—with an independent "producer" (i.e. an entrepreneur) selling investors on a "script idea" (a business plan)—only to dissolve soon after, with the "talent" (skilled professionals) moving on to mobilize around new ventures. In a sense, the Hollywood model is similar to the free-agent approach. As Dan Pink has written, "Large permanent organizations with fixed rosters of individuals are giving way to small flexible networks with ever changing talents." There is some truth in the Hollywood model. Companies are certainly coming to demand flexibility. And there are some strong similarities between the way Hollywood operates and the workings of high-tech areas like Silicon Valley.

But the Hollywood model suffers from several overblown claims. Clearly large organizations still matter a lot—both in Silicon Valley, where Stanford University was and still is a key hub, and in Hollywood, where corporations like Disney, Sony and Universal play key roles. In some ways a Hollywood-like system may well benefit large organizations—which can attract and shed labor at will—more than it does the majority of the people who work under it. But as the business writer James Surowiecki pointed out in a stinging *New Yorker* critique, the Hollywood model may not always be the most efficient way of doing business. Noting the dreadfully low rates of return at most Hollywood studios, Surowiecki writes: "Without a cadre of in-house performers studios lurch from movie to movie, wasting enormous amounts of time and money assembling the talent for each project. Hollywood needs to look more like a business and less like a crapshoot."[17] Likewise in high-technology industry, many researchers have noted the high cost of "churn"—the inefficiency, for instance, of constantly having to replace people who leave just after they've learned their way around the firm and become truly valuable.[18]

Yet in other senses the Hollywood analogy is, ironically, more potent than its advocates may realize. It actually applies—is valid, and useful and provocative—in two ways that most people have overlooked. Perhaps the most salient point is the fact that Hollywood is a *place*. Business gets done there because creative people congregate there, network with one another and are readily available. Ditto Silicon Valley or any other booming creative economy center. These places are talent magnets and talent aggregators. Their key economic function is to provide a regional talent pool into which firms can dip as needed, and from which new ideas and firms bubble up. The real economic sense in which we're "going Hollywood" is that places have replaced companies as the key organizing units in our economy. That's why much of my research, and much of the latter part of this book, has been devoted to learning what makes such places work and what makes them more or less attractive to creative people.

The other salient point is that we're also going Hollywood in a social sense. Hollywood is a place where social ties are notoriously tenuous and contingent. Similarly, many Creative Class people I study prefer loose ties, quasi-anonymous communities and shifting networks of social alliance. Does this mean we're turning into a nation of stereotypical Hollywood rats, hugging and kissing our associates before we stab them in the back? I don't believe so. But it's clear that our society is coming to look quite different from that of the past. We need to develop a clearer picture of where the new creative society seems to be taking us—so we can decide if we want to go there.

Dimensions of Creativity

Creativity is often viewed as a rather mystical affair. Our understanding of it has grown, however, through systematic study over the past few decades. Researchers have observed and analyzed creativity in subjects ranging from eminent scientists and artists to preschoolers and chimpanzees. Occasionally but notably, they have studied its workings across entire human societies. They have pored through the biographies, notebooks and letters of great creators of the past; modeled the creative process by computer; and tried to get computers to *be* creative.[19] From the existing body of literature I will abstract several main themes that surface repeatedly. As we trace these themes and begin to see what creativity really is, we will also begin to get a deeper sense of how and why the creative ethos is emerging in our lives today.

Let's start with a couple of basics. First, creativity is not the same as "intelligence." Says one scholarly review:

Many studies recognize creativity as cognitive ability separate from other mental functions and particularly independent from the complex of abilities grouped under the word intelligence. Although intelligence—the ability to deal with or process large amounts of data—favors creative potential, it is not synonymous with creativity.[20]

Creativity involves the ability to synthesize. Einstein captured it nicely when he called his own work "combinatory play." It is a matter of sifting through data, perceptions and materials to come up with combinations that are *new and useful.* A creative synthesis is useful in such varied ways as producing a practical device, or a theory or insight that can be applied to solve a problem, or a work of art that can be appreciated. [21]

Creativity requires self-assurance and the ability to take risks. In her comprehensive review of the field, *The Creative Mind,* Margaret Boden writes that creativity

involves not only a passionate interest but self-confidence too. A person needs a healthy self-respect to pursue novel ideas, and to make mistakes, despite criticism from others. Self-doubt there may be, but it cannot always win the day. Breaking generally accepted rules, or even stretching them, takes confidence. Continuing to do so, in the face of scepticism and scorn, takes even more.[22]

Small wonder that the creative ethos marks a strong departure from the conformist ethos of the past. Creative work in fact is often downright *subversive,* since it disrupts existing patterns of thought and life. It can feel subversive and unsettling even to the creator. One famous definition of creativity is "the process of destroying one's gestalt in favor of a better one." And to the economist Joseph Schumpeter, the "perennial gale of creative destruction" was the very essence of capitalism:

in capitalist reality as distinguished from its textbook picture, it is not [price] competition which counts but the competition from the new commodity, the new technology, the new source of supply, the new type of organization . . . competition which commands a decisive cost or quality advantage and which strikes not at the margins of the profits and the outputs of the existing firms but at their foundations and their very lives.[23]

The economic historian Joel Mokyr puts it even more bluntly in the preface to his landmark book *The Lever of Riches,* a sweeping study of technological creativity from classical antiquity through the Industrial Revolution. Drawing upon Schumpeter's famous distinction between the typical "adaptive response" and the disruptive and innovative "creative response," Mokyr writes:

> Economists and historians alike realize that there is a deep difference between *homo economicus* and *homo creativus.* One makes the most of what nature permits him to have. The other rebels against nature's dictates. Technological creativity, like all creativity, is an act of rebellion.[24]

Yet creativity is not the province of a few select geniuses who can get away with breaking the mold because they possess superhuman talents. It is a capacity inherent to varying degrees in virtually all people. According to Boden, who sums up a wealth of research: "Creativity draws crucially on our ordinary abilities. Noticing, remembering, seeing, speaking, hearing, understanding language, and recognizing analogies: all these talents of Everyman are important."[25] While the capacity to synthesize vast amounts of information and wrestle with very complex problems can be an advantage, Boden argues, genius can also cut both ways. "These rare individuals, then, can search—and transform—high-level space much larger and complex than those explored by other people. They are in a sense more free than us, for they can generate more possibilities than we can imagine. Yet they respect constraints *more* than we do." Later, she adds:

> The romantic myth of "creative genius" rarely helps. Often it is insidiously self-destructive. It can buttress the self-confidence of those individuals who believe themselves to be among the chosen few (perhaps it helped Beethoven to face his many troubles). But it undermines the self-regard of those who do not. Someone who believes that creativity is a rare or special power cannot sensibly hope that perseverance, or education, will enable them to join the creative elite. Either one is already a member, or will never be. Monolithic notions of creativity, talent, or intelligence are discouraging in the same way. Either one has got "it" or one hasn't. Why bother to try if one's efforts can lead only to a slightly less dispiriting level of mediocrity? . . . A very different

attitude is possible for someone who sees creativity as based in ordinary abilities we all share, and in practised expertise to which we can all aspire.[26]

Even though much about the creative process seems strange and elusive,
there does appear to be a consistent method underlying it. Many researchers see creative thinking as a four-step process: preparation, incubation, illumination and verification or revision.[27] Preparation is
consciously studying a task, and perhaps trying to attack it logically by
standard means. Incubation, the "mystical" step, is one in which both the
conscious mind and the subconscious mull over the problem in hard-to-
define ways. Illumination, the "Eureka!" step, is seeing a new synthesis;
and verification and revision include all the work that comes after. Anyone
who's done creative work *of any kind* will recognize the steps. Indeed more
of us today do precisely this sort of work, and that, for instance, is why so
many of us are moving to irregular work schedules: The alternating periods of different kinds of mental activity require it.

Creativity is multidimensional and experiential. The psychologist Dean
Keith Simonton, a leading scholar in the field, writes, "creativity is favored
by an intellect that has been enriched with diverse experiences and perspectives."[28] It is "associated with a mind that exhibits a variety of interests and knowledge." Thus, the varied forms of creativity that we typically
see as different from one another—technological creativity (or invention), economic creativity (entrepreneurship) and artistic and cultural
creativity, among others—are in fact deeply interrelated. Not only do they
share a common thought process, they reinforce each other through
cross-fertilization and mutual stimulation. And so through history practitioners of the different forms of creativity have tended to congregate and
feed off one another in teeming, multifaceted creative centers—Florence
in the early Renaissance; Vienna in the late 1800s and early 1900s; the
many fast-growing creative centers across the United States today.

Stimulating and glamorous as it may sometimes be, creativity is in fact
work. Both Thomas Edison (a paragon of technological creativity) and
George Bernard Shaw (a cultural creative) liked to say that genius is 90
percent perspiration and 10 percent inspiration.[29] Or as the journalist Red
Smith once said of the demands of his craft: "There's nothing to writing.
All you do is sit down at the typewriter and open a vein." Here we have an
inventor, a playwright and a sportswriter sounding a common theme: The
creative ethos is built on discipline and focus, sweat and blood. As Boden
observes,

a person needs time, and enormous effort, to amass mental structures and to explore their potential. It is not always easy (it was not easy for Beethoven). Even when it is, life has many other attractions. Only a strong commitment to the domain—music, maths, medicine—can prevent someone from dissipating their energies on other things.[30]

Creativity can take a long time—there are many stories of great mathematicians and scientists mulling a problem for months or more, to be finally "illuminated" while stepping onto a bus or staring into a fireplace—and even this apparent magic is the result of long preparation. Thus Louis Pasteur's famous dictum: "Chance favors only the prepared mind." Or as Wesley Cohen and Daniel Levinthal have put it in their studies of firm-based innovation: "Fortune favors the prepared firm."[31]

Moreover, it has been observed that because of the all-absorbing nature of creative work, many great thinkers of the past were people who "formed no close ties": They had lots of colleagues and acquaintances, but few close friends and often no spouse or children. In fact, muses the psychiatrist Anthony Storr, "if intense periods of concentration over long periods are required to attain fundamental insights, the family man is at a disadvantage." Quoting the famous bachelor Isaac Newton on his process of discovery—"I keep the subject constantly before me, and wait till the first dawnings open slowly by little and little into the full and clear light"—Storr notes that "If Newton had been subject to the demands of a wife for companionship or interrupted by the patter of tiny feet, it would certainly have been less easy for him."[32]

Creativity is largely driven by intrinsic rewards. Surely some creative people are driven by money, but studies find that truly creative individuals from artists and writers to scientists and open-source software developers are driven primarily by internal motivations. In a study of motivation and reward, Harvard Business School psychologist Teresa Amabile observed, "Intrinsic motivation is conducive to creativity, but extrinsic motivation is detrimental. It appears that when people are primarily motivated to do some creative activity by their own interest and enjoyment of that activity, they may be more creative than when they are primarily motivated by some goal imposed upon them by others."[33]

Although creativity is often viewed as an individual phenomenon, it is an inescapably social process. It is frequently exercised in creative teams. Even the lone creator relies heavily on contributors and collaborators. Successful creators have often organized themselves and others for systematic effort. When Edison opened his laboratory in Menlo Park, New Jersey, he called the lab an "invention factory" and announced his intention to produce "a minor invention every ten days and a big thing every six months or so."[34] The artist Andy Warhol similarly dubbed his Manhattan studio The Factory, and though Warhol liked to cultivate a public image of bemused indifference, he was a prolific organizer and worker—mobilizing friends and colleagues to publish a magazine and produce films and music, all while pursuing his own art.

Furthermore, creativity flourishes best in a unique kind of social environment: one that is stable enough to allow continuity of effort, yet diverse and broad-minded enough to nourish creativity in all its subversive forms. Simonton finds creativity flourishing in places and times marked by four characteristics: "domain activity, intellectual receptiveness, ethnic diversity, [and] political openness." In a study of the history of Japanese culture—a culture that has been "highly variable in its openness to outside influences"—Simonton found that "those periods in which Japan was receptive to alien influx were soon followed by periods of augmented creative activity."[35]

One final cautionary note is in order. Joel Mokyr notes that technological creativity has tended to rise and then fade dramatically at various times in various cultures, when social and economic institutions turn rigid and act against it. Spectacular fade-outs occurred, for instance, in late medieval times in the Islamic world and in China. Both societies, which had been leaders in fields from mathematics to mechanical invention, then proceeded to fall far behind Western Europe economically. When one takes the long view of human history, Mokyr writes, one sees that

> technological progress is like a fragile and vulnerable plant, whose flourishing is not only dependent on the appropriate surroundings and climate, but whose life is almost always short. It is highly sensitive to the social and economic environment and can easily be arrested.[36]

Thus a continued outpouring of creativity "cannot and should not be taken for granted," Mokyr warns—even today. Sustaining it over long periods is not automatic, but requires constant attention to and investment in the economic and social forms that feed the creative impulse. All the more reason to study the institutions of our emerging Creative Age closely, so that we can understand their inner workings and nourish them appropriately.

The Ultimate Source of Creativity

To the economist Paul Romer, not only is creativity inherent in humans, it is literally what distinguishes us, economically, from other species:

> We produce goods by rearranging physical objects, but so do other animals, often with remarkable precision. Birds build nests, bees build hives, and we build guns and cars. . . . Where people excel as economic animals is in their ability to produce ideas, not just physical goods. An ant will go through its life without ever coming up with even a slightly different idea about how to gather food. But people are almost incapable of this kind of rote adherence to instruction. We are incurable experimenters and problem solvers.[37]

Indeed it was a "different idea about how to gather food," the agricultural idea, that launched the beginnings of modern human society, as the next chapter will detail. It was experimenting and problem solving—proceeding in fits and starts over many centuries, then building rapidly since late medieval times—that led to a series of revolutionary scientific discoveries, followed by waves of practical invention. "We are not used to thinking of ideas as economic goods," writes Romer, "but they are surely the most significant ones that we produce. The only way for us to produce more economic value—and thereby generate economic growth—is to find ever more valuable ways to make use of the objects available to us."[38]

Romer is a leading proponent of an economic school of thought called New Growth Theory, which assigns a central role to creativity or idea generation.[39] He notes that ideas are especially potent "goods" because they are not like other goods, such as mineral deposits and machines, which deplete or wear out with use. A good idea, like the concept of the wheel, "can be used over and over again" and in fact grows in value the more it is used. It offers not diminishing returns, but *increasing returns.* Moreover, an idea can be built upon. As other people apply their own creativity to a new scientific theory or product design, they can tinker with it, improve it and combine it with other ideas in growing proliferations of new forms. This is what has happened in recent centuries. The early 1900s were a time when waves of invention—the accumulated fruits of that creativity—were being harnessed, mass-produced and widely promulgated through society as never before. What we are living through now is the next step. Not just the fruits or artifacts of the creativity, but human creativity itself is being widely harnessed on a truly massive scale and promulgated as never before.

Today we like to think that we clearly understand creativity as a source of economic value. Many commentators, for instance, trumpet the point that "intellectual property"—useful new knowledge embodied in computer programs, or patents or formulas—has now become more valuable than any kind of physical property. It's no surprise that we often litigate over intellectual property, and argue about the proper means of protecting it, as fiercely as miners in the California Gold Rush battling over a claim. But as Stanford University law professor Lawrence Lessing has powerfully argued, our penchant for overprotecting and overlitigating intellectual property may well serve to constrain and limit the creative impulse.[40] In the long run, we cannot forget what the fundamental cornerstone of our wealth is. Though useful knowledge may reside in programs or formulas, it does not originate there. It originates with people. The ultimate intellectual property—the one that really replaces land, labor and capital as the most valuable economic resource—is the human creative faculty.

To some degree, Karl Marx had it partly right when he foresaw that workers would someday control the means of production. This is now beginning to happen, although not as Marx thought it would, with the proletariat rising to take over factories. Rather, more workers than ever control the means of production because it is inside their heads; they *are* the means of production. Thus, the ultimate "control" issue is not who owns the patents that may result, nor is it whether the creative worker or the employer holds the balance of power in labor market negotiations. While those battles swing back and forth, the ultimate control issue—the one we have to stay focused on, individually and collectively—is how to keep stoking and tapping the creative furnace inside each human being.

The Creative Factory

Not just the scientific laboratory but the factory itself can be an arena for creative work. Factory workers, given the chance, often are the ones who come up with basic improvements in productivity and performance.[41] I saw this time and again in my studies of Japanese and U.S. factories. Even in areas such as environmental quality, it was line workers doing little things—like putting in drip pans—who were the key to making factories greener and more productive at the same time.[42] More and more factory jobs today require creativity as a condition of employment. At Sony's electronics plant outside Pittsburgh, as in many advanced manufacturing plants, even candidates for entry-level assembly jobs must pass a battery of tests screening them for aptitudes such as problem solving and the ability to work in self-directed teams.[43] And increasing numbers of factory workers no longer directly touch the products they make but essentially monitor, control and at times program computers that run the production process.[44] The manager of a fully automated steel mill in the American Midwest summed it up best when he told me, "This is not a traditional factory. It's a living laboratory with bright capable people."[45]

I first came to understand the power of creativity at work not from economic textbooks or from my research, but very early in life, from my father, Louis Florida. Born to Italian immigrant parents in Newark, New Jersey, he quit school at age fourteen to help support his family during the Great Depression. He took a job in a factory that made eyeglass frames. After fighting in the Second World War—he was one of those who stormed the beaches at Normandy—he returned to his previous line of work at a place called Victory Optical. By the early 1960s, when I was a small boy, he had worked his way up from laborer to a supervisory post. On some Saturdays he had to put in a few hours at work, and occasionally he would give in to my pants-tugging pleas to tag along. My eyes ablaze with youthful curiosity, we drove through Newark's sprawling, industrial Ironbound Section, so called because it was latticed with railroad lines, to the giant brick factory. Inside the plant, the energy was incredible. I would race on small legs to keep up with my father as he strode past the banks of machines: the presses, the lathes, the vats of plating solutions and the huge bins with eyeglass frames of all sorts. It was all a hurly-burly kaleidoscope of rapidly moving people, set amid the sounds of whirring machines and foreign-accented English, and the smells of cutting fluids, melted plastic and finely shaved metal chips.

I recall my father working on weekends with his colleague Karl, a German-born machinist, on new designs and layouts for various machines. I remember them discussing the latest machinery available from Italy and Germany and the advanced production systems used by their European competitors. But my father would always remind me that the productive power of the factory lay not in the machines and presses but in the intelligence and creativity of its workers. "Richard," he would say, "the factory does not run itself. It is those incredibly skilled men who are the heart, soul and mind of this factory."

My most vivid lesson on that score occurred when I was a Cub Scout about to enter the Pinewood Derby competition. This was a racing event for small model cars. Each Scout was given the same basic materials to work with: a rectangular block of wood, plastic wheels and metal axles. The instructions were to fashion a car from the materials supplied, and not to add additional weight in excess of five ounces. The cars would race by rolling down a sloped track. The week before my first race, I worked on the car with my father. We basically fastened the wheels to the block of wood, added a coat of paint and showed up. Suffice it to say we were badly beaten. Our primitive clunker came out of the gate down the track and literally fell apart, wheels flying in all directions, as the sleek cars of other Scouts flew by. Those sharp-looking cars fascinated me and I made my father promise to help me build one.

The next year we set to work early designing a streamlined racer. We started talking to the machinists and machine tool designers at Victory Optical, taking the car to the factory on weekends to seek advice. We honed that block of wood into an efficient aerodynamic design. We added a precise amount of lead weight, per the guidelines, to gain additional speed. We fashioned a little test track. In trial runs, the front axle began to crack under the strain of repeated nose-first impacts with the stopping barrier at the bottom. With the help of the skilled machinists, we developed an innovative solution, carving a bit of wood from the rear of the car and gluing it to the nose to protect the axle. We added a metallic paint job, decals, a roll bar and the *pièce de résistance*—a little plastic driver. The finished car looked like a Formula One racer. And with the collective ingenuity of Victory Optical in our corner, we went on to win every Pinewood Derby championship for the remainder of my Cub Scout career, at which point the dynasty passed along to my younger brother's racers. The creativity of the workers in the eyeglass-frame factory was multidimensional: It could be applied to my world, too.

The image of the factory as an arena only for rote physical labor was always wrong. It never gave a complete picture of the economic activity that went on inside. Workers always used their intellect and creative capabilities to get things done. And though they were increasingly stifled for a long period in many industries, factory workers today are coming to be valued more for these capabilities—for their ideas on quality and continuous improvement—than for their ability to perform routine manual tasks. Across the board, in a multitude of jobs, work has taken on a creative component.

Creativity Versus Organization

Creative people come in many different forms. Some are mercurial and intuitive in their work habits, others methodical. Some prefer to channel their energies into radical big ideas; others are tinkerers and improvers. Some like to move from job to job, whereas others like the security of a large organization. Some are best working in groups; others like nothing better than to be left alone. Moreover, many people don't fall at the extremes—and their work and lifestyle preferences may change as they mature.

What all of these people have in common is a strong desire for organizations and environments that let them be creative—that value their input, challenge them, have mechanisms for mobilizing resources around ideas and are receptive to both small changes and the occasional big idea. Companies and places that can provide this kind of environment, regardless of size, will have an edge in attracting, managing and motivating creative talent. The same companies and places will also tend to enjoy a flow of innovation, reaping competitive advantage in the short run and evolutionary advantage in the long run.

While certain environments promote creativity, others can most certainly kill it. Adam Smith noted this as early as 1776, in *The Wealth of Nations.* In his famous description of the pin factory, Smith praised the division of labor, a concept that allowed pins to be made efficiently by splitting the process into eighteen distinct steps, with each worker or group of workers typically doing only one step. But he also warned that this system—a creative achievement in its own right—had a downside:

> The man whose whole life is spent in performing a few simple operations . . .
> has no occasion to exert his understanding or to exercise his invention. . . .
> He naturally loses, therefore, the habit of such exertion, and generally becomes as stupid and ignorant as it is possible for a human creature to become. The torpor of his mind renders him, not only incapable of relishing or bearing a part in any rational conversation, but of conceiving any generous, noble, or tender sentiment.[46]

In their insightful book *The Social Life of Information,* John Seely Brown and Paul Duguid describe the inherent tug-of-war between how organizations generate knowledge and creativity, and how they translate those assets into actual products and services.[47] Creativity comes from individuals working in small groups, which Brown and Duguid refer to as "communities of practice." These communities emphasize exploration and discovery. Each develops distinctive habits, customs, priorities and insights that are the secrets of its creativity and inventiveness. But to link these communities to one another, transfer knowledge, achieve scale and generate growth requires process and structure. Practice without process becomes unmanageable, but process without practice damps out the creativity required for innovation; the two sides exist in perpetual tension. Only the most sophisticated and aware organizations are able to balance these countervailing forces in ways that lead to sustained creativity and long-run growth.

This fundamental tension between organization and creativity, which remains with us today, is reflected in a remarkable dialogue between two of the greatest chroniclers of everyday life in the mid-1900s, William Whyte and Jane Jacobs. Whyte's classic book, *The Organization Man,* published in 1956, documented the stifling effect of organization and bureaucracy on individuality and creativity.[48] A journalist at *Fortune* magazine, Whyte chronicled how big corporations of the time selected and favored the type of person who goes along to get along, rather than those who might go against the grain. The result, he wrote, was "a generation of bureaucrats." Even research and development, despite growing funds, was becoming bureaucratized: "Money, money everywhere...but not a cent to think." Whyte's organization man had an average workweek of 50 to 60 hours, was more interested in work than in his spouse and was dependent on the corporation for his very identity. He often lived in prepackaged suburban developments like Park Forest, Illinois, a place Whyte studied exhaustively. The new suburban communities were seen as more progressive and liberating than the old small towns. But as Whyte showed, they came to exert strong pressures of their own for social adaptation and conformity. In Park Forest, as in the corporations for whom many of its upwardly mobile residents worked, the idiosyncratic individual was quickly stigmatized.

Jane Jacobs's monumental work, *The Death and Life of Great American Cities,* published just five years later in 1961, celebrated the creativity and diversity of urban neighborhoods like her own Greenwich Village.[49] Whereas Whyte found conformity and homogeneity, Jacob's neighborhoods were veritable fountainheads of individuality, difference and social interaction. The miracle of these places, she argued, was found in the hurly-burly life of the street. The street, where many different kinds of people came together, was both a source of civility and a font for creativity. Since people lived close together in small private spaces, the street provided the venue for a more or less continuous conversation and interaction, kept alive by frequent random collisions of people and ideas. Jacobs documented in painstaking detail how this worked in and around Hudson Street where she lived, a neighborhood of tenement apartments and town houses, bars and shops, and her famed White Horse Tavern, where workers, writers, musicians and intellectuals gathered for relaxation, conversation and the occasional new idea.

What made Hudson Street work was its combination of physical and social environments. It had short blocks that generated the greatest variety in foot traffic. It had a wide diversity of people from virtually every ethnic background and walk of life. It had wide sidewalks and a tremendous variety of types of buildings—apartments, bars, shops, even small factories—which meant that there were always different kinds of people outside and on different schedules. And it had lots of old, underutilized buildings, ideal for individualistic and creative enterprises ranging from artists' studios to entrepreneurial shops. Hudson Street also fostered and attracted a certain type of person—Jacobs's all-important "public characters"—shopkeepers, merchants and neighborhood leaders of various sorts. These people, the antitheses of Whyte's organization men, played a critical role in resource mobilization. Performing a catalytic role in the community, they utilized their position in social networks to connect people and ideas. The creative community, Jacobs argued, required diversity, the appropriate physical environment and a certain kind of person to generate ideas, spur innovation and harness human creativity.

Ironically, but not surprisingly, Jacobs and Whyte were the closest of friends. When asked in March of 2001, on the fortieth anniversary of her classic book, to name her most admired contemporaries she had this to say: "Holly Whyte, William H. Whyte. . . . He was an important person to me and he was somebody whose ideas, yes, were on the same wavelength. And it was through Holly that I met my . . . publisher. . . . I told him what I wanted and he agreed to publish it [*The Death and Life of Great American Cities*] and gave me a contract."[50]

Upon closer examination, this bond is evident in their work. Whyte lamented the rise of organizational society and the alienation, isolation and conformity it carried with it. Jacobs showed the possibility of an alternative, a setting where difference, nonconformity and creativity could thrive. Who at the time could have guessed what history would render?

For much of the past half century, intelligent observers of modern life believed it was Whyte's world that had triumphed. But now it appears that Jacobs's world may well carry the day. Not only are urban neighborhoods similar to Hudson Street reviving across the country, but many of the principles that animated Hudson Street are diffusing through our economy and society. Workplaces, personal lives, entire industries and entire geographic regions are coming to operate on principles of constant, dynamic creative interaction.

CHAPTER 3

The Creative Economy

oday's economy is fundamentally a Creative Economy. I certainly agree with those who say that the advanced nations are shifting to information-based, knowledge-driven economies. Peter Drucker, who outlined the rise of the "knowledge economy," has been the most noted exponent of this view: "The basic economic resources—'the means of production,' to use the economist's term is no longer capital, nor natural resources . . . nor 'labor.' It is and will be knowledge," wrote the always-prescient Drucker.[1] Yet I see creativity—the creation of useful new forms out of that knowledge—as the key driver. In my formulation, "knowledge" and "information" are the tools and materials of creativity. "Innovation," whether in the form of a new technological artifact or a new business model or method, is its product.

The past century and in particular the years since 1950 have seen an explosion in creativity across the board in the United States. We have invested escalating amounts of money in research and development, reaped a growing number of patents as a result and seen growing numbers of our people work in creative occupations. None of this is totally new; humans of course have engaged in creative activities since antiquity, often with spectacular results. What we are doing now is mainstreaming these activities; building an entire economic infrastructure around them. Scientific and artistic endeavor, for instance, have become industries unto themselves, and they have combined in new ways to create still new industries. The joint expansion of technological innovation and creative content work has increasingly become the motor force of economic growth.

Consider the astounding growth in the following dimensions of the Creative Economy in the United States.

- Systematic investment in creativity, in the form of research and development spending, has increased consistently since the 1950s. R&D investments increased from roughly $5 billion in 1953 to more than

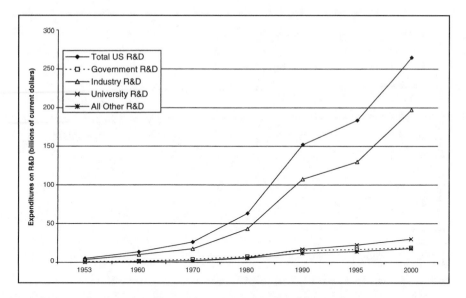

FIGURE 3.1   Investing in Creativity: R&D Spending, by Performer of Research, 1953–2000

(SOURCE: National Science Foundation, Division of Science Resource Studies.)

$250 billion in 2000 (Fig. 3.1). Controlling for inflation, R&D invest-
ments still grew by an amazing 800-plus percent over the period.[2]

- The fruits of research have also grown consistently over the course of
  the past century, accelerating in the years since 1950. The number of
  patents granted annually in the United States nearly doubled in the
  period 1900 to 1950, growing from 25,000 to 43,000. It has more
  than tripled since then, rising to 150,000 by 1999—an increase of
  some 250 percent (Fig. 3.2).[3]

- The workforce devoted to technical creativity, in the form of scientists
  and engineers, has also seen remarkable growth. Their numbers
  increased from 42,000 in 1900 to 625,000 in 1950, before expanding
  to 5 million by 1999—an eightfold increase since midcentury (Fig.
  3.3). The growth of the scientific and technically creative workforce
  becomes even clearer when we account for the growth in population.
  In 1900, there were just 55 scientists and engineers for every 100,000
  people in the United States. That figure increased to 400 by 1950, and
  to more than 1,000 in 1980. By 1999 there were more than 1,800
  scientists and engineers per 100,000 people.[4]

- The numbers of people making a living from artistic and cultural
  creativity also expanded dramatically over the course of the past

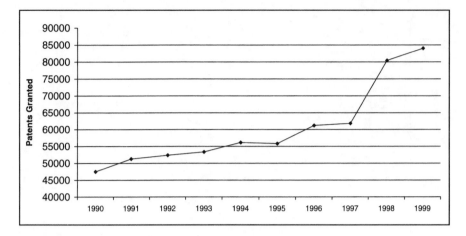

FIGURE 3.2   Rising Creative Output: Trends in Patents, 1900–1999

(SOURCE: U.S. Patent and Trademark Office.)

century, and particularly since 1950. Professional artists, writers and performers—so-called "bohemians"—increased from some 200,000 in 1900 to 525,000 in 1950 and to 2.5 million in 1999, an increase of more than 375 percent since 1950 (see Fig. 3.3). There were roughly 250 bohemians for every 100,000 Americans in 1900, a figure that increased to roughly 350 by 1950. That number crossed 500 in 1980, before reaching 900 for every 100,000 Americans in 1999.[5]

As far as I can tell, *Business Week* first introduced the concept of a "Creative Economy" in August 2000.[6] Since then, John Howkins has documented its global impact in his aptly titled 2001 book *The Creative Economy.*[7] His figures are worth noting even though his use of the term is somewhat different from mine. While I define the Creative Economy in terms of occupations, Howkins defines the Creative Economy to include fifteen "creative industry" sectors such as software, R&D and design, and creative-content industries like film and music. These industries produce intellectual property in the form of patents, copyrights, trademarks and proprietary designs.[8] In 1999, he estimated the annual revenue of these fifteen creative sectors worldwide to be $2.24 trillion dollars (Table 3.1). The United States is by far the world's leading Creative Economy with $960 billion dollars in revenue, more than 40 percent of the global total, and also accounts for more than 40 percent of all R&D spending worldwide. It is U.S. dominance in these creative fields—more so than productivity im-

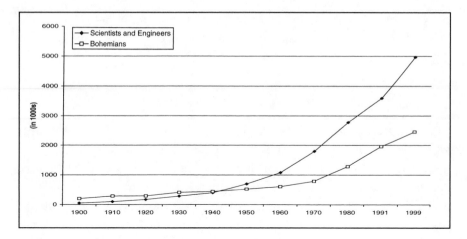

FIGURE 3.3   The Growing Creative Workforce, 1900–1999

(SOURCE: *Historical Statistics,* 1976; *Statistical Abstract,* various years.)

**Table 3.1   Core Industries of the Creative Economy
(by market size in billions of U.S. dollars, 1999)**

Sector	Global	U.S.	U.S. Share
R & D	$545	$243	44.6%
Publishing	506	137	27.1
Software	489	325	66.5
TV and Radio	195	82	42.1
Design	140	50	35.7
Music	70	25	35.7
Film	57	17	29.8
Toys and Games	55	21	38.2
Advertising	45	20	44.4
Architecture	40	17	42.5
Performing Arts	40	7	17.5
Crafts	20	2	10.0
Video Games	17	5	29.4
Fashion	12	5	41.7
Art	9	4	44.4
Total	$2,240	$960	42.8%

SOURCE: John Howkins, *The Creative Economy: How People Make Money from Ideas.* New York: Allen Lane, The Penguin Press, 2001, p. 116.

provements related to new technology and new manufacturing methods—that is responsible for a good deal of the nation's resurgence in global economic competitiveness since the 1980s.

Institutions of the Creative Economy

The Creative Economy of the United States has grown powerful and pervasive because it is supported by a formidable infrastructure. Paul Romer has argued that "the most important ideas of all are meta-ideas," which are "ideas about how to support the production and transmission of other ideas."[9] The Creative Economy is undergirded by a new set of institutions that have emerged to do just this. Taken together, they make up what I call the "social structure of creativity," comprising (1) new systems for technological creativity and entrepreneurship, (2) new and more effective models for producing goods and services, and (3) a broad social, cultural and geographic milieu conducive to creativity of all sorts.

New Systems for Technological Creativity and Entrepreneurship

I have already mentioned the dramatic growth of R&D investment. This has been particularly fruitful in spurring the rise of new industries like software and biotechnology, which have been closely tied to funded research at universities. In addition to this, the Creative Economy is supported by an extensive venture capital system that accelerates the processes of new firm formation and commercial innovation. The decade of the 1990s saw a remarkable increase in venture capital investments. These investments grew more than a hundredfold in real dollars over the course of the 1990s, increasing from less than a billion dollars in 1990 to roughly $100 billion in 2000, before falling back to less than $40 billion in the wake of the NASDAQ collapse and high-tech recession of 2001.[10]

This venture capital system, which Martin Kenney and I chronicled in our 1990 book *The Breakthrough Illusion*, evolved in response to the bureaucratic limits of the organizational age. It did much to unleash the talents and energies of creative people who previously might have chafed within the confines of big firms or research labs.[11] But venture capital is not necessarily a new development. In fact, its modern incarnation arose from a long period of experimentation with alternative mechanisms for providing support to entrepreneurial companies.[12] During the postwar period, even as Schumpeter and Whyte were railing against the stifling of innovation in large corporations, some of the most creative minds of the time were beginning to abandon these organizations for what would come to be called high-tech "startup" companies. A classic example is William Shockley, who with others developed the transistor at Bell Laboratories, then went west to California to start Shockley Semiconductor. A necessary ingredient for such a venture is venture finance.[13]

As Schumpeter noted long ago, people with ideas need money to turn those ideas into businesses. To Schumpeter, the provision of capital and credit to entrepreneurs was the vital element of a capitalist economy—"important enough to serve as its *differentia specifica*."[14] The early textile industry was built on venture finance. Merchants and bankers supplied the initial funding for people like Francis Cabot Lowell, founder of the Boston Manufacturing Company, who brought the British power loom to the United States.[15] Andrew Carnegie—the son, ironically, of a Scottish handweaver who had emigrated to the United States after being put out of work by power looms—became an entrepreneur and venture capitalist rolled into one. While working as a messenger boy, young Carnegie got to know powerful men, picked up business tips and grew rich trading in stocks and bonds. He then parlayed his wealth with that of others to build the most massive and efficient steel mills in the world. One of his contemporaries was Andrew Mellon, a precursor of modern-day venture capitalists. Mellon, a Pittsburgh banker, did more than lend money: He mobilized capital and often took equity stakes in his investments. Foreshadowing a practice that would later become the norm in Silicon Valley, Mellon in 1888 required a young Ohio inventor named Charles Martin Hall to relocate to Pittsburgh so that the company being built around his work could be monitored and nurtured more closely. Hall's invention was a process for smelting aluminum; the company became Alcoa.[16]

By the 1930s and 1940s, this arena of venture investing was stifled and to some extent forgotten, perhaps because there hadn't ever been a formal mechanism for venture finance; investors just did it. But as big firms grew—and as the barriers to entry that they raised, combined with the Great Depression, created a difficult climate for starting new companies—investors shifted their capital elsewhere. They began to favor blue-chip stocks and bonds issued by big companies that looked impregnable: Surely the Pennsylvania Railroad and AT&T would reign forever. There was considerable national debate during the Depression and World War II over mechanisms to stimulate innovation and entrepreneurship, and many ideas were floated, from major government investment in research and development to extensive small business assistance to government support for venture capital. Aside from undertaking public investments in R&D, government chose not to take these on in any significant way. Frustrated by the situation, a group of affluent Boston bankers and industrialists launched an investment scheme to help support new technology-based business ventures. Their creation was American Research and Development or ARD, established in 1946 as the United States' first formal venture capital fund. In 1958, Digital Equipment Corp. was formed with funding from ARD.[17]

Venture capital and high-tech industries reinforced each other's growth. In 1957, eight employees left Shockley Semiconductor in Palo Alto to form Fairchild Semiconductor. With a simple business plan they had contacted Arthur Rock, a New York investment banker, who then lined up Fairchild Camera to finance their endeavor. Fairchild Semiconductor and another firm, Texas Instruments, went on to produce the first integrated circuits— arrays of transistors and other electronic components etched into tiny pieces of layered metal that we now call "chips." And then the legend of the "Fairchildren" was born: spin-offs from Fairchild. Gordon Moore and others left Fairchild to start Intel. Eugene Kleiner then left Intel to start Kleiner Perkins—a dominant venture capital fund in Silicon Valley today, and one of the first of a new and improved breed.[18]

This new breed was the venture capital limited partnership. Before a venture capital company can give money to entrepreneurs, it has to raise the money. ARD had done this by selling stock in itself on the public stock market. The limited partnership drew a huge volume of funds from wealthy individuals and large institutions into venture capital, because it limited the liability of the partners to their investment in the fund. During the 1970s and 1980s, the success of funds like Kleiner Perkins, the Mayfield Fund, Sequoia and Institutional Venture Partners made the limited partnership the preferred vehicle for mobilizing venture capital. Powered by this financial innovation, the United States accumulated by far the world's largest formal system for developing and funding new companies. That's a big reason so many entrepreneurs come to the United States, and why American venture capital firms are often heavily involved in entrepreneurial activity abroad.[19]

In our research in the late 1980s, my colleague Martin Kenney and I clarified the mutually reinforcing character of venture capital and high-tech industry. In mapping the geography and flows of venture capital, we examined the conventional notion that venture capital was somehow an elixir that would magically lead to innovation, as some experts and policymakers seemed to think. A common assumption at the time was that simply by starting venture capital funds in places like Pittsburgh or Buffalo or Rochester, one could automatically trigger the creative process in that area. To test this assumption, we compared the places that had venture capital to those that were attracting the venture capital investments. And lo and behold we found a distinct geographic pattern. Two places that were home to scads of venture capital—New York City and Chicago—had very little venture capital-financed innovation. Rather, investment went to companies in locations like Silicon Valley or Boston's Route 128 corridor.[20]

The reason for this pattern was that venture capital, by itself, did not produce home-grown innovation. It flowed to places that had other elements of a well-developed "social structure of innovation," as Kenney and I then dubbed our initial version of what I now call the larger social structure of creativity. In such places, venture capital became an important part of that structure. As companies grew and became successful, their founders became investors in those regions, or venture capitalists from elsewhere moved offices into these growth regions. In places like Silicon Valley, Boston, Seattle and Austin, we found that these on-site venture capitalists were the key actors in the whole system of generating and investing funds. They would identify promising investments, develop partnerships with venture capitalists in New York or Chicago and then monitor the progress of the investments for all the venture capitalists in the pool.

The venture capital model is far from perfect. It runs in fits and starts, sometimes funding many ideas, sometimes not so many. The rapid rise and decline of the Internet sector in the late 1990s and early years of the new millennium is just the most recent illustration of this boom–bust cycle. There is a good deal of follow-the-leader investment, with venture capitalists chasing the trend *du jour,* just as investors in the public stock market do; and often they get similarly burned.[21] But the cycle has a cleansing effect, wiping away unproductive or redundant firms and activities and freeing up resources and talent for another round of investment and growth.

Notwithstanding the small-is-beautiful fantasy that some of its boosters promote,[22] the venture capital model has not killed off big companies. Most of the startups funded by venture capitalists fail. Only a few ever produce the stock-market bonanza of a successful initial public offering. Many of the rest are in fact bought by big companies; little software firms are gobbled up by big ones, and little biotech firms are absorbed by pharmaceutical giants. But that's okay with the venture capitalists, because as long as the sale pays them a healthy return on their investment, it's a perfectly acceptable "exit strategy." And it's okay in a larger sense, too. Creative work has been done and brought to market that otherwise wouldn't have been. The entrepreneurs themselves, often enriched by the sale, can move on to start something else. Venture capital and the broader system that surrounds it provide a powerful catalyst to the chain of creativity and an even more powerful mechanism for bringing its fruits to the commercial market.

New Models for Making Things:
The Creative Factory and Modular Manufacturing

Another key element of the social structure of creativity is the rise of new institutions and systems for actually producing things. The creative transformation is not limited to product innovation, but extends to manufacturing methods as well. Large Japanese firms like Toyota and Matsushita pioneered the first step of this manufacturing revolution in the years after World War II, and their basic principles have since diffused around the industrial world.[23] The result is the rise of the creative factory, where factory workers contribute their ideas and intellectual talent as well as their physical labor.

The Japanese admired the previous "taylorist" or "fordist" system of mass production, but saw the need to improve on it. One way was by eliminating the waste inherent in assembly lines—like inventories of parts and materials stacked up at key points to avoid a stoppage of the line. The Japanese perfected "zero-inventory" techniques with every part delivered and every operation done "just-in-time." They also perfected "total quality" techniques to cut the waste of turning out bad products that had to be scrapped, reworked or, worse yet, inflicted on the customer. Both of these efforts involved mobilizing the intelligence and creativity of all the people in the plant to engage in continuous improvement. A lowly factory worker could even—horror of horrors—stop the production line if he saw bad product being turned out.

Taiichi Ohno, chief architect of the famed Toyota Production System, wrote in the 1970s of the time that a manager of another firm visited his main production plant. The man was hoping to learn the secrets of Toyota's success and evidently expected to see a high-tech wonderland. Instead the amazed visitor "realized that the [kinds of] old machines he had discarded long ago were working well at Toyota." The key, Ohno explained, is to have a plant in which "worker activities harmonize with rather than impede production"—not to "rashly purchase the most advanced high-performance machine."[24] Akio Morita, the founder and former chairman of Sony, put it this way: "A company will get nowhere if all the thinking is left to management. Everybody in the company must contribute and for the lower level employees their contribution must be more than just manual labor. We insist that all our employees contribute their minds."[25] Gradually, the message began to penetrate other corporations. The venerable IBM slogan—"THINK"—was revived and became more than an ironic cliché. The factory thus became a creative factory.

Another key advance in making things came about with the growth of a system for outsourcing manufacturing to specialized subcontractors. To many people, outsourcing is a dirty word: It's what big companies do to cut costs and avoid carrying full-time employees. Certainly these are often prime reasons for jobbing out work. But outsourcing also has encouraged creativity. In many industries, the existence of good contract manufacturers makes it easier for new players to enter the field, and easier for all players to concentrate on their own creative work. As Timothy Sturgeon of MIT's Industrial Performance Center has shown, this system has two benefits. On the one hand, it allows creative firms to not worry so much about manufacturing and focus their efforts on innovative product design. It thus separates these activities into distinct modules and allows for specialization and a more efficient division of labor. On the other, it enables subcontract manufacturers to deepen and extend their own capabilities, spread risk and capitalize on economies of scale.[26]

This modular manufacturing system was developed by U.S. companies in response to the competitive advantages of large integrated Japanese producers. When I interviewed the founders of Fairchild Semiconductor in the mid-1980s, they told me that in their early days they had to build virtually all of the tools and equipment needed to make semiconductor chips.[27] That was necessary at the time because chips were a brand-new kind of product, requiring special manufacturing techniques. Since then, chips have grown far more complex, and a modern chip fabrication line (a "fab") is still very expensive, costing a minimum of two billion dollars in 2000. If you had to own one to be in business, there might be very few chip companies, just as there are only a few automakers. As it is, big firms like Intel and Motorola—which design the big CPU (central processing unit) chips for personal computers—have their own fab lines but also outsource growing amounts of production. A lot of the smaller special-purpose chips that go into cell phones, appliances and other products are designed by "fab-less semiconductor" companies, which contract out production to firms that specialize in silicon fabrication.

The assembly of electronic products—putting the chips together with all the other parts—is almost completely dominated by subcontract manufacturers. Companies like Solectron and Flextronics make virtually every electronic product we use, from laptops and PCs to cellular phones and game modules. Started in Silicon Valley in 1971, Solectron today has state-of-the-art plants around the world that put together precision electronic products. Again there is a double benefit. The company whose name is on the product gets to focus on product design, while the subcontract assembler focuses on improving the manufacturing. The Solectron plant that I visited in Guadalajara, Mexico, had won many quality awards, including the Malcolm Baldrige Award, often considered the Nobel Prize of manufacturing.

This subcontracting or modular system is not limited to high-tech electronics. It has helped unleash creativity in many economic sectors. The fashion industry is a prime example. Calvin Klein and Tommy Hilfiger are designers; they don't manufacture clothing. At a state-of-the-art garment factory I visited in the Karmiel-Misgav region of Israel outside Haifa in the summer of 1999, the production lines were making designer undergarments for virtually every major label from Ralph Lauren and Calvin Klein to Banana Republic, The Gap and countless others. Or consider the publishing industry, where the old saying that "freedom of the press belongs to those who own one" literally isn't true. Very few book, magazine or non-daily newspaper publishers actually own a printing press. Most simply contract their manufacturing out to printing companies.

Although the automotive industry does not make use of classic subcontractors per se, a network of global suppliers has taken on a similar function in the production of cars. At new-generation automotive plants that I visited with MIT's Sturgeon in the late 1990s, we saw workers assembling cars from complete "modules" provided by these suppliers.[28] In some of the plants, employees from suppliers actually put together the car; these assembly lines have few if any employees from the company whose name the car will bear. For example, two companies, Johnson Controls and Lear Corporation, make most of the seats—or complete interior subassemblies—used by automakers around the world. Germany's Bosch and

Japan's Denso provide a good deal of the advanced electronics. Charles Fine, co-director of MIT's International Motor Vehicle Program, goes so far as to suggest that this system of global suppliers may be causing a "power shift" in the automotive industry from the traditional assemblers (whose names go on the cars) to the new breed of subcontractors and global suppliers. A parallel according to Fine is Intel in high-tech electronics: The firm doesn't make computers, but most have "Intel inside," and Intel's influence is great.[29]

Of course clothing designers, publishers and electronics firms still have to pay the contractors who make their goods, and they have to spend money on items like marketing and distribution. But a lot of those services can be contracted for, too. The extreme of this phenomenon is the "virtual company," which contracts out everything—manufacturing, warehousing and fulfillment, advertising, accounting services—retaining only a small core of executives, marketers and designers as its own staff. Only the functions that generate intellectual property, creative designs or brand identity remain in-house. And even if subcontracting is not taken to such extremes, a big entry barrier is removed when you don't have to build a company from the ground up, brick by brick and department by department.

The Social and Cultural Milieu

The final element of the social structure of creativity, and the one that has received the least attention, is a supportive social milieu that is open to all forms of creativity—artistic and cultural as well as technological and economic. This milieu provides the underlying eco-system or habitat in which the multidimensional forms of creativity take root and flourish. By supporting lifestyle and cultural institutions like a cutting-edge music scene or vibrant artistic community, for instance, it helps to attract and stimulate those who create in business and technology. It also facilitates cross-fertilization between and among these forms, as is evident through history in the rise of creative-content industries from publishing and music to film and video games. The social and cultural milieu also provides a mechanism for attracting new and different kinds of people and facilitating the rapid transmission of knowledge and ideas. Taken together, these factors round out the social structure of creativity, on which I will have much more to say throughout this book.

The elements I have been discussing—the rise of spending on research, the high-tech startup company and the formal venture capital system, the systems of the creative factory and of subcontract manufacturing, and the new creative social milieu—all arose in parallel and are now converging. We are embarking on an age of pervasive creativity that permeates all sectors of the economy and society—not just seeing bursts of innovation from high-tech industries. We are truly in the midst of a creative transformation with the onset of a Creative Economy.

Creativity as an Economic Force in History

But the roots go deeper than I have yet described. Creativity was an economic force long before the twentieth century. Moreover if, as Paul Romer and Joel Mokyr argue, creativity underlies *all* economic advancement, then it seems to me that we can read economic history as a succession of new and better ways to harness creativity. That may seem a radical statement. My reasoning is as follows: While the creative impulse is universal, obviously there would arise from time to time systems, or general ways of organizing and carrying out society's work, that represented improvements in harnessing human creativity—in calling forth new ideas, putting them into action and rewarding them. These systems would take root, persist and eventually dominate.

Extrapolating what I know about recent economic history into the distant past, it seems to me that major new systems for harnessing creativity generally evolve from existing ones. The new systems do not necessarily replace or triumph over the old, but they always expand and alter the playing field. They tend to arise when the existing order has begun to reach certain limits—and as they emerge, they of course produce periods of great advance combined with great turbulence. For it is well established that major new economic systems lead to profound changes in work, social organization and geography.

Looking back across history, one can identify several watershed transformations of this type. Drawing from the remarkable body of historical scholarship by people such as Joel Mokyr, Nathan Rosenberg, David Landes, Jared Diamond and others,[30] I will now try to show that four crucial periods of transition were hinged on advances in the harnessing of human creativity: the rise of organized agriculture, the emergence of a modern system of trade and specialization, the rise of industrial capitalism and the organizational age. In the following pages, I provide a rough sketch of each, drawing from the relevant historical scholarship. These short sketches by no means do justice to the full range of economic, social and cultural forces at work in these great epochs. My intent here is not to rewrite economic history. I simply wish to highlight the role of human creativity in economic life—and show how previous developments led up to and informed our current fifth watershed transition, the emergence of the Creative Age.

So now let us leave the world of venture capital startups and the social structure of creativity and return to the dim days of prehistory, more than 10,000 years ago.

The Rise of Agriculture

The rise of organized agriculture was the first great shift in human society. Obtaining food is perhaps the most essential work we do, and agriculture represented a then new way of organizing and carrying out this work. Rather than gather wild grains and fruits we began to grow crops; rather than hunt animals we began to tame them, breed them, milk them and slaughter as desired. This system gave people access to wool, flax and other materials as well as to all sorts of food, and though agriculture never fully displaced hunting and gathering, gradually it took hold and came to prevail.

Why did our ancestors shift to the agricultural way of life? Some conventional economic motives can be deduced. For instance, in his award-winning book *Guns, Germs, and Steel,* Jared Diamond points out that agriculture is simply more productive per unit of land. An acre of cultivated cropland will give you much more food than an acre of wilderness, where most of the plant life is inedible. Moreover, not only can domesticated animals be eaten, some of them can be efficient sources of power and transportation—and as Diamond astutely argues, technically advanced civilizations tended to develop most rapidly in those parts of the world where there were large creatures that could be tamed and bred in captivity for a variety of uses. Agriculture also proved to be a more reliable system. Consider the story of Jacob and Esau in the book of *Genesis:* Esau the mighty hunter comes home famished from an unsuccessful hunt and literally gives up his birthright for a nice agricultural meal of "bread and lentil stew"—a striking allegory of the new system's superiority.

I would like to suggest another fundamental reason why agriculture came to prevail. It engaged and rewarded our ancestors' creative faculties, because as a system it is highly amenable to elaboration and improvement. Hunting and gathering is a matter of taking what nature offers. Although hunting does require ingenuity, the possibilities of the skill set are not so broad, and most of them seem to have been explored and mastered rather early in human history. When improved methods are applied to hunting, the result is often just depletion of the prey—as happened with the mammoths and giant ground sloths of ancient America in the face of the sophisticated spear technology known to archaeologists as the Clovis culture, and has also happened with many of the world's fishing grounds as commercial fleets began to use devices such as sonar and drift nets. Thus beyond certain limits, hunting actually provides a disincentive to creativity in the form of diminished returns.

Agriculture transcended the creative limits of the old system. Over the centuries it consistently rewarded creative tinkering with high returns in the form of increased yields or improved crops and livestock. Thus selective breeding has progressed from primitive methods to those of modern genetics. There have been waves of mechanical invention, from the iron plow and the horse collar to the massive crop-gathering combine. New ideas in soil management have ranged from artificial irrigation—one of the first major applications of civil engineering, with the building of complex networks of dikes and canals in ancient times—to various methods of crop rotation, raised-bed gardening and fertilization. Moreover, agricultural endeavors lent themselves to creative interactions with other industries. Draft animals were used for powering the machinery in early mills and factories. Edward Jenner developed his smallpox vaccine after noticing that milkmaids were unusually resistant to the disease—they had been inoculated by exposure to cowpox—and to this day, there is a rich scientific interplay between agriculture and medicine. Today the last economically important vestige of the old hunting and gathering system is commercial fishing. Though it is a major business, the greatest recent advance in the fish industry has been—what else?—fish farming. The trout and catfish you buy in the supermarket are bred and harvested, not caught in the wild; the tilapia is the product of genetic modification, and surely more developments lie ahead.

The agricultural transformation of long ago led to dramatic changes in everyday life and in society as well. A life attuned to the daily tending of crops and livestock, and to the seasonal activities of sowing and harvesting and animal breeding, is far different from a life organized around the shifting availability of game and fruit. Archaeological evidence shows that as the practice of agriculture spread, people gradually became more densely settled into villages and communities; the first city-states appeared, with urban administrative hubs surrounded by farmland. New class structures and power relations emerged, and new occupations proliferated and flourished, helping to set in motion yet another period of transition and advance.[31]

Trade and Specialization

The creative limit of the agricultural system was that it did not address the production of items other than food and certain materials. Yet the changes it triggered did seem to accelerate growing specialization in those other forms of production—the making of tools, textiles, clothing and household goods; the construction of public works; mining and metalworking.[32]

Concurrently with the spread of agriculture one can trace the growth of trade, the very concept that seems so basic and natural to us today, whereby there are producers who make certain things, consumers who use those things and merchants or market-makers in the middle. A system of specialization and trade has obvious advantages in terms of harnessing creativity. Focusing on one particular kind of activity (or as we've come to say, on one "trade") allows people to devise new and better ways to do it. They can tinker with materials and processes, come up with new product designs—and when successful, they're rewarded by a growing market for their work. Which of course is what happened in advancing societies. The vast majority of people remained farmers for a very long time. But specialized "tradespeople" began to drive the course and shape of society—partly, as some sources note, because they were the ones who tended to be close to the seat of power. Highly skilled craftsmen and merchants concentrated in towns and cities to serve the wealthy rulers who could pay for their services. In doing so they also found a brisk business serving each other. Farm families might grow their own food, make their own clothes and such, but specialized tradespeople living in cities had to buy goods other than their own. Cities became centers of specialization and diverse interaction—hubs of creativity.

Distinct class and social structures also evolved around the trades. Many cities in the Middle Ages, such as London, Paris and Brussels, were literally divided into streets and districts housing goldsmiths, tailors, furniture makers and the like.[33] The members of many trades organized into guilds, groups that controlled and formalized—or tried to control and formalize—various aspects of the work, such as entry into the trade through the taking and the training of apprentices, terms and prices of sale and employment, the settling of disputes and lobbying the aristocracy. The guilds were also social organizations: A member might have his wedding celebration in the guild hall, fraternize with his guild brothers and eventually be buried by them, having trusted them to look after his widow and children. There were merchant guilds as well as craft guilds, and both came to wield political power. One noted mayor of London in the 1300s was a member of the fishmongers' guild, which controlled the distribution and sale of fish in the city. Struggles among and within the guilds were common. And over the years, some guild members grew especially powerful and wealthy, helping to set the stage for the downfall of guild control and the emergence of a new system.

The guild system eventually came up against inherent limitations on the kinds of creativity it could call forth. Craftsmen continued to design and make increasingly refined wares, and apply new production methods, but their advances were mostly incremental. With most of them working in small shops—often within tight guidelines prescribed by a guild—there was no good mechanism for introducing leaps in efficiency or innovation. By the 1700s, the time was ripe for a new system to come to the fore.

Industrial Capitalism

The start of the Industrial Revolution is usually traced to England in the latter 1700s.[34] The term "industrial" conjures up images of machinery and smoke, and there was certainly plenty of both, but our focus here is the emergence of the system that made the massive machinery and smoke-belching power sources practical. That system was the factory system. The basic idea of a factory is to bring large numbers of workers together with all their various tools and materials in one place, with a high degree of division of labor, to produce goods efficiently. This idea actually can be said to date from antiquity—large operations with all its earmarks were necessary for building public works like the pyramids and extensive irrigation systems, and for mining and shipbuilding—and gradually, in some cases, it was applied to other forms of production as well. Joel Mokyr notes that by the 1600s, "large silk mills had been erected in the Piedmont and Tuscany regions of Italy that could be called factories in every respect."[35] But it takes a lot of money to pull together such an enterprise, and for quite a while not a great deal was done with the idea. Many of the first true capitalists—people amassing money and resources to make money—were not industrialists, but merchants pooling and borrowing capital to fund trading fleets, and to purchase goods for resale (think of Marco Polo and his forebears). The interests of merchants often focused not so much on how to make goods as on how to make money trading them. But by the 1700s in England, merchant capitalists had begun to tinker with the means of production, perhaps because many merchants were themselves former producers; some were wealthy master craftsmen who'd grown more interested in buying and selling than in laboring at the smithy or the carpenter's bench.

One early innovation was the "factoring system," literally a method for pulling together all the factors of production. A merchant would arrange for purchase of raw materials, have them distributed to numerous home workshops and individual craft workers scattered here and there, and then collect the goods, either for further processing or for sale. "The factoring system," writes the historian Marc Demarest, "offered the craft producer a release from the most culturally and emotionally damaging eventuality of the nineteenth century: moving house to get to work."[36]

But distributing work around to various places could be time-consuming and costly. Why not put the workers under one roof in a "factory"? This had the added benefit of allowing a very fine, step-by-step division of labor. The efficiency of such a setup may seem obvious today to anyone who's ever organized an envelope-stuffing party. But when applied to the making of goods in the 1700s, it was still such a new idea that Adam Smith, in *The Wealth of Nations,* felt compelled to explain it in detail for his readers. The factory system did not require automated machinery. In Josiah Wedgwood's factory, fine china was handmade by a division-of-labor process that employed well over a hundred people. Some workers prepared the clay and materials; others formed the various kinds of flatware and hollow-ware, or fired it in kilns, hand-painted it and so on. But the factory system was an ideal and in fact necessary prerequisite to the efficient use of automation.

As scientific and technical knowledge grew, inventors were developing devices like the power loom and Jacquard loom, new furnaces and machinery for ironmaking, and the steam engine, a truly versatile source of power. The value of such machines could only be realized, and their cost recovered, if they were applied in high-volume work. The first commercial steam engines, designed by Thomas Newcomen in the early 1700s, were used in mining—one of the few industries that had long been marked by large-scale organization for continuous high-volume output. Then in the late 1700s, James Watt developed a vastly improved steam engine, and its use quickly spread to other applications. The combination of automated machinery and a system for using it efficiently unleashed a wave of creativity by kicking off a long-running bull market in mechanical innovation.[37]

"The factory is a machine for driving cost out of the production process," writes Demarest.[38] Factory owners and their financiers, being in competition with one another, were ever on the lookout for new machines that could drive their costs down even further. The Bessemer converter and then the open-hearth furnace, along with many other machines, turned steel from a precious metal to a useful commodity. Factory owners and financiers were also on the lookout for inventions that would make new products and services possible: An improved steam engine called a turbine, hooked to a machine called a dynamo (or generator), ushered in the age of electricity. Clothing, tools, guns and many other items increasingly came to be mass-produced.[39] And the corollary of mass production was mass marketing and mass distribution.[40]

This new system profoundly altered the structures of society and the rhythms and patterns of everyday life. For the first time, large numbers of people worked in a different location from where they lived. Although old ways of life hardly vanished overnight, gradually fewer people worked on farms or in shops connected to their homes, while more worked in separate factories. Whereas the experience of time had been more or less natural in previous ages, the factory workday was organized into distinct periods of time or "working hours."[41] Cities not only grew but were subdivided into new sorts of districts: factory districts, commercial districts, housing for the factory workers and housing districts for the capitalists and managers.[42] Social life organized itself around the emergence and clash of new economic classes. The world, at least in the industrialized nations, began to change profoundly and rapidly.

The Organizational Age

The next great transition, in the late 1800s and early 1900s, marked the rise of large-scale organization. Its defining element is the shift to a modern, highly organized economy and society whose fundamental features are large-scale institutions, functional specialization and bureaucracy. This transition was premised on two basic principles: the breaking down of tasks into their most elemental components and the transformation of human productive activity into stable and predictable routines.[43]

While many have chronicled the production efficiencies of the organizational age, its creative advantages are often overlooked. There were two big ones. A huge creative advance was the basic idea that research and development could be organized and done systematically. In their quest to systematize everything, large corporations saw the benefits of systematizing the innovation process. Pioneering laboratories like those of Edison and the Mellon Institute were emulated across a wide range of industries from Bell Laboratories and RCA to Eastman Kodak and Dupont.[44] Universities were also transformed into centers for scientific and engineering research and new technical institutes like MIT, Carnegie Tech and CalTech were formed or expanded. This system grew dramatically with massive infusions of federal R&D funding after World War II.[45]

Second, advances in industrial production increased efficiency and reduced cost, bringing a host of new inventions to the masses. This was not limited to new products such as cars and home appliances, but also included the rapid expansion of the new creative-content industries— movies, radio and television—that would help to make the United States the world's creative center.

The productive efficiencies of the new age were premised on some fundamental innovations in the organization of work. Scientific management or taylorism—as it came to be called after its founder, Frederick Taylor— broke even a simple task down into simpler elements, with each step carefully timed and optimized. Under taylorism, a manager could not only tell a worker to stoke a furnace, or install a bolt, or type a business letter, but could arrange the task and show the worker exactly *how* to do it for maximum efficiency.[46]

Another key innovation was Henry Ford's moving assembly line. The automobile was by far the most complex consumer product yet devised, and early cars defied efficient mass production. Then Ford and his colleagues—drawing on early food-industry models like that of a meatpacking plant, where carcasses were moved through on hooks to be cleaned and dressed in steps—turned the game of building automobiles around. Instead of making workers carry parts to the car as it was assembled, Ford arranged for the chassis to be moved through the plant, with parts added and operations performed at specialized stations along the line. This vastly speeded up the process of making complex products of all kinds, and reduced their cost: The price of a Model T dropped from $950 in 1909 to $360 in 1916. The moving assembly line also offered (in fact demanded) unprecedented control over factory work. German manufacturers coined the term *Fordismus,* or fordism, for the overall organizational system. It was a system of total control, because for a moving line to work, every production step had to be exquisitely timed and orchestrated. "The line" now dictated the pace and content of work. Hordes of new supervisors, efficiency experts and other middlemen were needed to keep things moving, and work became more regimented and specialized than ever. It was the extraordinarily rigid, fine-grained control inherent in the Ford system that Charlie Chaplin satirized in *Modern Times,* and that led Aldous Huxley to deify the industrialist as "Our Ford" in *Brave New World.*

The organizational age was thus distinguished by the rise of giant "fordist" organizations—big, vertically integrated command-and-control bureaucracies. Automakers in the United States made most of their own parts, had "captive suppliers" for the rest and sold their cars through captive dealers. The big firms operated behind high barriers to entry. It had always taken a lot of capital to build a factory. It took even more to build a Ford-style factory, with attendant networks of suppliers. Thus the big got bigger while the small died out.

Still more significantly, the organizational model came to prevail in places other than factories and its spread had powerful social effects. The notions of a finely honed division of tasks, of hierarchy and of bureaucratic rules came to define work virtually everywhere. Whether people made things or pushed paper, they filled prescribed slots: "Work, don't think." Even if you had a high-order thinking job, you were paid to think only about certain things in certain ways. The giant office towers with massive administrative, managerial, executive and clerical staffs were the vertical equivalent of the factory. William H. Whyte's *The Organization Man,* as we have seen, captured the essence of this change on everyday life.

Whyte was not the only one to do so. Books like John Kenneth Galbraith's *The New Industrial State* chronicle the rise of large dominant corporate institutions in society. The iconoclastic sociologist C. Wright Mills bemoaned these trends, arguing that white-collar work was even more dehumanizing and degrading than work on the factory floor. Factory workers could leave their work at the factory gates, but the white-collar man carried his work home and sold his soul to the mega-corporation. In his 1961 book, *The Lonely Crowd,* David Reisman chronicled the rise of a new and more mobile workforce and its growing obsession with money. He divided people into two types: "inner-directed," with strong values and goals that enable them to effectively navigate this world, and "other-directed" people who, because of their intense need to be liked, were inclined to dutifully conform to organizational rules and norms. The attention these changes drew was not limited to social scientists and social critics, but reverberated through the literature of the period. Sloan Wilson's *Man in the Gray Flannel Suit* depicted the struggle of one man to protect his dignity in the face of the all-consuming organization. Willy Loman, the main character in Arthur Miller's *Death of a Salesman,* so personifies these themes that Mills saw Loman as the archetype of the "little man"—"a man who by the very virtue of his moderate success in business turns out to be a total failure in life." Richard Yates's *Revolutionary Road* chronicled the alienation and despair of the organizational life.[47]

Despite the initial creative efficiencies of this new system, the eventual creative limits of the organizational age are obvious to anyone who lived through this time. Large organizations were beset by the conflict between creativity and control. The bureaucratic values of the period often functioned to snuff out creativity on the factory floor, smother or ignore it in the R&D lab and discourage entrepreneurship by wiping out small competitors and raising high entry barriers. As a host of occupations were "deskilled," layers of command and control were imposed to keep workers in line and ensure efficiency. In offices as well as factories, cadres of managers and supervisors oversaw teams of workers who carried out their jobs within tightly prescribed limits. Scientists and engineers in corporate R&D labs saw their innovations scoffed at by corporate managers. Even corporations that invested in highly successful R&D centers, like Xerox's famed Palo Alto Research Center, ignored them or squandered their discoveries.[48] Others simply sold off their famed laboratories, as RCA did with its Sarnoff Labs.[49] The organizational system, as a means of harnessing human creativity, had proven to be inexorably self-limiting. The dominant form of organization was now the integrated, hierarchical, command-and-control behemoth—not a good form for eliciting creativity from vast ranks of pigeonholed employees.

Here again, I learned of this stifling of innovation directly from my father's factory. For years the Victory Optical plant had been an exception to the organizational age rule: It was operated entirely by foremen and self-made managers like my father, who had worked their way up from the shop floor. These managers had tremendous respect for the ideas of the factory workers. I can even remember the workers looking at samples of the latest designer eyeglass frames from overseas, and coming up with their own designs to improve on the high-priced imports. Then in the late 1960s and 1970s the plant owners began to hire college-educated engineers and MBAs to oversee the factory operations. With considerable book knowledge but little experience in the actual workings of the factory—without the intelligence of the men who ran the machines—these new recruits would propose complicated ideas and systems that inevitably failed and, at worst, brought production to a grinding halt. Their ideas not only were ineffective but created growing animosity among the workforce. The bitter standoff between workers and management finally became intolerable. One day in the late 1970s, when I was at college, my father called me on the phone and said, "Today, I quit."

At the time, I wasn't quite sure about my father's story: Could college-educated experts really have ruined the factory? I was a college student, after all, trying to use education to move up the socioeconomic ladder. But within a couple of years, I realized how right he had been. As the workforce grew more demoralized, problems mounted. Skilled people quit. Machinists left in droves. The self-taught foremen and supervisors who had worked their way up from the factory floor quickly followed. Without their storehouse of knowledge and institutional memory, the factory could not operate. Less than three years after my father's departure, Victory Optical was bankrupt. The huge, vibrant factory that had captivated me in my youth was shuttered, vacant, abandoned. And surely one contributing factor was this great irony. Just when the leading edge of the corporate world had begun moving toward the creative factory concept—the concept that Victory had always been run by—Victory had moved in the opposite direction: back to the past, to the deadly organizational age model that delegated creativity to the men at the top and denied it to the rank and file.

We are now living through another large-scale economic transformation, the creative transformation, the main contours of which I have already outlined. As we have seen, its roots can be traced to the 1940s and 1950s—many of its key systems arose in response to the creative limits of the organizational age—and it came to full bloom in the 1980s and 1990s. During this time we have seen the emergence of new economic systems explicitly designed to foster and harness human creativity, and the emergence of a new social milieu that supports it. And it has given rise to a new dominant class, the topic to which I now turn.

CHAPTER 4

The Creative Class

The rise of the Creative Economy has had a profound effect on the sorting of people into social groups or classes. Others have speculated over the years on the rise of new classes in the advanced industrial economies. During the 1960s, Peter Drucker and Fritz Machlup described the growing role and importance of the new group of workers they dubbed "knowledge workers."[1] Writing in the 1970s, Daniel Bell pointed to a new, more meritocratic class structure of scientists, engineers, managers and administrators brought on by the shift from a manufacturing to a "postindustrial" economy. The sociologist Erik Olin Wright has written for decades about the rise of what he called a new "professional-managerial" class.[2] Robert Reich more recently advanced the term "symbolic analysts" to describe the members of the workforce who manipulate ideas and symbols.[3] All of these observers caught economic aspects of the emerging class structure that I describe here.

Others have examined emerging social norms and value systems. Paul Fussell presciently captured many that I now attribute to the Creative Class in his theory of the "X Class." Near the end of his 1983 book *Class*—after a witty romp through status markers that delineate, say, the upper middle class from "high proles"—Fussell noted the presence of a growing "X" group that seemed to defy existing categories:

> [Y]ou are not born an X person . . . you earn X-personhood by a strenuous effort of discovery in which curiosity and originality are indispensable. . . . The young flocking to the cities to devote themselves to "art," "writing," "creative work"—anything, virtually, that liberates them from the presence of a boss or superior—are aspirant X people. . . . If, as [C. Wright] Mills has said, the middle-class person is "always somebody's man," the X person is nobody's. . . . X people are independent-minded. . . . They adore the work they do, and they do it until they are finally carried out, "retirement" being a con-

cept meaningful only to hired personnel or wage slaves who despise their work.[4]

Writing in 2000, David Brooks outlined the blending of bohemian and bourgeois values in a new social grouping he dubbed the Bobos. My take on Brooks's synthesis, which will come in Chapter 11, is rather different, stressing the very transcendence of these two categories in a new creative ethos.

The main point I want to make here is that the basis of the Creative Class is economic. I define it as an economic class and argue that its economic function both underpins and informs its members' social, cultural and lifestyle choices. The Creative Class consists of people who add economic value through their creativity. It thus includes a great many knowledge workers, symbolic analysts and professional and technical workers, but emphasizes their true role in the economy. My definition of class emphasizes the way people organize themselves into social groupings and common identities based principally on their economic function. Their social and cultural preferences, consumption and buying habits, and their social identities all flow from this.

I am not talking here about economic class in terms of the ownership of property, capital or the means of production. If we use class in this traditional Marxian sense, we are still talking about a basic structure of capitalists who own and control the means of production, and workers under their employ. But little analytical utility remains in these broad categories of bourgeoisie and proletarian, capitalist and worker. Most members of the Creative Class do not own and control any significant property in the physical sense. Their property—which stems from their creative capacity—is an intangible because it is literally in their heads. And it is increasingly clear from my field research and interviews that while the members of the Creative Class do not yet see themselves as a unique social grouping, they actually share many similar tastes, desires and preferences. This new class may not be as distinct in this regard as the industrial Working Class in its heyday, but it has an emerging coherence.

The New Class Structure

The distinguishing characteristic of the Creative Class is that its members engage in work whose function is to "create meaningful new forms." I define the Creative Class as consisting of two components. The Super-

Creative Core of this new class includes scientists and engineers, university professors, poets and novelists, artists, entertainers, actors, designers and architects, as well as the thought leadership of modern society: nonfiction writers, editors, cultural figures, think-tank researchers, analysts and other opinion-makers. Whether they are software programmers or engineers, architects or filmmakers, they fully engage in the creative process. I define the highest order of creative work as producing new forms or designs that are readily transferable and widely useful—such as designing a product that can be widely made, sold and used; coming up with a theorem or strategy that can be applied in many cases; or composing music that can be performed again and again. People at the core of the Creative Class engage in this kind of work regularly; it's what they are paid to do. Along with problem solving, their work may entail problem finding: not just building a better mousetrap, but noticing first that a better mousetrap would be a handy thing to have.

Beyond this core group, the Creative Class also includes "creative professionals" who work in a wide range of knowledge-intensive industries such as high-tech sectors, financial services, the legal and health care professions, and business management. These people engage in creative problem solving, drawing on complex bodies of knowledge to solve specific problems. Doing so typically requires a high degree of formal education and thus a high level of human capital. People who do this kind of work may sometimes come up with methods or products that turn out to be widely useful, but it's not part of the basic job description. What they *are* required to do regularly is think on their own. They apply or combine standard approaches in unique ways to fit the situation, exercise a great deal of judgment, perhaps try something radically new from time to time. Creative Class people such as physicians, lawyers and managers do this kind of work in dealing with the many varied cases they encounter. In the course of their work, they may also be involved in testing and refining new techniques, new treatment protocols, or new management methods and even develop such things themselves. As a person continues to do more of this latter work, perhaps through a career shift or promotion, that person moves up to the Super-Creative Core: producing transferable, widely usable new forms is now their primary function.

Much the same is true of the growing number of technicians and others who apply complex bodies of knowledge to working with physical materials. And they are sufficiently engaged in creative problem solving that I have included a large subset of them in the Creative Class. In an insightful

1996 study, Stephen Barley of Stanford University emphasized the growing importance and influence of this group of workers.[5] In fields such as
medicine and scientific research, technicians are taking on increased responsibility to interpret their work and make decisions, blurring the old
distinction between white-collar work (done by decisionmakers) and
blue-collar work (done by those who follow orders). Barley notes that in
medicine, for instance, "emergency medical technicians take action on the
basis of diagnoses made at the site," while sonographers and radiology
technicians draw on "knowledge of biological systems, pharmacology, and
disease processes to render diagnostically useful information"—all of
which encroaches on turf once reserved for the M.D.

   Barley also found that in some areas of biomedical work, like the
breeding of monoclonal antibodies, labs have had increasing difficulty
duplicating each other's work: They might use the same formulas and
well-documented procedures but not get the same results. The reason is
that although the lead scientists at the labs might be working from the
same theories, the lab technicians are called upon to make myriad inter-
pretations and on-the-spot decisions. And while different technicians
might all do these things according to accepted standards, they do them
differently. Each is drawing on an arcane knowledge base and exercising
his or her own judgment, by individual thought processes so complex and
elusive that they could not easily be documented or communicated.
Though counterproductive in this case, this individuality happens to be
one of the hallmarks of creative work. Lest you think this sort of thing
happens only in the rarefied world of the biomedical laboratory, Barley
notes a similar phenomenon among technicians who repair and maintain
copying machines. They acquire their own arcane bodies of knowledge
and develop their own unique ways of doing the job.

   As the creative content of other lines of work increases—as the relevant
body of knowledge becomes more complex, and people are more valued
for their ingenuity in applying it—some now in the Working Class or Service Class may move into the Creative Class and even the Super-Creative
Core. Alongside the growth in essentially creative occupations, then, we
are also seeing growth in creative content across other occupations. A
prime example is the secretary in today's pared-down offices. In many
cases this person not only takes on a host of tasks once performed by a
large secretarial staff, but becomes a true office manager—channeling
flows of information, devising and setting up new systems, often making
key decisions on the fly. This person contributes more than "intelligence"

or computer skills. She or he adds creative value. Everywhere we look, creativity is increasingly valued. Firms and organizations value it for the results that it can produce and individuals value it as a route to self-expression and job satisfaction. Bottom line: As creativity becomes more valued, the Creative Class grows.

Not all workers are on track to join, however. For instance in many lower-end service jobs we find the trend running the opposite way; the jobs continue to be "de-skilled" or "de-creatified." For a counter worker at a fast-food chain, literally every word and move is dictated by a corporate template: "Welcome to Food Fix, sir, may I take your order? Would you like nachos with that?" This job has been thoroughly taylorized—the worker is given far less latitude for exercising creativity than the waitress at the old, independent neighborhood diner enjoyed. Worse yet, there are many people who do not have jobs, and who are being left behind because they do not have the background and training to be part of this new system.

Growing alongside the Creative Class is another social grouping I call the Service Class—which contains low-end, typically low-wage and low-autonomy occupations in the so-called "service sector" of the economy: food-service workers, janitors and groundskeepers, personal care attendants, secretaries and clerical workers, and security guards and other service occupations. In U.S. Bureau of Labor Statistics projections from the late 1990s and 2000, the fastest-growing job categories included "janitors and cleaners" and "waiters and waitresses" alongside "computer support specialists" and "systems analysts." The growth of this Service Class is in large measure a response to the demands of the Creative Economy. Members of the Creative Class, because they are well compensated and work long and unpredictable hours, require a growing pool of low-end service workers to take care of them and do their chores. This class has thus been created out of economic necessity because of the way the Creative Economy operates. Some people are temporary members of the Service Class, have high upward mobility and will soon move into the Creative Class—college students working nights or summers as food clerks or office cleaners, and highly educated recent immigrants driving cabs in New York City or Washington, D.C. A few, entrepreneurial ones may be successful enough to open their own restaurants, lawn and garden services and the like. But many others have no way out and are stuck for life in menial jobs as food-service help, janitors, nursing home orderlies, security guards and delivery drivers. At its minimum-wage worst, life in the Service Class is a grueling struggle for existence amid the wealth of others. By going "undercover" as a service worker, Barbara Ehrenreich provided a moving chronicle of what life is like for people in these roles in her book *Nickel and Dimed.*[6]

A study of the Austin, Texas, economy sheds light on the growing gaps between the Creative and Service Classes. Austin is a leading center of the Creative Economy and consistently ranks among the top regions on my indicators. A study by Robert Cushing and Musseref Yetim of the University of Texas compared Austin, which in 1999 had a whopping 38 percent of its private-sector workforce in high-tech industries, to other regions in the state. Between 1990 and 1999, average private-sector wages in Austin grew by 65 percent, far and away the most in the state. During that same time, the gap between wages earned by the top fifth and the bottom fifth of the people in Austin grew by 70 percent—also far and away the most in the state. Remove the high-tech sector from the equation and both effects go away. There is a perfectly logical reason for the gap: High-tech specialists were in short supply so their wages were bid up. And in fairness, it should be noted that Austin's bottom fifth of wage earners weren't left out entirely. Their income did go up from 1990 to 1999, and more than for their counterparts in other Texas regions. Apparently Austin had a growing need for their services, too. But these trends do more than illustrate a widening income gap. They point to a real divide in terms of what people do with their lives—with the economic positions and lifestyle choices of some people driving and perpetuating the types of choices available to others.[7]

Counting the Creative Class

It is one thing to provide a compelling description of the changing class composition of society, as writers like Bell, Fussell or Reich have done. But I believe it is also important to calibrate and quantify the magnitude of the change at hand. In 1996, Steven Barley estimated that professional, technical and managerial occupations increased from 10 percent of the workforce in 1900 to 30 percent by 1991, while both blue-collar work and agricultural work fell precipitously.[8] In a 2001 article, the sociologist Steven Brint estimated that the "scientific, professional and knowledge economy" accounted for 36 percent of all U.S. employment in 1996—a human capital-based estimate including industries where at least 5 percent of the workforce has graduate degrees. His definition includes agricultural services, mass media, chemicals, plastics, pharmaceuticals, computers and

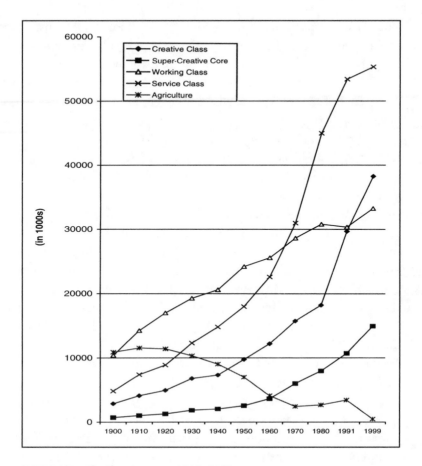

FIGURE 4.1   The Class Structure, 1900–1999

(SOURCE: See Appendix.)

electric equipment, scientific instruments, banking, accounting, consulting and other business services, health services and hospitals, education,
legal services and nearly all religious and governmental organizations.[9]

Working with colleagues and graduate students at Carnegie Mellon, I
developed a detailed statistical portrait of the rise of the Creative Class
and the changing class structure of the United States over the twentieth
century (see Figs. 4.1 and 4.2). I believe this definition is an improvement
over previous concepts of knowledge workers and the like. I base it on the
"standard occupational classifications" collected by the U.S. Census and
available in its historical statistics from 1900 to the present. (The Appendix provides a complete explanation of all data and sources.) Let's take a
look at the key trends.

- The *Creative Class* now includes some 38.3 million Americans, roughly 30 percent of the entire U.S. workforce. It has grown from roughly 3 million workers in 1900, an increase of more than tenfold. At the turn of the twentieth century, the Creative Class made up just 10 percent of the workforce, where it hovered until 1950 when it began a slow rise; it held steady around 20 percent in the 1970s and 1980s. Since that time, this new class has virtually exploded, increasing from less than 20 million to its current total, reaching 25 percent of the working population in 1991 before climbing to 30 percent by 1999.
- At the heart of the Creative Class is the *Super-Creative Core,* comprising 15 million workers, or 12 percent of the workforce. It is made up of people who work in science and engineering, computers and mathematics, education, and the arts, design and entertainment, people who work in directly creative activity, as we have seen. Over the past century, this segment rose from less than 1 million workers in 1900 to 2.5 million in 1950 before crossing 10 million in 1991. In doing so, it increased its share of the workforce from 2.5 percent in 1900 to 5 percent in 1960, 8 percent in 1980 and 9 percent in 1990, before reaching 12 percent by 1999.
- The traditional *Working Class* has today 33 million workers, or a quarter of the U.S. workforce. It consists of people in production operations, transportation and materials moving, and repair and maintenance and construction work. The percentage of the workforce in working-class occupations peaked at 40 percent in 1920, where it hovered until 1950, before slipping to 36 percent in 1970, and then declining sharply over the past two decades.
- The *Service Class* includes 55.2 million workers or 43 percent of the U.S. workforce, making it the largest group of all. It includes workers in lower-wage, lower-autonomy service occupations such as health care, food preparation, personal care, clerical work and other lower-end office work. Alongside the decline of the Working Class, the past century has seen a tremendous rise in the Service Class, from 5 million workers in 1900 to its current total of more than ten times that amount.

It's also useful to look at the changing composite picture of the U.S. class structure over the twentieth century. In 1900, there were some 10 million people in the Working Class, compared to 2.9 million in the Cre-

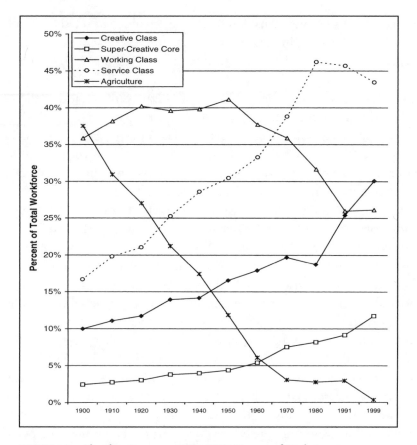

FIGURE 4.2 The Class Structure, 1900–1999 (Percent of Work Force)

(SOURCE: See Appendix.)

ative Class and 4.8 million in the Service Class. The Working Class was thus larger than the two other classes combined. Yet the largest class at that time was agricultural workers, who composed nearly 40 percent of the workforce but whose numbers rapidly declined to just a very small percentage today. In 1920, the Working Class accounted for 40 percent of the workforce, compared to slightly more than 12 percent for the Creative Class and 21 percent for the Service Class.

In 1950, the class structure remained remarkably similar. The Working Class was still in the majority, with 25 million workers, some 40 percent of the workforce, compared to 10 million in the Creative Class (16.5 percent) and 18 million in the Service Class (30 percent). In relative terms, the Working Class was as large as it was in 1920 and bigger than it was in 1900. Though the Creative Class had grown slightly in percentage terms, the

Service Class had grown considerably, taking up much of the slack coming from the steep decline in agriculture.

The tectonic shift in the U.S. class structure has taken place over the past two decades. In 1970, the Service Class pulled ahead of the Working Class, and by 1980 it was much larger (46 versus 32 percent), marking the first time in the twentieth century that the Working Class was not the dominant class. By 1999, both the Creative Class and the Service Class had pulled ahead of the Working Class. The Service Class, with 55 million workers (43.4 percent), was bigger in relative terms than the Working Class had been at any time in the past century.

These changes in American class structure reflect a deeper, more general process of economic and social change. The decline of the old Working Class is part and parcel of the decline of the industrial economy on which it was based, and of the social and demographic patterns upon which that old society was premised. The Working Class no longer has the hand it once did in setting the tone or establishing the values of American life—for that matter neither does the 1950s managerial class. Why, then, have the social functions of the Working Class not been taken over by the new largest class, the Service Class? As we have seen, the Service Class has little clout and its rise in numbers can be understood only alongside the rise of the Creative Class. The Creative Class—and the modern Creative Economy writ large—depends on this ever-larger Service Class to "outsource" functions that were previously provided within the family. The Service Class exists mainly as a supporting infrastructure for the Creative Class and the Creative Economy. The Creative Class also has considerably more economic power. Members earn substantially more than those in other classes. In 1999, the average salary for a member of the Creative Class was nearly $50,000 ($48,752) compared to roughly $28,000 for a Working Class member and $22,000 for a Service Class worker (see Table 4.1).

I see these trends vividly played out in my own life. I have a nice house with a nice kitchen but it's often mostly a fantasy kitchen—I eat out a lot, with "servants" preparing my food and waiting on me. My house is clean, but I don't clean it, a housekeeper does. I also have a gardener and a pool service; and (when I take a taxi) a chauffeur. I have, in short, just about all the servants of an English lord except that they're not mine full-time and they don't live below stairs; they are part-time and distributed in the local area. Not all of these "servants" are lowly serfs. The person who cuts my hair is a very creative stylist much in demand, and drives a new BMW. The woman who cleans my house is a gem: I trust her not only to clean but to

TABLE 4.1   Wages and Salaries for the Classes

Category	Total Workers	Average Hourly Wage	Average Annual Salary
Creative Class	38,278,110	$23.44	$48,752
Super-Creative Core	14,932,420	20.54	42,719
Working Class	33,238,810	13.36	27,799
Service Class	55,293,720	10.61	22,059
Agriculture	463,360	8.65	18,000
Entire US	127,274,000	15.18	31,571

SOURCE: Occupational Employment Statistics (OES) Survey, Bureau of Labor Statistics, Department of Labor, 1999, see Appendix.

rearrange and suggest ideas for redecorating; she takes on these things in an entrepreneurial manner. Her husband drives a Porsche. To some degree, these members of the Service Class have adopted many of the functions along with the tastes and values of the Creative Class, with which they see themselves sharing much in common. Both my hairdresser and my housekeeper have taken up their lines of work to get away from the regimentation of large organizations; both of them relish creative pursuits. Service Class people such as these are close to the mainstream of the Creative Economy and prime candidates for reclassification.

Creative Class Values

The rise of the Creative Class is reflected in powerful and significant shifts in values, norms and attitudes. Although these changes are still in process and certainly not fully played out, a number of key trends have been discerned by researchers who study values, and I have seen them displayed in my field research across the United States. Not all of these attitudes break with the past: Some represent a melding of traditional values and newer ones. They are also values that have long been associated with more highly educated and creative people. On the basis of my own interviews and focus groups, along with a close reading of statistical surveys conducted by others, I cluster these values along three basic lines.

Individuality.   The members of the Creative Class exhibit a strong preference for individuality and self-statement. They do not want to conform to organizational or institutional directives and resist traditional group-oriented norms. This has always been the case among creative people from "quirky" artists to "eccentric" scientists. But it has now become far more pervasive. In this sense, the increasing nonconformity to organizational norms may represent a new mainstream value. Members of the Creative Class endeavor to create individualistic identities that reflect their creativity. This can entail a mixing of multiple creative identities.

Meritocracy.   Merit is very strongly valued by the Creative Class, a quality shared with Whyte's class of organization men. The Creative Class favors hard work, challenge and stimulation. Its members have a propensity for goal-setting and achievement. They want to get ahead because they are good at what they do.

Creative Class people no longer define themselves mainly by the amount of money they make or their position in a financially delineated status order. While money may be looked upon as a marker of achievement, it is not the whole story. In interviews and focus groups, I consistently come across people valiantly trying to defy an economic class into which they were born. This is particularly true of the young descendants of the truly wealthy—the capitalist class—who frequently describe themselves as just "ordinary" creative people working on music, film or intellectual endeavors of one sort or another. Having absorbed the Creative Class value of merit, they no longer find true status in their wealth and thus try to downplay it.

There are many reasons for the emphasis on merit. Creative Class people are ambitious and want to move up based on their abilities and effort. Creative people have always been motivated by the respect of their peers. The companies that employ them are often under tremendous competitive pressure and thus cannot afford much dead wood on staff: Everyone has to contribute. The pressure is more intense than ever to hire the best people regardless of race, creed, sexual preference or other factors.

But meritocracy also has its dark side. Qualities that confer merit, such as technical knowledge and mental discipline, are socially acquired and cultivated. Yet those who have these qualities may easily start thinking they were born with them, or acquired them all on their own, or that others just "don't have it." By papering over the causes of cultural and educational advantage, meritocracy may subtly perpetuate the very prejudices it claims to renounce. On the bright side, of course, meritocracy ties into a host of values and beliefs we'd all agree are positive—from faith that virtue will be rewarded, to valuing self-determination and mistrusting rigid caste systems. Researchers have found such values to be on the rise, not only among the Creative Class in the United States, but throughout our society and other societies.

Diversity and Openness.   Diversity has become a politically charged buzzword. To some it is an ideal and rallying cry, to others a Trojan-horse concept that has brought us affirmative action and other liberal abominations. The Creative Class people I study use the word a lot, but not to press any political hot buttons. Diversity is simply something they value in all its manifestations. This is spoken of so often, and so matter-of-factly, that I take it to be a fundamental marker of Creative Class values. As my focus groups and interviews reveal, members of this class strongly favor organizations and environments in which they feel that anyone can fit in and can get ahead.

Diversity of peoples is favored first of all out of self-interest. Diversity can be a signal of meritocratic norms at work. Talented people defy classification based on race, ethnicity, gender, sexual preference or appearance. One indicator of this preference for diversity is reflected in the fact that Creative Class people tell me that at job interviews they like to ask if the company offers same-sex partner benefits, even when they are not themselves gay. What they're seeking is an environment open to differences. Many highly creative people, regardless of ethnic background or sexual orientation, grew up feeling like outsiders, different in some way from most of their schoolmates. They may have odd personal habits or extreme styles of dress. Also, Creative Class people are mobile and tend to move around to different parts of the country; they may not be "natives" of the place they live even if they are American-born. When they are sizing up a new company and community, acceptance of diversity and of gays in particular is a sign that reads "nonstandard people welcome here." It also registers itself in changed behaviors and organizational policies. For example, in some Creative Class centers like Silicon Valley and Austin, the traditional office Christmas party is giving way to more secular, inclusive celebrations. The big event at many firms is now the Halloween party: Just about anyone can relate to a holiday that involves dressing up in costume.

While the Creative Class favors openness and diversity, to some degree it is a diversity of elites, limited to highly educated, creative people. Even though the rise of the Creative Class has opened up new avenues of advancement for women and members of ethnic minorities, its existence has certainly failed to put an end to long-standing divisions of race and gender. Within high-tech industries in particular these divisions still seem to hold. The world of high-tech creativity doesn't include many African-Americans. Several of my interviewees noted that a typical high-tech company "looks like the United Nations minus the black faces." This is unfortunate but not surprising. For several reasons, U.S. blacks are under-represented in many professions, and this may be compounded today by the so-called digital divide—black families in the United States tend to be poorer than average, and thus their children are less likely to have access to computers. My own research shows a negative statistical correlation between concentrations of high-tech firms in a region and nonwhites as a percentage of the population, which is particularly disturbing in light of my other findings on the positive relationship between high-tech and other kinds of diversity—from foreign-born people to gays.

There are intriguing challenges to the kind of diversity that the members of the Creative Class are drawn to. Speaking of a small software company that had the usual assortment of Indian, Chinese, Arabic and other employees, an Indian technology professional said: "That's not diversity! They're all software engineers." Yet despite the holes in the picture, distinctive value changes are indeed afoot, as other researchers have clearly found.

The Post-Scarcity Effect

Ronald Inglehart, a political science professor at the University of Michigan, has documented the powerful shift in values and attitudes across the world in more than two decades of careful research. In three periods over the past twenty years, researchers participating in Inglehart's World Values Survey administered detailed questionnaires to random samples of adults in countries around the world.[10] By 1995–1998, the last survey period, the number of nations studied had grown to sixty-five, including about 75 percent of the world's population. Along with specific issues like divorce, abortion and suicide, the survey delved into matters such as deference to authority versus deciding for oneself, openness versus insularity (can strangers be trusted?), and what, ultimately, is important in life. Inglehart and his colleagues have sifted the resulting data to look for internal correlations (which kinds of values tend to go together) and for correlations with economic and social factors such as a nation's level of economic development, form of government and religious heritage. The researchers compared nations to one another, mapping out various similarities and differences—and they also looked for changes over time.

Among other things, Inglehart found a worldwide shift from economic growth issues to lifestyle values, which he sometimes refers to as a shift from "survival" to "self-expression" values. Moreover where lifestyle issues are rising or dominant, as in the United States and most European societies, people tend to be relatively tolerant of other groups and in favor of gender equality. This is very much in line with Creative Class values. In everything from sexual norms and gender roles to environmental values, Inglehart finds a continued movement away from traditional norms to more progressive ones. Furthermore, as economies grow, living standards improve and people grow less attached to large institutions, they become more open and tolerant in their views on personal relationships. Inglehart believes this new value system reflects a "shift in what people want out of life, transforming basic norms governing politics, work, religion, family and sexual behavior."

In their 2000 book *The Cultural Creatives,* sociologist Paul H. Ray and psychologist Ruth Anderson report similar conclusions. They estimate that some 50 million Americans fall into the category of cultural creatives, having neither "traditional" nor conventionally "modern" values. These people tend to be socially active on issues that concern them, pro-environment and in favor of gender equality. Many are spiritually oriented, though rejecting mainstream religious beliefs. Members of this group are more likely than others to be interested in personal development and relationships, have eclectic tastes, enjoy "foreign and exotic" experiences, and identify themselves as being "not financially materialistic."[11] In short, these cultural creatives have values that Inglehart refers to as "postmaterialist."

This shift in values and attitudes, Inglehart argues, is driven by changes in our material conditions. In agricultural societies and even for much of the industrial age, people basically lived under conditions of scarcity. We had to work simply to survive. The rise of an affluent or "post-scarcity" economy means that we no longer have to devote all our energies just to staying alive, but have the wealth, time and ability to enjoy other aspects of life. This in turn affords us choices we did not have before. "Precisely because they attained high levels of economic security," writes Inglehart, "the Western societies that were the first to industrialize have gradually come to emphasize post-materialist values, giving higher priority to the quality of life than to economic growth. In this respect, the rise of post-materialist values reverses the rise of the Protestant ethic."[12] The overriding trend appears to be an intergenerational shift from emphasis on economic and physical security toward increasing emphasis on self-expression, subjective well-being, and quality of life. . . . This cultural shift is found throughout advanced industrial societies; it seems to emerge among birth cohorts that have grown up under conditions in which survival is taken for granted.[13]

The Nobel Prize-winning economist Robert Fogel concurs: "Today, people are increasingly concerned with what life is all about. That was not true for the ordinary individual in 1885 when nearly the whole day was devoted to earning the food, clothing, and shelter needed to sustain life."[14] Even though many conservative commentators bemoan these shifts as hedonistic, narcissistic and damaging to society, the Creative Class is anything but radical or nonconformist. On the one hand, its members have taken what looked to be alternative values and made them mainstream. On the other, many of these values—such as the commitment to meritocracy and to hard work—are quite traditional and system-reinforcing. In my interviews, members of the Creative Class resist characterization as alternative or bohemian. These labels suggest being outside or even against the prevailing culture, and they insist they are part of the culture, working and living inside it. In this regard, the Creative Class has made certain symbols of nonconformity acceptable—even conformist. It is in this sense that they represent not an alternative group but a new and increasingly norm-setting mainstream of society.

Perhaps we are indeed witnessing the rise of what Mokyr calls *homo creativus*. We live differently and pursue new lifestyles because we see ourselves as a new kind of person. We are more tolerant and more liberal both because our material conditions allow it and because the new Creative Age tells us to be so. A new social class, in short, has risen to a position of dominance in the last two decades, and this shift has fundamentally transformed our economy and society—and continues to do so. The rest of this book will look at how these changes in our economy and society, in the class structure and in our values and identity are playing themselves out in the way we work and live in this new age.

PART TWO

Work

CHAPTER 5

The Machine Shop and the Hair Salon

During the late 1990s I served on the board of Team Pennsylvania, an economic development advisory group convened by then-Governor Tom Ridge. At one of our meetings, the state's Secretary of Labor and Industry, a big burly man, banged his fist on the table in frustration. "Our workforce is out of balance," he steamed. "We're turning out too many hairdressers and cosmetologists, and not enough skilled factory workers" like welders and machine-tool operators to meet the labor market's needs. "What's wrong?" he implored the group.

The problem is not limited to Pennsylvania. There have been acute shortages of skilled factory workers across the United States and many find this perplexing. Machinists, for example, earn good wages and benefits. They do important work. For many years, a machinist's job was considered an elite career for anyone not college-bound. It is the sort of "good job" that politicians and editorial writers fretted that our economy was losing. Yet as older machinists retire, there are not enough young people to fill the positions that exist. Trade schools that teach skills like machining and welding have had to cut back or close their programs for lack of interest. Meanwhile, young men and women flock to beauty academies.

At the Team Pennsylvania meeting, the clear diagnosis was that (a) guidance counselors at high schools have been steering the kids wrong, because (b) our job projections have been off. If we fixed the projections and worked with the high schools—and maybe did some public-image work—surely droves of young people would come back to those good, secure manufacturing jobs.

After the meeting, I laid out the problem to my first-year public policy students at Carnegie Mellon. Then I asked them: If you had just two career choices open to you, where would you work—in a machine shop, with high pay and a job for life, or in a hair salon, with less pay and where you were subject to the whims of the economy? Later I started putting the same question to audiences across the country.

Time and again, most people chose the hair salon, and always for the same reasons. Sure, the pay isn't as good, but the environment is more stimulating. It's more flexible; it's clean; you're scheduled to meet your clients and then left alone with them, instead of grinding away to meet quotas and schedules with bosses looking over your shoulder. You get to work with interesting people and you're always learning new things, the latest styles. You get to add your own touches and make creative decisions, because every customer is a new challenge, and you're the one in charge. When you do good work, you see the results right away: People look good; they're happy. If you are really talented, you can open your own salon. Maybe even become a hairdresser to the rich and famous, like Christophe, who kept Air Force One on the runway while he gave Bill Clinton a haircut, and get written up in celebrity magazines. Even when I pressed the issue of pay, most said the pay differential really didn't matter. In almost every case, the content of the job and the nature of the work environment mattered much more than compensation.

I don't think guidance counselors can change this. The people in my straw poll who chose the hair salon saw it as the more creative, exciting and satisfying place to work. It offers intrinsic rewards—rewards inherent in the nature of the job. I suspect that similar motives drive many of the people who choose the hair salon in real life—as well as the growing numbers of young people who are "good with their hands" but choose to wrap their hands around a tattooing needle, DJ turntable or landscaping tools rather than the controls of a turret lathe. Moreover, these values and attitudes have continually turned up in more structured interviews and focus groups I conducted with Creative Class people and others across the United States. The same values also top the list in various statistical surveys of what people desire in their jobs—including two major recent surveys of information-technology workers.

Why are people's desires so different from what the pundits and policymakers say we should want? The reason is basic. These new attitudes reflect both the changing nature of work and the shifting desires of the Creative Class. Conventional wisdom says people work for money; they will go where the financial opportunities are best and the shot at financial security is greatest. In the halcyon days of the New Economy, this was widely assumed to be true even of high-tech creative workers, who were working for the chance to translate their stock options into untold wealth.

That assumption was wrong. Writing at the apex of the New Economy, Peter Drucker had this to say:

> Bribing the knowledge workers on whom these industries depend will therefore simply not work. The key knowledge workers in these businesses will surely continue to expect to share financially in the fruits of their labor. But the financial fruits are likely to take much longer to ripen, if they ripen at all. . . . Increasingly, performance in these new knowledge-based industries will come to depend on running the institution so as to attract, hold, and motivate knowledge workers. When this can no longer be done by satisfying knowledge workers' greed, as we are now trying to do, it will have to be done by satisfying their values, and by giving them social recognition and social power. It will have to be done by turning them from subordinates into fellow executives, and from employees, however well paid, into partners.[1]

As this chapter will show, even dramatically changing economic conditions seem to have little effect on what most people, particularly creative people, want out of their work. Motivating creative people has always required more than money. It depends on intrinsic rewards and is tied to the very creative content of their work.

What Money Can't Buy

Of course people work to make money: It's necessary but not sufficient. During the NASDAQ crash, when mass layoffs were rampant at high-tech firms, I received the following e-mail from someone who had survived a round of head-cutting at the high-tech consulting company Sapient Systems: "Many of those I knew [who were laid off] have had little problem getting new jobs," he explained—but "we had a lot of really good people who wanted to work at Sapient because of the culture, and when they were let go it was like losing family." Then he added: "One of the most important things at Sapient is culture and hiring only the best people. Sapient does not pay the best, intentionally, because if you pay top dollar, then you get mercenaries and mercenaries don't help develop culture."[2] This was an astounding statement. Here was an employee writing at the darkest hour, with heads rolling all around him, and he was praising his employer for having the wisdom not to pay too highly. He also hints at another key point. For many people, the big worry during the high-tech downturn was not the loss of stock-option value or job security. It was that they might have to settle for "just a job," and perhaps not enjoy all the intrinsic rewards they'd grown accustomed to.

I am hardly the first observer to notice that money isn't the only thing people want. Yet my research has convinced me that many firms, scholars and business pundits still overrate money as a motivating factor, especially in the world of creative work. What I find generally is the following:

- Yes, people want enough money to live in the manner they prefer.
- Even if earning enough to pay the bills, they will be unhappy if they feel they are not being paid what they're worth, as gauged, for instance, by how much work they think they do or by what their colleagues are paid.
- But while the absence of enough money is sufficient, in itself, to make them unhappy with their work, money alone will not make most workers happy, or committed, or motivated.

Creative people require more than *compensation* for their time—a quid pro quo trade of time and effort for cash and other financial considerations. "You cannot motivate the best people with money," says Eric Raymond, author of *The Cathedral and the Bazaar* and a leading authority on open source software. "Money is just a way to keep score. The best people in any field are motivated by passion."[3] Yes, but passion for what? There is no one-size-fits-all answer. Passion varies because people are different. A number of books and studies on workplace motivation have tried to sort people into various groups on the basis of what they value most, and we'll look at some of these efforts shortly. I would also point out that people are complex. Most of us have mixed motives.

The *Information Week* Surveys

For all the attention given to workplace motivation over the years, surprisingly little hard numerical research or analysis has been done on what motivates today's creative workers.[4] In the summer of 2001, I had a chance to address this issue by analyzing data from what I believe are among the largest and most comprehensive extant surveys on the subject. As a columnist for *Information Week,* a print/on-line magazine covering the information-technology industry, I have access to the publication's research data. Every year *Information Week* conducts a Salary Survey that asks readers detailed questions not only about their pay and benefits, but about their job satisfaction and a host of work-related factors. Some 20,000 in-formation-technology (IT) workers completed the survey in both 2000 and 2001. Of these, approximately 11,000 identified themselves as IT staff and 9,000 as management. The sample is not scientifically random, since people self-select by choosing to respond. But it is extremely large and it reaches far beyond the computer and software industries per se, including IT workers in virtually every sector of the economy.

IT workers provide an interesting vantage point from which to examine these issues. On the one hand, they have been said to be a fairly conventional sector of the Creative Class. They are certainly a good deal more mainstream than artists, musicians or advertising copywriters. On the other, IT workers are said to care a great deal about money. They are a high-paid segment of the workforce to begin with, and during the late 1990s, companies went to great lengths to provide bonuses, stock options, six-figure salaries and other financial incentives to lure them. My colleague Kevin Stolarick and I combed through the raw data from the *Information Week* surveys and repeatedly resifted it to seek a better under-standing of what IT workers value.

One key question in the survey asked: "What matters most to you about your job?" It then listed thirty-eight factors from which respondents could check one or more. Just from glancing at the initial results, one bottom line is clear: Money is an important but insufficient motivator (see Fig. 5.1). Base pay ranked fourth as a key factor, selected by 38.5 percent of re-spondents. Nearly twice as many selected "challenge of job/responsibility," making it the top-ranked factor. Interestingly, the ability to share in the fi-nancial upside through stock options did not even make the top twenty: Fewer than 10 percent of all people selected it.

When we sorted the thirty-eight individual job factors in the *Informa-tion Week* survey into eleven broad clusters, challenge remained by far the top-ranked factor, followed by flexibility and job stability (see Fig. 5.2). Compensation was again fourth, followed by peer respect, technology and location; and further down the list were company orientation, organiza-tional culture, career orientation and benefits.

The things that matter to IT workers tend to stay fairly constant as eco-nomic conditions change. To determine this, I compared the *Information Week* surveys for two consecutive years. The surveys are taken early in the year and the one for 2000 was done before the high-tech downturn, when the stock-option dream was supposedly hottest. The 2001 survey came af-ter the NASDAQ crash had supposedly wiped out the dream. The same

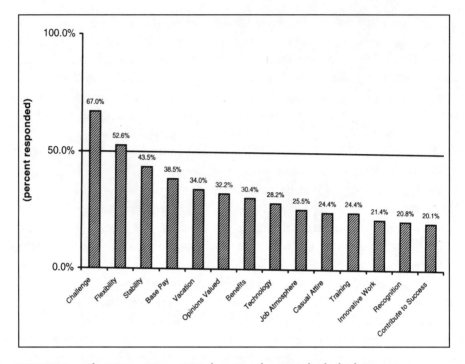

FIGURE 5.1   What Matters Most to IT Workers (Based on 38 Individual Job Factors)

IT workers value challenge, flexibility and stability over pay. (SOURCE: *Information Week Salary Survey, 2001, analysis by Richard Florida and Kevin Stolarick.)

three general attributes—a challenging job, a flexible workplace and job stability—topped the list in both years. Only a small percentage of people in each survey, the roughly 10 percent cited above, ranked stock options as being very important. Both before and after the crash, pay was generally important, but not nearly so much as intrinsic rewards. What people value and desire in their work is not contingent on the stock market or the rise and fall of the tech sector.

Beyond the Dollar

In the *Information Week* surveys as well as my own field research and statistical studies, certain job factors and workplace attributes keep showing up as highly valued. I digest them to a top-ten list as shown below. The list is not ranked. Suffice it to say that most people value one or more of these

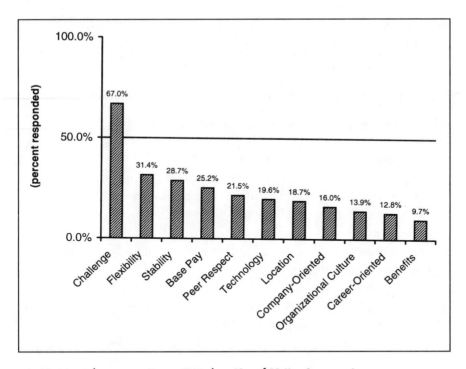

FIGURE 5.2   What Matters Most to IT Workers (Out of 11 Key Categories)

Challenge far outranks other criteria when individual job factors from the survey are clustered. (SOURCE: *Information Week* Salary Survey, 2001, analysis by Richard Florida and Kevin Stolarick.)

factors to varying degrees, with the mix varying from person to person. But note that nine of the ten highly valued job factors are intrinsic.

- *Challenge and responsibility*—being able to contribute and have impact; knowing that one's work makes a difference.
- *Flexibility*—a flexible schedule and a flexible work environment; the ability to shape one's work to some degree.
- *A stable work environment and a relatively secure job*—not lifetime security with mind-numbing sameness, but not a daily diet of chaos and uncertainty either.
- *Compensation*—especially base pay and core benefits: money you can count on.
- *Professional development*—the chance to learn and grow, to expand one's horizon for the future.

- *Peer recognition*—the chance to win the esteem and recognition of others in the know.
- *Stimulating colleagues and managers*—creative people like to be around other creative people, and they prefer leaders who neither micromanage nor ignore them.
- *Exciting job content*—the chance to work on projects and technologies that break new ground or pose interesting intellectual problems.
- *Organizational culture*—an elusive term that can include some factors already mentioned, plus more; perhaps best put for now as simply a culture in which the person feels at home, valued and supported.
- *Location and community*—a big factor on which I will say much more in later sections.

These factors can and frequently do overlap. Any sorting of human motives and values into categories is arbitrary; there are many ways to slice the pie. Keeping that in mind, let's bring the picture to life by looking in more detail at a few of these factors.

Challenge and Responsibility

Participants in my focus groups and interviews like to be on the front lines, doing work that makes a difference. They talk about wanting to work on "exciting projects," "great technology" and "important stuff." And it's very important for them to work on things that will see the light of day. One of the most frustrating events is having a project dropped, pecked to death or strangled in red tape. One person commented, "I would go crazy if I could not contribute. I would die if I had to deal with constant bureaucracy and could not contribute directly."[5] My respondents display a general disdain for the bureaucratic strictures and long career development paths of the past. I believe this was a key factor driving people to small companies during the high-tech boom. In a small firm, everyone counts. One young woman in Des Moines, Iowa, described the mind-numbing boredom of her first job after college. She worked in an insurance company and her entry-level post was essentially that of a better-paid secretary. "They had me Xeroxing paper all day and answering phones," she said. "So I quit, even though the pay was great, I had normal hours, and a secure job." She left for a job in a smaller company, where she could "use my skills, make a contribution, and not be bored silly all day."[6]

The young chief technology officer of a Seattle software startup offered yet another take on the subject. A boyish thirty-something of Asian-American descent, he had earned his Ph.D. in computer science at Carnegie Mellon and taught at Harvard. He then gave up a successful and promising career at the top of academia for the high-risk world of a startup because he wanted to see his ideas have an effect in the real world. "It's not enough to just publish papers and advance theory," he told me. "I did that. For me and for an increasing number of people of my generation, you have to show the impact of your work in the commercial market. You have to show that your technology can make a real difference in the market and in people's lives."[7]

Flexibility

The people in the focus groups and interviews blanched at the very idea of a 9-to-5 schedule or a standard dress code. How you use your time and how you dress and adorn yourself are intensely personal aspects of life. People are no longer so willing to compromise on these matters simply to get a job. Many spoke of wanting to be able to "bring themselves to work"—their real identities and selves—rather than create a separate, instrumental self to function in the workplace. This is nothing new. Creative people from artists to professors and even scientists in corporate R&D labs have always demanded flexibility of this sort.

Flexibility means more than the freedom to show up at the office at 10 A.M. wearing a nose ring. Creative people want the freedom and flexibility to pursue side projects and outside interests—some of which are directly related to their work, others perhaps less so, like being a musician or artist or being involved in community affairs. Regardless of whether they are directly work related, creative people see such activities as an important element by which they cultivate their creativity. In a detailed ethnographic study of high-tech design firms in Chicago, the sociologist Richard Lloyd quoted one person as saying: "The place where I'd want to work would support my creative endeavors and the kinds of creative things that I did on the side, and would recognize the fact that if I was continually building my skills with my own stuff, it would also benefit the company."[8]

Another key aspect of flexibility is having input in designing your work-space—and your role in the organization. Scientists have long controlled their work environments, setting up their own labs and designing their own experiments. The people in my focus groups and interviews want the same kinds of freedoms. In her research on high-tech startup firms, Laurie Levesque of Carnegie Mellon found that this process of role-making is highly valued by creative employees and their employers alike. Levesque studied eight firms in depth, interviewing both top executives and employees on their roles in the organization.[9] The most salient attributes, cited as desirable by both executives and workers, were "flexibility," meaning adapting to different responsibilities, and "defining one's own role" in the organization. Many of the employers said a key criterion for hiring an individual was that person's penchant for "wearing many hats." This was important because employers were often too busy to constantly monitor employees. The employees, meanwhile, thrived on "ambiguity" and the ability to "create" their own role in the enterprise, which they defined as being able to take on tasks and, on their own, figure out what they needed to accomplish. As one high-tech worker told Levesque: "My role is unclear, and that's how I like it." Much of this looseness is a function of size. Small emergent companies by their nature have less structure or hierarchy. People can make it up as they go along. But as a company grows, division of labor develops and people get pigeonholed in particular roles: Structure emerges inexorably.

Peer Recognition

As Eric Raymond notes, peer recognition and reputation provide powerful sources of motivation for open source software developers.[10] Most are paid nothing for the time they devote to such work. They post their contributions for free so that their peers will recognize them as competent and successful developers. They have evolved a complex, self-organizing, self-governing system of peer review that works much like that in academic science. The only difference is that open source software is a commercial activity.

Peer recognition has always been a strong motivator for thinkers and scientists. The sociologist Robert Merton long ago pointed to its importance in the work life of scientists, who he said were motivated more by reputation than by money.[11] Building on Merton's idea, the economists Partha Dasgupta and Paul David argue that peer recognition is the primary force in the "new economics of science" because it motivates scientists to be lauded as the first to discover something new.[12] The economist

Scott Stern has calculated that academic scientists actually "pay" to engage in science—sacrificing roughly 25 percent of their potential private-sector pay in order to pursue self-defined projects at prestigious universities.[13]

In one sense, these scientists are the polar opposite of the chief technology officer (CTO) at the Seattle software company, who left academia because he wanted his work to have commercial impact. But in another sense, they are the same. Both are choosing jobs that let them do what they want to do. Neither is motivated primarily by money or security, whether in the form of academic tenure or a fat corporate pension plan. The university researchers want to be able to do what interests them intellectually rather than what pays off commercially, whereas the CTO wants to see if he can do something practical, turning his research into a product that people will actually buy and use.

And when you're doing what you really want, for whatever personal reasons, it is the respect of your peers, the excitement and the challenge of the activity that really matter. This is the kind of work that keeps me at my keyboard for hours, hardly noticing that it's long past bedtime, or hardly caring that I've missed the chance to go to a party or have some other kind of "fun." The fun is the work itself—and this, I think, is a key element of the passion that Eric Raymond talks about. Can this passion come dangerously close to workaholism? Of course it can. But for me and many others, it is far better than work that has you counting the minutes until it's time to stop.

Location and Community Involvement

In contrast to the many techno-futurists who say the wired and wireless information age has made location and community irrelevant, the creative workers I talk with say they are vitally important. These people insist they need to live in places that offer stimulating, creative environments. Many will not even consider taking jobs in certain cities or regions—a stark contrast to the organizational age, when people moved to chase jobs and gladly let firms shuttle them from one backwater to another as part of the price of climbing the corporate ladder. I also meet Creative Class people who use location as their primary criterion in a proactive sense: They will pick a place they want to live, then focus their job search there.

Consider that nearly 20 percent of workers in the *Information Week* survey reported that geographic location of their workplace (18.7 percent) and the amount of time they have to commute (18.8 percent) are important factors. Both factors ranked ahead of the potential for promotion, bonus opportunities, financial stability, company prestige, stock options, on-site childcare, telecommuting and the ability to work from home. Other surveys, covering many types of workers, reinforce the importance of location. In a 2001 survey of U.S. workers by the public opinion firm Zogby International, nine out of ten reported quality of life (i.e. in the surrounding community) as being important in their decisions to take their current jobs. In a survey of 960 people looking to switch jobs, reported in the *Wall Street Journal* in July 2001, location ranked second only to salary (chosen by 25 percent versus 32 percent) as the prime motivation for switching.[14]

There are many reasons location is deemed so important, as Part 4 of this book will show. Let me note for now that members of the Creative Class are highly mobile and not bound to any particular place. My focus groups and interviews provided many examples of people who made employment decisions "for the money" and later left for "better locations." And every year I receive calls from former students who want to forego the high-paying consulting jobs they've landed for greater job quality and improved quality of life.

People also want to be involved in their communities. Numerous Creative Class people I have spoken with seek latitude to use work time and resources for community projects. To some degree, this is nothing new. Executives and highly skilled employees have long been enlisted to lead charitable campaigns, or to serve on the boards of nonprofit institutions. But Creative Class people today have new ideas on how to engage in community-building and civic action. They seek direct involvement on their own terms, in part because it is part of their creative identity—a point I will return to later in this book. For now the key point is: People use these extracurricular activities as a way of cultivating their interests, values and identities both in the workplace and in society more generally. In my view, they reflect a broader process of self-actualization and an attempt to use work as a platform for pushing forward an overall creative identity.

The Financial Side of Things

Compensation, of course, still matters, and it involves more than base pay. The past decade has seen a rapid run-up in the use of alternative forms such as stock options and bonuses. Many commentators favor these new forms, saying they align individual and organizational interests and provide more incentive for work effort. Furthermore, it has long been argued that workers trade off financial compensation against job security. Tenured professors, for instance, sacrifice short-term income for the long-term compensation that a secure lifetime position affords. Others trade job security for higher immediate pay and more risk. Either way, one could well say that security or stability is a form of compensation itself. It's the perceived ability to enjoy a fairly long-term income stream; one can project it, calculate it and weigh it against other forms.

So how do workers value these various forms of compensation? The *Information Week* survey data offered a number of insights.

- Job stability was more highly valued than any form of direct compensation. More than 40 percent of workers chose it as a key factor.
- Base pay was slightly less important, with 38.5 percent saying it is a key factor.
- Vacation and time off ranked next highest, chosen by slightly more than a third.
- Benefits (such as medical insurance and pension plans) matter almost as much as vacation time.
- Bonuses are not critical. The American Compensation Association reports that 83 percent of companies offer bonuses to upper management, 80 percent to middle management, and 74 percent to technical staff. Despite their extensive use, bonuses rate just twentieth of thirty-eight factors in the *Information Week* survey, with just 18 percent of workers identifying them as important. They rank lower than location, commute distance, casual attire and job atmosphere.
- Stock options are one of the least important factors in job satisfaction. Long offered to top management, they became popular for other employees as well during the New Economy boom because they allegedly enable employees to share in the company growth and thus better align individual and company interests. Compensation experts and financial economists have long predicted that such equity-based compensation will eclipse other forms of pay for top executives, outstanding technologists and other key people. Stock options are frequently said to serve three interrelated functions: to lure top candidates, to provide additional incentives for top people, and as "golden handcuffs" to keep key people on the job until they become vested. Yet despite all the hype, stock options ranked thirtieth in the *Information Week* surveys, with less than 10 percent of workers saying they are important.

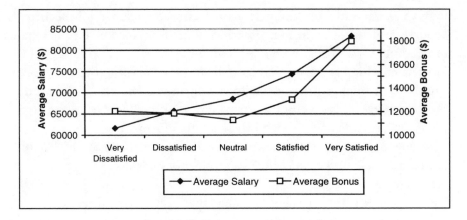

FIGURE 5.3   Job Satisfaction Rises Alongside Pay

(SOURCE: *Information Week* Salary Survey, 2001.)

The question remains: How does compensation interact with other factors to shape satisfaction? More than half of all IT workers were satisfied with their compensation and nearly two-thirds were satisfied overall. Of those who were satisfied with their compensation, roughly nine in ten were also satisfied with their jobs overall. But the story runs deeper. As Figure 5.3 shows, overall job satisfaction climbs steadily with compensation. The most satisfied workers are also the ones who make the most money. Perhaps they feel they can "afford" to focus on the other intrinsic aspects of their work because they are paid well. Or perhaps these workers have been performing better than their peers for a long time and so have earned raises, management approval and greater control over their jobs.

Whatever the cause, dissatisfied workers rate pay as one of the key elements of their being dissatisfied, as Figure 5.4 shows. Furthermore, people looking for work are also frequently looking for higher pay. More than three-quarters of the IT workers who were looking for work in 2000 and 2001 said "higher compensation" was the main reason, followed by dissatisfaction with management (42.4 percent), "more interesting work" (39.5 percent) and "more responsibility" (31.1 percent). Job stability ranked lower (18.5 percent), and stock options (13.4 percent) and the chance to join a startup company (2.9 percent) were among the lowest-rated answers. So pay is much more relevant to being dissatisfied with your job than to being satisfied.

Money, therefore, is important, but not the whole story. Creative people want challenging work and the ability to do their jobs flexibly, and as with

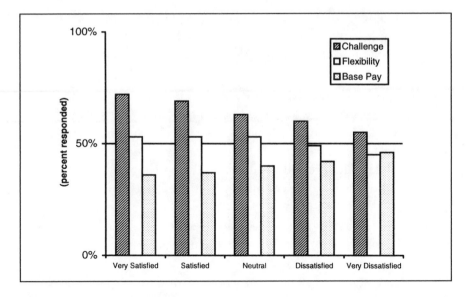

FIGURE 5.4   Challenge, Flexibility and Pay

Satisfied workers prefer challenge and responsibility; dissatisfied workers want higher pay.
(SOURCE: *Information Week* Salary Survey, 2001.)

anyone else, those who receive low pay are more likely to be unhappy. As Eric Raymond said, pay is essentially just a way to keep score. But Peter Drucker said it even better: bribing creative people just won't work.

Herding Squirrels

Unlike the traditional Working Class, Creative Class workers expect to be treated as distinct individuals. Harnessing them to do productive work thus can be very challenging, and there is no shortage of theories on how to wrangle a diverse herd of creative people into doing what the organization wants to have done, as we will see in Chapter 8. Let's close this chapter, meanwhile, with a look at some attempts to simplify the problem by classifying workers into broad attitudinal groups. *The McKinsey Quarterly*'s much-cited 1998 War for Talent Study surveyed more than 6,000 executives in seventy-seven large U.S. companies and found that while all survey respondents "care deeply about culture, values and autonomy," they could be divided into four distinct groups.

- "Go with a winner": This group preferred growth and advancement in a highly successful company and were less concerned with mission or location.

- "Big risk, big reward": A second group valued compensation and career advancement over the company's success or its active role in their professional development.
- "Save the world": Members of this group desired an inspiring mission and exciting challenges, caring less about compensation and personal development.
- "Lifestyle": This group valued flexibility, compatibility with their boss, and location over company growth or excitement.[15]

The 2001 *Towers Perrin Talent Report* likewise sampled a large group of professionals in various fields, dividing them by preference as follows:

- The largest group (42 percent) reported "work–life balance" as their priority.
- Twenty-eight percent said their chief desire was to develop their skills and advance in the company or companies they work for.
- Some 12 percent identified themselves as "fast-trackers" seeking quick advancement and high rewards.
- Another 12 percent saw themselves as "experimenters," interested in trying many things over the course of a career.
- Just 6 percent said they are "free agents" who desire to move quickly from job to job in search of greater financial rewards.[16]

Working from the raw data in the *Information Week* Salary Surveys, Kevin Stolarick and I sorted IT workers into six broad preference groups. Our percentages add up to more than a hundred, as many people fell into more than one category, and people in all the groups desired challenge in their work.

- About a third of the IT workforce sample (34.5 percent) value "flexibility" over other factors. Important job factors for them include a flexible work schedule and the ability to work from home when they like.
- Another third (34 percent) are "compensation-driven," favoring base pay, benefits and vacation time.
- About 20 percent are "technologists," motivated principally by the opportunity to work with leading-edge technology and highly talented peers, among other things.

- Roughly 15 percent are "professionals" who desire skill development, effective supervision and recognition for work well done.
- "Company men" (14 percent) tend to align their interests with the overall success of the company.
- "Entrepreneurs"(11 percent) are the smallest group. Among other things, they rate stock options as important, and prefer to work in startup companies.

Employers seeking to align such workers' needs with those of the organization must consider two additional points. The first is that while motivations have undoubtedly always varied, these variations can no longer be ignored as they could be in the past. The nature of the work, and thus of the workers, has changed. Second, employees' preferences are frequently mixed and subject to change over time. Our Seattle software CTO who left the faculty at Harvard apparently had felt, for a long stretch of his life, that academic research suited him. But he began to feel he had been there, done that, and so moved on to fulfill another yearning. Creative workers do not merely move up the scale in Abraham Maslow's classic hierarchy of needs. Most are not very worried about meeting the basic needs of subsistence; they're already on the upper rungs of the ladder, where intrinsic rewards such as esteem and self-actualization are sought. And having reached the high end, they can and do move laterally from seeking one form of esteem or actualization to another.

In *The Fourth Great Awakening,* Robert Fogel notes that in the advanced industrial nations, growing segments of the population work for challenge, enjoyment, to do good, to make a contribution, and to learn.[17] Such motivations, he suggests, will eventually eclipse compensation as the most important motivators for work. In the fast-growing Creative Class, where the job description includes creativity, I would say the surveys show this has already happened. It is even happening in the factory, where the rank and file do not merely follow orders and routines but are asked to take an active part in continuously rethinking and improving their work. If the trend continues, we may even hope to see young people migrating back to the machine shop. But only if the machine shop embraces the new values and structures of the creative age, acting on people's intrinsic motivations and allowing them to nurture and express their creativity—only, that is, if it becomes more like the hair salon.

CHAPTER 6

The Horizontal Labor Market

Hayes Clement did not seem the type of person who would someday be stuffing and delivering gift baskets for a living. Born into an upper-middle-class family in suburban Atlanta, he grew up tall and athletic, with Brooks Brothers good looks and a razor-sharp intelligence. Clement earned his undergraduate degree at Duke and an M.B.A. at the University of Virginia's Darden School. He was heavily recruited and took a prime offer from Price Waterhouse Coopers. The job was in New York City; his significant other from Darden had also landed a job there, with the pharmaceutical firm Pfizer, so they made the move together. And for about ten years, life in most respects was beautiful. With two healthy salaries, the pair was able to move from a cozy but cramped apartment in Greenwich Village to a large, stylishly redone place on a much-sought-after street. Clement was on the glamour side of PWC—consulting, not accounting—in a glamour division, media and entertainment. The work offered plenty of variety and challenge, and he was good at it. But he came to see consulting as a treadmill: the constant new assignments, the constant travel, the lurching from project to project and never actually seeing the end result of your labors. He wanted to build something.

Along came the perfect opportunity. One of his clients was a high-tech startup called MediaSite, a company with a technology for searching video and images much as text can be searched. An MIT survey had lauded it as one of the top ten emerging technologies that would change the world. Nor was MediaSite just an R&D project masquerading as a company: It had a real market, real customers and a bright, energetic staff. In early 2000, at the apex of the New Economy boom, Clement left PWC to become vice president of business development at MediaSite. The firm was in Pittsburgh, but that was only 400 miles from New York; he would commute between his work life and his social circle. The pay was much less than at PWC, but there were stock options, and the real upside was the chance to be part of a long-running success story. The honeymoon didn't last long. A new CEO was brought in from Silicon Valley to ready the firm for an IPO. But as the NASDAQ began to track downward, things got frantic and management, in Clement's view, lost focus. Changes of direction became so frequent that he stopped asking himself, "Do we have an executable strategy?" and began asking "Do we have a strategy?" One day barely six months into the job, Clement walked into the CEO's office and said: "I don't want to be here. You don't want me to be here. So let's make it easy and get an amicable divorce."

Back in New York, Clement was soon taking frequent calls from headhunters. But why rush the next step? He was about to turn forty and, thinking back, he realized he'd never had more than a week or so off at a time. His partner—the only member of their old Darden School gang still with the same firm since graduation—now held a high-paying executive post at Pfizer. So Clement decided to just hang for a while, do some reading and catch up with friends. One of those friends had a small gift-basket company. As the weeks passed and holiday orders began to stream in, the man asked if Clement might enjoy a little workplace slumming. He could help take the orders and get the baskets out. Clement said, "What the heck, I'll do it."

He found he enjoyed coming to work. The people were friendly; the place had energy; it seemed to fit. Before long, Clement was having ideas on how to grow the business. They could cultivate elite corporate accounts. Along with traditional baskets, they could put gourmet foods and digital goodies into fancy containers like leather-bound chests. They could expand into markets outside New York City. He had the contacts from his consulting days, he had the skills, and better yet, for the first time in years, he was having fun. Clement invested in the business, threw himself into the work and gradually the firm took off.[1]

A happy ending? No, more like a happy restart. Hayes Clement has since moved on to other ventures. But his story illustrates some key points on how people are charting career paths in the Creative Economy. The stereotype of the career path in recent years goes something like this: People leave boring, humdrum jobs at big company for high-tech startup because it's exciting and cool and free-floating, and offers instant wealth. Startup folds and people, chastened, look for job with more security. But Clement had already been in a cool, exciting industry. What he really wanted—what I consistently find most people want—was to exercise his creativity in building something, to experience the whole cycle of having ideas, putting them into action, and seeing the rewards. MediaSite hadn't come close to folding while Clement was there; in fact it was acquired by a successful publicly traded company in late 2001. What bugged him was the chaos and confusion. It wasn't shaping up as a place where he could enjoy that whole cycle of creativity any time soon. And once Clement recognized this, he was quick to move on. He never said "I've got to give it two years," or even one. He then found an environment in which he could be himself and feel at home. It was also, significantly, one in which he could do what he really wanted to do. But even then, after he had scratched that itch for a time, other opportunities beckoned and he was again quick to move on.

Horizontal Hypermobility

The most notable feature of the new labor market, as just about everyone agrees, is that people don't stay tied to companies anymore. Instead of moving up through the ranks of one organization, they move laterally from company to company in search of what they want. The playing field is horizontal and people are always on the roll. More than a decade ago, in our book *The Breakthrough Illusion*, Martin Kenney and I called attention to the hypermobility of high-tech labor in places like Silicon Valley and the Route 128 area.[2] Since then such hypermobility has become the norm across the entire economy. The statistics are striking:

- Americans now change jobs on average every 3.5 years—a figure that has been declining steadily for every age group; and workers in their twenties switch jobs on average every 1.1 years, according to 2001 figures from the Bureau of Labor Statistics.
- More than half of IT workers in the *Information Week* Salary Survey say they have been with their present employer for less than four years and expect to change jobs in less than three years. A quarter of these workers have been in their current job for two years or less and expect to change jobs in a year. More than 40 percent considered themselves "on the market" in 2001. And more than 60 percent say recruiters had contacted them in the past six months—on average, six times.[3]
- Fully 60 percent of respondents to a 2001 Towers Perrin survey said there is no longer *any* appropriate time an employee should stay with a company, and just 10 percent cited three to five years as

appropriate. More than half were actively in the job market at the time of the survey, and more than two-thirds said they thought it would be easy to get another job, even in late 2001, when layoffs hit a ten-year high.[4]

Companies once provided not only economic security but social identity. Many towns—even big cities like Detroit and Pittsburgh—were literally company towns, with a few big corporations providing most of the employment, and the social and economic infrastructure built around them. You were a company man, identifying with the company and often moving largely in the circles created or dictated by it.

Today workers carry risk that companies used to absorb, as the same companies now would rather add, drop and contract with people as needed. Nearly three-quarters of companies in the Towers Perrin survey said they continue to hire talented employees in the midst of overall downsizing. While Hayes Clement enjoyed the freedom to exercise his creativity how and where he wished, he took on a great deal of personal risk. Luckily he had a significant other with a stable job and steady salary. Like him, many of us have traded security and stability for greater autonomy, often accepting far greater levels of personal exposure and risk. And while these are daunting prospects, many people appear more than eager to take them on.

More Myths

As with many issues, the debate over the new labor market often tends to polarize into two extreme views. On one side are optimists who see the new labor market as a free-agent paradise, a way to cut loose from the corporate system for a more lucrative independent existence. On the other side are pessimists who believe the change in the market is just another sign of growing corporate oppression, social fragmentation and "the end of work." Even the more sober commentators have gotten caught up in the hype. A 1994 cover story in *Fortune* proclaimed "The End of the Job."[5] In a 1999 book Alan Burton-Jones tells us that in two generations people will ask their grandparents, "What was it like being employed?"[6] While both sides in this debate make some valid points, they overstate their cases and miss the deeper and more fundamental factors that are reshaping the world of work.

The Free-Agent Paradise

Dan Pink, author of the bestseller *Free Agent Nation,* is an astute observer of the new world of work. Many people I know identify with his upbeat free agent moniker.[7] But both the author and his fans tend to get carried away on the subject. According to Pink, free agency—defined as freedom from regular full-time employment—is the wave of the future, the state to which many aspire and in which most of us will soon be employed. Already there are some 33 million free agents, Pink claims, and the numbers are growing. "One fourth of the American workforce," he writes, "has declared its independence from traditional work." The real numbers, however, do not add up so neatly.

- According to the U.S. Bureau of Labor Statistics, the number of "self-employed" people was 12.9 million in 2000, roughly a third of Pink's estimate. The BLS found the number of "self-employed" Americans to be declining modestly. Adding in part-time and temporary workers may swell the ranks considerably and, according to some sources, give total numbers of the order that Pink claims. But those categories include low-end workers such as students and the elderly working part-time, and office temps, day laborers and seasonal farm workers.
- Only 6 percent of American workers identified themselves as free agents, according to the Towers Perrin survey.
- Just 1.1 percent of IT workers said they were "freelance or self-employed," and just 2.3 percent considered themselves "contract workers" according to *Information Week*'s Salary Survey. Over 95 percent in the survey classified themselves as full-time employees, and the great majority of these worked for big companies. More than half worked for companies with more than one thousand employees, and more than a quarter for companies with more than ten thousand employees.

The bottom line is clear: Most creative workers are not free agents. They work for companies or institutions. They move around frequently, but their fundamental condition is that of employees.

Among those who enjoy genuine free-agent status, the picture is hardly as bright as is typically painted. In Pink's view, the classic high-end free agents are people who work from their homes, perhaps commuting virtually and doing only the kinds of work they desire, picking the hours and conditions they want. In reality, such freedoms carry both a risk and a price. The kinds of work you want may not be widely available, especially in a market slump, and they may not always pay well. You then have a choice: be selective and settle for less money; or do a lot of things you don't really like, much as employees often do, and make more. You are also in competition with other free agents: If you turn down an onerous rush job because you've got a nice weekend planned, the client will call someone whom he or she has deemed more "responsive" and perhaps stick with that person in the future. Moreover, once you are on a project, guess what? You have to meet deadlines. You have to please the people in charge. You have to make it to meetings. You may work late into the night and wind up doing it not your way, but the client's way. As a reviewer of Pink's book aptly put it, "It takes more than a home office and temporary badge to build a workers' paradise."[8]

There is more. A detailed study of new media professionals by Rosemary Batt and Susan Christopherson of Cornell University and two colleagues found a huge gap in benefits between free agents and full-time workers.[9] Whereas roughly three-quarters of full-time employees enjoyed comprehensive health insurance (itself an alarmingly low rate), only 11 percent of free agents received health coverage from their primary employers or clients and just one-quarter received any sort of benefits from them.

Nor is it true that in the fast-moving free-agent world, companies become inconsequential and all that matter are "projects." Pink concedes that there is room for large permanent organizations in his "free agent universe." But as Rob Walker noted in his insightful *New York Times* review, Pink tends to see them as essentially "the clients of the graphic designers and copywriters who fill his anecdotes . . . and [he] considers such non-small companies as Kinko's, Starbucks, and Office Depot to be key elements of America's 'free agent infrastructure.'"[10] In a 2001 magazine article, Pink, noting the rapid rise and short corporate life span of Netscape, asked: "Was Netscape a company or a project? Does it make any difference?" Of course it does. Companies that persist and grow, like AOL Time Warner, which swallowed Netscape, wield great market influence and get to dictate the nature of future "projects." They thus dictate the kinds of work that will be available to free agents—many of whom survive by latching onto one or a handful of big clients that can provide a steady flow of work. It's hard to make a good living by catching nickel-and-dime projects from all over.

The free-agent world would be unthinkable without big companies. In fact it shifts a large share of economic risk from company to worker. And though free agency confers some benefits on companies, such as being able to readily adjust staffing levels to the market, it imposes costs on them as well, as the noted management scholar and Stanford professor Jeffrey Pfeffer has found. By relying heavily on freelance and contract workers, Pfeffer argues, companies implicitly accept high turnover, huge training costs, considerable productivity losses and significant leakage of intellectual property, in some cases virtually handing over key knowledge and ideas to competitors through turnover and defection.[11] So what can we conclude? There are free agents, but no free lunch.

The End of Work

On the other side of the debate, a growing chorus of social critics bemoans the very shifts that Pink revels in. According to Jeremy Rifkin and Stanley Aronowitz, the combination of advanced technology and globalization is bringing an end to meaningful work for much of the working population.[12] They contend that corporate downsizing of the past two decades has essentially turned high-paying "primary" sector jobs into lower-paying and less secure work in the "secondary" labor market. In their view, companies today use people as needed and then spit them out, leading to loss of security and social cohesion. Others, like Jill Fraser, the finance editor of *Inc.* magazine, argue that the office itself has been transformed into a "white-collar sweatshop."[13] Office workers are working longer hours, bringing more of their work home, and suffering from mounting economic insecurity and stress. This is the result, she contends, of a new style of management that uses layoffs and downsizing to instill fear in the white-collar world while squeezing the pay and benefits of those still at work and imposing ever-larger workloads.

These homilies seem as if they come from another age. Few people today face the end of work; most do not toil in an oppressive white-collar sweatshop, just as few enjoy the flexibility and autonomy of free agents. Most people today know intuitively that their working conditions are better than those available to their parents, not to mention their grandparents, who may have spent long days toiling in the grisliest of factories. The nature of work is changing for sure. But the driving force is not evil corporations taking aim at defenseless workers; rather it is a deep and fundamental shift in the nature of the economy.

The sociologist Richard Sennett takes the "end of work" line a step fur-

ther, asserting that the end of long-term attachment to the large corporation is leading to "corrosion of character" and thus the breakdown of
society.[14] Can we really believe that long-term employment in a large organization is a necessary element in building one's character? Or in defining
one's identity? Long-term jobs and reasonably stable careers with firms
were relatively recent phenomena, associated with the Industrial Revolution and the rise of modern unions and management. Before that, people
had well-defined identities through their occupations and their lives—as
farmer, craftsman, blacksmith or midwife. This is exactly the situation to
which many are reverting today: finding our identities elsewhere than in
the firm. Moreover, as Joanne Ciulla notes in her book *The Working Life,*

> [W]hile work is itself important for character, there is no reason to believe
> that changing employers frequently will harm one's character. Serial employ-
> ment does not necessarily have the same impact as chronic unemployment.
> People can still gain a sense of self-efficacy, discipline, integrity, and pride
> from the work they do and from the fact of employment itself.[15]

I find it fortunate that people today are no longer required to be loyal to
large corporations. Now people are free to direct their loyalties to more
meaningful aspects of life: their own personal development, their families
and friends, their communities and the things that truly interest and matter to them.

Deciding To Do It

Still, many people have the option of a stable, secure job and yet choose to
leave—whether by job-hopping or by going solo. In doing so they often
resist pay raises or other efforts to retain them. What really motivates these
people? Certainly part of the story lies in the demise of the old social contract: As companies began to breach it, people felt less inclined to keep
their end. As Ciulla writes,

> The downsizings of the 1990s were a wake-up call. The social compact—You
> do your job well and you stay employed—is dead, at least for the time being.
> Jobs were destroyed and lives were ruined, but one message came through
> loud and clear: Employment insecurity is the new way of life, even during
> times of low unemployment. Many workers have begun to rethink their
> commitment to employers, because their employers have changed their

commitment to them. The extra sacrifice of missed family birthdays because of long hours at the office no longer makes sense, and maybe never did. As the old saying goes, people on their deathbeds never wish they had spent more time at the office.[16]

Or as Stanford's Pfeffer likes to say: Loyalty isn't dead. Companies have driven it away.

This too is less a moral issue than a hard-nosed economic calculation. For companies, it's more efficient to exercise greater flexibility in staffing decisions. In fact some companies have reduced costs by terminating employees and then promptly hiring them back as independent contractors. The company no longer has to provide benefits, and doesn't have to promise, even implicitly, continued employment once a project is done.

But people also perceive advantages from this new system. To a large degree, it is what we "want." I have come across few who hanker for a return to the old one-company-for-life arrangement. Most believe that it's better to move around: They get more options that way, and it is easier to move up by moving on. They understand that their only real job security comes from their capabilities and continued productivity.

The new reality also is a result of people trying to take greater control over their work. The people in my interviews and focus groups cited this as their primary motivator. They get fed up with the office politics and bureaucracy of corporate life. Those in smaller, entrepreneurial companies grow tired of the stress and the management-by-chaos. People in both settings tire of worrying about losing their jobs. And while no person can achieve total control, many choose this route to take more control—in whatever areas may matter most to them. The following excerpt from an on-line dialogue on *Fast Company*'s website expresses it well.[17]

I never did fully understand the workaholics who put in 60+ hour weeks, working on weekends, and basically ignored the fact that some people have lives. . . . How many of them wound up with worthless options, marriages on the rocks, and lost jobs when their companies decided to downsize. . . . I worked for one company where it was not unusual for the CEO to call a trivial meeting for 6 PM on the Friday of a holiday weekend, and first announced the meeting at 2 PM while the family was already loading the car for a weekend trip. People were also called back from their vacations for minor matters that did not need immediate action. Folks were required to travel on their own (weekend) time to get cheaper airfares for the company.

There was no respect for the employees' own time or their families. Many of the corporate officers were based overseas, and would come to the states for two or three week stints, during which time they were living in hotels and thought nothing of calling long, evening meetings. Why not? It's not like they had a life. Just after my daughter was born, I decided that I wanted to be home for dinner on more than just weekends. I wanted to be a Dad, not a wallet. I wanted my daughter to know who I am, not just what I was able to provide for her.

By branching out on my own, I was able to meet my financial needs, decide how much is enough, and be able to say no to too much work. I don't have to "maximize" everything or answer to investors. I don't have to worry because the twenty-something workaholic urban dweller in the next cubicle thinks I'm a slacker because I start my one-hour drive home at 5 PM or 6 PM and resent a phone call during family time on Friday night or Saturday morning. It's just a job . . . it's what I do to pay my bills. . . . Sure, my revenues have slowed to a trickle too—and being old enough to remember the 80s and 90s, I think things will get a lot worse before they get better next year. I'll just have to try to tough it out.

The people I have come across in my research say that they leave jobs for the same sorts of reasons that the cartoon strip character Dilbert chronicles. It's not the amount of their salary or the number of stock options. It's management—inconsistent, incompetent or capricious. A big complaint is that management doesn't "get it" or fails to appreciate employee efforts. Even worse are major changes of direction that cause employees to think that all of their hard work has been for naught. This will drive even the most loyal of employees to abandon ship. I hear such comments not just from discombobulated "coolies" working in small high-tech companies, but from people in stable corporate jobs with good pay, and in nonprofit and government work, and from people who themselves have managerial duties. One person sent this e-mail after reading one of my *Information Week* columns:

Once again, I am working late, taking care of another disaster in my job as a biomedical engineer. . . . The management here is atrocious (I'm sure that you have heard it all before). The amazing thing to me is that valued, long-time employees are leaving my company at a frightening rate and the owners don't even seem to notice or care. As a middle manager, I have learned a considerable amount about how to (and how not to) treat one's employees. Unfortunately, there is a limit to how much I can insulate my team from the BS. . . . I have several offers now in private industry. . . . The front door code will once again be changed and everyone will wonder, "Who quit now?" as I join those ranks of "leaving in disgust."[18]

Gideon Kunda, Stephen Barley and James Evans, leading ethnographers of the workplace, have exhaustively studied the people who have left jobs with established companies to go out on their own.[19] Their study, titled "Why do Contractors Contract?" is based on in-depth interviews with fifty-two engineers and workers in information-technology fields. They organized the study to shed light on a series of hypotheses regarding the shift in the way people work. On the one hand, they wanted to test the claims derived from theories of the "contingent workforce." This is essentially the "company-as-oppressor" view that says people turn to freelance work only after being thrown out by big corporations. On the other hand, they wanted to test the counterclaims associated with the free-agent perspective. "Advocates of free agency," they write, "promote a post-industrial vision of economic individualism in which entrepreneurial workers regain independence and recapture a portion of the surplus value that employers formerly appropriated for themselves." What they found is similar to what I have reported.

The company-as-oppressor view, Kunda, Barley and Evans concluded, is dead wrong. The reasons why people struck out on their own had little to do with being thrown out of work. They did it to take control of their own lives, their time and the kinds of work they choose. Their decisions were in many respects liberating; they felt liberated from the constant *fear* of being thrown out. The study found three major types of complaints that precipitated workers leaving. Many were sick and tired of office politics. "You have to listen to a lot of people's agendas," noted one engineer in the study, "spend time in a lot of unnecessary meetings, trying to keep everybody happy, trying to play their game. It's not strictly work-related, it's very unproductive, and it can be very tense." Others left due to the Dilbert syndrome—a perception that higher-ups were incompetent or worse. "I was at the naval shipyard for a couple of years, and they were going nowhere," said another engineer. "I theoretically reported to the chief financial officer and they brought in a couple, how do we say, 'yo-yos.' We caught one of the CFOs funneling stuff into his condo in Florida." Still others left due to a sense of inequity. Skilled creative workers get upset when they perceive that merit is not the coin of the realm or that things are done for the wrong reasons. "I was getting the project done not for the goals of the project but for the goals of the people above," noted one participant in the study. And again, while striking out on one's own does not guarantee complete freedom, at least you become the person setting the goals and deciding how to play the cards. As a software developer put it, "I don't work for free anymore."

Life in the Horizontal Labor Market

The new labor market shaped by these trends has three chief characteristics. First, people today tend to pursue their careers horizontally rather than vertically. Climbing the corporate ladder is no longer so popular, perhaps partly because there isn't as much of a ladder in many of today's leaner, flatter firms—and it is liable to shift or vanish before you're halfway up. Instead, more of us swing from tree to tree in search of various fruit.

The early career of one young man I met is a good example. This man had come to the United States from Belarus. His first job, as a software developer, was in Norfolk, Virginia. He liked the work, but being young, he wanted to live in a bigger, more exciting city. New York and Miami, two popular havens for Russian émigrés, were among the options. But he judged Miami too hot and New York too expensive. So he settled on Pittsburgh—a city with a temperate climate, low cost of living, and big enough to provide the cultural stimulation he wanted. He took a full-time job with a growing young high-tech firm. After about a year he left to work for one of the city's old-line, industrial corporations—not as an employee but as a dedicated independent contractor. Now he was a free agent of sorts. Soon he became more of a free agent: As the work for the big firm tapered off a bit, he took on consulting for his previous employer. Then, having tired of the independent life, he went back to that employer full-time— less than a year after he left. That's a lot of moving in a short time, with a lot of different motivations. I could tell many similar stories. The point is that people like this young immigrant and Hayes Clement defy simple labels as free agents or job-hoppers. They are simply navigating the new realities of the horizontal labor market.

This shift is the product of powerful economic trends besides those already noted. As Barley observed in his 1996 study *The New World of Work,* the entire economy is moving toward "a more horizontal division of labor."[20] In the old days, bosses were people who knew their business better than the subordinates did, so both the typical organizational structure and the typical career path were vertical. As you stuck around and presumably learned more about the business, you moved up. But today, with growing specialization, this no longer holds: "[T]hose in authority," Barley writes, "no longer comprehend the work of their subordinates." Even the eminent research scientist can't boss the lab technicians around: They have knowledge and skills that he doesn't. Thus what we used to think of as jobs or occupations, Barley argues, devolve into "clusters of domain-specific knowledge." For things to go well in any organization, these clusters must interact on equal footing. This is why the vertical hierarchy and traditional career ladder have been replaced by a horizontal division of labor, sideways career moves between companies and a horizontal labor market. Once again, what appears to be self-indulgence (to conservatives) or new tactics of corporate oppression (to liberals) in fact turns out to be the result of the rational evolution of economic forces.

The second characteristic of the new labor market is that people have come to identify more with their occupation or profession than with a company. This is partly the product of the move to domain-specific knowledge. My focus groups and interviews show people increasingly defining themselves both by the creative content of their work and by their lifestyle interests: biker, climber, musician. In search of greater challenge, autonomy or satisfaction, people once again tend to move horizontally rather than vertically.

Third, people bear more responsibility for every aspect of their careers. We not only assume the risks of our job moves, we assume the task of taking care of our creativity—investing in it, supporting it and nurturing it. For instance, creative workers spend tremendous amounts of time and money on education. They go through basic port-of-entry education, education for a career-track change, and ongoing learning and upgrading of skills. People in my interviews and focus groups report that they, not their employers, have the responsibility for making sure their skills are current. This is particularly true for workers in rapidly changing high-technology fields. According to the study by Batt and Christopherson, new media professionals in New York City spent an average of 13.5 hours per week obtaining new skills—all of it unpaid.[21] That is one-third of a 40-hour workweek invested in taking care of their creativity. The report concludes that skill acquisition has become an individual responsibility, "both because the interactive nature of computer tools allows new media workers to learn new skills at their own pace and within their own learning styles and because formal learning programs have not kept pace with skill needs in this fast-changing industry." Moreover, in the new labor market it no longer pays for companies to invest significantly in developing their people's skills and capabilities, when people frequently leave for better opportunities and greater challenge. Just 30 percent of 262 "network professionals" in a Lucent Technologies survey of job satisfaction said that their company's formal training programs met their needs, even though nearly three-quarters (73 percent) said their careers required them to learn and grow.[22]

Perhaps the biggest change is that people now *expect* to manage their working lives in these ways. Fewer of us can even imagine a long-term career with one firm. When I was in graduate school in the 1980s, two years was considered the minimum acceptable tenure in a job. My focus groups and interviews, as well as the available statistics, suggest that the norm today is to bail out as quickly as possible if unhappy: Why waste your time and the firm's? Moreover, the new reality of chronic job changing has become internalized in the psyche of work. People have come to accept that they are on their own—that the traditional sources of security and entitlement no longer exist, or even matter. This is a sea change.

In the past, large-scale layoffs were met with outrage and horror. As recently as the late 1980s and early 1990s, corporate downsizings generated a national outcry, with waves of magazine cover stories and TV specials in which corporate spokesmen were called out to defend their actions. There were even street protests. Fast-forward to 2001: The jobless rolls numbered in the millions, their highest total in a decade or more. Thousands of people were thrown out of jobs not just by fly-by-night high-tech firms but in established companies like Ford, Lucent, Motorola, Merrill Lynch, Cisco and many others. And what was the reaction? Not much. Some scattered incidents of "white-collar rage," with laid-off people sabotaging the company computer or taking things home from work. But no picket signs, no demonstrations, not a peep from the politicians. "Protest does not even occur" to people who get fired anymore, wrote the *New York Times* in August 2001, quoting a woman who lost her job in Cincinnati: "If you talked to me a couple of months ago you might have heard some outrage, but now it's a matter of biting the bullet and going forward."[23]

This is perhaps the best indicator of how thoroughly we have come to terms with the new labor market. Like this woman, we simply accept it as the way things are and go about our busy lives. We acknowledge that there is no corporation or other large institution that will take care of us—that we are truly on our own.

CHAPTER 7

The No-Collar Workplace

One day recently I was running late for a meeting and called ahead to say so. The meeting was in the heart of Pittsburgh's downtown business district, with a securities lawyer and an accountant, so I asked the woman on the phone if I should take a few extra minutes to change from my typical jeans, black t-shirt and boots into something more professional. "That's unnecessary here," she said, "just come as you are." My heart sank as I parked my car and approached the grand stone building, a stunning exemplar of nineteenth-century corporate elegance. I walked sheepishly through the door, absolutely certain I should have changed. To my surprise people were dressed more casually than me, coming and going in khakis and polo shirts, some in sneakers and even sandals, others with gym bags in hand. Was I in the wrong place, maybe a high-tech company, or the lobby of a new clothing store? No, the receptionist assured me. I was where I was supposed to be—at the oldest and most prestigious corporate law firm in town.

The environments in which we work are changing and it isn't just the clothes. Many features of the workplace seem to be more open and user-friendly: open-office layouts and other new office designs, flexible schedules, new work rules and management methods. In these respects, firms of all types are coming to resemble high-tech startups. Some say it is a matter of competing for talent. As *Business Week* put it in April 2001: "Rather than sit back and take it, Big Five accounting firms, Rustbelt stalwarts, investment banks and law firms were forced to remake themselves in the image of their worker-snatching rivals."[1]

A passage from a *New York Times* article captured the magnitude of the change and hinted at the deeper forces behind it:

There is an iconic photograph from the 1950s that shows IBM offices, with row after row of secretaries and desks, and an apparently endless grid of regimented, soul-blistering cubicles symbolizing the corporate mindset of an earlier generation. These days, that conventional office layout is largely out-moded, a vestige of the command-and-control management mode of the corporate Dark Ages. The concept of the workplace has adapted to changes in the economy, technology, and the way people live.[2]

Welcome to the no-collar workplace. It is not merely the result of busi-ness trying to be hip and trendy, but an adaptation to the rise of creative work. Its core principles and practices are spreading because they are effi-cient, in the sense of being well suited to mobilizing talent around creative tasks. This workplace integrates elements of the flexible, open, interactive model of the scientist's lab or artist's studio more than the machine model of the factory or the traditional corporate office. And though championed by new high-tech firms, it did not erupt on the scene overnight. Many of its features have been evolving for decades and continue to do so.

A key element of this evolution is constant experimentation with new structures and practices, some of which "stick" while others amount to lit-tle more than passing fads. For instance, when the high-tech sector slumped in 2000 and 2001, many New Economy frivolities—on-site mas-sages, on-site dog-sitting services and the like—quickly vanished. The structures and practices that last are those that contribute to workplace performance, organizational efficiency and consequently profit. The no-collar workplace is thus the product of the ongoing movement of capital-ism toward more effective mechanisms for harnessing human creativity. Trends that feed creativity and harness it tend to dominate and persist— they have evolutionary survival value in the Creative Economy—while those that don't end up in history's dustbin.

The New Dress Code

Few workplace trends have drawn more attention than the loosening of dress codes. What started in small firms in chronically casual places like California is now everywhere. In the late 1980s, IBM, long known for re-quiring a necktie and *white* shirt (not blue or striped), endorsed business-casual dress, not just on Casual Fridays but every day. Roughly a quarter of information-technology workers report that the ability to wear "casual at-tire" is among the things that matter most to them on their jobs, according to the *Information Week* Salary Survey. As the *New York Times* noted, the shift has "complicated the lives of men who once thought they were immune to fashion gaffes"—no more simply grabbing a dark suit and tie from the closet in the dark early-morning hours.[3]

It has played equal havoc in the retail world. Retailers who once supplied the button-down-and-wingtip uniform, like Brooks Brothers, have scrambled to redefine themselves. In February 2001, 60 percent of the merchandise in Brooks Brothers' downtown Philadelphia store was "nouveau casual" v-neck sweaters, leather jackets and other business-casual staples, according to a report in the *Philadelphia Inquirer*; three years previously the stock had been 90 percent "conventional business attire" and "old casual" such as khakis and polo shirts.[4] Meanwhile Banana Republic, long positioned as a provider of casual and travel clothes, fortuitously found its goods accepted as business clothes and jumped at the opportunity. The firm struck partnerships with companies such as Home Box Office, First Boston and Credit Suisse to offer free advice on how to dress casually, along with discounts and free tailoring; mobile ministores were set up inside some workspaces, dispensing free drinks with fashion tips.[5] Retail chains and magazines alike have done a booming business in offering guidance on wardrobe selection.

The new codes have drawn a storm of reaction from those who don't like the look. During the late 1990s, the *Wall Street Journal* ran numerous stories on women who dress in clothes perceived to be "too risqué" for the office.[6] *USA Today* criticized casual dress as a recipe for slacking, calling it "the casualization of America."[7] "Some guys only have two kinds of clothes—suits and slob clothes," one female executive told the *New York Times*.[8] Dress at newer and smaller firms—which often pushes the envelope far beyond what you'll see at IBM or the law office—draws the most virulent reactions of all. And the reaction can go the opposite way. As one California lawyer told the *Wall Street Journal* in March 1999, "It's fascinating to watch the East Coast lawyers come through here. You've got British explorer types in suits, insisting on dressing up for dinner in the heart of darkest Africa. Then you've got the guys who take it all off and try to go native."[9]

What's really going on? First recall that for decades before office dress codes changed, dress outside the office had been growing more casual. In the early decades of the twentieth century, men wore suits and ties at baseball games, while women wore long dresses and fancy hats to picnics. As these standards faded for a variety of social reasons, the suit came to be primarily a business uniform, with less and less utility outside the office. By the 1990s, people were dressing down at church and even at weddings and wakes. Still, through most of the century a "uniform" seemed appropriate at work, since most work was organized along military lines. You put on the uniform to join the regiment. As you rose through the ranks, you acquired a finer and grander uniform to indicate your status as an "officer" of the firm.

Casual dress gradually crept in partly for the simple reason that it's more comfortable, but also because creative work came to be more highly valued in our economy. No longer did status accrue from being an officer or, at lower ranks, a good soldier. It accrued from being a member of the creative elite—and creative people don't wear uniforms. They dress to express themselves, as artists may do, or like scientists, they dress simply and practically so as to focus on the serious creative work at hand. They dress as they please.

In spring 2000, I visited the Seattle branch of Barney's, a high-end clothing store. On that night the store was jammed with young professionals sipping mineral water and chilled white wine as they browsed the racks.[10] The manager was a woman in her thirties, dressed in black, who had worked at the store since its inception. Over the last few years, she had noticed a significant change in the buying patterns of Seattle's Creative Class—particularly those who worked at Microsoft, long a haven for nerds. Sales of traditional suits had declined every year since the store opened, and sales of classic geekwear such as khakis, crewnecks and blue blazers had declined as well. But the store was doing well with New York-style fashion wear: black pants, Helmut Lang t-shirts, Prada outerwear and shoes, leather jackets and fashionable carry-all bags. The wardrobe was becoming more stylish, more urban. Noting the preference for Prada and other cutting-edge designers among some Microsoft executives, a September 2000 story in the *Wall Street Journal* dubbed the new look "geek chic."[11] Apparently techies don't want to be either soldiers or nerds. They want to dress like cosmopolitan, successful artists, befitting their status as the creative economic vanguard.

The Creative Economy no longer has one dress code; rather it has a diversity of them. One day in the summer of 2000, I looked around at the participants in a meeting room at a large Washington, D.C., law firm. One person wore a business suit; another had on a blazer and khakis. A third was in blue baggy pants and a t-shirt, and carrying a pair of roller blades. A young woman in a short skirt and funky blouse sported a tongue ring. The talk at that moment had in fact turned to dress codes, and when someone pointed out the range of attire it suddenly dawned on us that up to that point we'd barely even noticed it. We were all content to be ourselves, and no on particularly cared what others were wearing. The new code is evolving toward none at all, or more accurately, toward a code of diversity and tolerance.

Perhaps the only significant dividing line this code has created is the line between organizations that allow this diversity to flourish and those that try to stifle it. The latter run the risk of losing competitiveness, because they restrict the pool of creative talent from which they can draw. Cities and regions also may lose competitiveness if they do not reflect the new culture. Most have become more accommodating. I am frequently invited to speak to trade associations, Chambers of Commerce, community leadership groups and the like. For years I wore a business suit and tie when addressing them, but recently this has changed. Many groups, when asking me to speak on cultural and workplace changes, now explicitly add: "Would you please wear casual clothes to reinforce your message?" Not all do, however. In the winter of 2001, I was scheduled to speak to a group of business and political leaders in a large city. About a week before the event, a flurry of e-mail came across my computer screen, essentially inquiring about my dress as well as the contents of my speech. Some thought I should wear a suit and tie and not mention "controversial" subjects like gays. To which one of the principals responded to his worried corporate partners:

> I spoke with Dr. Florida and he assured me that there is no cause for concern. He will be giving his talk completely in ebonics, wearing a pink tutu, with a large sombrero. At the conclusion, he will stomp on a light bulb inside a white napkin. His only request is that everything in the ballroom be situated properly for positive feng shui.[12]

Much of the banter over dress codes misses the point. It is not about people's appearances, but about the acceptance of difference and diversity in the workplace, and this in turn is squarely in line with the shift to creativity and the demands of the Creative Class to work flexibly and express their identities in their appearance.

The New Work Schedule

The no-collar workplace has both a new schedule and a new sense of time. Instead of following the organizational age menu of core hours, growing numbers of workers in all industries are able to vary both the hours and the days they work. The U.S. Bureau of Labor Statistics reported that by 1997, more than 25 million workers—27.6 percent of all full-time wage and salary workers—varied their schedules to some degree, either formally or through informal arrangements with their employers.[13] More than two-thirds (68 percent) of workers were able to periodically change their starting and quitting times, according to a survey by the Families and Work Institute; more than half (55 percent) occasionally work at home. As Chapter 5 has shown, flexibility is among the attributes of a job that workers value most.

Flexible schedules are heavily concentrated in Creative Class occupations. More highly educated people are likely to have flexible hours than less-educated people, whereas workers who have not finished high school are most likely to have fixed schedules. Consider that more than 60 percent of natural scientists (60.2 percent) enjoy flexible schedules, followed by lawyers and judges (58.6 percent), high-end financial and business service salespeople (58.1 percent), mathematical scientists (55.9 percent), college and university professors (54.6 percent), other professionals (50.3 percent) and engineers and managers (both at 47.9 percent). In contrast, the lowest percentage by far is for machine tool operators (11.1 percent). Nearly 40 percent (39.5 percent) of people in personal service occupations have flexible schedules. And thus a major reason why many people prefer the hair salon to the machine shop.

The flexible schedule is partly a response to changing social needs. In households with two working parents, for instance, someone may have to bail out early to see the children home from school. But it is also tied to the very nature of creative work. Much creative work is project work and projects tend to run in cycles, with periods of crunch time followed by slower periods. Creative work requires enormous concentration, and people require flexibility so they can have some personal downtime even during the day. Many people tell me they like to work hard through lunch hour, then take a long run or bicycle ride in the afternoon to recharge themselves for what is almost a "second workday." Also, creative thinking is hard to turn on and off at will. It is an odd sort of activity: One often finds oneself percolating an idea, or hammering away desperately in search of a solution to a problem, only to see the answer begin clicking into place at unusual times.

Flexibility does not mean the end of long hours. One of the defining elements of the no-collar workplace is that Creative Class people work the longest hours. According to Bureau of Labor Statistics estimates, professional, technical and managerial workers are the most likely to put in "long work weeks" of more than 49 hours.[14] In the winter of 2000, I was in a corporate office tower when something strange happened. At 6 P.M., the lights automatically went out. While the people I was visiting appeared nonplussed, I was dumbfounded. This sort of thing simply does not happen anymore. The lights never go off; the computer never shuts down; the phone is never off. Everyone, everything is always on—even on those rare occasions when no one is there. The figures are squarely in line with my observations. Some 40 percent of the U.S. workforce is at work after 5 P.M., with about 25 percent on the job past 6 P.M., according to the BLS figures. My focus group participants and interview subjects report that they basically work anywhere and anytime. In fact, the long trajectory of modern capitalism has involved the relentless extension of the working day across time and space—first through electricity and the electric light and now via the personal computer, the mobile phone and the Internet.

The New Workspace

Offices look and feel different now. At some small high-tech or design firms, the ambience can seem downright raucous: bold wall-sized artwork and posters, broken surfaces with exposed pipes and beams, lounge areas and play areas, blaring rock music. But offices at mainstream firms are changing as well, often in dramatic and fundamental ways. Alcoa, Goldman Sachs, and the Chrysler division of Daimler Chrysler are among those that have abandoned corporate towers for new headquarters with radically new features. Traditional corporate office space had become obsessively neat and regular, and often subdued to the point of blandness.

Generally, space arrangement today tends to be traffic-oriented rather than hierarchical: lots of common spaces with offices opening onto them, instead of private spaces with locked doors for the big shots and rows of standardized cubes for the rank and file. The new workspace may have cubicles, but the inhabitants are encouraged to decorate and customize them. The new workspace also means space that is visually interesting and often a bit raw.[15] At some high-powered financial firms, I have seen contemporary touches blended with a more refined executive style. The office may have fine fixtures and furnishings, but a wall will be exposed or a bit of ceiling uncovered to show pipes—much like an expensive blouse or shirt with a couple of buttons left seductively open. According to Don

Carter, principal of UDA Architects, a leading architecture and urban design firm, the key elements of the new workspace include:[16]

- Open office design and layout
- High ceilings
- Exterior wall circulation path (everyone owns the views)
- Communal spaces (well designed, located and appointed)
- Abundant "hang out" spaces
- No clutter, lots of concealed storage
- An experiential environment (high-quality design, bold colors, exposed structural elements, etc.)
- Indirect lighting
- Abundant art

While there are infinite variations on the theme, creative workspace generally comes in two major types. Each has its own ways of delivering symbolic and functional value. In the suburbs and sprawling high-tech office parks of places like Silicon Valley and North Carolina's Research Triangle, one typically finds new architecture. Big firms that require lots of space—electronics design-and-assembly firms, for instance—often build expansive campuses in such locales. Exteriors may feature bold or unusual design elements. Buildings at the Marconi Communications campus outside Pittsburgh have canted exterior walls that make the structures look as if they were tilted or riding a rolling sea (perhaps a more apt metaphor for the telecom industry's turbulence than the architects realized).

Inside the newer suburban buildings, open arrangements for high traffic flow are mostly the rule. Occasional design touches that disrupt the slick newness of the interiors (such as ragged surfaces or exposed infrastructure) can help take the edge off the sterile feeling of new space, making it feel livable. As the new urbanist architect Andres Duany likes to tell his clients, "take the old-fashioned wall coverings off, but leave the glue on." Overall, the suburban campus may have virtually everything a worker would want or need—from espresso bars and free food to on-site day care, state-of-the-art health facilities, outdoor Frisbee fields and concierge services. The message and function are clear: No need to go wandering off; stay right here at work.

The other type is renovated space in older buildings found in downtowns and urban neighborhoods. Amazon.com, for example, took over an abandoned hospital in downtown Seattle. The company's head of real estate, Julie Benezet, said employees prefer the funky, unfinished character of older space. This kind of setting also is popular with smaller companies that require less space and perhaps want to establish their own identities. Older space of course has some obvious practical advantages. As long as extensive renovation isn't needed, it can be cheap—ideal for a small firm bursting with ideas but not money. This is why Jane Jacobs, noting the creative reuse of storefronts in the West Village, wrote: "Old ideas can sometimes use new buildings. New ideas must use old buildings."[17]

Old cheap space is also conducive to freewheeling workstyles: You don't have to worry about employees ruining the walls by tacking up posters and charts, or marring the floors when they wheel in their mountain bikes. If the space is in a loft-style building, it can be very flexible and easy to equip. If located in a bustling urban area, the company can rely on the surrounding neighborhood to provide services like cafes, shops and health facilities that big suburban companies provide on their campuses. Often, these older neighborhoods have a mix of large and small buildings that allow even a new firm to have a building of its own. Finally, for new firms, space in older buildings can provide credibility. It lets them draw on the historic character of the surroundings to say, in effect: Look, we're not fly-by-night. We have roots.

Form and Function: A Closer Look

Whether urban or suburban, new workspaces share a number of practical features. First, corporate real estate in every era has been meant to serve as a statement and a marketing vehicle for the firm, and the new workspace makes one statement consistently: "This company is on top of the times." Having a hip look and feel may not be everything, but it matters. Customers want to know that the company is a front-runner; prospective employees are ever looking for cues that the company "gets it." Second, the new workspace has an experiential component. Creative workers like visual stimulation; the informality encourages them to feel comfortable and expressive. And third, the new workspace is productive in the sense of being attuned to the flow of modern creative work.

Space design and space arrangement have always been crucial to productivity. But while factories have long been laid out scientifically, such thinking was not applied so rigorously to office space until recent times. Thomas Allen of MIT is considered one of the progenitors of modern office design. In a ten-year study of engineers in R&D labs, Allen found that proximity matters: People interact most with those located close to them; people seated more than seventy-five feet apart rarely interact at all.[18] Other studies found that software developers, like many creative workers, need both interaction and intense, focused concentration. When people had the "flow" of their creative work interrupted, it typically took them 20 to 30 minutes to refocus.

Such findings have not gone unnoticed. In the 1990s, I consulted for Steelcase, which had been a leading maker of the much-maligned cubicles of the corporate age. Familiar with Allen's work and other studies, Steelcase wanted new designs to help its clients take advantage of proximity without sacrificing privacy. One result was the new line of work modules called "Personal Harbors," private workspaces mounted on wheels, and more recently the technology-enabled Blue Space, developed jointly with IBM.[19] They can be rolled into groups around common areas as needed, to facilitate collaborative work, then rolled apart as people need to work alone, to limit unwanted interruptions. Companies like Knoll and Herman Miller also have introduced flexible, reconfigurable lines of furniture. From the *New York Times* in September 2001:

> In place of the file cabinets and cubicles of the *Man in the Gray Flannel Suit* era, Knoll is gambling on a new system called the A3. . . . Inspired by airplane interiors and camping equipment, the pod-like A3 unit is made from tubular steel framing covered by stretchy mesh fabric. It wraps around the officer worker with womblike curves. While providing some privacy, the A3's translucent envelope provides a sense of visual continuity. The A3 can be used alone in an open loft space or as part of a grouping in a more conventional office space. Herman Miller's new line of office furniture [includes] . . . the Red Grasshopper, a soft, adaptable system that has the look of NASA space equipment. Desks and storage units are wrapped in thick, protective padding. The Grasshopper uses what the company calls "soft docking"—and different components nuzzle together without precise configurations. Parts can be easily moved and reconfigured.[20]

Office layouts are changing as well. In a thoughtful *New Yorker* essay, Malcolm Gladwell connected the layout of the new workspace to the urban-vitality theories of Jane Jacobs. Jacobs in the 1960s had been vehemently opposed to urban renewal schemes that destroyed the organic nature of neighborhoods, replacing their bustling sidewalk life and diverse traffic flows with planned order that deadened creative interaction.[21] And while city planners largely ignored Jacobs, Gladwell argues that her ideas now form the basic principles of the new office design. "Who, after all, has a direct interest in creating diverse, vital spaces that foster creativity and empathy? Employers do. Offices need the sort of social milieu that Jane Jacobs found on the sidewalks of the West Village." And the new workspace, like Jacobs's West Village, stimulates creative interaction by being conducive to "the casual, nonthreatening encounter." Gladwell continues:

> When employees sit chained to their desks, quietly and industriously going about their business, an office is not functioning as it should. That's because innovation . . . is fundamentally social. Ideas arise as much out of casual conversations as they do out of formal meetings. More precisely, as one study after another has demonstrated, the best ideas in any workplace arise out of casual contacts among different groups within the same company.[22]

Ideal interactions, Gladwell notes, occur among people whose roles are different enough to give them different perspectives, but who have enough common knowledge and common interest to know what would be mutually useful. Very similar to Jane Jacobs's favored neighborhoods—where community leaders, the grocer and candy-store owner, parents and children, and many others all keep each other informed and share ideas on matters of public concern. Old-style workspaces don't foster such activity. They are like the suburbs—functions and people sequestered, important people in exclusive areas similar to gated communities—and these workspaces are often found in high-rise towers, where, as Gladwell notes,

> the center part of every floor is given over to the guts of the building: elevators, bathrooms, electrical and plumbing systems. Around the core are cubicles and interior offices, for support staff and lower management. And around the edges of the floor, against the windows, are rows of offices for senior staff. . . . The best research about office communication tells us that there is almost no worse way to lay out an office. The executive in one corner office will seldom bump into any other. . . . To maximize the amount of contact among employees, you really ought to put the most valuable staff members in the center of the room, where the highest number of people can be within their orbit. Or, even better, put all places where people tend to congregate—the public areas—in the center. . . . Is it any wonder that creative firms often prefer loft-style buildings, which have usable centers?[23]

The new workspace reflects Jacobs's notion that people are the source of creativity, and taps the productive efficiencies that come from concentration and co-location. "Forty years ago," Gladwell concludes, "people lived in neighborhoods like the West Village and went to work in the equivalent of the suburbs. Now, in one of the odd reversals that mark the current economy, they live in suburbs and, increasingly, go to work in the equivalent of the West Village."[24]

The traditional vertical corporation, with its top-down hierarchy, was based on a factory model of information flow and work flow. There were bosses who required separate areas for privileged communication, and workers who followed routines and thus must be put into standardized spaces to discourage deviation. Bosses and subordinates alike were literally required to think *inside* the box. The Creative Economy is premised on the rapid generation and transmission of ideas across the enterprise. This world of tight deadlines, uncertainty and discovery—of knowledge creation, teamwork and building off each other's ideas—requires the interactive space heretofore found in the design studio or scientific lab.

The new workspace is not universally wonderful. Companies that are rapidly expanding often crowd workers together. There is little privacy and workers frequently complain of noise. "Acoustical privacy" is a big concern, according to an August 2001 report in the *Wall Street Journal,* which ran under the headline "Shut Up So We Can Do Our Jobs!"[25] It told of companies going to great lengths to dampen the din associated with open-plan offices by wrapping cubicles in extra fabric, hanging sound-absorbing materials on ceilings, and affixing cork wallboards to hallways and conference rooms. Some people consider the new workspace an affront to their values and a threat to their status. A friend of mine, leaving an open-house party to preview the "cool space" at a new consulting firm, overheard one conservatively dressed professional saying to another: "I would never give up my office to work like *that!*"[26]

The New Perks

In recent years an array of new job perks have been offered widely. The Society for Human Resource Management found the following perks common in high-tech workplaces in the year 2000.

- Free food or subsidized cafeterias (provided by about 50 percent of firms surveyed)

- Free tickets to sporting events or performances (50 percent)
- Dry-cleaning service (31 percent)
- Paid maternity leave (19 percent)
- Free massages (15 percent)
- Concierge services (15 percent)

New perks are not limited to New Economy companies. By the year 2000, more than 3,500 companies nationwide, including more than 100 of the Fortune 500 and all of the Big Three automakers, offered health insurance and other benefits to the partners of gay and lesbian employees.

While they have generated much comment, the new perks have received little serious examination. There are no comprehensive studies of employees' attitudes toward them, but the *Information Week* Salary Survey suggests that even the more substantial new perks are not highly valued. Just 1 percent of IT workers cited domestic partner benefits as important, and less than half of 1 percent listed "on-site childcare" among the things that matter most to them.

Yet some perks may be more important for what they signal than for what they actually achieve. Same-sex partner benefits signal an open, tolerant workplace where one's own differences will be accepted. Also, it is obvious that the relative value of different perks depends on the employee: Paid maternity leave is likely to matter far more to some women of childbearing age than on-site massages. And many employers feel that perks like food and concierge services may pay for themselves by keeping valuable workers on site and focused, instead of tracking down food or taking their cars for repair.

Of this much we can be certain. Perks that fail to add to the bottom line will be short-lived, as we saw when the NASDAQ nosedive of 2000 and 2001 wiped out a lot of the fluffier freebies. Only perks that work to elicit and harness creativity and have value for both the employer and the employee will stick around.

CHAPTER 8

Managing Creativity

Exposed brick and Helmut Lang t-shirts, whatever their merit, do not equal an organizational structure designed and actively managed to harness creativity. We come therefore to the deeper issue of workplace culture.

Many views exist on how to manage and motivate for creativity. Some firms, even in so-called creative industries, still do it the old-fashioned way. They try to impose order and bureaucracy, and simply tally the returns by counting the time their employees put in. Others seek predictable procedures for eliciting creativity and making it more efficient. Some of these companies, like Motorola, take a page from Japanese-style quality management and actively manage and account for creativity. A system called the Capability Maturity Model (CMM), developed at the Software Engineering Institute at Carnegie Mellon, lays out extensive standards and guidelines for managing software developers, a special class of creative workers. Companies that use CMM march through a series of stages, with a scoring system to rate their productivity and performance as they move up the chart to more mature creative capabilities.

Other firms insist that creativity cannot be managed from above. In a recent interview, managers at Sun Microsystems railed against such attempts to manage or engineer creativity.[1] Their hands-off approach says that all you can do is hire talented people—technological virtuosos so to speak—give them the general outlines of a task, and then leave them alone. Most organizations fall somewhere between the extremes. Microsoft favors a blend of structure, self-motivation and peer pressure (see the following box). Yet far too many companies, particularly innovative ones, try to motivate people by lurching from crisis to crisis, launch to launch. Though this battlefield mentality may produce results for a while, it is not sustainable. It eventually leads to a vicious cycle of frustration, backlash and bitterness. In a 2001 Towers Perrin study, fewer than half of all professionals responded that "my company inspires me to do my best work." This implies we have far to go in both our knowledge and practice of how to

manage creative workers. But doing it right can generate considerable efficiencies. Stanford University's Jeffrey Pfeffer estimates a considerable performance payback, saying "all that separates you from your competitors
are the skills, knowledge, commitment and abilities of the people who
work for you. There is a very compelling business case for this idea: Companies that manage people right will outperform companies that don't by
30 percent to 40 percent."[2]

White-Collar Sweatshop Versus Caring Company

There is a highly polarized debate over what exactly is happening inside
the creative workplace. Jill Fraser's "white-collar sweatshop" perspective,
outlined in Chapter 6, depicts the workplace as a source of greater stress,
escalating time demands and increased insecurity.[3] On the other side is
the "caring company" point of view, which contends that the workplace
really is becoming a more supportive and nurturing environment for employees, and that it's a good thing. In her book *The Time Bind,* University
of California sociologist Arlie Russell Hochschild wrote of a large company known as a leader in programs designed to achieve "work-life balance."[4] After studying the company and interviewing scores of employees,
what she found was astounding. The company's practices were not leading
to a more effective balance of work and life. Rather, they were making
work more attractive than other aspects of life. Hochschild thus concluded that people were coming to work to avoid stress at home and in
other parts of their lives.

Another version of the caring-company perspective is Andrew Ross's
notion of the "bohemian workplace." After studying several Silicon Valley-
style dotcoms in New York City, Ross, the director of American Studies at
New York University, argues that the New Economy surge of the late 1990s
brought about a sweeping transformation of the workplace as a "giant
multipurpose playroom for ever-shifting teams of employees." Picking up
on David Brooks's cultural dialectic between bourgeoisie and bohemian,
Ross says the workplace itself has taken on formerly bohemian elements.

> Traditionally bohemian work styles were visible in everything from casual
> dress . . . to the endorsement of a kind of general hedonism and party cul-
> ture in the office. . . . A lot of these companies presented themselves as alter-
> natives to corporate America and took on all things bohemian. What's

HOW MICROSOFT MANAGES CREATIVITY[5]

according to David Thielen

1. Hire smart people who think. The company's interview process is designed to separate the people who think from those who simply perform tasks. . . . At Microsoft, the interviewing and final approval of job candidates is always done by the group that is doing the hiring. The most telling questions that Microsoft managers ask are highly unusual. Why are manholes round? Microsoft isn't actually interested in the correct answers. They want to see how the candidate goes about solving a problem. Example: Manholes are round so the covers cannot fall through the holes and so the covers, which are very heavy, can be rolled aside easily.

2. Expect employees to fail. If you work in an environment in which the best route to job security is by working to outdo the company's competition, you focus your energy on developing new products and new ways to solve problems.

3. Keep repercussions small when conquest-oriented employees make mistakes. You don't want them to feel as though their careers at the company or that their happiness is riding on just one mistake. At Microsoft, failure is expected. If employees don't fail, they're not taking enough risks. In some cases they've even been promoted because of what they learned from their failures.

4. Create an us versus them mentality. Microsoft employees are constantly reminded that their competition is other companies, not colleagues. Emphasize the company's goals, but let each individual figure out how to get there.

5. Sustain the company's start-up mentality. In a start-up company, there's an ever-present sense of urgency that the business must succeed. Make it everyone's responsibility to watch costs. There are no secretaries at Microsoft. And if a job needs five people to complete it, four are assigned. Frugality keeps employees from becoming too comfortable or lazy.

6. Make the office feel like home. Create a work environment that is as nice or nicer than home, and employees will want to be there. At Microsoft, everyone has his own office, and there's no dress code. Employees can walk around barefoot—except in the cafeteria. There's a big connection between enjoying your work and doing good work.

interesting is that both groups needed the other. The world of the bourgeoisie always needed a bohemian underside, a sort of fantasy demimonde, just as the bohemians always needed the bourgeoisie to define themselves against. . . . The fact that such a familiar dialogue has been played out in the business world is quite extraordinary.[6]

All of these views capture elements of the no-collar workplace discussed in the previous chapter, but miss the essential point. Workplaces are changing because the emphasis today is on creative work. And in the quest to elicit creativity, the typical workplace tends to become both more stressful *and* more caring. Stress increases because the Creative Economy is predicated on change and speed. If a firm is to survive, it must always top what it did yesterday. The employees must be constantly coming up with new ideas; constantly finding faster, cheaper or better ways to do things—and that's not easy. It's brutally stressful. At the same time, the smart firm will do its best to attract valuable creative workers and give them what they need to be creative. The result could be called a "caring sweatshop," but there's not really any contradiction here. It's just the reality of a workplace in a Creative Economy. As for the bohemian playroom: Many of the more frivolous, hedonistic aspects of this culture disappeared with the NASDAQ crash, and any that remained were swept away in the aftermath of September 11. But this does not mean that we are returning to the status quo ante. The no-collar workplace is not and never was just an old-style office hung with bohemian trappings or jazzed up with the thrill of a fantasy underside. As I will argue more fully in Chapter 11, the modern world is fusing aspects of bourgeois and bohemian so deeply that those old categories no longer apply. The fundamental fact about this new workplace, again, is that it's geared to harness creativity—and the best ways to do this are still being worked out.

Sculpting, Zen and Common Sense

Two increasingly popular strategies for eliciting creativity in the workplace, touted in publications like the *Harvard Business Review* and *Fast Company,* are "job enrichment" and "job enlargement." More recently, the concept of "job sculpting" has been advanced. According to a 1999 article in the *Harvard Business Review,* "Many talented professionals leave their organizations because senior managers don't understand the psychology of work satisfaction; they assume that people who excel at their work are necessarily happy in their jobs. Sounds logical enough. But the fact is, strong skills don't always lead to job satisfaction."[7] So companies strive to "sculpt" jobs in ways that reflect employees' deeply embedded life interests. It is as if we have discovered the Zen of job design.

This is a noble undertaking, and it certainly makes sense to try to fit each job to what the person does best and likes to do. But job sculpting will work only if it is implemented in a culture that is strong on the fundamentals. As we have seen, most people do not quest after some workplace Zen: They desire challenging work, good pay and reasonably competent management that does not get in their way. There is a vast literature on effective organizational cultures. And despite a lot of academic jargon, this perspective says that creative people and knowledge workers respond well to organizations with solid values, clear rules, open communication, good working conditions and fair treatment. People don't want to be abandoned and they don't want to be micromanaged. They don't want to take orders, but they do want direction.

These are not easy lines to walk. All we know for sure is that creative work cannot be taylorized like rote work in the old factory or office, for several reasons. First, creative work is not repetitive. Second, because a lot of it goes on inside people's heads, you literally cannot see it happening— and you can't taylorize what you can't see. Finally, creative people tend to rebel at efforts to manage them overly systematically. We have seen this all too often in the universities, where many a dean and administrator have learned hard lessons about trying to manage highly independent-minded faculty and researchers.

Peter Drucker captured it best when he said that knowledge workers do not respond to financial incentives, orders or negative sanctions the way blue-collar workers are expected to. I particularly like Drucker's observation that the key to motivating creative people is to treat them as "de facto volunteers," tied to the firm by commitment to its aims and purposes, and often expecting to participate in its administration and its governance. "What motivates knowledge workers," writes Drucker, "is what motivates volunteers. Volunteers, we know, have to get more satisfaction from their work than paid employees precisely because they do not get a paycheck."[8] The commitment of creative people is highly contingent, and their motivation comes largely from within.

Soft Control

The no-collar workplace is not being imposed on us from above; we are bringing it on ourselves. For Jack Beatty of *The Atlantic Monthly*, the legions toiling in the no-collar workplace are not victims of corporate oppression. He dubs this new reality "cannibalistic capitalism,"[9] citing a designer quoted in Fraser's *White-Collar Sweatshop*: "We are all devouring ourselves. . . . We all own stock, and as stockholders, all we care about is profits. So we are the ones who are encouraging the conditions that make our work lives so awful." As one high-tech worker wrote to *Fast Company*: "Nobody held a gun to anyone's head. . . . It seems as if the American work ethic of the New Economy . . . turned us into such whores that it's all for sale if the price is right!"[10] More than four of ten American workers described themselves as workaholics, according to a 1999 Gallup Poll.[11] But the real reasons for our present workplace conditions go deeper. Unlike these two people, most of us are not even doing it for the money. Members of the Creative Class do it for the challenge, the responsibility, for recognition and the respect it brings. We do it because we long to work on exciting projects with exciting people. We do it because as creative people, it is a central part of who we are or want to be.

The no-collar workplace runs on very subtle models of control that rely on people's intrinsic motivations. As companies try to motivate and persuade us rather than boss us or bribe us, they're basically seducing us to work harder—and we are most willing to be seduced. As *Business Week* bluntly put it, "The smartest companies know this. Instead of ensnaring employees with more signing bonuses and huge salaries, they are trying to hook them emotionally."[12] I call this "soft control."

One very effective form of soft control is challenge. Recall that more than two-thirds of workers in the *Information Week* survey report that challenge and responsibility are what matter most to them in their jobs. So the no-collar workplace seeks to act on these motivations by allowing workers to define their tasks, assume greater responsibility and confront ever-greater challenge. There are always new and more advanced products to launch, new deadlines to meet, new competitors to beat back. Another effective form of soft control is peer recognition and the pressure it can bring. Nearly one-fifth of workers in the *Information Week* survey report that "working with talented peers" is among the things that matter most to them at work. The no-collar workplace acts on a complex dynamic of peer recognition and competitive peer pressure to harness the talents of creative people.

A New Employment Contract

For all of these reasons, the nature of the employment contract between firms and people is undergoing dramatic change. The old employment contract was group oriented and emphasized job security. The new one is tailored to the needs and desires of the individual. The old organizational age system was truly a package deal, literally a comprehensive "social contract" in which people traded their working lives for money, security and the sense of identity that came from belonging to the firm. They took their places in the hierarchy, followed bureaucratic rules and worked their way up the ladder. In the words of William Whyte, an "ultimate harmony" developed between the managerial class and the large companies they worked for, causing the members of this class to give themselves over more completely to the organization.[13]

The new employment contract could not be more different. Creative people trade their ideas and creative energy for money. But they also want the flexibility to pursue things that interest them on terms that fit them. Thus they trade security for autonomy, and conformity for the freedom to move from job to job and to pursue interesting projects and activities. The shift to self-motivation and personal autonomy in the workplace is bound up with the fact that we no longer take our identity from the company we work for, but find it in the kind of work we do, our profession, our lifestyle interests and the community we live in.

The new reality turns Whyte's ultimate harmony on its head. Instead of a broad social contract, a key feature of today's employment relationship is that employees are seeking out and getting what my Carnegie Mellon University colleague Denise Rousseau calls "idiosyncratic deals." These deals may include not only a "sculpted" job description, but terms of employment tailored to the individual as well. The aim is to provide the mix of security, flexibility, type of challenge and whatnot that a valued person may be seeking.[14] A 2001 Towers Perrin survey of more than 5,500 professionals strongly advised companies to strike such deals, both to retain key people and to capture "the discretionary effort that produces top performance."

The rise of this new employment contract, according to Rousseau, is the result of two interrelated factors. One is that workers are more likely to look for specific short-term deals. The old long-term employment system gave workers more reason to believe their hard work early on would be rewarded with higher pay later in their careers. With little reason to believe they will be with the company for very long, today's workers want their rewards *now*. The other reason is that creative people typically see themselves as unique individuals with unique skill sets and expect to be rewarded accordingly.

The Open Source Example

Open source software development provides an interesting model of how intrinsic motivation, horizontal structure and voluntary membership can be used to motivate creative people and get work done.[15] Open source developers are not a tight-knit community but a far-flung network of individuals—yet together they have created high-quality products like the Linux operating system and the Apache netserver, which powers the computer networks of many large companies. The open source community uses a subtle discipline and structure to mobilize the creativity of thousands of independent software developers. Eric Raymond, a present-day open source guru, argues that while coding remains a solitary activity, the really great contributions or "hacks" come from harnessing the brain power of many. Open source development, in his view, works less like the orchestrated building of a cathedral and more like the chaotic interplay of a bazaar.

At first glance, the production of open source software appears completely unstructured. It is based on voluntary cooperation of developers in many different locations and organizational affiliations around the world. While a shared "hacker culture" may develop across this diffuse community, it contains none of the formal attributes we associate with productive work—no reporting relationships, assignments or clear responsibilities. But look deeper and a clear structure and discipline emerge. In place of the bureaucratic hierarchy of traditional organizations, the structure here is based on performance, capability and peer review. Yet open source software reflects a distinct division of labor. The software itself is "modular"—composed of many smaller, decomposable and well-defined tasks to which individuals and groups contribute. This allows people with different skill sets and capabilities to work on different elements.

Open source projects are structured around a stable group of core contributors who perform key tasks and play a key role in governance, while harnessing the temporary efforts of a much larger group of volunteers. In his research tracking 13,000 open source developers, the economist Josh Lerner of the Harvard Business School found that less than one-tenth of 1 percent of them contributed nearly three-quarters of all code. Nearly three-fourths made only one contribution.[16]

Members of the core group are typically people with extensive professional credentials—usually individuals who have proven themselves as programmers and have contributed to the original source code, though as the project progresses they may do less and less coding themselves. These core people provide the overall vision for the project and also serve as gatekeepers. They review submissions to decide which contributions will be incorporated into the code, and control their own membership by deciding which volunteers shall be elevated to the core group. Yet in contrast to traditional hierarchies—where those in charge can easily exclude or stifle bright, creative people—the members of the core have a strong incentive to actively recruit and harness the very best programmers, for their control exists only so long as the rest of the community supports them. If they behave unwisely or if their vision fails, "forking" may occur, whereby the disgruntled group takes the project's source code (which of course is not protected by any copyright or patent) and starts a new project with a different vision—as has sometimes happened.

An open source software project takes the form of a voluntary membership organization, but with clear rules governing the behavior of the volunteers. There are clear if unwritten principles for how they can enter the community and remain within it. Membership is fluid but only to some extent, and is contingent on performance of tasks, as well as on adhering to norms of appropriate conduct and fair play.

A complex yet subtle system of monitoring and sanctions reinforces the rules and keeps everyone contributing. Members exert strong pressures against noncompliance, for example through "flaming" (sending someone an angry or hostile e-mail), "spamming" (flooding someone with unsolicited e-mail) or "shunning" (deliberate refusal to respond). Faced with such sanctions, members often leave the community of their own initiative; there is frequently no need to expel them.

Open source software development thus relies on the intrinsic motivations of volunteers. Its structure is horizontal to a certain degree, but organized around a core group that provides direction and review. The work, which is complex and difficult, is rewarded largely by peer recognition as opposed to financial compensation. While the opportunity to gain recognition is an important motivation for joining an open source project, the desire to maintain and enhance one's reputation is the key mechanism for ensuring progress. Performance is always visible and transparent. All members can see whether someone has done a good job. Code is reviewed in ways that resemble scientific peer review, except that the process is completely open: The reviewers' names are public. Despite this, their comments can be nothing short of brutal. Posting bad code can elicit vehemently negative and even career-damaging feedback. Contributors accept this risk in exchange for the challenge and recognition that come from being associated with an elite creative community. And in this sense, the open source model reflects two other core values of the Creative Economy: openness to new ideas and meritocracy.

Where It All Began

The no-collar workplace is not new; rather it is a stage in the ongoing evolution toward more efficient ways of harnessing ideas and creativity. It aims to accomplish what John Seely Brown, the former director of Xerox PARC, called "the ability to leverage the community mind" by providing the physical and social context required for creativity.[17] "This place feels just like my graduate engineering lab," exclaimed one of my Carnegie Mellon colleagues upon entering the offices of one of our university spin-off companies. His comment cuts to the heart of where the no-collar workplace comes from: It is derived from older, more established systems for organizing creative work—the artist's studio and the university lab. Artists have long worked in open studio environments, but they tended to work alone. Andy Warhol's "Factory" transformed the isolated studio into a multidimensional creative laboratory for art. The original Factory was a raw, open space. It was entirely covered in silver foil, including the exposed pipes, to provide a "space age" look. Filling it out was a mélange of equipment for silk-screening, filmmaking and other art forms—and a constant parade of friends and associates trooping in and out at all hours. Floating through it all was Warhol himself, the archetypal modern soft-control manager: sometimes coddling or nudging, sometimes merely observing or recording what was going on, sometimes retreating into his own work. Architects and designers extended the studio environment to creative group work, with open-plan offices to encourage collaboration, peer review and feedback.

The laboratories of university professors were also developed on the open-plan model, where professors could come and go as they pleased, engage their students and colleagues, work could be done on a collaborative basis, and ideas could flow. Even the large mega-corporations of the mid-1900s created a special place for the scientists and engineers who were seen as the source of innovation. Theirs was the space of the research and development laboratory, often at a campus explicitly modeled on that of the university. The R&D lab was far removed from the factory or the downtown headquarters, both to encourage flexibility and openness and to ensure that the eccentric ways of scientists and engineers would not infect the executives and managers or, worse, be seen by customers. A casual dress code was accepted at the R&D labs, too. Yet even here, bureaucracy and micromanagement often crept in. In *The Organization Man,* Whyte noted that few corporate R&D labs were able to be truly creative:

> In the great slough of mediocrity that is most corporation research, what two laboratories are conspicuous exceptions in the rate of discovery? They are General Electric's research department and Bell Labs: exactly the two laboratories most famous for their encouragement of individualism—the most tolerant of individual differences, the most patient with off-tangent ideas, the least given to the immediate, closely supervised team project. By all accounts, the scientists in them get along quite well, but they do not make a business of it, and neither do the people who run the labs. They care not a whit if scientists' eyes fail to grow moist at company anthems; it is enough that the scientists do superbly well what they want to do, for though the consequences of profit for The Organization are secondary to the scientist, eventually there are these consequences, and as long as the interests of the group and the individual touch at this vital point, such questions as belongingness are irrelevant.[18]

What could have motivated the corporate leaders to create such labs in the first place? Simply put, they needed such places to attract top scientific talent from leading academic centers. To get such people they had to establish environments and procedures similar to those in academic settings—allowing scientists to pursue their own lines of interest, host visitors in their labs, and freely publish their results in scientific journals.[19] These labs were incredibly productive and many of them still are, making major advances from the development of nylon (Dupont) and the transistor (Bell Labs) to the flat-panel display (RCA and Westinghouse) and much of modern personal computing (Xerox PARC). It was the culture of the R&D labs, born at laboratories like GE, Bell and many others, that later companies like Fairchild Semiconductor, Digital Equipment and Hewlett-Packard, and even Apple and Microsoft, sought to emulate and build upon.[20] Gradually, these norms and practices began to seep into technical divisions of large companies, their IT staffs, and their engineers. Before long they would penetrate larger and larger segments of the economy.

And these practices offered one great efficiency to firms—and one incredible advantage to capitalism—which ultimately assured their further diffusion. They enabled firms and the economy as a whole to capture the creative talents of people who would have been considered oddballs, eccentrics or worse during the high period of the organizational age. Richard Lloyd quotes the founder of one of the Chicago high-tech firms he studied as saying: "Lots of people who fell between the cracks in another generation and who were more marginalized are [now] highly employable and catered to by businesses that tend to be flexible with their lifestyles and lifecycles."[21]

The Real Legacy of the New Economy

The practices and structures of creativity would have permeated corporate life on their own, but the meteoric rise and equally meteoric decline of the New Economy accelerated their diffusion. The New Economy created an additional social and cultural force that pushed these practices to the fore. As *Business Week* commented in April 2001:

> Far from being fads that will evaporate like so many market caps, many of these workplace revolutions developed to coddle employee and warehouse them in offices for as long as possible might very well strengthen during the next 15 years. Part of the reason is economic. Even with the slowdown, companies must still compete for valued knowledge workers. And as employees are forced to clock workaholic hours in the global 24/7 economy, companies will have to make offices seem more like home.[22]

Like the early days of Silicon Valley before it, the New Economy unleashed a powerful cultural force for business change, but in an even more pervasive way. The rapid rise of the New Economy uprooted the age-old distinction between appropriate business norms and alternative culture. As Andrew Ross has noted, the New Economy redirected a powerful passion for change away from social and political issues and directly into the business world itself. In those heady days, joining a company became a form of self-expression and self-actualization. Many companies actively embraced this by combining commercial zeal with a mission to transform business culture.[23] A clear distinction was drawn between the outmoded, staid and constricting practices of the "Old" economy and the open, progressive, liberating practice of the "New." In propagating the myth of the New Economy as social force, this period raised people's expectations about what they wanted in a company and a job. As Ross sums it up:

> One of the most interesting stories is about the role of young people. How their passion for change, which is endemic to youth in general, somehow got channeled into a passion for corporate change. Which meant that a lot of activism, or socially productive work that they otherwise might have done, was redirected into a kind of infatuation with changing the shape of corporate America. That could only have happened, of course, because of the particularly bohemian cast—the sort of counterculture cast—of the companies that recruited these employees, for better or worse.[24]

In my view, however, it was mostly worse—amounting, in many cases, to little more than a well-choreographed charade. Many companies merely presented a cheap facade of the "alternative"—a ping-pong table, perhaps an espresso machine. And many otherwise sensible people bought into it because they were starved for something different. It wasn't about the money after all. As countless people in my focus groups and interviews have told me, they made these moves in the hopes of being part of a different, more inclusive, more progressive culture. Most of them, however, were quickly disappointed.

Many of these companies failed to reflect even the most basic elements of good management. These were the sorts of places that eat people alive—beset with near constant stress, continuous uncertainty, chronic management turnover, frequent changes of direction and general chaos. They came to resemble "toxic workplaces," a phrase coined by Jeffrey Pfeffer. According to Pfeffer, a key sign that a company is toxic is that:

> It requires people to choose between having a life and having a career. A toxic company says to people, "We want to own you." . . . A toxic company says, "We're going to put you in a situation where you have to work in a style and on a pace that is not sustainable. We want you to come in here and burn yourself out—and then you can leave."[25]

In 1999 and 2000, there was hardly a day that I did not receive a call or e-mail from an employee at a high-tech company complaining of some sort of organizational dysfunction: "Three of our top people left and nobody said anything." "Our COO contradicted what he said last week." "They let five developers go and people are scared; and we have no clue what's happening." "How can I keep my people motivated and engaged in an environment like this? I'm afraid everybody may just up and leave." Or one of my favorites: "Yesterday I received a Microsoft Project schedule e-mail from 'our leaders' for three projects that I never heard of before that need to be done in a couple of weeks and will easily require 50 to 75 percent of my time. I of course flipped. . . . But what else is new." The once great New Economy migration became a great exodus, captured in the telling epitaph: "I'd rather work at Starbucks."[26]

In the summer of 2000, I was asked to address the top management of a major regional bank on how to attract and retain creative and talented workers. We selected an edgy high-tech company as the venue for our workshop and invited two of their top executives to join in the discussion. Within the first half hour of the meeting, after I had given a short introduction to the subject, discussion began in earnest. The bank managers wanted to know what creative people care about, and seemed particularly interested in younger employees. They asked questions about the role of dress codes, workspace design, perks, compensation, location and the like. It became very clear to me that these people were genuinely concerned with managing and motivating their employees—if truth be told with treating them like human beings.

As we got further into it, the two high-tech executives began to chime in with their views, which essentially amounted to a high-tech version of "management by stress"—working people as long and as hard as they could stand. It quickly became clear to the group that these two did not have the foggiest idea of how to motivate or even treat creative people, let alone build an effective and enduring organizational culture. As the end of the workshop drew near and the clock edged toward 6 P.M., the high-tech pair, seemingly unaware of the time, began an extended harangue. As the rest of us sat uncomfortably in our seats, one of the bank managers interrupted the two: "At our company," he said, "we respect the flexibility and the right of our people to go home, if need be, to their spouses, significant others and families, so I think we should draw this meeting to a close."

The NASDAQ crash and subsequent New Economy collapse were a giant wake-up call for people to look beyond the hype, a point that was reinforced by September 11, 2001, and its repercussions. People got smart quickly, becoming much savvier about what they really require in a workplace and an employer, and no longer being entranced by the myth of striking it big. Young people saw their elder siblings' plight in sharp relief. "Working for a startup has a certain stigma associated with it," said one 2001 graduate from Carnegie Mellon. Added another: "People are attracted to big companies for two reasons: job security and not having to work crazy hours." Like creative workers in general, these younger workers expressed a preference for companies that combine the flexibility and openness of the no-collar workplace with job stability, reasonable expectations about working hours, talented peers and responsible management. "You have to remember I grew up in the most insane job market in recent memory. Now it's just a normal job market," is how a 2001 college graduate summed up the change.[27] The real legacy of the rise and fall of the New Economy is that it recalibrated people's expectations about what really matters about their jobs. For this alone, it was an invaluable collective learning experience.

Here and Now

All of which brings us to the present day. The always silly distinction between the New and Old Economies has collapsed. Different types of workplaces are converging and becoming more similar in their quest to attract talented people and harness creativity. People want to work for a company that values them, provides a challenging yet stable work environment, nurtures and supports their creativity, and allows them to realize their full potential. They desire flexibility on matters such as hours, dress and personal work habits. They seek a workplace that incorporates both the freedom and flexibility of a smaller startup and the stability and direction of a larger firm. But the trajectory is not backward to the boredom and drudgery of a traditional corporate bureaucracy.

People have come to expect the key features of the no-collar workplace and simply won't work in places that don't offer them. And this is part of a broader pattern. Improvements in workplace conditions tend to be sticky. Once instituted, they are not easily reversed, even when the job market is lean. Companies of all types are converging on a new style of managing creative work. If we find this new style more suited to our needs than the old, so much the better.

CHAPTER 9

The Time Warp

If the very word "time" evokes a tight, edgy feeling in your chest and makes your temples throb, you are not alone. Many surveys show that growing numbers of Americans feel pressed for time. We often attribute this to our status as "overworked Americans," as Juliet Schor's influential 1991 book had it, but the case is not so simple.[1] While Creative Class people do tend to work long hours, many other factors contribute to the feeling of being crunched for time. Moreover the big news about time goes deeper than our simply working more.

The key change is that our use of time has intensified. We now try to pack every moment full of activities and experiences—at work, at home and at leisure. In the process, the ways in which we think about time as well as use it are being warped into new configurations. This is true over the course of a day or a week, as we move to more flexible, interwoven schedules. It is true over the long trajectory of a life, as growing numbers of us "front-load" our careers and lives, deferring marriage and children, or make major changes in midlife. The Creative Class is at the forefront of these trends in the use of time. And this in turn is leading to a new divide: We are becoming a society in which Creative Class people literally live in a different kind of time from the rest of the nation.

The intensification of the experience of time is a long-running phenomenon. In agricultural societies, people lived and worked by the sun and the seasons. The clock, as the British historian E. P. Thompson has written, changed the nature of work and subsequently the rest of life.[2] The introduction of the clock led to a new way of thinking about and allocating time by creating a more finely divided day. The Industrial Revolution brought demarcation of time into distinct compartments of work-time and off-time. Frederick Taylor's scientific management at the turn of the twentieth century was predicated on using time more efficiently and intensively during working hours, while new technologies like electricity facilitated the extension of the workday. Scientific management, which came to include timing and setting standards for each movement in the performance of a task, extended the division of labor into the division of time itself. The organizational age led to a further ordering and intensification of time, and also helped promote the notion of a steady chronological climb up the corporate and status ladders as the normal life course.

Time is not just a physical given but a social construction that shapes our lives in deeply ingrained ways. Joanne Ciulla writes:

> Cultures change and adapt their concepts of time, just as they can revise and change their notion of work. Every society has its own social time. Social time determines a general path of life—when you do what. It tells you when to eat, when you should go to school, when you are old enough to drink, drive, get married, or retire.[3]

Today our sense of time is changing again. And the story is more multifaceted than you might think.

Has Overwork Been Overhyped?

When Juliet Schor's *The Overworked American* was published in 1991, her findings seemed to resonate with what many people intuitively felt. In recent years, the average American had been working increasingly longer hours, and we were finding it the main source of stress in our lives. Blue-collar people, as usual, were taking it on the chin hardest.

Let's now take a closer, updated look at the story. It does appear that Americans on average work more hours per year than people in other advanced nations. Led by the Creative Class, the United States surged ahead of even Japan, long thought to be a nation of workaholics, in average hours worked. A 2001 report by the International Labour Organization showed us taking an unenviable first place in this regard among the advanced industrial nations. American workers averaged 137 more hours (almost 3 1/2 more weeks) per year than their Japanese counterparts, 260 hours (6 1/2 weeks) more than British workers, and nearly 500 hours (12 1/2 weeks) more than German workers.[4] We're more willing to put in a longer day, and we take shorter vacations. An American private-sector professional who asked for a month off from work—the norm for many Europeans—would generally be told to take a hike.

Meanwhile, a detailed time-use survey has challenged many of Schor's original findings. John Robinson and Geoffrey Godbey's book *Time for*

Life: The Surprising Ways Americans Use Their Time, published in 1993 and reissued with updated figures in 1997, paints a more complex picture. The book summarizes the findings of a four-decade research study, the Americans' Use of Time Project. At ten-year intervals between 1965 and 1995, research teams at the University of Maryland, University of Michigan and elsewhere asked thousands of Americans to keep detailed time diaries for extended periods. Schor in fact used research from the 1975 and 1985 surveys in her book, along with other data, to show a hefty run-up in average hours worked from the late 1960s to the late 1980s. But Robinson and Godbey argue that she mishandled the data in numerous ways.[5] From their work and other studies and data, the following conclusions can be drawn:

- Americans on average have not been working substantially longer hours over recent decades. According to the time-diary studies, average hours worked per week by employed men declined from 46.5 hours in 1965 to 42.3 hours in 1995, while hours worked by employed women inched up a bit from 36.8 to 37.3 hours over this period. Using a measure of "total productive activity" which combines paid work and house work, Robinson and Godbey found that working women actually worked fewer hours per week, as their total productive activity fell from 66.6 hours in 1965 to 62.9 hours in 1995, while employed men put in 1.6 fewer hours, a decline from 62.5 hours to 60.9 hours per week. And, the reductions were even greater when non-working people were taken into account.[6]
- Free time also increased over this period, according to the time-diary studies. Between 1965 and 1995, free time increased by more than 6 hours, from 34.8 to 41 hours per week. On average, Americans today have roughly as much free time as they do work time.[7]
- *The Creative Class, however, is by far most likely to work the longest hours.* Although exact comparisons cannot be made with the available data, people in professional, technical and managerial occupations were most likely to work "long work weeks" of 49 hours or more, according to figures collected by the Bureau of Labor Statistics (BLS).[8] Nearly half of all managers and nearly 40 percent of all professional people did so.
- The Working Class tends to have shorter work weeks. Only 30 percent of people in "skilled blue collar" occupations worked more than 49 hours per week, according to the BLS; only 15 percent of laborers did so.

- *The Creative Class is the most likely to feel stress and time pressure.*
  Nearly two-thirds of college-educated Americans reported moderate
  to high levels of stress, compared to roughly half of those with a
  high-school education or less, as Robinson and Godbey show.

In his foreword to *Time for Life,* Harvard's Robert Putnam noted the
irony of these findings:

> The most worrisome social trend in America over the last several decades
> has been the widening gap in wealth and income between the social classes.
> Robinson and Godbey report a less noticed counterpart trend: Less well-ed-
> ucated Americans appear to be enjoying more free time, whereas their col-
> lege-educated counterparts, for the most part, are not. Paradoxically, as the
> authors put it, the "working class" is spending fewer hours at work, while the
> erstwhile "leisure class" has less leisure.[9]

For avoiding overwork, the real winners appear to be people in higher-
paid Working Class jobs, like skilled workers in factories and the building
trades. They can put in their standard 40-hour week, go home at the end
of each day, and take down a decent wage. Higher-end Service Class people also can do this. For lower-paid people in both classes, earning a decent wage is the problem: thus the tendency of many low-wage workers to
moonlight on a second job. The real losers, in terms of overwork, are those
holding two full-time minimum-wage jobs to support a family. They work
an 80-hour week, still don't earn much, and are a modern-day equivalent
of the nineteenth century's burned-out factory laborers.

As for creative workers: Why do these people work so much?

Why the Creative Class Works Long Hours

In the Creative Economy, time is the only nonrenewable resource. The
three big factors driving this economy, along with the need for creativity,
are the prevalence of change, the need for flexibility and the importance of
speed. We are all familiar with the stories of companies racing around the
clock to turn out a new computer or piece of software. But more than just
the occasional race is at work here. The pressures of change and speed are
pervasive. Every product from sneakers to software is constantly being up-
graded, and everything from mutual funds to potato chips now comes in
an ever-proliferating variety of types—because the Creative Economy is

largely based on selling novelty, variety and customization. A lot of people need to put in a lot of time doing all of that upgrading and product-differentiating.

So why can't these things be done in standard 40-hour weeks? If constant change and speed are so important, why don't companies hire enough people to spread the work and get it done fast? One reason is that some fast-growing and still-emerging fields, like computer programming, face shortages of qualified people. Note also that creative workers tend to be salaried workers. The Americans' Use of Time surveys and other studies have found that people on salaries are much more likely than hourly-wage workers to put in long weeks. The BLS figures also show that among salaried people, average hours worked rise dramatically as salary goes up. Certainly one explanation may be that high-salaried people like executives have many responsibilities. Work can be delegated, but in any business unit or on any project there is usually one person in the lead, and a lot of bucks are going to stop at that person's desk.

But simple economics likely comes into play here as well. If you are an employer, you must pay your hourly workers a premium for overtime. With "exempt" people on monthly salaries, the overtime is essentially "free." Why not get as much as you can out of each one? If someone regularly works a 50-hour week, that amounts to a donation of 25 percent in extra time. Over the course of a full year, this person is working the equivalent of three months for free. If you regularly work a 60-hour week, it's like throwing in an extra 50 percent.

Workers put in longer hours for a wide variety of reasons. As earlier chapters have shown, many creative people do it because they are intrinsically motivated and like their work. When the researchers in the *Time for Life* study asked people to rate how much they enjoyed various activities, seven of ten scored work as average to above-average. Work in fact was one of the most enjoyable activities people cited. Others put in long hours because they are "ambitious." Many observers, too, have noted the power of peer pressure—you don't feel right punching out at 5 P.M. if your coworkers are still there, hunkered down for a long evening. Still others may work hard to make contributions that will gain the respect and recognition of their peers.

There are also more insidious factors. In a fascinating study of engineers at a leading electronics high-tech company, Leslie Perlow of the University of Michigan pointed to a number of factors that help enforce long hours among creative workers. Not surprisingly, for instance, she found a good bit of work being done inefficiently. The crisis mentality—don't deal with it until it's a crisis—was a noticeable time-waster.[10] Some of the best people had trouble getting work done during normal hours because they were interrupted frequently by others turning to them for help. And perhaps the most insidious factor of all: With creative work often being hard to measure and manage, supervisors turn to time on the job as a visible, easily quantifiable measure of whether their people are doing all they can. In one research paper, Perlow quoted Rosabeth Kanter's book *Men and Women of the Corporation* on this topic.

> *Question:* How does the organization know managers are doing their jobs and that they are making the best possible decisions?
> *Answer:* Because they are spending every moment at it and thus working to the limits of human possibility.[11]

In her own book *Finding Time,* Perlow tells the story of an engineer at the electronics firm she studied. This woman, a project leader and a rising star at the firm, had struck an arrangement whereby she would work from home one day per week. It seemed to pay off splendidly. The woman was able to do her own work uninterrupted. Her long commuting time was cut down so she could spend more time with her family; her team members enjoyed added autonomy on her days away; her six-month performance review was her best yet. Then suddenly she was reassigned to what coworkers agreed was a much lesser job—one that required her to be in the office every day. After further difficulties, such as not getting an expected raise, she transferred to another division and said she was considering leaving the firm. Perlow notes that workers at this firm were generally granted "ad hoc flexibility" to do things like run personal errands at midday. But overall, the pressure to put in a great deal of visible time on the premises was so strong that some "resort[ed] to tricks, leaving a coat in the office, say, or a car in the parking lot to give the appearance of 'being present.'"

Yet another factor is the relentless march of technologies that extend the workday. While many have noted how cell phones, laptops and wireless networks allow our work to follow us wherever we are, they also invade our time: Our work can follow us *whenever* we are. Then too, creative work tends to follow you around in the sense of inhabiting your head. At the end of each day there are usually problems remaining unsolved or decisions waiting to be made. These things may not occupy the foreground of your time off, but they linger in the background, to be mulled over. Are you "working" at such times? If you mulled while riding a bike or eating dinner, would you record it as work in a time diary? Creative workers may actually "work" more than statistics show.

Many factors, then, conspire to make creative people work long hours. If they are made to do so unwillingly, then surely they qualify as "over-worked Americans." But many of us are more than willing to put in the time. Few people in my focus groups and interviews complained of work-ing long hours. Many took on new time-consuming challenges even when they didn't have to: leaving a settled routine to join a time-eating startup firm, or piling volunteer work on top of their paid work. They complained that there wasn't *enough* time to do all they wanted—quite different from feeling that one works too much—or they complained when they put in the time but were frustrated with the results because of management in-competence or other reasons.

The Time Famine

Time-use scholars agree on one overwhelming fact about today's world. It is not so much that we are "overworked," but that we suffer from a con-stant feeling of being rushed—of generally not having enough time in our lives. "Time has become the most precious commodity," write Robinson and Godbey, "and the ultimate scarcity for millions of Americans."[12] They cite a 1996 *Wall Street Journal* survey that found that 40 percent of Ameri-cans believe that lack of time is a bigger problem for them than lack of money. Robinson and Godbey describe this as the "time famine." Looking at a variety of surveys done between 1965 and 1995, they note an across-the-board increase in people saying they felt "hurried" or "rushed" in their daily activities. The number reporting they "always feel rushed" increased from 24 percent of working age (18–64 years old) respondents in 1965 to 38 percent by 1992.[13] And the people most likely to feel rushed are the col-lege-educated members of the Creative Class. Consider the following:

- High levels of stress were again most prevalent among the college educated and more affluent people likely to be members of the Creative Class. Nearly two-thirds (65 percent) of college-educated Americans reported moderate to high stress levels, compared to roughly half of those with a high school education or less (55 percent

for high school, 48 percent for some high school and 36 percent for those with an eighth grade education or less).
- Reported stress also rose with income: Nearly two-thirds of those with incomes over $50,000 reported moderate to high stress, compared to roughly half of those with incomes of $20,000 or less.[14]
- When asked in separate surveys whether they wanted an "extra day off," the highest percentage of respondents saying they would take the extra day were college-educated people (58 percent)—the average for all respondents being about half.

Creative work is time-consuming and stressful, and more of us are feeling it. But the long workday is not the only thing making us feel short of time. Households with two working parents or a working single parent are increasingly numerous, and the absence of a support spouse crunches time tremendously. The Americans' Use of Time Project found that in 1995 the average (nonemployed) housewife was spending some 42 hours per week on family care, household chores and commuting duties—the equivalent of a full-time job, though this was down from 54 hours in 1965. It also found that women continued to provide more than two-thirds of all family care. When the housewife vanishes, paid caretakers like maids and childcare workers can pick up some of the slack but not all. (Do you have a chauffeur for your children?)

Stanford's Paul Romer makes the intriguing argument that even when we are not actually pressed for time, we may perceive that we are because our time is literally worth more than it used to be. In advanced nations, Romer explains, the long-term trend is for average real income to increase. There are fluctuations, to be sure—real wages may stagnate or fall at times for various sectors of the workforce—but overall, adjusting for inflation, the dominant trend is for most of us to earn more per hour than our counterparts of previous years. This ought to make us feel pretty good about the returns we're getting on our time. But our minds don't work that way. Instead, we assign an ever-increasing cost to every minute that we spend outside work—and thus worry constantly about the minutes slipping away. It is, says Romer, an unavoidable side effect of our economy:

Our children will have more of almost everything, with one glaring exception: They won't have more time in the day. As income and wages increase, the cost of time will continue to grow and so will the sense that time is scarce and that life proceeds at a faster pace than in the past.[15]

Even within a lifetime, the effect grows as one's income grows. Waiting rooms become excruciating—"My time is worth $100 an hour; I ought to charge the doctor"—and loose change is left on counters in stores because it doesn't justify the time-cost of dealing with it. Over the years, Brad Templeton has tracked the rise of a number he calls the Bill Gates Wealth Index. The idea is to imagine Gates seeing or dropping a piece of paper money on the ground: How large a denomination would the bill have to be to make it worth his time to stop and pick it up? Assuming four seconds to do so, and using Gates's income statements for each year to estimate his average earning rate in dollars per second of working time, Templeton calculated that during 1986—the year Microsoft went public— a $5 bill would have been "too small a bill for Bill" to bother with. By 1998, a $10,000 bill wasn't worth the trouble.[16]

Flexibility and Interweaving

The way we organize and use time is also shuffled, warped and interwoven. I noted in Chapter 7 that the proportion of U.S. workers on flexible schedules doubled between 1985 and 1997, according to the Bureau of Labor Statistics. And yet again, statistical breakouts show the Creative Class in the forefront of the trend. Much of the increased flexibility is in occupational categories marked by project-oriented creative work as opposed to routine operating work, as the previous chapter has shown. For instance, roughly three in five research scientists had flexible work schedules. Only one in nine machine tool operators did.

Moreover, Creative Class people tend to enjoy richer kinds of flexibility. One earmark of a flexible schedule is the freedom to periodically change one's starting and quitting times. This can be done either by a formal agreement that lets the worker regularly come in, say, an hour later or earlier than usual, or by ad hoc informal arrangement. It is popular for a number of obvious reasons—like the desire to avoid rush-hour traffic, or the need to chauffeur children—and in many workplaces, creative workers and others enjoy this kind of start-and-quit flexibility.

But there is also the flexibility of being able to come and go as one pleases throughout the workday, or to vary one's work hours greatly according to the workload. Usually these kinds of flexibility are only possible for people in project-oriented creative work. Increasingly I find creative workers demanding these kinds of flexibility and employers giving it to them. In 2000, the recruiting portion of a website at a major software firm promised a warm and fuzzy policy:

> We want you to be as comfortable as possible and feel at liberty to take time off when you need to. Only you know the optimum hours necessary to excel at your job.[17]

Whether managers always adhere to this policy may be questioned, but many employers have come to offer similar terms, and employees are quick to take them up on it.

Many people thus arrive at a complex interweaving of work and personal life: working to meet the demands of the job, certainly, but in patterns attuned to their own creative rhythms. From morning to night and from workplace to home, they intersperse bursts of work with chunks of personal time for exercise, errands, socializing, family time or just plain downtime. The folks sitting in the coffee shop with their laptops—are they working or are they socializing? Well, both, sort of. Working now, but ready to shift quickly into social mode when someone interesting walks in, they very much resemble the old craftsman in his shop on the village main street—busy but always ready to chat with a friend who drops in, maybe nipping into the back room for a pot of tea to share with him. Indeed many people see interweaving as a natural way of operating, a sort of throwback to the cottage-industry days when life was integrated and whole. It seems a healthy reaction to the organizational age system, which split work and life into compartments and required you to be one person here, another there.

Unfortunately the flexible, interwoven life can frequently be more hectic than idyllic. The standard 9-to-5 workstyle requires only a few transitions of mindset or location during the day. You show up at work and stay there, then switch off and go home. Maybe you run a few errands on the way. An interwoven day—with midday run or bike ride, late-night work, and meals and errands scattered across different times and places—requires many transitions. While some of these are easy, many are taxing. They take *time.* You need to shift focus, remember where you put your papers and materials, be sure you've got everything—and be sure you're dressed properly. One driver of the move to casual dress, I suspect, is that people got tired of changing in and out of their business attire. Moreover there are times in the interwoven day when parallel worlds collide. It can happen in the coffee shop or at home with the children: You want to work, but someone is standing before you who demands something else. Do you get that tight, edgy feeling in your chest? That's the pang of the time famine.

And though your personal allocation of time may be flexible, scheduled events are not. A good bit of time stress comes from trying to make it to scheduled events: The meeting is at 4 P.M., the soccer game is at 6, the plane leaves without you if you're not there. I think the stress is exacerbated if, like many creative workers, you spend much of the day working at a self-dictated pace and schedule, and then suddenly have to switch to a mode dictated by the clock. This may be the most jarring transition of all. It reflects, in the realm of time, the ongoing tension between creativity and organization. Finally, the flexible life of creative workers helps to create a demand for a 24/7 corps of service workers. The all-night restaurant is wonderful for the code writer who wants a hamburger at 3 A.M. It may not be wonderful for the waitress. She isn't on a flexible schedule, just the night shift.

The Front-Loaded Career and the Deferred Life

In most Creative Class occupations, people manage their careers by "front-loading"—working excruciatingly long and hard at the outset of their professional lives in the hopes it will pay off in greater income, marketability and mobility later. Granted, young people often have worked hard in the past. Young executive-track hopefuls in the organizational age were certainly expected to be diligent, but in those days the responsibilities and the time demands grew as you climbed the ladder. Besides, you wanted to start a family early because it showed the company that you were a stable person and a belonger. Today that has all been turned upside down. Indicative of the trend, the median age for marriage among men has risen to twenty-seven from twenty-two a generation ago, and to twenty-five from twenty for women.[18] The growing number of women in the professions—along with the fact that a lot of employers still don't care to see their young professional women on the mommy track—surely has been one factor driving the trend to front-load work and defer the rest of life, but it runs deeper.

Think of the forks in the career track facing any young creative person, man or woman. In the universities, post-docs and assistant professors have long been noted for working fiendishly at their research. Often they forego family aspirations and other nice things in life through their twenties because they are aiming for the tenure track. Academic tenure provides more than a secure lifetime position. It puts you in the ranks of the privileged. You get choice teaching assignments, a higher salary, a nicer office. As you build your reputation, it becomes easier to secure research funds, to generate novel findings and to publish. Other universities bid for your talent. Something similar has long been the case with artists. A musician, painter, writer or actor may not aim for academic tenure at a university, but for all of these people, it makes a big difference if you can come barreling out of your youth tagged as a star or at least a comer. You still have to keep working hard, but the returns on your early investment are high. Now that you are noticed, you can get the choice commissions, the savvy agents, the nice gigs. I would submit that a similar phenomenon is taking hold today in the private sector. It is particularly true in the so-called "up-or-out" professions like law or consulting, where great advantages accrue to those who make partner status, while those who do not are essentially out of luck. But it is also becoming true more generally.

There are several reasons for this. Young recent graduates are the workhorses of many sectors of the Creative Economy. Often they have the most up-to-date skills in fields like computing, or consulting or turbo-finance, and being young and unattached they are able to work ridiculous hours. Rather than being groomed slowly for advancement, they are thrown quickly to the front lines to see what they can do. And the young people set to it with a vengeance. They do so partly because they relish the challenge but also because, in a fluid market, this is the time to make your mark. You are hot now. If you want to be hot later—if you want to be calling the shots rather than waiting for calls, and have people bidding for you rather than screening your résumé—you need to be on the star track. Whereas if you acquire a reputation as just another hacker, you may spend the rest of your days on the hack track.

Even those who do not turn workaholic feel a strong pressure to front-load their careers and defer at least the more time-consuming aspects of personal life. The pressure reached its height in the boom days of the New Economy. The explosive growth of the Internet created the sense of a once-in-a-lifetime opportunity, a chance to be part of building something really big. Moreover, with tech stocks skyrocketing there was the IPO pipe dream: Start or join a new company, get rich, retire young.

Performance artist Steve Tomlinson of Austin—himself an adjunct faculty member at the University of Texas—captured the whole dynamic perfectly in a satiric monologue titled *Perfect Pitch,* which I heard him perform in early 2001 at a high-tech gathering called the Austin 360 Summit. The piece isn't long; I reprint the script here, with the artist's permission. He wrote and performed it at a time when the high-tech and Internet companies were imploding and the NASDAQ was tumbling.

PERFECT PITCH
(A PERFORMANCE PIECE FOR THE AUSTIN 360 SUMMIT, JANUARY 11, 2001)

© 2000 by Steven Tomlinson

The Pitch

For almost a decade, we've been offering our customers a deal that's literally too good to be true. "If you've got one brilliant idea, you can roll the dice for a shot at immortality." For almost a decade, we've been talking to talented, driven people. We've been talking big money, fast, with no sweat. Limitless, exponential growth. Perfect security. And the envy and admiration of the Big Boys and all the lesser mortals who don't have the guts or the brains to play. We've been talking about our satisfied customers—start-up stars and dot.Commandants—and millions of the best and the brightest have been listening. They've seen the vision, they've caught the fever and they've bought in to our non-diversified *Deferred-Life Plan.*

We've got great brand recognition. [Projected slide: IPO] Read *Upside. Red Herring.* Pick up anything at the airport. Our message is everywhere [Slide: Improved Professional Outlook]—"If you're not rich by now, you must be dumb or lazy. Or maybe you don't know the right people. Because once you're on the right team, it's just a matter of catching the money as it falls from Heaven."

We've got buzz. [Slide: Impress Peers Overnight] Almost everyone knows someone who knows someone who's hit the jackpot. And the stories of instant wealth are always streaming through our wireless broadband peer-to-peer network, gathering decimal places along the way.

And we've got soul. In fact we've got hundreds of thousands of souls. We've got the souls of people who've put their lives on hold to pursue a dream. [Slide: Instant Permanent Optimism] We're holding their souls in escrow while they chase after sparkling visions of pure happiness. Because what we're really selling is fantasy. And the great thing about fantasy is the customer does all the work. The customer designs it. The customer builds it. We're just the ASP. In fact, the customer is the product. That's why fantasy is good business.

And that's why we have to do whatever it takes to defend our market share in the face of recent developments. People won't buy into the Deferred-Life Plan unless they see the payoff—and suddenly it's a tough sell. We're having trouble closing deals—and unless we adapt our pitch, some of our best customers may pull out and go with the competition. Now no one's forecasting an epidemic of intellectual honesty, but the customers are asking questions—[Slide: Is the Party Over?]—so we need to have answers.

The Market

Remember, we can divide the market into three segments. [Slide: Spectrum graph] Over here we've got people with passion. People on a mission from God. People who actually believe in what they're doing because they love it. People curing diseases and fighting injustice and writing poetry and making the world a better place, even if it means working for free. Forget these people. We can't afford them.

Over here we've got people with drive. Greedy people—people who wouldn't know passion if it crashed their server—mercenaries, chasing the herd from one gold rush to another, trampling each other on the way. Forget these people. We've got them locked up.

I want to talk about *these* people. [Points to the middle of the graph] Reasonable people. People with passion *and* drive. Here's a guy who starts with passion—an idea, something useful and beautiful. It comes to him late one night and fills him with joy, because it's cool. And he's sure that other people will want this cool thing—so he starts a little business—and sure enough some people want it. So the business grows, and that means more people and investors and the market. And when the herd gets involved—*cool* isn't enough. It's got to be *hot*. It's got to be The Next Big Thing. And so our guy with a cool idea is suddenly riding the buzz of the next big, hot, *scalable* thing and people he's seen in magazines are talking to *him*—promising fame and more money than he and his family could ever spend. And surely the prospect of that security is worth some overtime.

So he's ready to sacrifice. We offer him stock in Deferred-Life, and he makes a rational calculation, and as long as his upside fantasy covers the costs, he buys in—he outsources his fulfillment, and he shifts from cool to hot. And from here on, he's driven. His vital signs follow the NASDAQ, his vision clouds, and before long he's making bets with his life that even the craziest VCs wouldn't touch. And we've got him. So we focus our efforts right here. On this calculation. Ignore the bears. We simply put the costs and benefits in perspective, and the customer sees that he needs us now more than ever.

The Plan

Strategy 1. Denial. The simplest strategy is focus on the fundamentals. Shine the spotlight on some hot prospects and watch the soul-searching evaporate. So what if the market's moody. Blame it on the Fed. Blame it on sunspots. Blame it on Florida. Nothing's really changed. Technology rules. So e-commerce is having a rough adolescence. Why worry? Biotech and soft cells and code-morphing optical microsystems are just around the corner. [Slide: Nanotechnology] Miniaturization is the next big thing—and you can't win if you don't keep playing. Keep in mind, we're talking about desperate customers who can barely afford the minimum monthly payments on their maxed-out self-delusion. We're offering to bump up their limit. And they'll buy it, because they can't afford the alternative.

Strategy 2. Sunk Costs. They're having unauthorized fantasies about a simpler life, but we're going to remind them what's at stake. We're going to rattle their golden handcuffs until we've dispelled all doubt. There is *no* exit strategy. They've invested too many sleepless nights and frayed nerves and lost opportunities. They've sold their friends and family on Deferred-Life. And they're fully vested in *our* definition of success. "If you crap out now, you lose everything—money, respect, and your Elite Status in our Preferred-Customer program. Of course, the successful people may still be polite to you, but they won't pay quite so much attention—they'll always be looking over your shoulder." We have to remind our customers of the penalty for early withdrawal. They'll conclude for themselves that [Slide: Survival] is the next big thing. And here's the secret of our success: If fear is your dividend, your shareholders always reinvest.

Strategy 3. Speed. Fear's great, but frenzy is better. And that's the real problem with this slump. No frenzy. When the market cools, our customers have time on their hands. Real time. And real time means real reflection. What am I doing? Am I crazy? What does it all *mean?* And believe me, reflection is the last thing we want. People reflecting in real time recover their passions. They look around and see—real people, real needs—and they may do something surprising. Real time is bad, bad for business. So we're going to punch the accelerator. Get the wheels spinning again. Fast. Get people back on autopilot. Always on. 24/7. Focused on success, filtering out irrelevant information, impervious to surprise. Deferred-Life customers like speed, because the less they think, the better they feel.

The Payoff

So, the NASDAQ's down, everyone's holding their breath, and our competition smells blood. They're betting that our customers are ready to switch back to reality. They're going to start phoning at dinner time with their best pitch. [Slide: Important Personal Opportunity] "Do you remember how it all started? How exciting it is to have a good idea? Something cool? Purpose, meaning, a mission that your idea could make someone's life better? Now that the fog has lifted, do you see where you are? How far you've drifted from where you started? Well, for a limited time only, you can come back. Back to passion. Back to people and balance. Back to your life. It's just as good as you remember." It's great marketing—it's retro, it appeals to self-doubt. It's *good*. So we've got to be better.

I'd say it's time to pay some big dividends. Let's bundle our services and offer our customers a new package deal of fear and fantasy. They'll double down because they're in too deep—and we'll pack up their loyal souls and their frozen assets and ride the bear to The Next Big Thing. And what might that be? Does it matter? As long as it's not REALITY, we'll be just fine.

Tomlinson is saying in this monologue that while the IPO pipe dream may have cooled off, the desires that motivate people to a front-loaded career—and the "deferred-life plan"—persist. This is the new way to make it: Exploit the inherent, fundamental features of an economy in which creative work is valued, labor markets are fluid, and an early splash makes a big difference in one's career path. The star track is the hook in the mouth of the young Creative Class person on the make.

Cynicism aside, I believe it is natural and logical for people to adjust to prevailing market mechanisms. Happiness and peace of mind are not precluded but they must be sought in new forms. Our society, as a whole, is still adapting to the front-loaded career and deferred life. Meanwhile, the widespread adoption of this life pattern by creative workers sets the Creative Class apart from many others in the society. Their lives unfold to the tick of different clock.

Life-Shifting

Another trend in the use of time is the growing prevalence of the life-shift—for instance, not just a job change but a career change, not just a career change but a way-of-life change. While it frequently involves a change of work venue or status, such as from employee to freelancer, or from entrepreneur back to employee, it is often coupled with a broader change of lifestyle. But it is not what people called dropping out in the 1960s. Although it is sometimes accompanied by time off, extensive travel or a major geographic move, like the professor's sabbatical, it's back to work after awhile. Some people shift more than once: It is now common to speak of the "quarter-life" and "three-quarter-life" shifts.[19]

The archetypal multiple shifter is Bob Metcalfe, inventor of the Ethernet technology and founder of the networking company 3Com. Born in 1946, Metcalfe spent the early part of his career, through the 1970s, as a research scientist. During the 1980s he was an entrepreneur and executive with 3Com. He left the firm in 1990, spent the following years as a journalist and publisher with *InfoWorld*—pulling back to write about a scene in which he'd been a hands-on player—and meanwhile moved with his wife and young children from Silicon Valley to a farm near Lincolnville, Maine. Then in 2000, Metcalfe wrote a farewell column in *InfoWorld* (lamenting, by the way, that he hadn't achieved his journalistic goal of winning a Pulitzer Prize) and joined a venture capital firm in the Boston area. The turn of each decade, for this man, is a cue to try a new way of life.

What's going on here? Life-shifting may partly be a reaction to the ultra-specialization of the organizational age. There is a natural creative desire to seek multiple outlets for one's creativity, to be a Renaissance person. Hobbies and leisure pursuits can help to satisfy this need, but it becomes hard to seriously practice more than one profession at the same time, because the knowledge bases are more complex than they were in the Renaissance. So we try different fields in serial order in part to satisfy our multidimensional creative urges.

Life-shifting also can be seen as a logical economic attempt to get the most from a limited resource. The bohemian painters in the garrets of Montmarte in the 1800s often didn't have much money. Canvas costs money. So what they would sometimes do, as painters today still do, is take an existing canvas, already painted, and paint a new picture on the back side. Then perhaps flip again to the front and start over-painting. Similarly, to the Western mind, the allotment of lives we get is severely limited: one per person. And for many who feel called to go on creating, the solution is to flip sides; paint over.

The one-life-per-person rule is the ultimate time constraint and people have never been very happy with it. A good bit of intellectual and social history can be read as a series of attempts to get around it. In addition to life-shifting, with its strategy of stacking two or more lives into one end-to-end, modern-day attempts would include the war on death and aging—an ongoing campaign to extend life—and parallel processing, which is the strategy of trying to live several lives simultaneously by combining a vocation with longtime avocations: thus the programmer–rock climber–rock musician.

Deepening the Moment

With so many people feeling chronically pressed for time, a new set of moment-to-moment strategies has emerged. The intent is what scholars call "time deepening"—if one cannot elongate time, perhaps one can deepen or intensify it, getting more from each bit. To me this is the key difference in our use of time, and it can be far more insidious than long hours. Because we are unable to physically extend the day, we pack each moment full. In *Time for Life,* Robinson and Godbey were notably dry-eyed about this trend:

> Time-deepening fools people into thinking they can avoid sacrificing one activity for another. We instead seek to do it all, and see it all, and to do it and see it now. In effect, time has become a commodity, and time viewed as a commodity seems to have made people's lives shorter and less tranquil. The experience of life is increasingly catalogued in terms of a patternless checklist of "been there, done that."[20]

The authors suggest that there are four basic strategies for time deepening:

- The *speeding up* of activities.
- *Substituting* a leisure activity that can be done more quickly for one that takes longer, such as getting take-out or home delivery rather than cooking, playing racquetball rather than a slower game like tennis—or, in my case, an hour of spinning in the gym as opposed to a two- or three-hour bike ride with friends.
- *Multitasking,* or doing more than one thing at once: watching TV while reading the paper, eating dinner while editing a chapter, using the cell phone while driving.
- *Detailed time planning and budgeting*—especially for leisure or recreational activities; compartmentalizing time so as to get a handle

on it. What astounds me more than anything is that my students now carry personal organizers with their days parceled into half-hour chunks. I certainly did not need to schedule my time like this when I was a student, and did not even carry a calendar until I became an assistant professor.

In general, write Robinson and Godbey, we are shifting from the "consumption of goods" to the "consumption of experiences." This is a theme that takes us from the sphere of work to the sphere of life as a whole. In the next part of this book, I will describe how a key facet of the Creative Class lifestyle is a quest for experiences that are in themselves rich and multidimensional. In this classic creative view, time is truly deep not when it is rushed or crammed, but rather when it fully engages every faculty of one's being in every waking moment.

PART THREE

Life

and

Leisure

CHAPTER 10

The Experiential Life

At the dawn of the millennium, on the morning of January 1, 2000, a new avatar of the New Economy made his debut. He was a twenty-six-year-old former systems analyst who had legally changed his name to DotComGuy. His website, DotComGuy.com, logged an astounding 10 million hits that New Year's Day. People around the world watched on their computer screens, via webcam, as the bland-looking young man moved into a bland suburban house in North Dallas, Texas. There he would remain for the rest of the year, living entirely on goods and services ordered over the Internet: groceries from Food.com, housecleaning by TheMaids.com, point-and-click pizza delivery and much more.

The secret of DotComGuy's appeal could not have been his daily routine, which often resembled that of an elderly shut-in waiting for Meals on Wheels. Nothing kinky here: no webcam sex or moody personal revelations. He spent much of his time playing with his dog, DotComDog, or watching TV, or surfing the web. Yet he drew a devoted on-line following, including a chat room frequented by young girls commenting on his cuteness. News reporters and eager visitors came to call. What made Dot-ComGuy so fascinating was that he perfectly embodied all the myths of *homo new economicus* in the Internet age. Here was the quintessential maverick using the Internet to turn the system upside down. He was a free agent and entrepreneur, out on his own, doing it his way. He had lined up corporate sponsors to provide everything he needed free, in exchange for publicity and banner ads on his website. The sponsors included long-established firms like UPS; equipment and tech support for the website were donated by technology giants such as Gateway and 3Com. Rather than hold a faceless job in corporate America, DotComGuy had the big companies beating a path to *his* door. Rather than travel for what he wanted, he had the world brought to him. He was a virtual Horatio Alger, a housebound king of infinite cyberspace.

DotComGuy's *über*-virtual lifestyle provoked two kinds of reactions. Some reveled in the prospect of the new world it represented. New Economy pundits had preached the virtues of business going virtual, and to true believers, much of life would be better that way as well: We would come together in on-line communities of like-minded individuals. New technologies and business models were converging to link everyone in a gigantic virtual global village, with virtual storefronts, virtual offices, virtual playgrounds and even virtual singles bars. When DotComGuy left his house at the end of the year 2000, he announced that he planned to marry a woman he had "met" in his website chat room.

Then there were the cynics. *Salon* called DotComGuy the "Poster Child for Internet Idiocy."[1] Other critics worried that the virtual lifestyle would tear apart an already fraying social fabric and bring an end to real community. In this dark view, we were becoming isolated and divided into a nation of lonesome cowboys, hunkered down with our PC screens.

Both perspectives miss the point. Virtual community is not replacing real community. Chat rooms have proliferated, but so have real coffee shops. And while DotComGuy's entrepreneurial spirit may be admired by many, his virtual lifestyle is not at all what vast and growing numbers of people want. Members of the Creative Class are not looking for a life delivered through a modem. They want one that is heart-throbbingly real.

Creativity and Experience

On many fronts, the Creative Class lifestyle comes down to a passionate quest for experience. The ideal, as a number of my subjects succinctly put it, is to "live the life"—a creative life packed full of intense, high-quality, multidimensional experiences. And the *kinds* of experiences they crave reflect and reinforce their identities as creative people. My interviews and focus groups indicate that they favor active, participatory recreation over passive spectator sports. They like indigenous street-level culture—a teeming blend of cafes, sidewalk musicians, and small galleries and bistros, where it is hard to draw the line between participant and observer, or between creativity and its creators. They crave creative stimulation but not escape. As one young man told me, explaining why he and his friends favored nonalcoholic hangouts: "We can't afford the recovery time." Moreover, while many members of the Creative Class actively use computers, shop online, participate in chat rooms and even have virtual personas, I repeatedly find that the most computer-savvy people of all—high-technology

professionals and computer-science-oriented students at schools like
Carnegie Mellon—have interests extending well beyond the virtual. More
than anything, they crave intense experiences in the real world.

In their insightful book *The Experience Economy,* Joseph Pine and James
Gilmore observe that consumers are coming to favor the consumption of
experiences over traditional goods and services.

> Experiences are a fourth economic offering, as distinct from services as ser-
> vices are from goods. . . . Experiences have always been around but con-
> sumers, businesses, and economists lumped them into the service sector
> along with such uneventful activities as dry cleaning, auto repair, wholesale
> distribution, and telephone access. When a person buys a service he pur-
> chases a set of intangible activities carried out on his behalf. But when he
> buys an experience, he pays to spend time enjoying a series of memorable
> events that a company stages—as in a theatrical play—to engage him in a
> personal way. . . .
>
> The newly identified offering of experiences occurs whenever a company
> intentionally uses services as the stage and goods as props to engage an indi-
> vidual. While commodities are fungible, goods tangible, and services intan-
> gible, experiences are *memorable.* Buyers of experiences—we'll follow
> Disney's lead and call them *guests*—value being engaged by what the com-
> pany reveals over a duration of time. Just as people have cut back on goods
> to spend more money on services, now they also scrutinize the time and
> money they spend on services to make way for more memorable—and
> highly valued—experiences.[2]

But Pines and Gilmore are talking here mainly about pre-packaged experiences of the sort Disney provides. Members of the Creative Class prefer more active, authentic and participatory experiences, which they can
have a hand in structuring. In practical everyday terms, this means running, rock climbing or cycling rather than watching a game on TV; it
means travel to interesting locations that engage one physically or intellectually; it means the purchase of unique antique pieces or original "midcentury modern" furniture as opposed to just buying something to sit on.

The quest for experiences extends far beyond the point of purchase.
Some commentators suggest that anticipation is more important than the
actual consumption of experiences, dubbing this "imaginative hedonism."[3] Ben Malbon's book on the British club scene, *Clubbing,* highlights
the role of such "experiential consuming." For the young people he studied,

the actual visit to a dance club is only part of the scene, Malbon notes. He describes, in detail, the lengthy and intricate processes of clubbers debating where and when to go, laying out clothes for the event, and discussing and creating "histories" of their experiences afterward.[4] However one views it, this much is certain: Experiences are replacing goods and services because they stimulate our creative faculties and enhance our creative capacities. This active, experiential lifestyle is spreading and becoming more prevalent in society as the structures and institutions of the Creative Economy spread.

Writing in the 1950s, the psychologist Carl Rogers called attention to the relationship between creativity and experiences. At one point in his well-known book *On Becoming a Person* he criticized the overly rigid, bureaucratic society of his day for its stifling effect, arguing for the "desperate social need" for creativity.

> In our leisure time activities, passive entertainment and regimented group action are overwhelmingly predominant while creative activities are much less in evidence. . . . In individual and family life the same picture holds true. In the clothes we wear, the food we eat, and the ideas we hold, there is a strong tendency toward conformity, toward stereotypy. To be original, or different, is felt to be "dangerous."[5]

The creative or experiential lifestyle is a direct reaction to this predicament, as the economic need for creativity has grown. After outlining the dimensions of the creative process and offering his basic theory of creativity, Rogers went on to detail what he saw as the necessary connection between creativity and experiences.

> It has been found that when the individual is "open" to all his experience . . . then his behavior will be creative, and his creativity may be trusted to be essentially constructive. . . . In a person who is open to experience each stimulus is freely relayed . . . without being distorted by any process of defensiveness. Whether the stimulus originates in the environment, in the impact of form, color, or sound on the sensory nerves, or whether it originates in the viscera . . . it is available to awareness. . . . This last suggests another way of describing openness to experience. It means lack of rigidity and permeability of boundaries in concepts, beliefs, perceptions, and hypotheses. It means a tolerance for ambiguity where ambiguity exists. It means the ability to receive much conflicting information without forcing closure upon the

situation. . . . This complete openness of awareness to what exists at this moment is, I believe, an important condition of constructive creativity.[6]

All of which brings us to the role that experiences play today in stimulating creativity. The old conformist lifestyle that Rogers disparaged has given way to a more creative one based on the eyes-wide-open pursuit of wide-ranging, highly engaging activities and stimuli.

Some might say the appeal of this lifestyle will necessarily diminish in the wake of the World Trade Center tragedy of September 11, 2001—that these pursuits were the markers of a self-centered, fun-chasing and essentially aimless mindset, and that people are now becoming more serious and no longer so interested in such frivolities. I do not think that is the case. The new lifestyle is not mainly about "fun." Rather it complements the way members of the Creative Class work and is a fundamental part of the way they go about their lives.

Let me tell you a personal story that may help put this in perspective. The events of September 11 affected me powerfully. For two weeks I was unable to concentrate on my work or focus on my writing. I canceled a number of speaking engagements, because literally I could not speak. Like millions of Americans I sat in front of the television for hours on end watching news broadcasts. But there was one thing I wanted to do— that I was pulled to do. And that was to ride my bicycle. I am an avid road cyclist, and I took several hours each day to just go out and ride . . . and ride . . . and ride. It had little to do with my passion for cycling or an effort to stay fit. The pull toward my bike came from the release it afforded, the ability to stop thinking and let go, to stop my brain from turning, to do something physical, to just ride. And I suspect that much the same impulse drives the new lifestyle and the new leisure. As a way of both disconnecting and recharging, it is part of what we *need to do* as creative people.

Writing at the turn of the twentieth century, the iconoclastic economist Thorstein Veblen outlined his famous theory of the wealthy "leisure class."[7] Calling attention to the "conspicuous consumption" of the *nouveaux riche* capitalists and their families, Veblen found the new elite displaying their power and values through what their money bought. As the historian Gary Cross shows in his comprehensive review of consumption in the twentieth century, the consumption habits of this new elite revolved around giant mansions and estates, "vicarious consumption" through their wives' purchases of luxuries, and participation in "ostentatious time-killing activities" like golf.[8] Thus they were a leisure class indeed, flaunting not only their goods but their indolence.

The members of the Creative Class are less a leisure class in Veblen's sense of the term and more an "active class." Their consumption is not so crudely conspicuous and they certainly do not participate in time-killing activities of any sort, for as the last chapter has shown they do not have the time to kill. Moreover, status and identity for these people come not so much from the goods they have, but from the experiences they have. As Julie Blick, a Wharton School graduate, retired Microsoft engineer and author of a 1995 book on her experiences, wrote: "Conspicuous consumption isn't the style. People don't have jets or huge vacation homes. They have a cabin in the woods furnished by Ikea."[9] There are good economic reasons for this shift. As economic historians have shown, average American living standards have risen to such an extent that material goods no longer confer the status they once did. In her detailed survey of American living standards in the twentieth century, the University of California–Berkeley labor economist Clair Brown wrote:

> By the late 1980s, daily material life had improved in ways that could not have been imagined in 1918. Working-class families had a richer material life in 1988 than the salaried class had in 1918. Their food, transportation, medical care, and home comforts provided a material quality of life that was not attainable even by the elite in any previous era. . . . [L]eisure time activities became an important part of life. Working-class families owned sports equipment and toys, attended sporting and cultural events, and even took vacation trips.[10]

The Nobel Prize-winning economic historian Robert Fogel sums up the situation this way: "Today, ordinary people wish to use their liberated time to buy those amenities of life that only the rich could afford in abundance a century ago. . . . The principal cost of these activities is not measured by cash outlays, but by outlays of time."[11] And with life itself having become the scarce and precious commodity, many increasingly define the quality of their lives by the quality of experiences they consume.

The Active Life

"In the early 1960s, there was no such thing as a middle-aged man jogging on the street," writes the journalist Andy Sheehan in *Chasing the Hawk*, a book about his father, Dr. George Sheehan, the physician-turned-author and well-known "running guru" of the 1960s and 1970s.[12] The elder Sheehan, a successful doctor in Red Bank, New Jersey, began running in 1963 at the age of forty-five. At the time, grown men simply did not exercise in public; doing so meant one was frivolous or even "subversive." So Sheehan ran in his backyard. "It was with no small amount of wonder," his son writes, "that I stood on my back porch one day . . . and watched my father running the perimeter of our backyard. The backyard covered two acres, and I watched as he ran the length of the house, trotted down a small slope, turned right at a neighbor's fence." When his father eventually took to the streets he did so "despite the honking horns and the sounds of laughter from the cars that passed him." The jibes were sometimes directed at the younger Sheehan and his siblings: "'Why does your father run around town in his underwear?' we children were asked." But through it all, according to his son, running helped establish George Sheehan as a creative person. "My father attributed a whole host of astonishing personal transformations to running. It made him stop drinking, freed him from anger, got him in touch with himself, and made him a creative being."

Few of us, of course, achieve such a radical makeover from running or any other single activity. But we are engaging in many new behaviors that add up to a radical makeover of leisure in our society. And while Sheehan claimed that his pastime made him creative, I would suggest that for us, the causality runs the other way as well. Because we relate to the economy through our creativity and thus identify ourselves as "creative beings," we pursue pastimes and cultural forms that express and nurture our creativity.

The ensuing decades have witnessed a virtual revolution in active recreation. In 1964, when Sheehan entered his first Boston Marathon, there were just 225 runners. Today the event is limited to 15,000 qualifiers. According to a 2000 Roper Starch survey, 67 percent of all Americans participated in active outdoor recreation on a monthly basis in 1999, up from 50 percent in 1994. The study also noted that an increasing number of people, some 30 percent, participate in more than five different active recreational activities per year.[13] Figures from the Outdoor Recreation Coalition of America highlight the shift to so-called adventure or extreme sports. Counting people who engage in an activity nine or more times a year, it found 300 percent increases in snowshoeing and telemark skiing, and more than 50 percent increases in rafting and kayaking from 1998 to 1999.[14] According to the U.S. Bureau of Economic Analysis, Americans spent approximately $535 billion on recreation in 1999.[15] Buried in this

TABLE 10.1   How Americans Use Their Free Time, 1965-1995 (average hours per week)

Activity	1965	1995	Change	% Change
Television viewing	10.4	16.5	+6.1	+ 58.6
Socializing	8.2	7.3	−1.5	−18.5
Communication	3.6	3.7	+0.1	+ 2.8
Active sports and exercise	1.0	3.0	+2.0	+200.0
Hobbies	2.2	2.6	+0.4	+18.2
Religion	0.9	0.9	0.0	0.0
Other organizations	1.3	0.9	−0.4	−30.8
Sports and cultural events	1.2	1.3	+0.1	+ 8.3
Continuing education	1.8	2.7	+0.9	+50.0
Subtotal	20.2	22.4	+2.2	+10.9
Total free time	34.8	41.0	+6.2	+17.8

SOURCE: John P. Robinson and Geoffrey Godbey, *Time for Life: The Surprising Ways Americans Use Their Time*, 2nd ed. University Park, PA: The Pennsylvania State University Press, 1997, p. 343.

staggering figure is the extent to which people—particularly Creative Class people—have come to participate in active sports and physical exercise. It is increasingly normal and even expected that Creative Class people, well into middle age and beyond, will engage in these activities once deemed juvenile or deviant. The average age of customers of the sporting goods retailer REI is forty-four. Health club memberships in the United States grew from virtually nothing in the early 1960s to more than 15 million by the mid-1980s, reaching 32.8 million by 2000.[16] Many larger companies provide on-site physical exercise facilities. Some even reduce the employee contribution for health care benefits for those who engage in regular exercise.

As noted in the last chapter, the Americans' Use of Time surveys show that on average we now have roughly as much free time as work time—nearly 40 hours per week—and enjoyed an average free time gain of 6.2 hours between 1965 and 1995. Interestingly, women picked up 4.5 hours of free time over that period while men gained 7.9 hours.[17] Though much has been made of the increase in television viewing, active sports and exercise registered the largest percentage increase of all free time activities, *tripling* over the period (see Table 10.1).

Reliable data sources on the varied lifestyle activities of Americans in general and the Creative Class in particular are very hard to come by. But using data collected from a nationwide survey of some 15.3 million American consumers by Equifax, some interesting trends are apparent. Although these data are by no means definitive, some intriguing patterns in the lifestyle and leisure preferences of the Creative Class can be inferred.[18]

- High-income people between eighteen and thirty-four years of age (with incomes of more than $75,000) are more than two times as likely as the average person to scuba dive, snow ski, travel, play tennis, fly frequently or jog, whereas low-income people in this age group (those with incomes of $30,000 or less) are more likely to play home video games, horseback ride, fiddle with electronics, camp, ride a motorcycle or do automotive work.
- The same basic pattern holds for people in the thirty-five- to forty-four-year-old age group. High-income people in this age group are more than two times more likely than average to travel, ski or scuba dive, and are more than one and a half times more likely to play tennis, golf, jog and enjoy wines. Lower-income people in this age group are more likely to horseback ride, play video games, collect stamps, ride motorcycles, camp and do automotive work.
- Affluent middle-aged Americans between the ages of forty-five and sixty-four are significantly more likely than average to own a vacation home, travel, enjoy wines, golf, sail and attend arts and cultural events, whereas lower-income people in this age group are more likely to spend time with their grandchildren, enter sweepstakes, sew and do needlework, collect stamps, coins and other things, read the Bible and engage in crafts.

My focus groups and interviews with Creative Class people reveal that they value active outdoor recreation very highly. They are drawn to places and communities where many outdoor activities are prevalent—both because they enjoy these activities, and because their presence is seen as a signal that the place is amenable to the broader creative lifestyle. The Creative Class people in my studies are into a variety of active sports, from traditional ones like bicycling, jogging and kayaking to newer, more extreme ones like trail running and snowboarding. My favorite, bicycling, has grown dramatically in the past few decades. While people in other nations regularly use bicycles for commuting and errand-running, most people in the United States long thought of bicycles mainly as children's toys. Through the 1950s and into the 1960s, old-line American makers like Schwinn and Huffy targeted their products heavily to children. Today we have a host of new manufacturers—Cannondale, Trek, Gary Fisher and many others—plus new genres of the sport and new types of bicycles, everything from road bikes and mountain bikes to cross-bikes and BMX bikes, along with other even more specialized types. Mountain biking, the off-road form pioneered by Gary Fisher in California, has skyrocketed and split into genres such as single versus dual suspension, downhill and cross-country. For the creative people and high-tech professionals in my field studies, riding a mountain bike has become almost a *de rigueur* social skill—much as horseback riding was for the members of the old elite. And this is not just among the young. I have come across countless forty- and fifty-somethings who are avid mountain bike riders. Quite a cultural transformation: forty years ago the bicycle was a childish symbol of small-town squareness; today it is cool.

What accounts for the interest in active recreation? Part of it is the changing nature of work itself. Members of the traditional Working Class spent the day engaged in physical labor and thus were inclined to relax in their time off. Creative work is largely intellectual and sedentary; thus Creative Class people seek to recharge through physical activity. If you spend your workday in front of a computer screen or an artist's canvas, you probably are not eager to spend your leisure in front of a TV screen. You are much more likely to want to get out and be active. As one person I interviewed put it, "Recreation is stress relief away from everyday work."[19] Time and again, when people in my interviews and focus groups speak of active sports, they use the word "release." Climbing a rock face or pedaling a bike releases the physical energy pent up through long hours of sitting, and is also a form of mental release. As the wife of a high-powered executive put it: "He is compelled to engage in these kinds of activities simply to release the incredible energy he has."[20]

Similar reasoning may help explain why motorsports today have blue-collar appeal, whereas the Creative Class favors active sports. A friend who canoes the rivers in Pittsburgh tells me of his frequent encounters with motorboaters. Many will slow down or stop to chat with him. Often the people aboard the motorboats turn out to be blue-collar individuals such as steelworkers or construction workers, and my friend says that as he paddles toward them, the greeting they call out is almost always the same: "Looks like work!" Meanwhile, many of these modern-day Working Class people are enjoying themselves much as Veblen's leisure class once did: relaxing in a deck chair on a big, well-appointed boat that will roar into action, at their command, with a touch of the throttle.

Another curious reversal is apparent. Generally, the active sports most popular with the masses in the early and mid-1900s were competitive, highly structured game sports. Working Class neighborhoods then were full of the bowling leagues whose passing is so lamented by Robert Putnam; and they were also full of amateur baseball teams and sandlot football teams, boxing gyms and public swimming pools. They had church-league basketball and local track and field clubs for women and men alike. Most of the fast-growing active sports for adults today are the less structured ones. In running, for instance, there are organized races, but most people, most of the time, run informally. The same is true of rollerblading, mountain cycling and many other such sports. One might say this is a classic case of the creative impulse coming to the fore, as growing numbers of people wish to set their own pace and create their own rules.

Few of my Creative Class subjects show significant interest in spectator sports. They want to participate directly. While they may take in an occasional game, in dozens of focus groups and countless interviews, not one Creative Class person ever mentioned being drawn to a city for the professional sports teams it offers. A 2000 survey by Bear Stearns highlighted the shift toward individual over team sports. The study forecasted a 44 percent increase in active outdoor exercise by adults over the ten-year period 2000–2010, with much of the growth driven by active individual sports such as jogging, aerobics, swimming and weight training.[21] Among the spectator sports, members of the Creative Class appear to favor continuous-action sports like basketball and even hockey over football or baseball. Part of the reason is that continuous-action sports are more packed with experience. But beyond this, an even broader reason—highlighted in a fair number of my interviews—is that basketball and hockey games are played in the evening during times of year when the weather is cold and daylight ends early. These people say that they can simply not afford to "sacrifice" a warm summer evening to watch baseball, or an entire Sunday afternoon to attend a football game. In his irreverent 1983 book *Class*—full of barbed but often perceptive comments on everyone from the "proles" to the "out-of-sight" wealthy—Paul Fussell of the University of Pennsylvania noted that obsession with spectator sports tends to be a marker of Working Class status for two reasons:

One is their need . . . to identify with winners, the need to dance and scream "We're number one!" while holding an index finger erect. One hockey player says: "The whole object of a pro game is to win. That is what we sell. We sell it to a lot of people who don't win at all in their regular lives.". . . In addition to this appeal through vicarious success, sports are popular for middles and proles to follow because they sanction a flux of pedantry, dogmatism, record-keeping, wise secret knowledge, and pseudo-scholarship of the sort usually associated with the "decision-making" or "executive" or "opinion-molding" classes. The World Series and the Super Bowl give every man his opportunity to . . . play for the moment the impressive barroom pedant, to imitate for a brief season the superior classes identified by their practice of weighty utterance and informed opinion. . . . If the prole doesn't know what might cause Union Carbide to go up or down, as a master of "the fine points of the game" he can affect to know why the Chargers or the Dodgers are go-ing to win this time, and that's a powerful need satisfied.[22]

Of course we are dealing here in generalities. Some Working Class people have no interest in spectator sports or motorsports. Some wealthy and Cre-ative Class people love them: think of Malcolm Forbes on his motorcycle, or Spike Lee in his courtside seat at New York Knicks games. The sociology of sport and class contains many nuances. Nonetheless, as we have seen, there is considerable evidence that the more active, individual forms of recreation are most popular at the high end of the socioeconomic ladder.

There are other logical reasons why spectator sports are less popular among the Creative Class. High levels of mobility are one. When people move frequently to pursue careers and lifestyle interests, it becomes harder to sustain the home-team allegiances built in youth. Also, as we have seen, more and more of the Creative Class are immigrants. Those who grow up with cricket or field hockey or soccer may not take to American-style sports. The campus at Carnegie Mellon is built around a wide green lawn called the Cut. For generations it has been common to see students out on the Cut playing touch football or tossing a baseball, but the games are changing. Growing activities now are impromptu soccer games, led by for-eign students, and Ultimate Frisbee, an American-invented game that, like soccer and unlike American football or baseball, features nonstop action.

The Body as Art

Noting the toned bodies on many young members of the Creative Class, my brother Robert, himself a fellow who likes to stay fit, says that "college students today look like they major in staying in shape." Much the same is true of another Creative Class subgroup, performing artists. A number of middle-aged rock stars, such as Bruce Springsteen and Madonna, now appear much fitter than when they started out. Some musicians have bigger biceps than pro athletes did forty years ago; if Bob Dylan were to come along today, his agent would probably send him to the weight room.

In its January 2000 issue, *Men's Fitness* magazine issued its "Fitness Index," which ranked fifty large American cities on how fit or fat they were, and made an immediate sensation in newspaper headlines and on talk shows across the country.[23] The Index examined twenty-nine separate categories, from obesity and smoking to the percentage of adults who exercise in a given day. While I will have much more to say on indicators of creative cities in the next part of the book, Table 10.2 lists the "fittest" and "fattest" cities alongside their ranking on my Creativity Index. By and large, the fittest cities were leading Creative Centers—San Diego, Minneapolis, Seattle, Washington, D.C., and San Francisco—whereas the fattest cities were not. Along with Philadelphia (whose mayor challenged his entire city to a weight-loss diet), the fattest cities included Kansas City, Houston, Indianapolis and New Orleans. The fittest cities had an average ranking of 30 on the Creativity Index, while the fattest were more than 20 places behind with an average rank of 53.

Even though the *Men's Fitness* sample is somewhat small, I ran some basic correlations just to see what the relationship might be between the Fitness Index and various indicators of a creative city, such as my Creativity Index and other measures. In all cases, the correlations were both strongly positive and statistically significant. The fittest cities were those that scored highly on my Creativity Index, had high levels of innovation and high-tech industries, and flourishing gay and bohemian populations.[24]

The force behind the Creative Class obsession with being in shape is more than a concern with health. Nor is it a mere shifting of the aesthetic standard to favor, say, big biceps. I see it as a growing awareness of the body as an arena for creative expression. It is no coincidence that tattooing and piercing also have exploded in popularity, and that health clubs offer classes called "body sculpting." What we're seeing is the emergence of the body as art form. The trend may seem narcissistic to some, but there are practical reasons for it. With marriage often deferred and divorce more common, Creative Class people spend a lot of time on the mating market. And in many species, not just humans, physical display is a key aspect of mating: You are more marketable if you look your best. Being economically mobile and entrepreneurial, members of the Creative Class also spend a lot of time marketing themselves to prospective employers, part-

TABLE 10.2   Fit Regions Are also Creative Regions

Region	Fitness Rank	Creativity Index Score	Creativity Index Rank
25 "Fittest" Regions			
San Diego	1	1015	3
Minneapolis	2	960	11
Seattle	3	1008	5
Washington, D.C.	4	964	9
San Francisco	5	1057	1
Portland, Oregon	6	929	18
Denver	7	940	14
Honolulu	8	580	111
Colorado Springs	9	756	48
Los Angeles	10	942	14
Oakland, CA[a]	11	1057	1
Virginia Beach, VA	12	555	120
Long Beach, CA[b]	13	942	13
Tucson, AZ	14	853	21
Boston, MA	15	1015	3
Mesa, AZ[c]	16	909	22
San Jose, CA[a]	17	1057	1
Albuquerque	18	965	8
Fresno, CA	19	516	138
Phoenix	20	909	22
Charlotte, NC	21	787	42
Tulsa	22	721	61
Austin	23	1028	2
Miami	24	775	43
Atlanta	25	940	14
Average	–	887	30
25 "Fattest" Regions			
Sacramento	26	872	26
Jacksonville, FL	27	715	64
Milwaukee, WI	28	736	56
Fort Worth, TX[d]	29	960	11
Las Vegas	30	561	117
New York	31	962	10
St. Louis	32	770	45
Baltimore[e]	33	964	9
Cleveland	34	774	44
San Antonio	35	737	55
Dallas	36	960	11
Pittsburgh	37	734	57
Oklahoma City	38	668	83

TABLE 10.2   (continued)

Region	Fitness Rank	Creativity Index Score	Creativity Index Rank
Nashville	39	711	67
Omaha	40	637	97
El Paso	40	464	156
Memphis	42	530	132
Columbus, OH	43	832	33
Detroit	44	708	68
Chicago	45	935	16
New Orleans	46	668	83
Indianapolis	47	891	24
Houston	48	980	7
Kansas City	49	816	35
Philadelphia	50	927	19
Average		781	53

SOURCES: The Fitness Index score is from *Men's Fitness*, January 2001. The Creativity Index is by the author.

NOTES: [a]Part of San Francisco region; [b]Los Angeles region; [c]Phoenix region; [d]Dallas region; [e]Washington, D.C. region.

ners and clients. And though it may be a pernicious stereotype, an in-shape person is often perceived to be more reliable and more presentable to the public than someone who is, say, overweight.

The notion of oneself as a work of art has a long tradition among creative people. When a new class of self-styled bohemian artists and writers emerged in Paris in the early to mid-1800s, many observers of the time remarked on the great attention that these people paid to looking good, looking unusual, looking creative:

> When Thackeray first came on the Paris Bohemia, he was astonished enough to make a careful record of their appearance—their ringlets, single locks, toupees, English, Greek, and Spanish nets, and the variety of their beards and jackets. . . . Theophile Gautier's red waistcoat staggered the bourgeois at the premiere of *Hernani*, though by Bohemian standards such apparel was in no way extraordinary.[25]

The writer Baudelaire wrote essays on an ideal character type he called "The Dandy," and Baudelaire himself always took care to go out into the streets of Paris dressed impeccably:

He was meticulously careful to avoid the mud, and if it was raining, hopped on the pointed toes of his pumps. . . . He wore a soft collar of snowy white that could be seen above the collar of his cloak.[26]

In today's Creative Class we are seeing a similar phenomenon, the main difference being that presentation is now extended to the body beneath the clothing. Modern clothes are more revealing—Baudelaire never had to think about how his arms would look in a tank top, nor his mistress Jeanne Duval how her legs would look in shorts—and thus the creative impulse addresses the body.

The Efficient Use of Leisure

There are more factors involved in this shift in leisure activities and they run even deeper. Asked why he and his peers favor highly active forms of recreation, one young member of the Creative Class gave a succinct reply: "You get more entertainment value per unit of time." The young man went on to explain that in his view, even a relatively tame pastime like hiking or simply going for a walk is more continuously engaging, on more levels, than watching baseball or playing a sport like golf. You are in motion every minute. The scenery is varied and changing; the world is unfolding around you. You can stop to sightsee or window-shop or talk with people along the way, or get deep into conversation with a walking companion, or just walk solo and let your mind range.

Extreme sports like rock climbing offer the same catalog of benefits, albeit in a much more demanding form. Climbing gives you continuous engagement on both the physical and mental planes. You get variety and novelty, and the possibilities expand as you grow more skilled, because you can try new and more difficult climbs. The mental engagement of climbing, intense as it may be, is a profound release from work: One does not think about tomorrow's meeting while clutching for a piton a hundred feet in the air. Yet once you reach a secure perch, you can indulge in sightseeing and reverie as well. All told, a lot of experience per unit of time.

Many outdoor pursuits favored by the Creative Class are adventure-oriented. The essence of climbing, hiking and a host of similar sports is to enter some other world, away from your workaday world, and explore it and experience it while performing a task that is often challenging in itself. In short, the idea is to have an adventure. Game sports like baseball are fun-

damentally different. Baseball also offers an other-world to enter, whether
you are playing or watching, but the other world in this case is a highly
structured one: four bases ninety feet apart, three strikes and you're out.
And while rock climbing has its own rules and limits—you can't, for instance, violate the law of gravity—there are thousands of ways to apply the
basic skills in picking your way up any given rock face; it's more of a freelance thing. Game sports are competitive: It's you against the opponent.
Adventure sports are you against the task; you against nature; you against
your own physical and mental limits.

My sport of choice is the traditional form of bicycling, touring on a
skinny-tired road bike. Summer evenings are a delight, because they give
me a couple hours' daylight after work to put on my helmet, head for the
hills and ride until dusk. And it has struck me that the demographics of
my sport are almost obscenely skewed. Nearly every rider I meet on my
journeys is a graduate student, professor, transplant surgeon, corporate
lawyer, engineer, entrepreneur or something similar. Why is the sport so
Creative Class? It can't be the expense. Although some bikes, like my tita-
nium model, are pricey, an adequate machine can be had for much less.
Bicycles cost little to maintain and nothing to ride. They are far less expensive than motorcycles.

Again I think the answer lies in aspects of the sport that appeal to the
creative ethos. Bicycling is multidimensional. A long ride combines physical exertion and challenge, release, exploration and communing with nature. As you focus on pedaling you get into a rhythm and flow, losing track
of whatever was on your mind, dumping the garbage. The mind's shelves
are cleared for restocking while the body, the crucial infrastructure that
sustains the mind, is reinvigorated. Sensory inputs are exquisite, for without the speed and roar of a motorized vehicle, you can really see and hear
the world. Because you're breathing deeply, you can smell the world—
damp earth in the countryside, fresh leaves and grass. There is also the
"I'm doing it" factor: The joy for instance of moving as fast as it is possible
for a human to move under his or her own power, upward of 30 mph on
level ground, 50-plus downhill; the joy of conquering one of Pittsburgh's
long hellish hills. Think too of the nature of the act of powering a bicycle.
The up-and-down pumping of the legs, translated into the smooth rotation of the wheels, is very similar to the mesmerizing, almost mystical
mechanism by which our beloved internal-combustion engine works: the
explosive, up-and-down motion of the pistons flowing out through the
crankshaft as rotary power. Except on a bicycle, it's you making it happen

and feeling it happen. Certainly motorcycles offer thrills of their own. To sit astride a motorcycle and control the powerful engine between your legs can be gratifying, I'm sure. But to climb onto a bicycle and *become* the engine is a fundamentally transforming experience—a creative experience.

The Hegemony of the Street

For more than a century, the mark of a cultured city in the United States has been to have a major art museum plus an "SOB"—the high-art triumvirate of a symphony orchestra, an opera company and a ballet company. In many cities recently, museums and the SOB have fallen on hard times. Attendance figures have declined and audiences are aging: too many gray heads, not enough purple ones. Consultants have descended to identify the problems and offer solutions. One problem is static repertoire. In a museum, for instance, the permanent collection is, well, permanent: It just hangs there. A typical solution is more packaged traveling exhibits, preferably interactive multimedia exhibits, with lots of bells and whistles. In the SOB, not a lot of new symphonies and operas are being written and fewer are performed, because staging them is expensive. One solution is to augment the experience. It's not just a night at the symphony; now it's Singles Night at the Symphony. At other times, orchestras bring in offbeat guest performers—a jazz or pop soloist, or a comedian for the kids. Or musicians are sent out to play in exotic locales—the symphony in the park, a chamber group at an art gallery, the symphony playing the *1812 Overture* at the Fourth of July fireworks. All this is reminiscent of the efforts of old-line churches to fill seats by augmenting the experience—how about a guitar and drumset with the organ?—or the efforts of many professional sports teams, with their mascots and exploding scoreboards.

Meanwhile, the Creative Class is drawn to more organic and indigenous street-level culture.[27] This form is typically found not in large venues like New York's Lincoln Center or in designated "cultural districts" like the Washington, D.C., museum district, but in multiuse urban neighborhoods. The neighborhood can be upscale like D.C.'s Georgetown or Boston's Back Bay, or reviving-downscale like D.C.'s Adams Morgan, New York's East Village, or Pittsburgh's South Side. Either way, it grows organically from its surroundings, and a sizable number of the creators and patrons of the culture live close by. This is what makes it "indigenous." Much of it is native and of-the-moment, rather than art imported from another century for audiences imported from the suburbs. Certainly people may come from outside the neighborhood to partake of the culture, and certainly they will find things that are foreign in origin or influence, such as German films or Senegalese music. But they come with a sense that they are entering a cultural community, not just attending an event. I think this is a key part of the form's creative appeal. You may not paint, write or play music, yet if you are at an art-show opening or in a nightspot where you can mingle and talk with artists and aficionados, you might be more creatively stimulated than if you merely walked into a museum or concert hall, were handed a program, and proceeded to spectate. The people in my focus groups and interviews say they like street-level culture partly because it gives them a chance to experience the creators along with their creations.

The culture is "street-level" because it tends to cluster along certain streets lined with a multitude of small venues. These may include coffee shops, restaurants and bars, some of which offer performance or exhibits along with the food and drink; art galleries; bookstores and other stores; small to mid-sized theaters for film or live performance or both; and various hybrid spaces—like a bookstore/tearoom/little theater or gallery/studio/live music space—often in storefronts or old buildings converted from other purposes. The scene may spill out onto the sidewalks, with dining tables, musicians, vendors, panhandlers, performers and plenty of passersby at all hours of the day and night. Ben Malbon provides a vivid description of the late-night street scene in London's Soho drawn directly from his research diary:

> We stumble out of the club at around 3-ish—Soho is packed with people, crowding pavements and roads, looking and laughing—everyone appears happy. Some are in groups, bustling their way along noisily—others are alone, silent and walking purposefully on their way. . . . Cars crawl down narrow streets which are already impossibly full of cars, Vespas, people, thronging crowds. This wasn't "late night" for Soho—the night had hardly started.[28]

It is not just *a* scene but many: a music scene, an art scene, a film scene, outdoor recreation scene, nightlife scene, and so on—all reinforcing one another. I have visited such places in cities across the United States, and they are invariably full of Creative Class people.[29] My interview subjects tell me that this kind of "scene of scenes" provides another set of visual and aural cues they look for in a place to live and work. Many of them also visit the big-ticket, high-art cultural venues, at least occasionally, as well as consuming mass-market culture like Hollywood movies and rock or pop concerts. But for them, street-level culture is a must.

Consider just the practical reasons for this. Big-ticket, high-art events are strictly scheduled, often only on certain nights of the week, whereas the street-level scene is fluid and ongoing. As a large number of my interview subjects have told me, this is a big benefit for creative types who may work late and not be free until 9 or 10 P.M., or work through the weekend and want to go out Monday night. Moreover, creative workers with busy schedules want to use their cultural time "efficiently." Attending a large-venue event, be it a symphony concert or a professional basketball game, is a single, one-dimensional experience that consumes a lot of recreational resources: It is expensive and takes a big chunk of time. Visiting a street-level scene puts you in the middle of a smorgasbord; you can easily do several things in one excursion. The street scene also allows you to modulate the level and intensity of your experience. You can do active, high-energy things—immerse yourself in the bustle of the sidewalks or head into an energized club and dance until dawn—or find a quiet cozy spot to listen to jazz while sipping a brandy, or a coffee shop for some espresso, or retreat into a bookstore where it is quiet.

Everything Interesting Happens at the Margins

Consider, too, the nature of the offerings in the street-level smorgasbord. In culture as in business, the most radical and interesting stuff starts in garages and small rooms. And lots of this creativity stays in small rooms. Aside from Garrison Keillor and Spalding Gray, for instance, not many serious monologue artists have hit it big in the United States; you've got to go to the street-level venues to find them. These venues in Austin, Seattle and other cities offer a dense spectrum of musical genres from blues, R&B, country, rockabilly, world music and their various hybrids to newer forms of electronic music, from techno and deep house to trance and drum and bass. Nor is everything new. The street-level scene is often the best place to find seldom-performed or little-known works of the past. Recent offerings in Pittsburgh alone have included a small theater company staging Richard Brinsley Sheridan's eighteenth-century play *The Rivals*; a gallery specializing in historic photography; a local jazz-rock group performing old American political songs such as "For Jefferson and Liberty" and "The Farmer Is the Man Who Feeds Us All"; and a street musician who plays violin pieces you won't hear on the classical radio programs that endlessly recycle the equivalent of the symphonic "Top Forty."

The street scene is *eclectic*. This is another part of its appeal. Consider that eclecticism is also a strong theme within many of today's art forms. Think of DJs in Harlem nightclubs of the 1970s who started the technique known as "sampling"—frenetically mixing snatches of music from different records, on different turntables, for the crowd to dance to. Think of the proliferation of hyphenated music genres like Afro-Celt. Think of Warhol, Rauschenberg and a host of visual artists after them appropriating images from news photos, comic strips, food packages, wherever. Eclectic scavenging for creativity is not new. Picasso borrowed from African art as well as Greco-Roman classical forms; rock and roll pioneers melded blues and R&B; and one could argue that the literary DJ who really pioneered sampling was T. S. Eliot in *The Waste Land*, a poem built largely by stringing together, and playing upon, quotations and allusions from all corners of the world's literature. Today, however, eclecticism is rampant and spreading to a degree that seems unprecedented. It is a key element of street-level culture—and eclectic taste is a social marker that can usually be counted on to distinguish a Creative Class person. Eclecticism in the form of cultural intermixing, when done right, can be a powerful creative stimulus.

Furthermore, street-level culture involves more than taking in staged performances and looking at art. It is social and interactive. One can meet people, hang out and talk, or just sit back to watch tonight's episodes of the human comedy. To many the social milieu is indeed the street's main attraction. If that sounds a bit vapid and superficial, sometimes it is. This is not high art; it admits amateurs. Hanging in a sidewalk café does not deliver the exquisite and carefully crafted artistic intensity of Beethoven's *Ninth*. It is also true that for some people, hitting the street-level cultural scene devolves into little more than cruising the singles scene. And even when experiencing culture is truly the goal, if hanging out in nightspots frequented by artists and aficionados is how you choose to pick up your creative stimulation, you are going to pick up a lot of chaff along with it. You run the risk of becoming chaff yourself: a dilettante, a *poseur*, a gallery gadfly, a coffee-shop talker.

At the same time, let's not be too quick to belittle the social aspect of the street. Conversation, to begin with, is a valid art form. Dorothy Parker and Oscar Wilde are quoted more from their repartee than from their writing. Few people today read what Samuel Johnson wrote, but many have read Boswell's *Life* for its accounts of Dr. Johnson shooting the breeze with

Oliver Goldsmith and Joshua Reynolds. All Socrates did was talk. I am not suggesting that you can routinely hear Socratic wisdom in a bar in Adams-Morgan at two o'clock in the morning. But though it may not produce deathless epigrams reliably, good conversation has creative possibilities. In my own work I often learn a great deal from talking with people in coffee shops and other such venues. I pick up observations and anecdotes from people who feel free to ramble. I listen to their ideas about work, leisure and community and this stimulates my own thinking. The creative faculties are fed by meeting and talking informally, by chance, with a diverse range of creative-minded others.

Just people-watching is arguably a valid form of cultural exchange. It is certainly one of my favorites, and as Andy Warhol noted, he didn't go to restaurants only to eat. Take the experience of strolling through a good street scene in, say, New York, or the city of your choice. The first thing that strikes you is the sheer visual variety of the people. Many ethnic groups are present, of course, in various ages, conditions and sizes, and this alone is thought-provoking. You may find yourself drawn to meditate on the history of our species—the many so-called races of humans, and how they came to grow apart as they spread across the globe, and how they endlessly intermix. You may find yourself meditating on your own history—how you were once as young as that one, and may someday be as old as that one, and are liable to look like that one if you don't mend your wicked ways. And then, if it is a proper street scene, there will be many people of exotic appearance: foreigners in long skirts and bright robes; young Americans with hair in colors and configurations that bend the laws of physics, at least Newtonian physics; people dressed as cowboys, Goths, Victorians, hippies—you get the picture. And for many people, the experience of this picture is exhilarating, liberating. It is similar to the thrill of a costume party, when people literally put on new identities—including masks that obliterate or alter the social "masks" they normally wear—and there is a delicious sense of adventure in the air. One has an awareness of the possibilities of life.

I would further argue, following Rogers and others, that this kind of experience is essential to the creative process. We humans are not godlike; we cannot create out of nothing. Creativity for us is an act of synthesis, and in order to create and synthesize, we need stimuli—bits and pieces to put together in new and unfamiliar ways, existing frameworks to deconstruct and transcend. I also feel it is inherent to the creative mindset to want to maximize choices and options, to always be looking for new ones, because in the game that Einstein called combinatory play, this increases your chances of coming up with novel combinations. And as more people earn their keep by creating, the more these aspects of experience are likely to be highly valued and just plain necessary.

Pitfalls of the Experiential World

There is much that seems good about living a quest for experience. It seems an energetic and productive way to live. It can even be a more humane and benevolent way to live. The emphasis on active, participatory recreation seems healthy physically and psychologically, as well as more satisfying than the thin diet of the TV junkie. Done properly it should lead to good experiences all around. So where exactly does the insidiousness come in?

First with the fact that the packaging and selling of experience is often perceived to be—and often is—inauthentic. As Tom Frank and others have noted, the commercialization of experience can empty it of its original creative content.[30] Retailers from Banana Republic to Prada do this with clothes. They try to create brand recognition around experience, and in doing so sell you experience as brand: just wearing the clothes supposedly makes you cool and with-it. Or, to paraphrase what numerous Creative Class people have told me in my interviews: "You can't just enjoy a ballgame; you have to go to a 'state-of-the-art' $500 million stadium for a multimedia circus that distracts you from the very game you paid to see." Many Creative Class people are acutely aware of this pitfall. They thus tend to shun the heavily packaged commercial venues that they call "generica"—the chain restaurants and nightclubs, the stadiums with bells and whistles, and the like—or they patronize them with a conscious note of irony, as in the obligatory trip to a business conference in Las Vegas. They prefer more authentic, indigenous or organic venues that offer a wide range of options and where they can have a hand in creating the options.

Finding such venues can be an ongoing struggle, because generica has a way of creeping in everywhere. One of the last areas of social life where a modicum of authenticity can be found is the music scene. But today music clubs that used to be dynamic, street-level places to enjoy "real" music are being replaced by late-night versions of those multimedia circuses. Not only do you immerse yourself in booming music, but you get digital lighting, smoke machines, water sprinklers activated in concert with peaks in the music—everything you need to be hot and cool. Some such clubs have even become chains. What began as an organic development from the street has become a Disneyland facsimile of itself—safe, secure and predictable—trafficking not in a series of unique experiences of different styles of music and performance, but in the same generic experience night after night. There are deeper concerns as well. In his book *Clubbing*, Malbon focuses on the elaborate society that clubbers have woven for themselves. The book is a highly detailed study of the young people who frequent the club scene in Britain. (Malbon admits that he spent "150 nights out" researching the book, and as he puts it, "many of these were the best nights out I have had.") He notes that:

> Clubbers distinguish themselves from others through their tastes in clothing, music, dancing techniques, clubbing genre and so on. . . . These tastes are trained and refined, and constantly monitored not only in order to distinguish oneself from another, but also in identifying with those that share one's distinctive styles and preferences.[31]

In all of these ways they are, he says, constructing identities. Not to be too judgmental here: I did some of these things myself once upon a time and I still occasionally visit music venues and clubs. But one could well say that Malbon's clubbers sound like little more than trendy sheep. If the goal is to construct an identity or discover an identity, there are other, better ways to do it.

Marketplace attempts to satisfy the craving for experience can turn weirdly self-contradictory in many ways. The "fantasy kitchen" is a useful example. The showpiece of my eclectically decorated home is a kitchen full of everything a professional chef needs to make a meal—seldom used, of course. I sometimes refer to the stainless-steel All-Clad cookware hanging from a rack in my kitchen as my "giant charm bracelet." Kara Swisher, the *Wall Street Journal* columnist, wrote a column chronicling the renovation of her San Francisco home. Tallying the thousands of dollars she spent outfitting her fantasy kitchen, she concluded that she spent the equivalent of "about 1,000 takeout meals or at least 600 outings at pretty good restaurants."[32] The point is these are no longer appliances and cookware in the traditional utilitarian sense. They are part of the food *experience.* They are there to provide experiences—the visual experience of looking at them, the status experience of owning them, and the experience of cooking "like a professional" on those infrequent occasions when we actually do use them to whip up a dinner that mixes Pan-Asian, Italian and home-grown influences. A new experiential service, "Impromptu Gourmet," has taken the food experience to a new extreme. It allows you to purchase the ingredients for a meal from a roster of America's leading chefs. When the ingredients arrive in the mail, you can then have the experience of "cooking" this designer meal in your very own kitchen.

In short, if we crave experiences we will be sold experiences, and in the process we may find ourselves buying a bill of goods. The final pitfall is that even in the attempt to avoid packaged-and-sold experiences, we may pack our lives so full that we overdo it. While we scorn the couch potatoes hooked on TV, the desire for constant stimulation and experiences can itself come close to looking like addiction. But no way of life is perfect, and the trend is inexorable. The experiential life is more than a pastiche of recreational fads and marketing gimmicks. As I've shown, it is a product of the rising creative ethos—which, as the next chapter will argue, is born from a deep new cultural fusion.

CHAPTER 11

The Big Morph
(a Rant)

O n a blustery winter day in 2001, I boarded a plane and emerged a couple of hours later into warm southwestern air. I was in Austin, Texas, one of the country's leading creative centers, where I would soon find that more than the weather was different. I was to be a guest speaker at the Austin 360 Summit, an annual conference of local business and civic leaders to discuss economic development. I had been to many such meetings in other cities, not to mention countless professional conventions and meetings of U.S. mayors and governors. The Austin 360 Summit was not like any of them.

Typically, this sort of meeting takes place at the city's most lavish hotel or convention center, or perhaps amid the classic Greek columns and Beaux Arts decor of grand old buildings. Here we gathered at the funky, folksy Austin Music Hall. Usually at such a conference, you check the agenda for keynote speaker. They're the really important people who get prime time at the podium on their own. Here, Michael Dell, founder and chair of Dell Computers, was a mere panelist in a panel discussion. Of course he didn't wear a tie, nor did anyone. If you wanted to interrupt him with a question or comment in midspeech you went right ahead. All trappings of status and privilege had been left at home.

The usual drill at a convention is to endure a long day of stuffy presentations and working-group sessions, then head out to the local nightspots and cut loose. At the Austin 360 Summit it was work and play together all day long. When we filed into the noisy main meeting room in the morning we were issued plastic wiffle balls. If you didn't like what a speaker was saying, even Michael Dell, you could pelt him with one. The lunchtime keynote speech on the first day—typically given by a gray-headed pillar of the community—was a satiric monologue by performance artist Steve Tomlinson, who appeared only because Sandra Bullock, originally scheduled, was on location making a film.* In interludes between conference sessions at the Austin 360 Summit, a rock band played—and not the kind of watered-down, easy-listening rock band you sometimes find at business functions. This was an excellent, hard-driving band, full of guys with real chops. Austin, after all, is the music capital of the Southwest.

After a full half-day of this, it was my turn. I was moderator of a panel of CEOs and venture capital types, addressing a question that I believed central to the region's future economic development. I had gotten the idea from a cab driver, who worried that the crush of high-tech industry and people threatened to drive out the ethnic and cultural diversity that had fueled Austin's creativity to begin with. So I organized the panel around the question: "Is Austin losing its soul?" After some predictable back-and-forth among the panelists about their investments in the music and cultural scene, I used the moderator's prerogative to interject. "Creativity is multidimensional," I boomed. "It's not something you can keep in a box and trot out at work. You can't have high-tech innovation without art and music. All forms of creativity feed off each other"—and so on. Then a sudden inspiration struck me. "If you really want to know how important this is," I said, "don't ask your fellow high-tech CEOs or the mayor or the head of the Chamber of Commerce. Ask the guys in the band!" I gestured grandly to the musicians seated at the edge of the stage, who looked like the members of Conan O'Brien's late-night ensemble. Then one of the panelists cued me in. The guys in the band, now grinning broadly at me, were not local grungers. They *were* high-tech CEOs and venture capitalists. Not only were they top-notch musicians on the side, they had felt perfectly comfortable bringing their instruments and playing for their peers at an economic summit. It was as if Jack Welch, George Soros and Warren Buffett had agreed to jam for the crowd at Davos.

When the old markers that distinguished one type of person from another begin to fade and blur, it is a clear sign that profound social change is afoot. Highbrow and lowbrow, alternative and mainstream, work and play, CEO and hipster all are morphing together today. Although this trend cuts across many aspects of our life and culture, it is not dramatic or sudden enough to be labeled a revolution. It is not a Big Bang but a *Big Morph,* an evolutionary process that flowered first and strongest in certain enclaves and is now gradually filtering through the rest of society. It is also

---

*You can find Tomlinson's monologue on page 156 of this book.

a dialectical process, with major elements of society either fighting the shifts or at least passively resisting them. The Big Morph is not merely cultural and recreational. It also has a strong economic component. It encompasses the sphere of work and involves an interpenetration of new work forms with new lifestyle forms. This is what makes it so powerful. Changes in taste and lifestyle that at first glance seem superficial and unrelated turn out to be rooted in a widespread, fundamental economic change.

At the heart of the Big Morph is a new resolution of the centuries-old tension between two value systems: the Protestant work ethic and the bohemian ethic. Many observers have noted the clashing of these two value systems, and recently some have commented on their blending—usually with the conclusion that one or the other has been watered down, or spoiled, in the process. These are short-sighted views that result from clinging to old categories and values. The Big Morph is a synthesis so deep that it has moved beyond the old categories to produce something new: the shared work and lifestyle ethic that I call the creative ethos. To trace its evolution, let's start by defining the two defining ethics of the past.

The *Protestant work ethic* says meaning is to be found in hard work. And work in this ethic is essentially a duty. We are put here to serve others; we serve them by making ourselves productive and useful, and from this— inexorably, but almost as a side effect—come the personal rewards that mark us as worthy. Writing at the turn of the twentieth century, Max Weber, the great German sociologist, considered this ethic the very "spirit of capitalism."[1] The Protestant work ethic called for a great deal of conscious structuring and budgeting—managing one's time, practicing thrift and so forth. It was traditionally pursued within the structure of social institutions, like the large corporations that grew economically and socially dominant in the late 1800s and well into the twentieth century. And thus this ethic became an organizational and social ideology. One is productive and efficient so that the organization can be productive and efficient. As such, this ethic is also essentially mainstream and conformist. One accepts the social structure as the way things are. As Paul admonished the early Christians, one obeys the secular authorities and observes the laws of the land—one does one's duty.[2]

The *bohemian ethic* is more hedonistic. It says value is to be found in pleasure and happiness—not necessarily in gross indulgence or gluttonous excess, but in experiencing and appreciating what life has to offer. The bohemian ethic has its own form of discipline, which is largely aesthetic. In his classic but too-little-read book *Bohemian Versus Bourgeois,* the cultural historian Cesar Graña notes that Baudelaire "gave his praises to cats because they appeared to him as the very embodiment of well-managed voluptuousness."[3] But the bohemian ethic is not merely sensuous. It too has spiritual and sociopolitical dimensions. On these fronts, it tends to be intuitive rather than logical, and individualistic rather than conformist. In the cosmology of the English poet William Blake, the "dark Satanic mills" of the early Industrial Revolution were not just England's physical smoke-belching factories. They could also be seen as evoking the mills of cold logic and clockwork materialism—the mental grindstones that, like flour mills, ground men's souls to dust. In Blake's eyes they had to be countered by unleashing the "Poetic Genius" that lay divinely planted in every human breast. Over time, as writers and artists since Blake carried this theme forward, the bohemian ethic came to signify everything the Protestant work ethic was not.

Thus the great culture wars of recent decades. Conservative scholars worried long and loud about the experiential, bohemian culture that washed across America in the 1960s. They worried even that the Protestant work ethic was undermining itself by succeeding too well—bathing us in such a flood of material goods and leisure that we were turning soft and hedonistic. Salvos were fired from the bohemian side as well. In the patois of Rastafarian reggae musicians, the dark Satanic world of offices and factories was simply "Babylon"—the great whore that must someday fall.

The so-called culture wars were not merely a product of the twentieth century, however. Almost since the time of its emergence, modern industrial society has been seen as a house divided.

The Great Divide

In Karl Marx's seminal analysis, capitalist society was the battleground for a war between two great classes, the bourgeoisie and the proletariat. The bourgeoisie were the true, literal capitalists who owned and controlled the means of production. The proletarians were the mostly poorer majority, who lived by selling their labor. Marx's sympathies of course lay with the proletariat, but his salient point for our purpose is this. The ongoing tension between these classes was the mainspring driving the course of modern history and shaping modern society—and that tension was almost entirely over economic matters. Later cultural and social theorists believed that Marx had neglected the cultural dimensions of the struggle. Some of his disciples, from Georg Lukas and Antonio Gramsci to the members of the Frankfurt School, tried to construct a theory that dealt sufficiently with culture.[4]

Others, meanwhile, identified a second divide coinciding with the rise of capitalism—the divide between the bourgeoisie and the bohemian that concerns us here. Graña argues in *Bohemian Versus Bourgeois* that this conflict came to life after the French Revolution. The toppling of the aristocracy frightened writers, artists and intellectuals, who had, after all, depended on the aristocrats as their patrons. The new capitalist bourgeoisie were evidently more concerned with amassing wealth than with advancing the arts or becoming culturally literate. They had brought to power with them the businesslike grinding of the Protestant ethic, combined with the gross materialistic tastes of what Thorstein Veblen would later dub conspicuous consumption. In response, according to Graña, the self-styled bohemians of France in the early to mid-1800s created an ideology of artistic beauty, alternative values and a distaste for material things. It was to be a powerful and enduring brew—as well as a direct assault on the bourgeois values. Graña, who by the way was quite critical of bohemian values, writes:

> The industrious man who shouldered his way into the leadership of modern society threatened all three ideals of intellectual aristocracy—the heroic, the formal, and the introspective. By making new and unexpected demands on human vitality, modern pragmatism was also likely to undermine man's total sensitivity, his emotional free play, and that capacity for physical pleasure which in the past had represented a means both of biological and of aesthetic fulfillment.[5]

In the bohemian subculture of Paris—and in its later American counterpart, the café society of Greenwich Village that sprang up in the early 1900s—there were plenty of Marxists, anarchists and labor radicals rubbing shoulders with the artists and writers.[6] All had a common opponent, the bourgeois juggernaut. But in Graña's view, the essence of bohemianism was apolitical. The real enemy was not the oppressive capitalist economic order but the suppression of key elements of the human spirit by the prevailing culture. Near the end of his book Graña notes that the twentieth-century poet and novelist D. H. Lawrence was equally disenchanted with Western-style capitalism and Russian-style communism: "Lawrence . . .

said that all of modern society was 'a steady sort of Bolshevism; just killing the human thing and worshiping the mechanical thing.'"[7]

Thus the essence of the bohemian response, whether in Paris or Greenwich Village, was to celebrate or at least desperately seek the "human thing." Many values and credos espoused by the early bohemians are the same ones animating today's Creative Class—for instance, the desire to be "always on" and make life a broad-ranging quest for experience. Graña notes that the novelist Marie Henri Stendahl strove for a state of "animated intellectual suspension."

> This capacity to keep himself in animated intellectual suspension he called "the English manner" which, coupled with "the Italian heart"—the alertness of a skilled sensitivity always allowing the beautiful to play upon the mind "like a bow"—guided his great purpose of becoming a virtuoso of delectable discoveries. . . . It is the life program of the perfect intellectual tourist, the observer on the loose, the man who says to life: "Here I am; please me, amuse me, intrigue me."[8]

Early bohemian circles also valued cultural eclecticism—or, as Graña calls it, exoticism:

> Borel, the frustrated Caribbean Indian, also wanted to be a Tahitian (a reverie later put into effect by Paul Gauguin). Flaubert . . . wanted to be an Andalusian muleteer, a Neapolitan rogue. . . . From literary underlings to famous authors the talk was filled with black gondolas in the night, cathedral shadows, the southern sky and, always, the East. "Alhambra," "Moorish," were shouted as words of praise at literary soirees.[9]

The bohemians not only valued creativity but were responsible for a vast and substantial outpouring of it: paintings in a succession of new styles, for instance, which saw the world in different ways, and a flood tide of novels and poetry depicting the struggles of modern men and women in their search for identity, love and meaning—from Madame Bovary to J. Alfred Prufrock, Lady Chatterley and Dean Moriarty. Though championed at first by small circles of thinkers, the bohemian response came to have wide currency. As the historian Jackson Lears points out in a review of Christine Stansell's book *American Moderns,* which examines the role of the early twentieth-century bohemia of New York, historians and social critics have long looked to the bohemian avant-garde as the source of everything they either like or dislike about American society: "a freer (or more promiscuous) attitude toward sexuality, a more sympathetic (or a more sentimental) relationship between intellectuals and the working class, and a more open and honest (or a more cloying and narcissistic) preoccupation with inner life."[10]

Let us now turn to the latter-day critics of the bohemian, starting with one of the most eloquent, Daniel Bell.

Bewailers of the Bohemian

Daniel Bell likes to describe himself as a social conservative and an economic liberal. To me he is a remarkably prescient thinker who has influenced my own thinking in powerful ways. His book *The Post-Industrial Society* put a label on our times that has stuck to the present day.[11] In his lectures at Harvard, he foresaw that the coffeehouses and bohemian enclaves around Harvard Square could also become meeting places for the exchange of practical ideas on new technologies and business plans as well as intellectual constructs. But Bell also worried a lot about bohemianism. In his great book *The Cultural Contradictions of Capitalism,* he fired salvo after salvo at bohemian values of open-mindedness and eclecticism, which he viewed as little more than a cover for self-centeredness:

> Modern culture is defined by this extraordinary freedom to ransack the world storehouse and to engorge any and every style it comes upon. Such freedom comes from the fact that the axial principle of modern culture is the expression and remaking of the "self" in order to achieve self-realization and self-fulfillment.[12]

Note that the word "self" is put in ironic quotation marks, as if it were a suspect construct. Not only were our modern-day bohemians narcissistic,[13] according to Bell, they were also childish and unoriginal; he dubbed their lifestyle "pop hedonism."

> The so-called counter-culture [of the 1960s] was a children's crusade that sought to eliminate the line between fantasy and reality and act out in life its impulses under a banner of liberation. It claimed to mock bourgeois prudishness, when it was only flaunting the closet behavior of liberal parents. It claimed to be new and daring when it was only repeating in more raucous form—its rock noise amplified in the electronic echo-chamber of the mass

media—the youthful japes of a Greenwich Village bohemia a half century before. It was less a counter-culture than a counterfeit culture.[14]

Worse yet, capitalism had brought this upon itself:

> In brief not work but the "life style" became the source of satisfaction and the criterion for desirable behavior. . . . What has happened in society in the last fifty years—as a result of the erosion of the religious ethic and the increase in discretionary income—*is that culture has taken the initiative in promoting change,* and the economy has been geared to meeting these new wants. [italics in original][15]

Is that necessarily a bad thing? Isn't a free-market economy supposed to be geared to meeting our wants? It's bad, says Bell, because the economy is what supports all the other activity, and the economy will not work well if its ethical bedrock is undercut:

> When the Protestant ethic was sundered from bourgeois society, only the hedonism remained, and the capitalist system lost its transcendental ethic. ... The cultural, if not moral, justification of capitalism has become hedonism, the idea of pleasure as a way of life.[16]

The great fault in this line of thinking is that it persists in seeing work and life, or the economy and the culture, as separate spheres with distinct value systems that should be allowed to interact only in certain ways—such as, work first, then live in your spare time. The possibility of synthesis between the bohemian ethic and the Protestant ethic, or of actually moving beyond these categories, is never admitted. Instead it almost appears we should keep them quarantined, because if bohemian pseudoconcepts like "lifestyle" or the "self" keep spreading, we're done for.

Synthesis Lite

But wait, here come the Bobos. In his writerly and at times captivating bestseller *Bobos in Paradise*, David Brooks caught onto the synthesis and even gave its avatars a handy shorthand name. Bobos are, of course, the bourgeoisie-bohemian.[17] Drawing, as I have, from the classic typology outlined by Graña, Brooks chronicled the melding of these two groups into a new class.

It used to be pretty easy to distinguish between the bourgeois world of capitalism and the bohemian counterculture. The bourgeois worked for corporations, wore gray and went to church. The bohemians were artists and
intellectuals. Bohemians championed the values of the liberated 1960s; the
bourgeois were the enterprising yuppies of the 1980s. But now the bohemian
and the bourgeois are all mixed up. . . . It is hard to tell an espresso-sipping
professor from a cappuccino-gulping banker.[18]

Brooks also notes factors like the rise of the meritocratic ethic and diversity in the new Bobo world. He provides a long section describing how
student populations on Ivy League campuses changed after World War II
from predominately upper-class WASP to a mix of ethnicities and economic backgrounds. Much of the book, however, is best read as social
satire. Brooks takes us on a detailed tour of the lifestyles and consumption
habits of this new class. Bobos, for instance, buy food at upscale grocery
stores like Fresh Fields, Whole Foods or Bread and Circus; furnish their
homes at Pottery Barn and Restoration Hardware; and wear clothing from
Banana Republic and J. Crew (or if they are a little edgier, or a little more
affluent, perhaps Gucci or Helmut Lang).

Brooks's descriptions of these adventures in consumption are often
wickedly funny. Since reading the book, I keep having what I refer to as
"Bobo moments." Late one summer night in 2001, for instance, I was at a
stylish restaurant in Pittsburgh's upscale Shadyside district. The restaurant
is in a renovated old building; the decor is an eclectic mix of antique furniture, thrift-store finds and postmodern fixtures. My dinner partner and
I were the last customers remaining. As we relaxed over dessert and
espresso in the outdoor dining area, our young, black-clad waitress came
to us and asked, "Did all the commotion inside bother you?" We had been
unaware of it, but peering through the large glass window we could see the
owner chastising the staff. The woman had a problem, it seemed, with
how the staff had tidied up. As our waitress explained: "You know we are
quite bohemian here. She was so upset that all of the chairs at the tables
matched." I asked if the waitress had read *Bobos in Paradise*. She hadn't,
but she had heard about it and caught the drift. "That's just how it is here,"
she said. "You pay expensive prices to eat in this funky place with mis-
matched chairs."

David Brooks caught a great deal, but he also missed a great deal. His Bobos, for instance, are mostly aging baby boomers. They are the ones leading

the charge. They buy all these things, eat at these places, jog and work out in the hopes of staying youthful, edgy and alternative. Thus they mostly come across as bourgeoisie in bohemian clothing. Gone over now to the bourgeois side, they are bankers and professors trailing the incongruous trappings of their bohemian youth and giving us many of the bizarre social phenomena we see today. But the synthesis is not a boomer thing. Nor, when decked in tattoos and piercings, is it a Generation-whatever thing.

Neither is the bohemian-bourgeois synthesis primarily a lifestyle-and-consumer thing. Brooks has missed the import of the deep economic shifts that shaped his Bobos and made them possible. When he does follow them to work, he fastens mostly on the trappings of the new workplace and misses the ways in which work has become fundamentally different, in content and meaning, to the people at the heart of this synthesis.

Brooks added a grim coda to *Bobos in Paradise* with an April 2001 article in *The Atlantic Monthly* titled "The Organization Kid."[19] To see what kinds of children the Bobos had been rearing, he visited students at Princeton and found them to be grimly workaholic, obsessively career-conscious and deferent to any authority that will help them get ahead—a reversion to Whyte's organization man of the 1950s. The message here is subtle but straightforward: The crazy sixties are gone; it's back to business as usual. The only difference is that these kids are deader inside than the old businessmen ever were. Not only don't they have much fun, they have no uplifting sense of purpose or higher calling; they are merely driven by personal achievement for its own sake—or for *one's* own sake. These kids, writes Brooks, are "missing [the] conceptions of character and virtue"; they've been reared in "a country that has lost, in its frenetic seeking after happiness and success, the language of sin and character-building."[20] And that's the dropping of the other shoe, the grim shoe: If the sixties left any legacy at all, it wasn't a good one.

I can't imagine how Brooks came to such conclusions. Perhaps he didn't stay up long enough to see what the Princeton students do late at night. Perhaps he should have come to Carnegie Mellon and spent some time with our students. Mine work hard, as they say, but they also play hard. And they do not see any conflict between organization, discipline and enjoying themselves: They simply reflect the creative ethos. Or perhaps the problem is that Brooks, like his forebears, is just intent on drilling home the conservative message. Bohemianism was a child of the sixties—an unoriginal adopted child that never amounted to much—and it's a shame we ever let it into the house, because all that the synthesis has done is suck out our souls.[21]

The Co-opting of Bohemia

Critics at the liberal end of the spectrum, ironically, have also found the bohemian-bourgeois synthesis to be soul-sucking, but in a different sense. "Hip is how business understands itself," writes the cultural critic Tom Frank, suggesting that the rise of new alternative cultures is just another aspect of capitalism. There is no counterculture anymore—if there ever really was.[22]

The term itself is a misnomer. The "counterculture" was—and is—just popular culture, and popular culture is a ticket to sell things and make money. In his best-selling *One Market Under God* and earlier *The Commodification of Cool,* Frank bemoans how capitalism has co-opted counterculture symbols in an onslaught of hip new products and advertising themes that target consumers who want to associate themselves with youth and alternative culture.[23] Thus we have all the neo-bohemian stores that David Brooks made fun of, plus so much more and so much worse. It's evident in the co-opting of alternative music—the sounds of Nick Drake, an underground jazz-rock cult hero, being used to sell Volkswagens. Generations of edgy new musicians, from sixties bands to punks to reggae and hip-hop artists, have had their creative integrity compromised and their hard-edged political messages blunted by major labels that turned them into mass-market commodities. Then this music is played in workplaces to make people feel alternative, when all they're doing is grinding away at a desk in Babylon.

The liberal bemoaning of the co-optation of bohemianism sounds just as off-key as the tired conservative tune. There are several objections to be raised. In the first place, millions of people would never have gotten to hear any number of fine musicians, either recorded or live, had these musicians not been mass-marketed. In the second place, many of them *want* to be mass-marketed. The hip-hop artists who wear dollar signs on gold chains around their necks and chant lyrics about money and fine cars aren't indulging in poetic irony. They really want a little of your cash.

Nor does mass marketing necessarily compromise artistic integrity. Bob Dylan heard that complaint loud and often. Dylan first hit it big as a folk and Southern-style blues balladeer in the traditional vein, armed only with an acoustic guitar and harmonica. Then came the infamous 1966 concert in Manchester, England, where he took the stage with an electric guitar and rock-style backup band. People in the audience were outraged. One man memorably screamed "Judas!" at the top of his lungs. But what Dylan was doing wasn't selling out. On the contrary: By this time, he already had built a global reputation on the basis of hot-selling albums in the traditional style. Not only was he taking an artistic risk, he was taking a bit of a commercial risk in departing from a proven, and still viable, brand image. Indeed the Manchester concert is now regarded as a seminal event in contemporary music, with one critic claiming that the torrent of sound unleashed by Dylan and his mates that night amounted to a proto-version of punk rock—"ten years before Johnny Rotten" and "rather better played." Dylan of course went on to experiment again and again, with forays into the Nashville-style country sound, Christian music and numerous other subgenres. Artistic integrity doesn't only mean doing the same things you used to. And the security that comes from hitting it big can make it easier to conduct such experiments.[24]

As for the fear that mass marketing kills the artist's political message: Reports of that death have been greatly exaggerated. Few cultural products have much political content to begin with. Many cultural theorists like to see cultural forms such as graffiti art and rap as political movements expressing the voices of the oppressed. This absurd notion does a disservice to both politics and art. True political movements, from the civil rights movement to the grassroots organizing of the right wing, are serious entities, laboriously put together and directed to specific political ends. These movements sometimes adopt art forms but are not generated by them. Meanwhile, most good graffiti artists and rappers are like good artists of any kind. They mainly want to hone their skills and do their art. They spend a lot of time practicing, as you may know if you live near any. If they can make money in the process, that's wonderful.

A final argument, heard from both the right and left, is that the mass marketing of alternative culture is producing an unwanted leveling effect, dragging high art down toward the gutter and elevating low or gross art to a stature it doesn't deserve. This complaint relies on the always questionable assumption that art comes in "high" and "low" varieties to begin with. And as the writer John Seabrook has told us, it is all really just "NoBrow."[25] In reality, the rise of the Creative Economy is drawing the spheres of innovation (technological creativity), business (economic creativity) and culture (artistic and cultural creativity) into one another, in more intimate and more powerful combinations than ever.

The Real Legacy of the Sixties

Conservative scholars exulted and liberal scholars lamented during the 1980s when the fruits of the so-called sixties revolution seemed to be withering. Not only were many legislative measures of the sixties being rolled back by the Reagan and Bush administrations, the bohemian cultural leaders of the sixties were fading to obscurity along with their movements. Timothy Leary had become a sideshow attraction on the lecture circuit. His former colleague Baba Ram Dass (née Richard Alpert) was off somewhere chanting at an ashram. Abbie Hoffman and Richard Brautigan died during the 1980s; Jimi Hendrix, Jim Morrison, Janis Joplin and many others already were dead. For a brief while, the old corporate system based on the Protestant work ethic seemed to be firmly back in the driver's seat, with the surviving bohemians of the Woodstock generation relegated to cranking out tribute albums. The barbarians having been beaten back from the gates, we could all resume business as usual.

It didn't turn out that way. What happened instead was neither sixties nor eighties, neither bourgeois nor bohemian, but the opening of a path to something new. The great cultural legacy of the sixties, as it turned out, was not Woodstock after all, but something that had evolved at the other end of the continent. It was Silicon Valley. This place in the very heart of the San Francisco Bay area became the proving ground for the new ethos of creativity. If work could be made more aesthetic and experiential; if it could be spiritual and "useful" in the poetic sense rather than in the duty-bound sense; if the organizational strictures and rigidity of the old system could be transcended and if bohemian values like individuality—which also happens to be tried-and-true all-American value—could be brought to the workplace, then we could move beyond the old categories. And though the Valley itself has now mushroomed into something quite different than it was, the ethos that it pioneered has spread and endured, and continues to permeate our society. It does so because, unlike Woodstock or Haight-Ashbury—and equally unlike the Beat subculture of the 1950s or the bohemian café society of Paris, from Baudelaire to Gertrude Stein—it has a wide and sustainable economic base. It engages the world of work and the world of life and weaves them together, profoundly changing both.

The sixties are too easily stereotyped. They were not simple times, nor was what happened then merely a generational phenomenon. Many diverse movements and schools of thought—some of which had been building for decades and were spearheaded by people a lot older than the baby boomers, such as Martin Luther King, Jr., and Betty Friedan—came to the fore during a period of social ferment that actually stretched from the mid-1950s, with the launching of a serious civil rights movement in the South, well into the 1970s. One common thread, however, is that few of these movements sought to fundamentally transform the world of work and economics. The civil rights movement and the women's movement affected the world of work mainly by crusading for equal workplace rights and treatment for certain groups of people. Ringing speeches often called for fundamental transformation of the economic system, but this never quite made it to the top of the practical agenda. Similarly the peace movement assailed the "military–industrial complex" that former president Dwight Eisenhower had famously warned of, but mainly aimed to lessen its influence, not to make the system function differently. Pure socialism never gained much of a foothold in the United States, even in the years of the Great Depression. And organized labor, though it eventually proved quite successful in pushing its agenda, concerned itself mostly with the balance of power in the workplace. Largely through union efforts over many decades, rank-and-file working people gained higher pay, shorter hours, better benefits and working conditions, and powers such as the right to bargain collectively or contest an individual firing. But these were all powers and rights *within* the framework of the existing economic system.

The bohemian counterculture of the San Francisco Bay Area—which had given rise to phenomena as diverse as the Beat poets of the 1950s, the highly political Free Speech Movement at Berkeley in the early 1960s, and the Summer of Love in 1966—included a wide spectrum of views on work and economics. Some in the hippie milieu preferred to simply ignore the world of work, perhaps living by their wits or the generosity of friends or parents. Some sought to rob "the system," as described how-to-do-it style in Abbie Hoffman's *Steal This Book.* For many the strategy was to grudgingly coexist with the system. Get a job, even a haircut if you must; earn the money you need and do what you have to do, but no more.

Then there were various attempts to create alternative economic systems: farming-based communes, often in remote rural areas; plus urban experiments like that of the Diggers in San Francisco. Drawing their name from a seventeenth-century communal experiment in England, the Diggers promoted the building of a system within the system, based on a literally "free" market. Money was not to be used, nor were any barter accounts to be kept. If you worked at the Free Clinic, you would give your services without charge, but you could also take any goods you wanted at the free stores, or have your car repaired for free, and so forth. With both the need and the incentive to make money removed, ideally people would do what they were truly moved to do—whether by the calling of their own muses or by a sense of service. The Diggers actually put parts of their system into effect, but never achieved the critical mass to sustain it in the midst of a larger system running by quite different rules.

And so it was with many other economic experiments of the time. Interesting as they were, they were small and highly localized. Most folded after a few years; they became footnotes to the history of the period. Still, some common bohemian themes that fired the experiments persisted, including a general dislike of large organizations and bureaucracy. Many so-called sixties radicals, like earlier bohemians before them, found the existing capitalist system to be oppressive and dehumanizing, regardless of how the balance of power played out. The increase of human happiness and well-being, they believed, should be the primary purpose of both work and the products of work—not some side effect of the workings of an Invisible Hand.

Another common theme, curiously enough, was an intense interest in the then-new technology of computers. One of the early Digger publications featured Richard Brautigan's poem "All Watched Over by Machines of Loving Grace"—a playful vision of a "cybernetic ecology" of "pines and electronics," a world "where mammals and computers/live together in mutually/programming harmony." Techno-utopian fantasy, perhaps, but the poem reflected a widespread feeling in the counterculture of the time: Computing was surely emerging as the next "revolution," and we couldn't let it be turned into just a tool for corporate efficiency—or for war. We had to seize it and make it our own. It had to be integrated into a new and better way of life.

Moreover the Bay Area in the late 1960s and 1970s was full of eccentric technology types from Berkeley and Stanford. The broad valley south of San Francisco, then emerging as a major electronics center, was a natural gathering point for many of these folks. It was midway between Haight-Ashbury and close-by hippie havens like Monterey and Big Sur. It already had a fair number of firms that would hire you without worrying much about your long hair and jeans, or your weird personal habits and beliefs. The older engineers who populated companies like Hewlett-Packard, Fairchild Semiconductor and Intel found it relatively easy to tolerate this new counterculture breed. Certainly they were more open to idiosyncrasies of personal style than their East Coast corporate counterparts. The engineering culture tends to be meritocratic—you are what you produce—and this was, after all, the West Coast, where previous generations had come to escape the traditional norms of more established society. And it so happened that just as the younger counterculture computer people were infiltrating the Valley, a new dream was emerging. Computers were becoming both more powerful and more compact and affordable. By the late 1960s the massive mainframes already had been joined by a new generation of refrigerator-sized or smaller minicomputers built by companies like DEC. The next step, said the dream, would be computers that anyone could own and create with. Yet most people still considered this a radical idea, even a silly or pointless one: Who would buy such a thing? The book *Fire in the Valley: The Making of the Personal Computer,* by Paul Frieberger and Michael Swaine, chronicles how things unfolded. At the dawn of the 1970s,

> The mainframe computer and minicomputer companies had the money, the expertise, and the unequaled opportunity to place computers in everyone's hands. It did not take a visionary to look down the path of miniaturization and see at the end a personal computer, one that would fit on a desktop or in a briefcase. . . . But it didn't happen. Without exception, the existing computer companies passed up the chance to bring computers into the home and onto the desk. The next generation of computers . . . was created entirely by individual entrepreneurs working outside the established corporations.[26]

These entrepreneurs were farther outside the corporate and cultural mainstream than is commonly known. Lee Felsenstein, a prolific inventor and moderator of the Valley's legendary Homebrew Club, where early personal-computer buffs met, had been a writer for the radical paper *The Berkeley Barb.*[27] The Club's first meeting occurred in March 1975, when an anarchic cadre of thirty-two engineers, inventors, tinkerers and programmers met in the Palo Alto garage of Frederick Moore—but only after Moore had spent the earlier part of the evening tacking up peace-activist notices on local bulletin boards and telephone poles. Homebrew Club members, many with their own tenuously financed garage firms, freely traded ideas and designs without worrying overly much about competitive considerations—a "hacker ethic" that would persist in the open source software community and elsewhere. Many were associated with counterculture ventures like the People's Computer Company, a users' collective that published a newspaper. IMSAI, one of the first personal-computer makers in the Valley, was run by graduates of Werner Erhard's est training, a San Francisco-based consciousness-raising and personal-improvement program.

At one Homebrew Club meeting, when Steven Dompier, a hobbyist hacker, played a rendition of the Beatles' "Fool on the Hill" on an Altair computer he had laboriously programmed, the members gave him a rousing ovation. Early members Paul Allen and Bill Gates had done some mischief hacking in their teens, exploiting their ability to find bugs in mainframe systems. Others like John Draper were phone hackers who tapped into the inner workings of the telephone system in the 1960s and 1970s. Draper earned his nickname "Cap'n Crunch" after he discovered that the tone produced by the whistle prize in the cereal box could unlock the AT&T long-distance system. In the old photos reproduced in *Fire in the Valley*, Steven Jobs and Steven Wozniak look like a couple of sixties hippie-boppers who had refused to straighten up—which is exactly what they were. In their jeans and long scraggly hair, if they had tried to raise investment capital in New York, Chicago or Pittsburgh, they wouldn't have made it past the receptionist. Yet in Silicon Valley they and others like them found a warm reception. As Donald Valentine, one of the original venture capitalists behind Apple Computer, told me some years ago, he didn't care what Steve Jobs looked like; the guy had an idea worth backing.[28] When Wozniak eventually left Apple "to pursue other interests," he launched not another high-tech company but the Woz Music Festival.

What set Silicon Valley apart was not just Stanford University or the warm climate. It was that the place was open to and supportive of the creative, the different and the downright weird. The Valley was able to integrate those who were offbeat, not ostracize them or discourage them. Thus its growth can only be understood in relation to the place that was a focal point of the "sixties revolution"—San Francisco. The same basic pattern can be found in almost every other high-growth technology region. Before these regions were high-tech hotspots, they were places where creativity and eccentricity could be accepted and celebrated. Boston has always had Cambridge. Seattle was the home of Jimi Hendrix and later Nirvana and Pearl Jam as well as Microsoft and Amazon. Austin was home to Willie Nelson and its fabulous Sixth Street music scene long before Michael Dell ever stepped into his now famous University of Texas fraternity house. New York had Christopher Street and SoHo long before Silicon Alley erupted. All of these places were open, diverse and culturally creative first. *Then* they became technologically creative and subsequently gave rise to new high-tech firms and industries.

Thus the tone of the Creative Economy was set. Bohemian values met the Protestant work ethic head-on, and the two did more than survive the collision. They morphed into a new work ethic—the creative ethos—steeped in the cultivation of creativity. People from software developers to circuit designers could now work as creative people, coming and going virtually as they pleased, taking breaks to exercise, working to blaring rock music if they so desired. Employees at Apple wore t-shirts that read "90 Hours a Week and Loving It," and why not? Their work was fun to them, and besides, they were changing the world. Not everything stayed as it was in those early days—nothing ever does. Big firms like IBM and the Valley's own Hewlett-Packard belatedly entered the personal-computer market, of course, and soon made their presence strongly felt. Silicon Valley has now been turned into a massively congested and high-priced suburban megalopolis. Nevertheless, the synthesis pioneered in those early days took root and spread through many elements of our economy and society. It even gave us a new cultural role model.

Microsoft and Jimi Hendrix

American society over the years has romanticized some most unlikely occupations. In the early 1800s young men read *Two Years Before the Mast* and dreamed of becoming lowly merchant seamen. Well into the 1900s, the hero of thousands upon thousands of books, plays, films and cigarette ads was that miserable wage slave of the Western plains, the cowboy. Other occupations traditionally have not fared so well. Through long centuries, from Shylock to Scrooge to Willy Loman, the businessman in drama and literature was either hard-hearted or heartsick. And tell me this: How many well-known novels can you think of that were written before, say, 1980, or major films or plays before that time, in which the hero was an engineer? Even in works of science fiction, the hero typically was the pilot who flew the space ship, not the engineer who designed it. The engineer was kept in the background because he was a geek. Engineers were rather useful people but not cool, the opposite of cool, the very definition of the absence of cool. They had thick glasses and no sex lives. They told bad jokes, wore bad clothes and toted slide rules in holsters. They worked for *businessmen,* for heaven's sake.

And now the picture has been reversed. Business people are no longer vilified. Today, they and so-called bohemians not only get along, they often inhabit each others' worlds; they are often the same people. Jobs, Wozniak, Gates, Allen and others have inserted the idea of *entrepreneur* into the fabric of popular mythology. They created a powerful new identity that broke with the old images of the robber baron and the organization man. They became celebrities in the truest sense of the term and continue to rank among the most well-known and popular people in the world. They hobnob with movie stars and rock stars, invite the latter to play at their parties; they appear on late-night TV. Paul Allen, cofounder of Microsoft and one of the world's richest men, embodies this fusion in identity. Allen is the creator of Seattle's Experience Music Project, an interactive music museum designed by Frank Gehry and initially created as a tribute to Jimi Hendrix, but now expanded to encompass genres from jazz and blues to hip-hop.[29] Think of the implications of Allen's museum. Unlike powerful businessmen before him, he did not build an opera house or high-culture art museum. He built a museum that celebrates the music of people who wrote lyrics like:

> White-collar conservative flashing down the street
> Pointing your plastic finger at me
> You're hoping soon my kind will drop and die
> But I'm gonna wave my freak flag high[30]

Other factors helped change the image of the engineer. A key early development was the massive infusion of technology into popular music—a blending of technological and artistic creativity. Les Paul, a tinkerer and inventor as well as master musician, launched the process in the 1940s when he began producing unearthly sounds with his revolutionary solid-body electric guitar. He also pioneered techniques such as overdubbing and multitrack recording. Then came inventor-entrepreneurs like Robert Moog and Raymond Kurzweil with the synthesizer, and Amar Bose and Henry Kloss with their high-fidelity sound equipment. All became cult figures in the music world. So did the techno-wizards who put together the light shows for concerts in the 1960s and worked ever-greater magic with recorded tracks in the studios. Many of the most famous musicians of the 1960s, from the Beatles to Hendrix, experimented with new sounds and recording techniques in state-of-the-art studios built expressly for such experiments.

Another key development, of course, was the growth of computing. Here was a technology with double-feature appeal to the popular imagination. The big supercomputers were perceived as remote and mysterious, even dangerous, like rockets or H-bombs, while personal computers were ubiquitous and charming, like TV. But unlike TV, these computers and their software kept changing and metamorphosing before our eyes, right there on our desks. And it was these maverick engineers working the miracles. They were members of a new and awesome fellowship of the elect. They wrote code—a secret language!—and with it, they could do just about anything: start a company, make art, play games. Better still, you too could join the elect. Exactly as in rock music, you could hack away in your basement or garage with a couple of friends and dream of hitting it big.

Thus today we have the engineer as pop-culture hero. The very word *geek*, which Webster's dictionary defines as "a person of intellectual bent who is disapproved of," has lost its pejorative connotation, becoming a term of endearment and status. One of the hottest social events in Pittsburgh in the late 1990s was a bimonthly Geek Nite, packing upward of five hundred people into a local microbrewery. The event began drawing so many hangers-on and groupies, not to mention headhunters and service providers, that its organizers created a more exclusive event, Shadow Geek Nite, for the engineers, programmers and other "real" geeks who wished to party in peace. As films like *Neuromancer* and *The Matrix* glamorized cyber-culture, computer nerds or "geeks" found their way into literature as well. In Richard Powers's acclaimed 2000 novel *Plowing the Dark*, the heroes are Stevie, an ex-poet who finds the essence of poetry in computer code, and Adie, a disillusioned painter, whose passion for art is rekindled when she discovers computer graphics. This plot line would have been unthinkable just a few years previously: Artists become geeks and reconnect with their artistic creativity through technology.[31] Jon Katz's 2000 bestseller *Geeks* celebrated the term in its very title.[32]

Cultural icons in past eras had tended to fall into two general types. The first was the romantic, rebellious outsider. Included here were the sailors and cowboys of the 1800s—lowly blue-collar types, but men who eschewed the common workaday world to roam the wide sea or the Great Plains—as well as twentieth-century drifters like the characters played by Marlene Dietrich, Humphrey Bogart and James Dean. In real life these icons were the bohemian artists and writers themselves, from Poe and Van Gogh to the punk rockers: rebels, with or without causes, but questing on against the grain. The other type was the straight-arrow good guy. Included in this genre were young pulp-fiction heroes like Tom Brown and Nancy Drew, many of the movie characters played by Jimmy Stewart, the Cleaver parents in TV's *Leave it to Beaver,* and real-life pop heroes such as Eisenhower. The heroes on this side were builders and problem solvers: exemplars and upholders of the Protestant ethic, welcome in any living room or boardroom. And then, in a unique and unprecedented role, came the geek. Neither outsider nor insider, neither bohemian nor bourgeois, the geek is simply a technologically creative person.

A New Mainstream

Moreover, whether people define themselves as geeks or not, they are coming to see themselves as having a deeply fused identity. This was brought home to me rather forcefully as I was working on this book. I noticed that the Creative Class people I was interviewing, particularly the younger ones, did not like to be called Bobos—and they bridled at the suggestion that they were in any way bohemian.[33] A product of the sixties who always liked to consider myself a bit edgy or cool, I had thought the term a compliment. Not so, I quickly learned. Many of these people hated the word: Some urged me to find another one to use in the book.

At first I thought the problem was that bohemian sounded passé to them, conjuring up old images of beatniks with bongos or spaced-out hippies strumming acoustic guitars. Perhaps they wanted something more with it, something that belonged to their generation. But that wasn't it. They also disliked terms like "alternative." Thus the real issue came out. Bohemians are alienated people, living in the culture but not of it, and these people didn't see themselves that way—not even the immigrants who really *were* aliens. What they liked, however, was the notion that in whatever they did, they could be thought to be creative.

Are they cutting-edge? Definitely. On top of it all, open to new ideas and rediscovering old ones, too? Yes. Youthfully inventive and at times youthfully rebellious, walking into a situation and wondering why it has to be that way? Absolutely. At a fall 2001 meeting in Providence, organized to help the city become more of a Creative Class center, one young man stood up in front of the city's leadership and said: "You say you want us here so long as we don't cause 'trouble.' It's our very nature to ask tough questions; so by our very nature, we're trouble-makers."[34] The point is that these people want to contribute; they want to be heard. They are not drifters in our midst, nor by any means are they barbarians at the gates. They see no need to overthrow the established order when they will soon be joining their older counterparts at events like the Austin 360 Summit. They will be helping society run, and run on an even more powerful new work ethic—not on some nitro-burning strain of pure hedonism or narcissism.

The people we're seeing today are neither Baudelaire nor Babbitt. The synthesis that they are living is not just a matter of sticking a bohemian lifestyle onto an organization man value set, like a bike rack on a chrome-bumpered Country Squire station wagon. The melding has become so deep that the old components are no longer recognizable; the old categories no longer apply at all. The people of the Big Morph see themselves simply as "creative people" with creative values, working in increasingly creative workplaces, living essentially creative lifestyles. And, in this sense, they represent a new mainstream setting the norms and pace for much of society.

PART FOUR

Community

CHAPTER 12

The Power of Place

As I walked across the campus of Carnegie Mellon University on a delightful spring day, I came upon a table filled with young people chatting and enjoying the spectacular weather. Several had on identical blue t-shirts with "Trilogy@CMU" written across them—Trilogy being an Austin-based software company that often recruited our top students. I walked over to the table. "Are you guys here to recruit?" I asked. "No, absolutely not," they answered, seeming taken aback by the very question. "We're not recruiters. We're just hangin' out, playing a little Frisbee with our friends." How interesting, I thought. They've come to campus on a workday, all the way from Austin to Pittsburgh, just to hang out with some new friends.

I noticed one member of the group sitting slouched over on the grass, dressed in a tank top. This young man had spiked multicolored hair, full-body tattoos and multiple piercings in his ears—an obvious slacker. "So what's your story?" I asked. "Hey man, I just signed on with these guys." As I would later learn, he was a gifted student who had just inked the highest-paying deal of any graduating student in the history of his department, right at that table on the grass, with the recruiters who do not "recruit," because of course that would be pushy and not cool.

What a change from my own college days, when students would put on their dressiest clothes and carefully hide any counterculture symptoms, in order to show recruiters that they could fit in. Here the company was trying to fit in with the student. Trilogy had wined and dined this young man over margaritas in Pittsburgh and flown him to Austin for private parties in hip nightspots and aboard company boats. When I called the recruiters to ask why, they answered, "That's easy. We wanted him because he's a rock star." Moreover, "when big East Coast companies trek down here to see who is working on *their* project, we'll wheel him out"—blowing the customers' minds with his skill and coolness.

But something bigger struck me: Here was another talented young person leaving Pittsburgh. That was exactly the problem that had started me on this line of research in the first place. My adopted hometown has a huge number of assets. Carnegie Mellon is one of the world's leading centers for research in information technology. The University of Pittsburgh, right down the street, has a world-class medical center. Pittsburgh attracts hundreds of millions of dollars per year in university research funding and is the sixth largest center for college and university students, on a per capita basis, in the country. It is hardly a cultural backwater. The city is home to three major sports franchises, renowned museums and cultural venues, a spectacular network of urban parks, remarkable industrial-age architecture, and truly great urban neighborhoods with an abundance of charming yet affordable housing. It is a friendly city, defined by strong communities and a strong sense of pride. In the 1985 Rand McNally survey, Pittsburgh was ranked "America's Most Livable City," and it has continued to score high on such lists ever since.

Yet the economy putters along in a middling flat-line pattern. Both the core city and the surrounding metropolitan area lost population in the 2000 census. And those bright young university people keep leaving. Most of Carnegie Mellon's prominent alumni of recent decades—like Vinod Khosla, among the best known of Silicon Valley's venture capitalists, and former faculty member Rick Rashid, now head of R&D at Microsoft—went elsewhere to make their marks. Pitt's vaunted medical center, the place where Jonas Salk created his polio vaccine and the site of the world's premier organ-transplant program, has inspired only a handful of entrepreneurs to build biotech companies in Pittsburgh.

Over the years I have seen the community try just about everything possible to remake itself, and I was personally involved in many of these efforts. The region has launched a multitude of programs to diversify its economy away from heavy industry into high technology. It rebuilt its downtown virtually from scratch, invested in a new airport and developed a massive new sports complex for the baseball Pirates and the football Steelers. It devotes considerable effort to attracting and retaining talented young people. But nothing, it seems, can reverse the tide of people and companies leaving.

I vividly recall the day one of our university's most famous spin-off companies, Lycos, left town. I was on leave at Harvard's Kennedy School and opened the morning paper only to find a story reporting the company's relocation to Boston. Carnegie Mellon researchers had developed the Lycos catalog-and-search technology in the earliest days of the commercial Internet. The technology had then been licensed to the Boston-based venture capital firm CMGI, which built a company around it. At first, Lycos headquarters were in Boston but the engineering offices and the technical operations, a considerable enterprise, were kept in Pittsburgh. But now that was moving as well. According to a number of my colleagues who were close to the situation, the main reason was that Boston offered lifestyle options that made it much easier to attract top managerial and technical talent.

With all of this whirring in the back of my brain, I asked the young man with the spiked hair why he was going to a smaller city in the middle of Texas, a place with a small airport and no professional sports teams, without museums and high-art cultural amenities comparable to Pittsburgh's. The company is excellent, he told me. It has terrific people and the work is challenging. But the clincher was: "It's in *Austin!*" "Why is that good?" I asked. There are lots of young people, he explained, and a tremendous amount to do, a thriving music scene, ethnic and cultural diversity, fabulous outdoor recreation, and great nightlife. That's what mattered—not the symphony or the opera, which he enjoyed but would not feel comfortable attending. What's more, Austin is affordable, unlike Silicon Valley, another place that offered the kinds of work he desired. He was right: Austin ranked as the fourth most affordable place for information-technology workers like him, with a pay differential of more than $18,000 over the San Francisco Bay area, when cost-of-living differences are taken into account.[1]

"I can have a life in Austin," he concluded, not merely a job. When I asked him about Pittsburgh, where he had chosen to go to college, he replied that he had lived in the city for four years and knew it well. Though he had several good offers from Pittsburgh high-tech firms, he felt the city lacked the lifestyle options, cultural diversity and tolerant attitude that would make it attractive to him. As he summed it up, "How would I fit in here?"

Thus a question that lies at the heart of our age, and that would drive much of the research for this book:

How do we decide where to live and work? What really matters to us in making this kind of life decision? How has this changed—and why?

The usual answer is "jobs." That certainly is what most economists would say. People go to places in pursuit of the most attractive positions and the greatest financial rewards. But jobs are not the whole story. People balance a host of considerations in making decisions on where to work and live. What they want today is different from what our parents wanted, and even from what many of us once thought we wanted. And while the young man with spiked hair and impressive tattoos is not representative of everyone in the Creative Class, my research shows that the same basic kinds of things he liked about Austin are representative of the traits many look for in choosing a place to live. A number of consistent themes emerge from my research:

- The Creative Class is moving away from traditional corporate communities, Working Class centers and even many Sunbelt regions to a set of places I call Creative Centers.
- The Creative Centers tend to be the economic winners of our age. Not only do they have high concentrations of Creative Class people, they have high concentrations of creative economic outcomes, in the form of innovations and high-tech industry growth. They also show strong signs of overall regional vitality, such as increases in regional employment and population.
- The Creative Centers are not thriving for such traditional economic reasons as access to natural resources or transportation routes. Nor are they thriving because their local governments have given away the store through tax breaks and other incentives to lure business. They are succeeding largely because creative people want to live there. The companies then follow the people—or, in many cases, are started by them. Creative centers provide the integrated eco-system or habitat where all forms of creativity— artistic and cultural, technological and economic—can take root and flourish.
- Creative people are not moving to these places for traditional reasons. The physical attractions that most cities focus on building— sports stadiums, freeways, urban malls and tourism-and-entertainment districts that resemble theme parks—are irrelevant, insufficient or actually unattractive to many Creative Class people. What they look for in communities are abundant high-quality amenities and experiences, an openness to diversity of all kinds, and above all else the opportunity to validate their identities as creative people.

Limits of the Conventional View

Several perspectives dominate the debate over the role of place in our economy and society. While not opposed to each other in every respect, they are seldom in agreement. Perhaps the greatest of all the New Economy myths is that "geography is dead." With the Internet and modern telecommunication and transportation systems, the thinking goes, it is no longer necessary for people who work together to *be* together, so they won't be. This end-of-geography theme has been with us since experts predicted that technologies from the telegraph and the telephone to the automobile and the airplane would essentially kill off the cities. In his widely read 1998 book *New Rules for the New Economy,* Kevin Kelly wrote, "The New Economy operates in a 'space' rather than a place, and over time more and more economic transactions will migrate to this new space."[2] Kelly then qualifies this to some degree: "Geography and real estate, however, will remain, well . . . real. Cities will flourish, and the value of a distinctive place, such as a wilderness area, or a charming hill village, will only increase." Still he reiterates that "People will inhabit places, but increasingly the economy inhabits a space."

Never has a myth been easier to deflate. Not only do people remain highly concentrated, but the economy itself—the high-tech, knowledge-based and creative-content industries that drive so much of economic growth—continues to concentrate in specific places from Austin and Silicon Valley to New York City and Hollywood, just as the automobile industry once concentrated in Detroit. Students of urban and regional growth from Robert Park and Jane Jacobs to Wilbur Thompson have long pointed to the role of places as incubators of creativity, innovation and new industries.[3] Moreover, the death-of-place prognostications simply do not square with the countless people I have interviewed, the focus groups I've observed, and the statistical research I've done. Place and community are more critical factors than ever before. And a good deal of the reason for this is that rather than inhabiting an abstract "space" as Kelly suggests, the economy itself increasingly takes form around real concentrations of people in real places. There are several theories that seek to account for the continued importance of place in economic and social life. Let's take a look.

One view suggests that place remains important as a locus of economic activity because of the tendency of firms to cluster together. This view builds on the seminal insights of the economist Alfred Marshall, who argued that firms cluster in "agglomerations" to gain productive efficiencies. The contemporary variant of this view, advanced by Harvard Business School professor Michael Porter, has many proponents in academia and in the practice of economic development.[4] It is clear that similar firms tend to cluster. Examples of this sort of agglomeration include not only Detroit and Silicon Valley, but the *maquiladora* electronics- and auto-parts districts in Mexico, the clustering of makers of disk drives in Singapore and of flat-panel displays in Japan, and the garment district and Broadway theater district in New York City.

The question is not whether firms cluster but why. Several answers have been offered. Some experts believe that clustering captures efficiencies generated from tight linkages between firms. Others say it has to do with the positive benefits of co-location, or what they call "spillovers." Still others claim it is because certain kinds of activity require face-to-face contact.[5] But these are only partial answers. As I have already noted and will show in greater detail, the real force behind this clustering is people. Companies cluster in order to draw from concentrations of talented people who power innovation and economic growth. The ability to rapidly mobilize talent from such concentrations is a tremendous source of competitive advantage for companies in the time-driven Creative Economy.

An alternative view is based on Robert Putnam's social capital theory. It basically says that regional economic growth is associated with tight-knit communities where people and firms form and share strong ties.[6] Putnam and others have tried to use social capital theory to account for the performance of high-tech industrial clusters like Silicon Valley, arguing that the networks of people and firms in these places constitute a form of social capital. But these high-tech centers do not approximate the classic social capital model. Rather they are centers of loose ties, of economic and social diversity. The Creative Class people I have interviewed in these places do not desire the strong ties and long-term commitments associated with traditional social capital. Rather they prefer a more flexible, quasi-anonymous community—where they can quickly plug in, pursue opportunities and build a wide range of relationships.

Human Capital and Economic Growth

Over the past decade or so, a potentially more powerful theory for city and regional growth has emerged. The basic idea behind this theory is that people are the motor force behind regional growth. Its proponents thus refer to it as the "human capital" theory of regional development.

Economists and geographers have always accepted that economic growth is regional—that it is driven by and spreads from specific regions, cities or even neighborhoods. The traditional view, however, is that places grow either because they are located on transportation routes or because they have endowments of natural resources that encourage firms to locate there. According to this conventional view, the economic importance of a place is tied to the efficiency with which it can make things and do business. Governments employ this theory when they use tax breaks and highway construction to attract business. But these cost-related factors are no longer the key to success.

The proponents of the human capital theory argue that the key to regional growth lies not in reducing the costs of doing business, but in endowments of highly educated and productive people. This clustering of human capital is even more important to economic growth than the clustering of companies, because as Ross DeVol of the Milken Institute points out, "You attract these people and you attract the industries that employ them and the investors who put money into the companies." Joel Kotkin captures the essence of the human capital view when he writes that:

Traditionally, human intelligence tends to cluster in places where industry and commerce draw them. This has been true from the time of ancient Mesopotamia and Rome through early modern Amsterdam and New York. Yet at the same time brainpower could be highly concentrated in certain places—like New England or the Minneapolis region, other regions with more relative brawn—such as industrial Detroit or Buffalo, would still lead economic growth, luring highly skilled workers when needed. . . . This "brawn to brain" shift profoundly alters the importance of "place." Under the new regime of geography, wherever intelligence clusters evolve, in the small town or the big city, so too will wealth accumulate. Moreover, these clusters are far less constrained by traditional determinants such as strategic waterway location, the abundance of raw materials or the proximity to dense concentrations of populations.[7]

The human capital theory—like many theories of cities and urban areas—owes a debt to Jane Jacobs. For a long time academic economists ignored her ideas, but in the past decade or two, some very prestigious ones have taken them up in earnest and tried to develop empirical proof of their validity. Decades ago, Jacobs noted the ability of cities to attract creative people and thus spur economic growth.[8] The Nobel Prize-winning economist Robert Lucas sees the productivity effects that come from the clustering of human capital as the critical factor in regional economic growth, referring to this as a "Jane Jacobs externality." In a widely circulated e-mail he went so far as to suggest that she should be considered for a Nobel in economics herself. Building on Jacobs's seminal insight, Lucas contends that cities would be economically infeasible if not for the productivity effects associated with endowments of human capital:

> If we postulate only the usual list of economic forces, cities should fly apart. The theory of production contains nothing to hold a city together. A city is simply a collection of factors of production—capital, people and land—and land is always far cheaper outside cities than inside. . . . It seems to me that the "force" we need to postulate to account for the central role of cities in economic life is of exactly the same character as the "external human capital." . . . What can people be paying Manhattan or downtown Chicago rents for, if not for being near other people?[9]

Studies of national growth find a clear connection between the economic success of nations and their human capital, as measured by the level of education. This connection has also been found in regional studies of the United States. In a series of studies, Harvard University economist Edward Glaeser and his collaborators found considerable empirical evidence that human capital is the central factor in regional growth.[10] According to Glaeser, such clustering of human capital is the ultimate cause of regional agglomerations of firms: Firms concentrate to reap the advantages that stem from common labor pools—not merely, according to Glaeser, to tap the advantages from linked networks of customers and suppliers as is more typically argued. Research by one of Glaeser's Harvard graduate students, Spencer Glendon, shows that a good deal of city growth over the twentieth century can be traced to those cities' levels of human capital at the beginning of the century.[11] Places with greater numbers of highly educated people grew faster and were better able to attract more talent. Research by Patricia Beeson, an urban economist at the University of Pittsburgh, supports this view. Her ongoing work explores how investments in various sorts of infrastructure have affected city and regional growth since the mid-nineteenth century. She finds that investments in higher education infrastructure predict subsequent growth far better than investments in physical infrastructure like canals, railroads or highways.[12]

Creativity and Place

The human capital theory says that economic growth will occur in places that have highly educated people. This begs the question: Why do creative people cluster in certain places? In a world where people are highly mobile, why do they choose to live in and concentrate in some cities over others and for what reasons?

While economists and social scientists have paid a lot of attention to how companies decide where to locate, they have virtually ignored how people do so. This is the fundamental question I sought to answer. With little in the way of academic studies or literature to guide me, I began simply by asking people how they make their decisions about where to live and work. I started with my students and colleagues at Carnegie Mellon and then turned to friends and associates in other cities. Eventually I began to ask virtually everyone I met about this. The same answer kept coming back. People said that economic and lifestyle considerations both matter, and so does the mix. In reality, people were not making the career decisions or geographic moves that the standard theories said they should: They were not slavishly following jobs to places.

Gradually I came to see my perspective as distinct from the human capital theory. A colleague of mine even gave it a name, the "creative capital theory." Essentially my theory says that regional economic growth is driven by the location choices of creative people—the holders of creative capital—who prefer places that are diverse, tolerant and open to new ideas. It thus differs from the human capital theory in two respects: (1) It identifies a type of human capital, creative people, as being key to economic growth; and (2) it identifies the underlying factors that shape the location decisions of these people, instead of merely saying that regions are blessed with certain endowments of them. I will explain more about my theory and the various ways I test it in Chapter 14, but for now let me share the findings from my interviews and focus groups that provide invaluable insights on what creative people actually value in locations.

Thick Labor Markets

When asked about the importance of employment, the people in my interviews and focus groups repeatedly say they are not looking just for a single job but for many employment opportunities. The reason, they tell me, is simple. They do not expect to stay with the same company for very long. Companies are disloyal and careers are increasingly horizontal. To be attractive, places need to offer a job market that is conducive to a horizontal career path. In other words, places have to offer a *thick labor market.*

In this way, place solves a basic puzzle of our economic order: It facilitates the matching of creative people to economic opportunities. Place thus provides a labor pool for companies who need people and a thick labor market for people who need jobs. The gathering of people, companies and resources into particular places with particular specialties and capabilities generates efficiencies that power economic growth. It is for this reason that I say place is becoming the central organizing unit of our economy and society, taking on a role that used to be played by the large corporation.

Lifestyle

The people in my focus groups tell me that lifestyle frequently trumps employment when they're choosing where to live. Many said they had turned down jobs, or decided not to look for them, in places that did not afford the variety of "scenes" they desired—music scene, art scene, technology scene, outdoor sports scene and so on. Some recounted how they or their friends had taken jobs for economic reasons, only to move elsewhere for lifestyle reasons. In the course of my research, I have come across many people who moved somewhere for the lifestyle and only *then* set out to look for employment there.

People today expect more from the places they live. In the past, many were content to work in one place and vacation somewhere else, while frequently getting away for weekends to ski, enjoy a day in the country or sample nightlife and culture in another city. The idea seemed to be that some places are for making money and others are for fun. This is no longer sufficient. The sociologists Richard Lloyd and Terry Nichols Clark of the University of Chicago note that "workers in the elite sectors of the postindustrial city make 'quality of life' demands, and . . . increasingly act like tourists in their own city."[13] One reason is the nature of modern creative work. Of course people still go away at times, but given their flexible and unpredictable work schedules, they want ready access to recreation on a "just-in-time" basis. When putting in a long day, for instance, they may need an extended break in the middle to recharge their batteries. Many who do this tell me a bike ride or run is a staple of their day-to-day productivity. And for this, a beach house or country getaway spot doesn't do them much good. They require trails or parks close at hand.

Nightlife is an important part of the mix. The people I talked to desired nightlife with a wide mix of options. The most highly valued options were experiential ones—interesting music venues, neighborhood art galleries, performance spaces and theaters. A vibrant, varied nightlife was viewed by many as another signal that a city "gets it," even by those who infrequently partake in nightlife. Interestingly, one of the biggest complaints of my focus groups had to do with cities where the nightlife closes down too early. The reason is not that most of these people are all-night partyers, but with long work hours and late nights, they need to have options around the clock. Many stressed the importance of nonalcoholic options, like the young man in Chapter 10 who said he "can't afford the recovery time." This is an illuminating comment about the value of time to creative people. As one person in a focus group summed it up: "I want the option available, when I want to do it."

A survey by one of my students, Erica Coslor, found that nightlife is indeed an important component of a city's lifestyle and amenity mix. Defining nightlife as "all entertainment activities that happen after dark," Coslor examined what younger Creative Class people (her respondents ranged in age from early twenties into their thirties) desire in urban nightlife. The highest-rated nightlife options were cultural attractions (from the symphony and theater to music venues) and late-night dining, followed by small jazz and music clubs and coffee shops. Bars, large dance clubs and after-hours clubs ranked much farther down the list. Most of her respondents desired a mix of entertainment options and safe and reliable "after-hours transportation." She also identified a strong preference for "on-demand entertainment." A third of Coslor's survey respondents said that "nightlife" plays a role in where they choose to live and work. She found that it takes a variety of activities coming together to create that *gestalt* that is nightlife.[14] Time and again, the people I speak with say these things are signals that a place "gets it"—that it embraces the culture of the Creative Age; that it is a place where they can fit in.

Social Interaction

People have always, of course, found social interaction in their communities. But a community's ability to facilitate this interaction appears to be more important in a highly mobile, quasi-anonymous society. In his book *A Great Good Place,* Ray Oldenburg notes the importance of what he calls "third places" in modern society. Third places are neither home nor work—the "first two" places—but venues like coffee shops, bookstores and cafés in which we find less formal acquaintances. According to Oldenburg, these third places comprise "the heart of a community's social vitality" where people "hang out simply for the pleasures of good company and lively conversation."[15]

Creative Class people in my focus groups and interviews report that such third places play key roles in making a community attractive. This is because the two other sources of interaction and stability, the family and workplace, have become less secure and stable. People are more likely to live alone, and more likely to change jobs frequently. Third places fill a void by providing a ready venue for acquaintance and human interaction.

The importance of third places also arises from the changing nature of work. More of us do not work on fixed schedules and many of us work in relative isolation—for instance, in front of a keyboard at home, as I often do. Reliable human contact is thus hard to come by, and e-mail or phone interruptions provide only a limited form. So I frequently take a break and head to the coffee shop down the street just to see people on the street; or I take a bike ride to recharge, then head to the café to see my associates there. Many people I interview say they do much the same thing.

Diversity

My focus group and interview participants consistently listed diversity as among the most important factors in their choice of locations. People were drawn to places known for diversity of thought and open-mindedness. They actively seek out places for diversity and look for signs of it when evaluating communities. These signs include people of different ethnic groups and races, different ages, different sexual orientations and alternative appearances such as significant body piercings or tattoos.

Small wonder that when a group of students visited my house recently, and I asked them where they wanted to live after graduation, highly diverse Washington, D.C., was the favorite. A Korean student liked it "because there's a big Korean community," meaning Korean religious institutions, Korean grocery stores and Korean children for his children to play with. Likewise an Indian student favored it for its large Indian population, an African-American for its large black professional class, and a gay student for the community around DuPont Circle.

But there's more at work here than expatriates who only want to be around people like themselves. It's the differences, not just the sameness, that are the benefit. A young female premedical student of Persian descent summarized the many criteria for diversity:

> I was driving across the country with my sister and some friends. We were commenting on what makes a place the kind of place we want to go, or the kind of place we would live. And we tried to list [the factors].. . . We said: It has to be open. It has to be diverse. . . . It has to have a visible gay community; it has to have lots of different races and ethnic groups. It has to have people of all ages and be open to young people. It has to have people who *look* different.[16]

Like the diverse workplace, a diverse community is a sign of a place open to outsiders. And just as domestic partner benefits convey that a potential employer is open and tolerant, places with a visible gay presence convey the same kind of signal. Some said they oriented their location search to such places, even though they are not gay themselves. Others actively sought out gay neighborhoods for their amenities, energy, safety and sense of community. Younger women in particular said they liked to live in gay neighborhoods because they are "safe." As with employers, visible diversity serves as a signal that a community embraces the open meritocratic values of the Creative Age.

Diversity also means "excitement" and "energy." Creative-minded people enjoy a mix of influences. They want to hear different kinds of music and try different kinds of food. They want to meet and socialize with people unlike themselves, to trade views and spar over issues. A person's circle of closest friends may not resemble the Rainbow Coalition—in fact it usually does not—but he or she wants the rainbow to be available.

An attractive place doesn't have to be a big city, but it has to be cosmopolitan—a place where anyone can find a peer group to be comfortable with, and also find other groups to be stimulated by; a place seething with the interplay of cultures and ideas; a place where outsiders can quickly become insiders. In her book *Cosmopolitan City,* Bonnie Menes Kahn puts it very simply.[17] She says a great city has two hallmarks: tolerance for strangers and intolerance for mediocrity. These are precisely the qualities that appeal to members of the Creative Class—and they also happen to be qualities conducive to innovation, risk-taking and the formation of new businesses.

Authenticity

Places are also valued for authenticity and uniqueness, as I have heard many times in my studies. Authenticity comes from several aspects of a community—historic buildings, established neighborhoods, a unique music scene or specific cultural attributes. It comes from the mix—from urban grit alongside renovated buildings, from the commingling of young and old, long-time neighborhood characters and yuppies, fashion models and "bag ladies."

People in my interviews and focus groups often define "authenticity" as the opposite of generic. They equate authentic with being "real," as in a place that has real buildings, real people, real history. An authentic place also offers unique and original experiences. Thus a place full of chain stores, chain restaurants and nightclubs is not authentic: Not only do these venues look pretty much the same everywhere, they offer the same experience you could have anywhere. One of my Creative Class subjects, emphasizing the way people are attracted to the authenticity and uniqueness of a city, used the two terms together as a combined phrase.

> I'm thinking in particular of the Detroit Electronic Music Festival. Here was a free concert that drew a million people the first year . . . and featured a stellar lineup of Detroit and some national performers and DJs, a great boon to the city and its image. This year, they . . . start to drop Detroit artists in favor of more well-known national acts. So more people come, but the event is losing much of the uniqueness/authenticity that makes people want to come to this event from around the world.[18]

Music is a key part of what makes a place authentic, in effect providing a sound or "audio identity."[19] Audio identity refers to the identifiable musical genre or sound associated with local bands, clubs and so on that make up a city's music scene: blues in Chicago, Motown in Detroit, grunge in Seattle, Austin's Sixth Street. This is what many people know about these cities and the terms in which they think of them; it is also the way these cities promote themselves.

Music in fact plays a central role in the creation of identity and the formation of real communities. Sounds, songs and musical memories are some of the strongest and most easily evoked. You can often remember events in your life by what songs were playing at the time. Simon Frith writes that music "provides us with an intensely subjective sense of being sociable. It both articulates and offers the immediate *experience* of collective identity. Music regularly soundtracks our search for ourselves and for spaces in which we can feel at home."[20]

In fact, it is hard to think of a major high-tech region that doesn't have a distinct audio identity. In addition to Seattle and Austin, consider the San Francisco Bay Area. It was home to perhaps the most creative music scene of the 1960s with the Grateful Dead, Jefferson Airplane, Mamas and the Papas, Haight-Ashbury and the seminal Monterey Pop Festival. Chapel Hill, North Carolina, at the heart of the Research Triangle, was recently named as having one of the best local music scenes in the country. Technology and the music scene go together because together they reflect a place that is open to new ideas, new people and creativity. And it is for this reason that frequently I like to tell city leaders that finding ways to help support a local music scene can be just as important as investing in high-tech business and far more effective than building a downtown mall.

Other kinds of "soundtracks" are important besides music. As Creative Class people like to say, an authentic place has a distinct "buzz." The sociologists Lloyd and Clark write of a sculptor who told them, "I came to Chicago because that was where the conversation was." This kind of soundtrack cannot be dubbed into a place. It is played and sustained by the creative people who live there—who *choose* to live there.

Identity

Place provides an increasingly important dimension of our identity. Fewer people today find lifelong identity in the company for which they work. We live in a world where many traditional institutions have ceased to provide meaning, stability and support. In the old corporate-driven economy, many people took their cues from the corporation and found their identity there. Others lived in the towns where they grew up and could draw on the strong ties of family and long-term friends. As the Berkeley sociologist Manuel Castells has noted, "the power of identity" has become a defining feature of the insecure, constantly changing postmodern world.[21]

The combination of where we live and what we do has come to replace who we work for as a main element of identity. Forty years ago, some would likely identify themselves by saying "I work for General Motors" or "I'm with IBM." Today our tattooed friend is more likely to identify himself by saying "I'm a software developer and I live in Austin" rather than "I work for Trilogy." I travel by plane a lot and have noticed that the standard conversation-starter has changed. Ten years ago, people were likely to ask, "Where do you work?" Today it's "Where do you live?"

With the demise of the company-dominated life, a new kind of pecking order has developed around places. Place is becoming an important source of status. To some extent, this has always been true. Places like Paris, London and New York City have always been high on the status order. Elsewhere, people were content to substitute the economic status that came from a good job with a prestigious company for the status of place. But now the people in my focus groups and interviews tell me they are likely to move to places that convey high status.

Many Creative Class people I've studied also express a desire to be involved in their communities. This is not so much the result of a "do-good" mentality, but reflects their desire to both actively establish their own identity in places, and also to contribute to actively building places that reflect and validate that identity. In Pittsburgh, for instance, a group of young people in creative fields, ranging from architecture and urban design to graphics and high-tech, has formed a loose association that they dubbed "Ground Zero" (the group was formed and took its name before the World Trade Center tragedy). The group emerged on its own out of a series of brainstorming sessions that I organized in early 2000 to gain insight into the lifestyle and other concerns of young Creative Class people. While the initial impetus for the group was to combat a redevelopment plan that would have replaced an authentic downtown shopping district with a generic urban mall, they quickly began to focus their efforts on shaping the creative climate and identity of the city. Their initial "manifesto" speaks so directly to the nexus of creativity, place and identity that it is worth reproducing here in full.

> Creative Friends,
> Now is the time for us to come together to Speak Up and Act Up.
> We the people who make things, who make the culture of this city,
> need to connect and engage. We want you to come and join us.
> We all hear about how to make Pittsburgh a better place to be a
> consumer or a sports fan or an entrepreneur. We hear about
> strategies to suck in the young suburban consumers so they can
> park their cars, shop and leave.
>   This isn't us. We are already here. We are actively creating, whether
> it be food, stories, photographs, music, video games, paintings,
> buildings, performance or communities. We are making the culture

of this city. We already know what makes Pittsburgh unique, interesting and attractive to people of all ages. We want to work to preserve its authenticity as a place, to make it more authentic.

We want to capitalize on what is already here, not destroy, demolish or suppress it. We want City policy that encourages culture to grow from within instead of promoting removal and replacement. We will then work proactively through ALL forms of media to make our voice heard. To make our city better.

We want to provoke awareness, discussion, argument, debate, and maybe even local pride (?) through what we will accomplish. And we want the voice of young creators to be heard loud and clear by those who make public policy.

The Ground Zero people have launched a variety of efforts to realize their vision, from organizing edgy community arts events to working to organize a shuttle-bus system, the "Ultra-Violet Loop," to establish "connectivity" between the various neighborhoods that make up Pittsburgh's street-level cultural mix. In doing so, they have sought to implant their creative identity into the urban fabric of the city.

The role of place in our identity is also evident in the growing struggles over who controls places. Some of the great conflicts of our age are the displacement of existing residents from their communities—their identities. I got a first-hand taste of this on a warm night in Seattle's up-and-coming Belltown neighborhood in May 2000. Walking down newly fashionable First Avenue with its mix of high-tech companies, high-end residences and nice restaurants, our group came upon a rag-tag band banging on drums and bellowing: "Say no to the construction noise." Jolted by the commotion, well-dressed yuppies emerged onto the street to see what it was about. A boisterous debate broke out between them and the protesters over who were the neighborhood's "true" residents.

Quality of Place

All of the factors that go into Creative Class location decisions are, together, so powerful that I have coined a term to sum them up: *quality of place.* I use the term in contrast to the more traditional concept of quality of life. It refers to the unique set of characteristics that define a place and make it attractive. Generally, one can think of quality of place as having three dimensions:

- *What's there:* the combination of the built environment and the natural environment; a proper setting for pursuit of creative lives.
- *Who's there:* the diverse kinds of people, interacting and providing cues that anyone can plug into and make a life in that community.
- *What's going on:* the vibrancy of street life, café culture, arts, music and people engaging in outdoor activities—altogether a lot of active, exciting, creative endeavors.

The quality of place a city offers can be summed up as an interrelated set of experiences. Many of them, like the street-level scene, are dynamic and participatory. You can do more than be a spectator; you can be part of the scene. And the city allows you to modulate the experience: to choose the mix, to turn the intensity level up or down as desired, and to have a hand in creating the experience rather than merely consuming it. The street buzz is right nearby if you want it, but you can also retreat to your home or other quiet place, or go into an urban park, or even set out for the country. This is one reason canned experiences are not so popular. A chain theme restaurant, a multimedia-circus sports stadium or a prepackaged entertainment-and-tourism district is like a packaged tour: You do not get to help create your experience or modulate the intensity; it is thrust upon you.

Many members of the Creative Class also want to have a hand in actively shaping the quality of place of their communities. When I addressed a high-level downtown revitalization group in Providence, Rhode Island, in the fall of 2001, a thirty-something professional captured the essence of this when he said: "My friends and I came to Providence because it already has the authenticity that we like—its established neighborhoods, historic architecture and ethnic mix." He then implored the city leaders to make these qualities the basis of their revitalization efforts and to do so in ways that actively harness the energy of him and his peers. He said that Creative Class people like him seek places that are themselves a challenge and where they can help craft the future. Or as he aptly put it: "We want a place that's not done."

Quality of place does not occur automatically; rather it is an ongoing dynamic process involving the coming together of several different aspects of a community. The sociologist Richard Lloyd of the University of Chicago provides a vivid description of how this occurred in Chicago's Wicker Park neighborhood.

Wicker Park was a relatively obscure, low-income neighborhood in the 1980s populated largely by Puerto Rican and Mexican immigrants who struggled against receding opportunities in the postindustrial landscape. With its relatively high crime rates and its abundance of derelict buildings leftover from a bygone era, the neighborhood would have seemed a poor candidate for the current proliferation of high-tech enterprises. However in the 1990s it underwent a striking transition. In 1989, the Northwest Tower lent its nickname to an annual "Around the Coyote" festival, designed to advertise the growing numbers of young artists who lived and worked in the neighborhood. The local rock-and-roll scene gained national recognition in the early part of the decade, leading *Billboard* magazine to anoint Wicker Park "cutting edge's new capital." The concentration of young artists, along with the establishment of associated amenities including boutiques, performance venues, coffee shops and galleries transformed the image of the neighborhood from a space of postindustrial decay to a privileged site of urban culture. This in turn has abetted the development of new profit-generating practices.[22]

It has also given rise to gentrification and displacement of long-term residents as Lloyd notes—an issue I will return to in Chapter 16.

Some of my critics like to argue that many people who work in high-tech industries tend to be blandly conservative and prefer homogeneous communities and traditional lifestyles of the sort found in middle-class suburbs. They find evidence in the fact that so many high-tech people live in suburban enclaves like northern Virginia, the heart of Silicon Valley or the Seattle suburbs. My response is simple. These places are all located within major metropolitan areas that are among the most diverse in the country and offer a wide array of lifestyle amenities. In fact, these places are themselves a product of the openness and diversity of the broader areas. Had the Silicon Valley–San Francisco area not been receptive years ago to offbeat people like the young Steven Jobs, it could not have become what it is.

What people want is not an either/or proposition. Successful places do not provide just one thing; rather they provide a range of quality of place options for different kinds of people at different stages in the life course. Great cities are not monoliths; as Jane Jacobs said long ago, they are federations of neighborhoods. Think about New York City and its environs. Young people, when they first move to New York, live in places like the East Village, Park Slope, Williamsburg or Hoboken, where rents are more affordable and there are lots of other young people. When they get a little older and earn a little more, they move the Upper West Side or maybe to SoHo; earn a little more and they can go to the West Village or the Upper East Side. Once marriage and children come along, some stay in the city while others relocate to bedroom communities in places like Westchester County, Connecticut or the New Jersey suburbs. Later when the kids are gone, some of these people then move back to the city and buy a co-op overlooking the park or a duplex on the Upper East Side.

Members of the Creative Class come in all shapes, sizes, colors and lifestyles; and to be truly successful, cities and regions have to offer something for them all.

CHAPTER 13

The Geography of Creativity

M any people like lists and I'm one of them. This is the chapter where I list the Creative Economy's winners, losers and also-rans. To show where various cities and regions stand, I'll turn in this chapter and the next to statistical analysis. Toward the end of the chapter I introduce my baseline indicator for evaluating a region's position in the Creative Economy, the *Creativity Index.* Using this measure and a number of others, and correlating them in a variety of ways, I consistently find two major trends.

The first is a new geographic sorting along class lines. Different classes of people have long sorted themselves into neighborhoods within a city or region. But now we find a large-scale resorting of people among cities and regions nationwide, with some regions becoming centers of the Creative Class, while others are composed of larger shares of Working Class or Service Class people. To some extent this has always been true. For instance there have always been artistic and cultural communities like Greenwich Village, college towns like Madison and Boulder, and manufacturing centers like Pittsburgh and Detroit. The news is that such sorting is becoming even more widespread and pronounced.

The second trend is that the centers of the Creative Class are more likely to be economic winners. The larger Working Class centers tend to be economically stagnant, while many smaller ones are locked in grim downward spirals. Some Service Class centers—mainly tourist destinations like Las Vegas—are attracting people and creating jobs rapidly. But many of these are low-wage dead-end jobs. A job cleaning hotel rooms or even dealing cards in Las Vegas does not offer much of a ladder up into our economy's jetstream. I suspect the Service Class centers too will become increasingly separated from the economic engine of our society.

The New Geography of Class

Table 13.1 provides the 1999 Creative Class rankings for the forty-nine larger regions, those with more than one million people. (Appendix Table 4 provides the rankings for the remaining regions across the country.)[1] In the leading centers, the Creative Class makes up more than 35 percent of the workforce. This is already the case in the greater Washington, D.C. region, Raleigh-Durham, Boston and Austin. Rounding out the top ten are San Francisco, Minneapolis, Hartford, Denver, Seattle and Houston.

Despite their considerable advantages, large regions have not exclusively cornered the market as Creative Class locations. In fact, a number of smaller regions have among the highest Creative Class concentrations in the nation—notably college towns like Gainesville, Florida; East Lansing, Michigan and Madison, Wisconsin; and other regions like Bloomington, Illinois; Melbourne, Florida; Huntsville, Alabama; Santa Fe, New Mexico; and Boise, Idaho.

Furthermore, the Creative Class is not limited only to well-known high-tech and artistic centers. Kansas City, Rochester and Detroit, for instance, number among the top twenty centers for the Creative Class among large regions. Albany, New York; Omaha, Nebraska; Little Rock, Arkansas; Birmingham, Alabama; and Baton Rouge, Louisiana, rank alongside Albuquerque, New Mexico, as leading Creative Class locations among medium-sized regions with populations between 500,000 and one million. Boise, Idaho; Provo, Utah; Jackson, Mississippi; and Des Moines, Iowa, rank among the top regions with populations between 250,000 and 500,000; while Bloomington, Illinois; Gainesville, Florida; Bryan–College Station, Texas; Santa Fe, New Mexico; and Springfield, Illinois top the list of regions with less than 250,000 people. A number of these regions are home to major universities, research facilities or state governments that certainly help to boost their Creative Class standings.

At the other end of the spectrum are regions that are being bypassed by the Creative Class. Among large regions, Las Vegas, Grand Rapids and Memphis harbor the smallest concentrations of the Creative Class. Members of this class have nearly abandoned a wide range of smaller regions in the outskirts of the South and Midwest. In small metropolitan areas like Victoria, Texas; Jackson, Tennessee; and Houma, Louisiana, the Creative Class comprises less than 15 percent of the workforce.

The nucleus of the Creative Class, its Super-Creative Core, is also rather

TABLE 13.1 The Class Structure by Region, 1999 (for regions over 1 million people)

Rank[a] (Large regions)	Overall Rank[b]	Creative Class Share	Employment	Super-Creative Core Share	Employment	Working Class Share	Employment	Service Class Share	Employment	Total Employment
1 Washington, D.C.	4	38.4%	1,458,580	15.0%	570,320	17.8%	676,080	43.8%	1,666,480	3,803,260
2 Raleigh-Durham	5	38.2%	241,700	16.9%	106,630	22.0%	139,340	39.7%	250,910	632,420
3 Boston	6	38.0%	746,230	14.6%	287,910	17.7%	347,030	44.3%	871,240	1,965,980
4 Austin	7	36.4%	231,190	14.6%	92,600	18.8%	119,420	44.8%	284,650	635,260
5 San Francisco	12	34.8%	1,211,520	15.4%	535,860	22.3%	776,500	42.6%	1,485,250	3,482,430
6 Minneapolis	14	33.9%	578,520	13.2%	225,750	24.6%	419,380	41.4%	706,330	1,705,750
7 Hartford, CT	16	33.4%	202,930	14.2%	86,550	23.2%	140,930	43.4%	263,590	607,950
8 Denver	17	33.0%	451,070	13.5%	184,960	23.3%	317,670	43.7%	596,300	1,365,970
9 Seattle	20	32.7%	561,730	14.6%	250,190	23.4%	401,660	43.8%	753,080	1,719,130
10 Houston	22	32.5%	691,600	13.3%	282,610	26.1%	555,500	41.3%	877,900	2,126,520
11 Kansas City	24	32.4%	307,660	10.9%	103,350	24.2%	229,110	43.3%	410,860	948,230
12 New York	25	32.3%	2,688,810	12.1%	1,007,620	20.9%	1,739,590	46.8%	3,903,110	8,336,310
13 Philadelphia	27	32.2%	927,090	11.8%	338,800	22.0%	633,170	45.7%	1,316,180	2,878,880
14 Chicago	29	32.2%	1,389,160	10.8%	467,320	27.2%	1,175,430	40.5%	1,750,650	4,318,330
15 San Diego	30	32.1%	369,470	13.8%	158,240	22.6%	260,190	45.0%	517,230	1,150,270
16 Atlanta	32	32.0%	641,700	12.3%	246,810	26.4%	529,120	41.5%	830,550	2,002,640
17 Rochester, NY	34	31.6%	176,590	15.8%	88,500	26.2%	146,590	42.2%	235,990	559,380
18 Sacramento	40	31.1%	222,630	11.1%	79,650	20.4%	146,350	47.9%	343,610	716,770
19 Detroit	42	31.0%	776,540	13.3%	332,350	28.9%	722,740	40.1%	1,002,310	2,501,670
20 Los Angeles	46	30.7%	1,984,700	11.5%	740,490	26.9%	1,737,010	42.1%	2,723,950	6,462,960

(continues)

TABLE 13.1 (continued)

Rank[a] (Large regions)	Overall Rank[b]	Creative Class		Super-Creative Core		Working Class		Service Class		Total Employment
		Share	Employment	Share	Employment	Share	Employment	Share	Employment	
21 Jacksonville, FL	50	30.3%	149,670	11.0%	54,380	22.7%	111,900	46.9%	231,230	493,430
22 Pittsburgh	53	30.3%	322,230	10.6%	112,850	25.9%	275,410	43.8%	465,830	1,063,880
23 Dallas	55	30.2%	825,390	11.2%	307,220	26.3%	718,960	43.5%	1,188,550	2,735,150
24 St. Louis	57	30.1%	393,240	11.5%	150,340	26.3%	343,300	43.5%	567,070	1,304,530
25 Indianapolis	68	29.7%	265,040	9.6%	86,030	28.9%	257,800	41.5%	370,260	893,100
26 Charlotte, NC	69	29.7%	253,140	9.5%	80,770	28.6%	244,210	41.7%	355,560	853,660
27 Columbus, OH	70	29.5%	250,500	11.2%	95,080	25.3%	214,440	45.1%	382,020	847,830
28 Cleveland	71	29.5%	430,130	10.1%	147,110	28.2%	412,070	42.3%	617,410	1,460,300
29 Oklahoma City	72	29.4%	147,740	11.1%	55,720	26.4%	132,610	44.2%	221,710	502,060
30 Portland, OR	73	29.4%	314,240	12.2%	130,150	28.0%	299,860	42.3%	452,260	1,069,950
31 Tampa	76	29.2%	337,960	10.9%	126,220	23.0%	265,670	47.6%	550,040	1,156,150
32 Nashville	79	29.1%	188,850	8.2%	53,330	29.5%	191,120	41.4%	268,600	648,880
33 Buffalo	83	28.9%	163,580	12.6%	71,210	24.3%	137,370	46.8%	265,100	566,340
34 San Antonio	84	28.8%	196,670	11.0%	74,970	23.2%	158,470	47.9%	326,770	682,160
35 Phoenix	92	28.6%	440,290	10.6%	163,790	26.0%	400,290	45.2%	696,310	1,539,040
36 Norfolk, VA	97	28.4%	192,250	12.0%	81,330	25.8%	174,460	45.8%	310,170	677,130
37 Miami	99	28.3%	440,450	8.5%	132,420	22.0%	342,190	49.5%	768,660	1,553,700
38 Orlando	108	28.0%	238,600	11.0%	93,480	20.8%	177,010	50.8%	432,530	850,840
39 Milwaukee	111	27.9%	284,250	10.0%	101,600	29.8%	303,300	42.1%	429,070	1,018,100
40 Cincinnati	119	27.7%	277,600	9.5%	95,400	27.8%	278,910	44.4%	444,500	1,002,080
41 Providence, RI	120	27.6%	138,370	10.3%	51,510	26.5%	133,060	45.8%	229,370	501,210

		Rank									
42	New Orleans	122	27.5%	168,250	9.4%	57,660	25.0%	152,960	47.4%	290,030	612,010
43	West Palm Beach	123	27.5%	116,030	8.5%	35,900	20.1%	84,750	51.8%	219,110	422,610
44	Greensboro, NC	128	27.3%	177,360	10.7%	69,500	36.2%	235,470	36.4%	236,580	649,820
45	Salt Lake City	139	26.8%	186,210	9.7%	67,190	28.6%	198,810	44.7%	310,890	695,910
46	Louisville	150	26.5%	143,500	7.8%	42,130	28.4%	154,080	45.1%	244,280	542,170
47	Memphis	184	24.8%	140,540	7.8%	44,140	32.7%	185,340	42.5%	240,410	566,290
48	Grand Rapids, MI	197	24.3%	137,160	9.0%	50,560	36.2%	204,040	39.5%	222,780	563,980
49	Las Vegas	257	18.5%	131,560	4.9%	34,860	23.5%	167,410	58.0%	413,650	712,820

NOTES: In some cases, the names of Standard Metropolitan Statistical Areas have been shortened to reflect their core city.

[a]Rank is based on forty-nine large regions over 1 million people.

[b]Overall Rank is based on the Creative Class share for the 268 regions of all sizes for which data are available.

concentrated. Among large regions, Raleigh-Durham, San Francisco, Washington, D.C., and Rochester have the largest concentrations of these super-creative people—more than 15 percent of their workforces. Boston, Seattle, Austin and Hartford, Connecticut, are close behind. Smaller cities like Bloomington, Illinois; Gainesville, Florida; Bryan–College Station, Texas; Madison, Wisconsin; Provo, Utah; Lafayette, Indiana; Melbourne, Florida; and Huntsville, Alabama, also boast significant concentrations of the Super-Creative Core.

Yet there are many places where these super-creative people have virtually no presence. In places like Lawton, Oklahoma; Jacksonville, North Carolina; Enid, Oklahoma; Decatur, Illinois; Jackson, Tennessee; and Victoria, Texas, the Super-Creative Core makes up less than 2 percent of the workforce—a concentration five to ten times less than the leading locations.

Working Class Enclaves

The leading centers for the Working Class among large regions are Greensboro, North Carolina; Grand Rapids, Michigan; and Memphis, Tennessee, where the Working Class makes up more than 30 percent of the workforce. Milwaukee, Buffalo, Detroit, Nashville, Louisville, Charlotte, Portland and Salt Lake City are close behind, with between 28 and 30 percent in the Working Class. Several smaller regions in the South and Midwest are veritable Working Class enclaves with 40 to 50 percent or more of their workforce in the traditional industrial occupations. Elkhart, Indiana, for instance, has 55 percent of its workforce in Working Class occupations, while Decatur, Alabama; Fort Smith, Arkansas; Hickory, North Carolina; and Houma, Louisiana, exceed 40 percent. The Working Class makes up 35 percent or more of the workforce in a dozen other small regions across the nation.

These places have among the most minuscule concentrations of the Creative Class in the nation. They are symptomatic of a general lack of overlap between the major Creative Class centers and those of the Working Class. Of the twenty-six large cities where the Working Class comprises more than one-quarter of the population, only one, Houston, ranks among the top ten destinations for the Creative Class. Just six others— Chicago, Los Angeles, Atlanta, Dallas, Detroit and Rochester—rank among the top twenty. Chicago is interesting because it shows how the Creative Class and the traditional Working Class can coexist. But Chicago has an advantage in that it is a big city, with more than a million members of the Creative Class. The University of Chicago sociologist Terry Clark likes to say Chicago developed an innovative political and cultural solution to this issue. Under the second Mayor Daley, the city integrated the members of the Creative Class into the city's culture and politics by treating them essentially as just another "ethnic group" that needed sufficient space to express its identity.[2]

Service Class Locations

Las Vegas has the highest concentration of the Service Class among large cities, 58 percent, while West Palm Beach, Orlando and Miami also have around half. These regions rank near the bottom of the list for the Creative Class. More troubling is that a large number of smaller regions across the nation are becoming virtual Service Class bastions. The Service Class makes up more than half the workforce in nearly fifty small and medium-size regions across the country. Few of them boast any significant concentrations of the Creative Class save as vacation visitors and offer little prospect for upward mobility. They include resort towns like Honolulu, Hawaii; Naples, Fort Myers, Daytona Beach, Panama City and Sarasota, Florida; Myrtle Beach, South Carolina; and Cape Cod (Barnstable), Massachusetts. But they also include places like Shreveport, Louisiana; Rapid City and Sioux Falls, South Dakota; Bismarck and Grand Forks, North Dakota; Pittsfield, Massachusetts; Utica, New York; Chico, California; and Victoria, Laredo, Killeen and Lubbock, Texas. For these places that are not tourist destinations, the economic and social future is troubling to contemplate.

The Great Class Sorting

Taken together, these findings suggest that a vast and disturbing change is afoot. The U.S. working population is re-sorting itself geographically along class lines. This emerging geography defies categories like East Coast versus West Coast or Sunbelt versus Frostbelt. Significant concentrations of the Creative Class can be found in places like Omaha, Little Rock, Bloomington, Gainesville, Albany and Boise, as well as in more obvious high-tech centers like San Francisco, Austin and Seattle. The correlations between Creative Class and Working Class regions, and also between Creative Class and Service Class regions, are consistently *negative* and significant, indicating that the different classes are sorting themselves into distinct regional centers.[3] The new geography of class in America may well be giving rise to a new form of segregation—different from racial segregation or the old schism between central city and suburb, and perhaps more threatening to national unity.

I see these geographic patterns powerfully expressed in my everyday life in Pittsburgh. Despite its respectable 22nd-place ranking among large regions and 53rd-place ranking among all regions on the Creative Class, Pittsburgh consistently still has trouble attracting and retaining members of the Creative Class, particularly younger ones. Pittsburgh is home to more than 91,000 college and university students. In percentage terms, it is the sixth largest college town in America with some thirty-nine students per thousand residents—a ratio in a class with places like Boston (45.8), San Francisco (45.5), San Diego (46.2) and Denver (44.0). Only Austin (72.2) has appreciably more, and Pittsburgh ranks ahead of cities like Washington, D.C., Seattle, Chicago and New York on this score.[4] But so many of these talented people leave town that the community's leadership has identified their outflow and the need to attract others from outside as among the region's biggest problems.

My focus groups and interviews suggest that the overriding reason these people leave is that they do not feel the city provides a comfortable home for them—a place where they can construct and validate their identities as creative people. When the participants in these groups point to the absence of certain lifestyle amenities, and when they say things like "I don't fit in" or "the city does not get it" or "it's not for me," what they are saying is that Pittsburgh lacks the patterns of everyday life that signal a Creative Class lifestyle. The same sorts of findings are confirmed by the research of others. My Carnegie Mellon colleague Susan McElroy has found that talented African-Americans are leaving the city for places like Atlanta and Washington, D.C. This is perfectly understandable. These places have large middle-class black communities and they are also centers for the Creative Class.[5] Elizabeth Currid, one of my Carnegie Mellon graduate students, has found that foreign-born students are also leaving Pittsburgh for Creative Class centers like New York, San Francisco and Washington, D.C. Another student found much the same pattern for gays.[6]

Thus, the migratory patterns of the Creative Class cut across the lines of race, nationality and sexual orientation. Creative Class people of varied backgrounds are all migrating to the same *kinds* of cities. While more African-American members of the Creative Class may head for Washington, D.C., and Atlanta, and while gay members may favor San Francisco, all are heading to regions that have considerable concentrations of their class. Their decisions, I am convinced, are not dictated merely by economic opportunity but a desire for a distinctly different way of life. Pittsburgh's problem exemplifies the great shifting and resorting of the Creative Class into distinct geographic pockets across our nation. And if Pittsburgh is having problems, what will be the plight of regions like Buffalo and Grand Rapids, Youngstown and El Paso, Lubbock and Kokomo, which rank much farther down the list? Members of the Creative Class are moving away from places like these that do not reflect their interests in favor of those that validate their identities in the very structure of daily life.

Creativity and Regional Advantage

The emerging geography of the Creative Class is dramatically affecting the competitive advantage of regions across the United States. Significant competitive advantage goes to regions that are home to substantial concentrations of this class, whereas regions that are home to large concentrations of the Working and Service Classes are by and large being left behind (see Table 13.2).

Places that are home to large concentrations of the Creative Class also rank highly as centers of innovation and high-tech industry. Three of the top five large Creative Class regions are among the top five high-tech regions. Three of the top five are also among the top five most innovative regions (measured as patents granted per capita). And, the *same five* large regions top the list on the Talent Index (measured as the percentage of people with a bachelor's degree or above) and Creative Class concentration: Washington, D.C., Boston, Austin, Raleigh-Durham and San Francisco. (The Appendix provides complete definitions and data sources for all indicators.) The statistical correlations comparing Creative Class locations to rates of patenting and high-tech industry are uniformly positive and statistically significant.[7]

Working Class centers by contrast have low levels of high-tech industry, innovation, human capital and employment growth. The correlations between Working Class concentration and these factors are uniformly negative and statistically significant.[8] Service Class regions also have low levels of innovation, low levels of high-tech industry, and low levels of economic growth.

244   THE RISE OF THE CREATIVE CLASS

TABLE 13.2   Creative Class Regions Are Innovative, High-Tech Centers

Creative Class Rank	Region	Innovation Rank[a]	High-Tech Rank
1	Washington, D.C.	30	5
2	Raleigh-Durham	4	14
3	Boston	6	2
4	Austin	3	11
5	San Francisco	2	1
6	Minneapolis	5	21
7	Hartford, CT	13	26
8	Denver	10	38
9	Seattle	12	3
10	Houston	16	16
40	Cincinnati	8	31
41	Providence	34	44
42	New Orleans	48	45
43	West Palm Beach	19	25
44	Greensboro, NC	35	33
45	Salt Lake City	20	24
46	Louisville	39	46
47	Memphis	42	48
48	Grand Rapids, MI	23	43
49	Las Vegas	47	42

NOTES: This list is based on the forty-nine regions with over 1 million in population in the 2000 Census.
[a]Innovation rank is based on patents per population; high-tech rank is from the Milken Institute of forty-nine large regions.

The Creativity Index

The key to economic growth lies not just in the ability to attract the Creative Class, but to translate that underlying advantage into creative economic outcomes in the form of new ideas, new high-tech businesses and regional growth. To better gauge these capabilities, I developed a new measure called the *Creativity Index*. The Creativity Index is a mix of four equally weighted factors: (1) the Creative Class share of the workforce; (2) innovation, measured as patents per capita; (3) high-tech industry, using the Milken Institute's widely accepted Tech Pole Index (which I refer to as the High-Tech Index); and (4) diversity, measured by the Gay Index, a reasonable proxy for an area's openness to different kinds of people and ideas. This composite indicator is a better measure of a region's underlying creative capabilities than the simple measure of the Creative Class, because it reflects the joint effects of its concentration *and* of innovative economic outcomes. The Creativity Index is thus my baseline indicator of a region's overall standing in the Creative Economy and I offer it as a barometer of a region's longer run economic potential. I refer to regions that score high on the Creativity Index as Creative Centers.

My Creativity Index rankings for the forty-nine largest regions are presented in Table 13.3. (Appendix Table 5 provides these rankings for the remaining regions.) Some key findings:

- The San Francisco Bay Area is the nation's undisputed leader in creativity. When the major subregions that make up the broad San Francisco Bay Area are looked at individually, each of them ranks among the top ten Creative Centers: Silicon Valley is No. 1; San Francisco proper is No. 2; and the Berkeley/Oakland area is No. 7.
- Other winners include established East Coast regions like Boston, New York and Washington, D.C., as well as younger high-tech regions like Austin, Seattle, San Diego and Raleigh-Durham. Texas is a bigger winner, with three regions—Austin, Dallas and Houston— in the top ten. Two Midwestern regions—Minneapolis and Chicago—also do well.
- Large places have an apparent advantage in spawning and capturing creativity. Of the nation's twenty leading Creative Centers, all but three are large regions with over one million people. Perhaps this is because large regions can offer abundant options.
- Still, large places do not have an exclusive hold on creativity. Several smaller regions—Santa Fe, Madison and Albany—score highly on the Creativity Index. Santa Barbara, Melbourne, Des Moines and Boise also do reasonably well.
- Some cities that are parts of broader metropolitan areas—such as Ann Arbor and Boulder—are significant Creative Centers in their own right. These cities are frequently home to major research universities.
- Creativity is not limited to established high-tech and cultural centers. Regions like Des Moines, Boise, Albany, Gainesville, Portland, Maine; and Allentown, Pennsylvania, do quite well on the Creativity Index. While these regions do not make the typical lists of high-tech

TABLE 13.3 Ranking Regions in the Creative Economy: The Creativity Index (for regions over 1 million people)

Rank^a (Large regions)	Region	Creativity Index	Overall (All regions) Rank^b	Rank			
				Creative Class	High Tech	Innovation	Diversity
1	San Francisco	1057	1	12	1	5	1
2	Austin	1028	2	7	13	6	23
3	San Diego	1015	3	30	14	13	4
3	Boston	1015	3	6	2	12	41
5	Seattle	1008	5	20	3	34	11
6	Raleigh–Durham	996	6	5	16	8	52
7	Houston	980	7	22	19	39	16
8	Washington–Baltimore	964	9	4	5	85	18
9	New York	962	10	25	15	54	20
10	Dallas	960	11	55	6	40	15
10	Minneapolis–St. Paul	960	11	14	28	11	60
12	Los Angeles	942	13	46	4	79	5
13	Denver	940	14	17	65	29	25
13	Atlanta	940	14	32	7	87	10
15	Chicago	935	16	29	10	56	46
16	Portland, OR	929	18	73	11	32	31
17	Philadelphia	927	19	27	17	36	70
18	Hartford, CT	922	21	16	41	35	61
19	Phoenix	909	22	92	8	46	21
20	Indianapolis	891	24	68	20	55	42
21	Rochester, NY	877	25	34	51	4	115
22	Sacramento	872	26	40	26	103	34
23	West Palm Beach	852	32	123	40	44	17
24	Columbus, OH	832	33	70	48	102	24

25	Kansas City	818	35	24	25	135	73
26	Tampa	804	38	76	42	128	26
27	Salt Lake City	798	41	139	35	45	59
28	Charlotte, NC	787	42	69	46	124	51
29	Miami	775	43	99	62	138	2
30	Cleveland	774	44	71	57	42	134
31	St. Louis	770	45	57	24	76	153
32	Orlando	752	49	108	43	164	9
33	Cincinnati	742	52	119	50	23	141
34	San Antonio	737	55	84	34	126	93
35	Milwaukee	736	56	111	61	38	128
36	Pittsburgh	734	57	53	31	50	210
37	Jacksonville, FL	715	64	50	95	168	47
38	Nashville	711	67	79	70	171	45
39	Detroit	708	68	42	147	27	150
40	Providence, RI	698	70	120	80	108	71
41	Greensboro, NC	697	71	128	53	119	78
42	Oklahoma City	668	83	72	72	150	113
42	New Orleans	668	83	122	87	180	19
44	Grand Rapids, MI	639	95	197	76	52	110
45	Louisville	622	100	150	91	131	83
46	Buffalo	609	105	83	71	73	240
47	Las Vegas	561	117	257	74	178	8
48	Norfolk, VA	555	120	97	60	200	162
49	Memphis	530	132	184	100	141	119

NOTES: In some cases, the names of Standard Metropolitan Statistical Areas have been shortened to reflect their core city.

[a]Rank is based on forty-nine regions over 1 million people.

[b]Overall Rank is based on the 268 regions of all sizes for which data are available.

centers, their rankings here suggest that their economic futures may be brighter than otherwise thought.

- Many regions are being bypassed in the shift to the Creative Economy. Although their ranks include a number of older industrial regions, like Buffalo and Grand Rapids, Michigan, Sunbelt regions like Norfolk, Las Vegas, Louisville, Oklahoma City, New Orleans and Greensboro, North Carolina are also in precarious positions. The big losers in this emerging geography are smaller cities and regions in the South and Midwest that are being left almost totally behind.

This is why it is so important to understand the factors and processes that are shaping the nation's emerging geography of creativity. The emergence of distinct Creative Centers is having a dramatic effect on innovation, high-tech growth and the potential for longer-run economic growth.

CHAPTER 14

Technology, Talent and Tolerance

The 3 T's of
Economic Development

The key to understanding the new economic geography of creativity and its effects on economic outcomes lies in what I call the 3T's of economic development: *Technology, Talent and Tolerance.* Each is a necessary but by itself insufficient condition: To attract creative people, generate innovation and stimulate economic growth, a place must have all three.

There are several explanations for regional growth, as we saw in Chapter 12. The conventional firm-driven view held by mayors and economic development professionals is that regional growth comes from attracting companies or building clusters of industries. Then there is the social capital theory of Robert Putnam, which views economic growth as a product of social cohesion, trust and community connectedness. The human capital theory advanced by economists like Robert Lucas and Edward Glaeser says that concentrations of educated people drive regional growth.[1] Each of these views makes intuitive sense. A place with more industry, more community cohesiveness and more educated people is likely to grow faster than a place with less.

But I believe my creative capital theory does an even better job. Recall its basic argument: that regional economic growth is powered by creative people, who prefer places that are diverse, tolerant and open to new ideas. Diversity increases the odds that a place will attract different types of creative people with different skill sets and ideas. Places with diverse mixes of creative people are more likely to generate new combinations. Furthermore, diversity and concentration work together to speed the flow of knowledge. Greater and more diverse concentrations of creative capital in turn lead to higher rates of innovation, high-technology business formation, job generation and economic growth.

Economists have long argued that diversity is important to economic performance, but they have usually meant the diversity of firms or industries. The economist John Quigley, for instance, argues that regional economies benefit from the location of a diverse set of firms and industries.[2] Jane Jacobs long ago highlighted the role of diversity of both firms and people in powering innovation and city growth. As Jacobs saw it, great cities are places where people from virtually any background are welcome to turn their energy and ideas into innovations and wealth.[3]

Economists also speak of the importance of industries having "low entry barriers," so that new firms can easily enter and keep the industry vital. Similarly, I think it's important for a place to have *low entry barriers for people*—that is, to be a place where newcomers are accepted quickly into all sorts of social and economic arrangements. Such places gain a creativity advantage. All else being equal, they are likely to attract greater numbers of talented and creative people—the sort of people who power innovation and growth.

In more pragmatic terms, the creative capital theory says that regional growth comes from the 3T's of economic development, and to spur innovation and economic growth a region must offer all three of them. The 3T's explain why cities like Baltimore, St. Louis and Pittsburgh fail to grow despite their deep reservoirs of technology and world-class universities: They have not been sufficiently tolerant and open to attract and retain top creative talent. The interdependence of the 3T's also explains why cities like Miami and New Orleans do not make the grade even though they are lifestyle meccas: They lack the required technology base. The most successful places—such as the San Francisco Bay Area, Boston, Washington, D.C., Austin and Seattle—put all 3T's together. They are truly creative places.

My colleagues and I have conducted a great deal of statistical research to test the creative capital theory by looking at the way these 3T's work together to power economic growth. In a nutshell, we found that creative people are attracted to, and high-tech industry takes root in, places that score high on our basic indicators of diversity—the Gay, Bohemian and other indexes (see Table 14.1). Why would this be so? It is not because high-tech industries are populated by great numbers of bohemians and gay people. Rather, artists, musicians, gay people and the members of the Creative Class in general prefer places that are open and diverse. Low entry barriers are especially important because today places grow not just through higher birth rates (in fact virtually all U.S. cities are declining on this measure), but by their ability to attract people from the outside.

TABLE 14.1   Technology, Talent and Tolerance

Technology (High-Tech Index)	Talent	Tolerance (Gay Index)	Creativity Index
Large Regions[a]			
1 San Francisco	Raleigh-Durham	San Francisco	San Francisco
2 Boston	Washington, D.C.	San Diego	Austin
3 Seattle	Boston	Los Angeles	Boston[c]
4 Los Angeles	Austin	Austin	San Diego[c]
5 Washington, D.C.	San Francisco	Seattle	Seattle
6 Dallas	Hartford	Sacramento	Raleigh-Durham
7 Atlanta	Atlanta	Washington, D.C.	Houston
8 Phoenix	Denver	Atlanta	Washington, D.C.
9 Chicago	Minneapolis	Minneapolis	New York
10 Portland	Dallas	Houston	Minneapolis
All Regions[b]			
1 San Francisco	Santa Fe	San Francisco	San Francisco
2 Boston	Raleigh-Durham	San Diego	Austin
3 Seattle	Columbia MO	Los Angeles	Boston[c]
4 Los Angeles	Washington, D.C.	Austin	San Diego[c]
5 Washington, D.C.	Boston	Seattle	Seattle
6 Dallas	Gainesville, FL	Sacramento	Raleigh-Durham
7 Atlanta	Madison, WI	Madison, WI	Houston
8 Phoenix	Champaign-Urbana	Washington, D.C.	Albuquerque
9 Albuquerque	Austin	Atlanta	Washington, D.C.
10 Chicago	State College, PA	Minneapolis	New York

[a]Based on the forty-nine regions with over 1 million in population.
[b]Based on all regions for which complete data are available.
[c]Boston and San Diego are tied for third place on the Creativity Index.

Technology and Talent

Let's now look at the first two T's—technology and talent—and how they are interrelated. As we have already seen, human capital theorists have shown that economic growth is closely associated with concentrations of highly educated people. But few studies had specifically looked at the relationship between talent and technology, between clusters of educated and creative people and concentrations of innovation and high-tech industry. My team and I addressed this by developing and using four regional measures: the relative concentration of the Creative Class in a region, plus its Talent Index (a simple human–capital measure of the percentage of the population with a bachelor's degree or above), its Innovation Index (patents granted per capita), and its High-Tech Index—a number based on the Milken Institute's Tech Pole Index, which measures both the size and concentration of a region's economy in growth sectors such as software, electronics, biomedical products and engineering services. We examined the relationships among these factors for both the forty-nine regions with more than 1 million people and the more than 200 regions for which data are available. Along with some well-known technology centers, smaller college and university towns rank highly on the Talent Index—places like Santa Fe, Madison, Champaign-Urbana, State College, Pennsylvania and Bloomington, Indiana. When I look at the subregional level, Ann Arbor (part of the Detroit region) and Boulder (part of the Denver region) rank first and third, respectively.

The findings show that both innovation and high-tech industry are strongly associated with locations of the Creative Class and of talent in general. The high-tech leaders are San Francisco, Boston, Seattle, Los Angeles and Washington, D.C., while the innovation leaders are Rochester, San Francisco, Austin, Boston and Raleigh-Durham. Fifteen of the top twenty high-tech regions also rank among the top twenty Creative Class Centers, while fourteen of the top twenty regions on the Innovation Index do so as well. Furthermore, seventeen of the top twenty Talent Index regions also rank in the top twenty of the Creative Class. The statistical correlations between the Talent Index and the Creative Class Centers are understandably among the strongest of any variables in my analysis—because Creative Class people tend to have high levels of education. But the correlations between Talent and Working Class regions are just the opposite—negative and highly significant, suggesting that Working Class regions possess among the lowest levels of human capital.[4]

The New Outsiders

A large number of studies point to the role of immigrants in economic development. In the book *The Global Me,* the *Wall Street Journal* reporter Pascal Zachary argues that openness to immigration is the cornerstone of innovation and economic growth. He contends that America's successful economic performance is directly linked to its openness to innovative and energetic people from around the world, and attributes the decline of once prospering countries, such as Japan and Germany, to the homogeneity of their populations.[5]

Openness to entrepreneurial individuals from around the globe has long been a hallmark of our nation. The 1990s saw the largest wave of immigration in U.S. history, more than 9 million people. Immigrants now make up more than 12 percent of the U.S. workforce—in certain regions more than 30 percent.[6]

Immigrants have also powered a good deal of recent growth in U.S. cities and regions. A 2000 study by the Milken Institute identified immigration as one of the two most powerful demographic trends reshaping the nation's cities and regions. Its list of "Melting Pot Metros" ranks the most diverse regions in the country.[7] The 2000 Census makes it abundantly clear that a large share of regional growth over the 1990s was driven by immigration. Immigrants have fueled the rebound of older established regions like New York and Chicago, as well as powering growth in younger cities from Atlanta to Phoenix. Between 1990 and 2000, New York City added 1 million immigrants, pushing its population over 8 million for the first time in history.[8] More than 40 percent of all New York City residents were foreign-born in 1999, up from 28 percent in 1990.[9] Immigration also enabled Chicago to grow over the decade of the 1990s for the first time in fifty years. In Silicon Valley, the world's leading high-tech center, nearly a quarter of the population and a third of high-tech scientists and engineers are foreign-born, according to Annalee Saxenian of the University of California at Berkeley.[10]

From Andrew Carnegie in steel to Andy Grove in semiconductors, immigrants have also been a powerful source of innovation and entrepreneurship. Those who choose to leave their countries are predisposed to risk and can be thought of as "innovative outsiders." It seems obvious too that people and groups facing obstacles in traditional organizations are more likely to start their own enterprises, and the facts bear this out. Roughly one-quarter of new Silicon Valley businesses started since 1980 were founded by immigrants, according to Saxenian's study, a figure that increased to 30 percent for businesses started after 1995. In my hometown of Pittsburgh, Indian entrepreneurs have founded a large share of high-tech startup companies. As a result, cities across the United States have stepped up their efforts to attract immigrants. While companies scramble to obtain visas for new recruits, entire inland regions in the United States—which normally don't get many immigrants—are actively encouraging immigration to build their economies. The Minneapolis–St. Paul region is one example, and the state of Iowa has declared its intention to be "the Ellis Island of the Midwest," while Philadelphia wants to attract im-

Table 14.2   Immigrants and High-Tech Industry

High-Tech Index Rank	Region	Melting Pot Index Rank
1	San Francisco	4
2	Boston	8
3	Seattle	16
4	Los Angeles	2
5	Washington, D.C.	14
6	Dallas	17
7	Atlanta	31
8	Phoenix	21
9	Chicago	7
10	Portland	24
40	Buffalo	28
41	Oklahoma City	38
42	Las Vegas	13
43	Grand Rapids	36
44	Providence	6
45	New Orleans	26
46	Louisville	49
47	Jacksonville	34
48	Memphis	46
49	Detroit	22

NOTE: Rank based on the forty-nine regions with over 1 million in population.

migrants as "replacement people." Pittsburgh leaders are trying to attract more immigrants from India.[11]

My team and I examined the relationships between immigration, or percent foreign-born, and the presence of high-tech industry (see Table 14.2). Inspired by the Milken Institute study, we dubbed this the Melting Pot Index. The effect of openness to immigration on regions is mixed. Four out of the top ten regions on the Melting Pot Index are also among the nation's top ten high-technology regions; and the Melting Pot Index is positively associated with the High-Tech Index statistically. Clearly, as Saxenian argued, immigration is associated with high-tech industry. But immigration is *not* strongly associated with innovation: The Melting Pot Index is not statistically correlated with the Innovation Index, measured as rates of patenting. While it is positively associated with population growth, it is not correlated with job growth.[12] Furthermore, places that are open to immigration do not necessarily number among the leading Creative Class Centers. While twelve of the top twenty Melting Pot regions number in the top twenty centers for the Creative Class, there is no significant statistical relationship between the Melting Pot Index and the Creative Class.[13]

The Gay Index

While immigrants are important to regional growth, there are other types of diversity that are even more important. In the late 1990s, Gary Gates, now at the Urban Institute in Washington, D.C., used information from the United States Census of Population to measure the concentrations of gay people in various regions. When I came back to Carnegie Mellon in 1998 from a leave at Harvard's Kennedy School of Government, I happened to mention to my dean the research I was conducting on the location decisions of people and high-tech industries. He suggested I meet Gates, then a doctoral student at Carnegie Mellon, who was working on the demography of the gay population. As soon as we met, the parallel became obvious: The same places that were popular among gays were also the ones where high-tech industry located. Gates and I quickly became collaborators and friends.

Working with the economists Dan Black, Seth Sanders and Lowell Taylor, Gates had created a new measure that he called the Gay Index.[14] Before this, nobody really had a good statistical handle on where gay people were located. The U.S. Census Bureau collects detailed information on the American population, but until the 2000 Census it did not ask people to identify their sexual orientation. Gates and his collaborators had come up with an ingenious solution. A student of public policy with interest in gay issues, Gates had two advantages over other researchers. He was a "sworn Census Investigator," meaning he had access to the raw census data. He also had extensive experience in computer programming. The 1990 Census allowed couples that were not married to identify themselves as "unmarried partners," different from "roommates" or "unrelated adults." By determining which unmarried partners were of the same sex, he identified gay and lesbian couples. He then used this data to come up with the Gay Index, which ranks regions by their concentrations of gay people. Gates later updated it to include the year 2000.

Almost immediately, we got to work comparing innovation and high-tech industry to the Gay Index ranking. There are several reasons why the Gay Index is a good measure for diversity. As a group, gays have been sub-

TABLE 14.3 The Gay Index and High-Tech Industry

High-Tech Index Rank	Region	1990 Gay Index Rank	2000 Gay Index Rank
1	San Francisco	1	1
2	Boston	18	22
3	Seattle	5	8
4	Los Angeles	3	4
5	Washington, D.C.	7	11
6	Dallas	12	9
7	Atlanta	8	7
8	Phoenix	23	15
9	Chicago	17	24
10	Portland	22	20
40	Buffalo	49	49
41	Oklahoma City	40	40
42	Las Vegas	28	5
43	Grand Rapids	32	38
44	Providence	31	32
45	New Orleans	25	11
46	Louisville	47	36
47	Jacksonville	38	24
48	Memphis	43	41
49	Detroit	42	45

NOTE: Rank based on the forty-nine regions with over 1 million in population.

ject to a particularly high level of discrimination. Attempts by gays to integrate into the mainstream of society have met substantial opposition. To some extent, homosexuality represents the last frontier of diversity in our society, and thus a place that welcomes the gay community welcomes all kinds of people.[15] As Gates sometimes says, gays can be said to be the "canaries of the Creative Age."[16] For these reasons, openness to the gay community is a good indicator of the low entry barriers to human capital that are so important to spurring creativity and generating high-tech growth.

In addition to the large regions listed in Table 14.3, smaller places like Iowa City, Iowa; Madison, Wisconsin; Eugene, Oregon; East Lansing, Michigan; and Bloomington, Indiana, rank among the top twenty of all regions on the Gay Index. The results of our analysis are squarely in line with the Creative Capital theory (see Table 14.3). The Gay Index is a very strong predictor of a region's high-tech industry concentration. Six of the

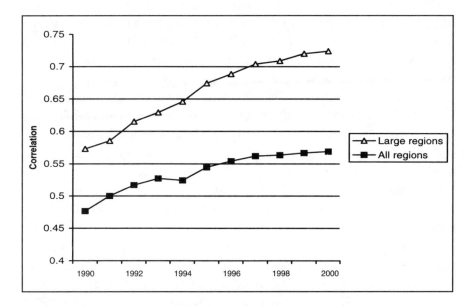

FIGURE 14.1   The Gay Index–High-Tech Connection Increases over Time

top ten 1990 and five of the top ten 2000 Gay Index regions also rank
among the nation's top ten high-tech regions. In virtually all of our statistical analysis, the Gay Index did better than any other individual measure
of diversity as a predictor of high-tech industry.[17] Gays predict not only
the concentration of high-tech industry, they also predict its growth. Four
of the regions that rank in the top ten for high-technology growth from
1990 to 1998 also rank in the top ten on the Gay Index in both 1990 and
2000.[18] In addition, the correlation between the Gay Index (measured in
1990) and the High-Tech Index (calculated for each year from 1990–2000)
increases over time (see Fig. 14.1). This suggests that the benefits of diversity may actually compound.

Some of our critics argued that our results might be biased by the
unique situation of San Francisco, which ranks highly (No. 1 in fact) on
both measures. To check for this, we removed San Francisco from the
analysis. Still, the basic findings remained virtually the same.[19] In fact, the
influence of the Gay Index on high-tech industry was strengthened when
San Francisco was removed from the analysis. This increases our confidence in the strength of the concentration of gays as a predictor of high-
tech industry. These results even held up after the 2000 Census when a
number of resort cities like Miami, Las Vegas and Orlando made it to the
top of the list of gay regions. Despite this, twelve of the top twenty Gay

Index regions continued to rank among the top twenty high-tech regions. In addition, ten of the top twenty Gay Index regions numbered among the top twenty centers for the Creative Class. The Gay Index was positively associated with the Creative Class in both periods; but it was negatively associated with the Working Class.[20] There is also a strong relationship between the concentration of gays in a metropolitan area and other measures of diversity, notably the percent of foreign-born residents. These results reiterate the impact of diversity on a broad section of society. Low barriers to entry thus seem to be good for the whole economy.

It is amazing how many times people misconstrue what Gates and I have to say on this score. Many people, both in academe and in the general public, seem to think we are saying there is a direct connection between being gay and being in high-tech industry. They say things like: "So what you mean is that more high-tech people than average are gay." Or, others add even more ludicrous things like: "Engineers and high-tech types are a conservative bunch, how can you say they're gay?" That's not what we're saying. The predictive power of the Gay Index does not somehow depend on the prevalence of gays in high-tech industry. It simply represents a leading indicator of a place that is open and tolerant. These qualities are important to high-tech workers and Creative Class people in general for a couple of reasons. To begin with, many are immigrants or people moving from one region of the country to another. Many grew up being stereotyped as nerds; some have extreme habits and dress. All want places where they can fit in and live as they please without raising eyebrows. As my friend Bill Bishop, a reporter with the *Austin American-Statesman,* put it, "Where gay households abound, geeks follow."

Lifestyle Matters

In the late 1990s, the Richard King Mellon Foundation commissioned me to study the role of lifestyle amenities in the location decisions of talented and creative people. The foundation was concerned about the outflow of young talented people from the Pittsburgh region and wanted to see if it could use its funding for arts, culture and land conservation to help turn it around. Previous studies had found that lifestyle amenities were a powerful draw for companies that require higher-skilled, more talented labor. The reason seemed to be that such people had higher income and thus could afford a higher quality of life. A pioneering Princeton University doctoral dissertation by Paul Gottlieb, now at Case Western Reserve University in Cleveland, had found this to be true in early studies of the location of high-tech companies in New Jersey.[21] Two economists associated with the National Bureau of Economic Research later found that high-income "power couples" preferred locations with high levels of amenities.[22] Gates and his collaborators found the same to be true among gay people. It was also clear to me that cities have long used amenities as a tool to spur economic development. Mayors and city leaders often tout the "high quality of life" their cities have to offer. Cities across the country have spent countless billions of dollars to build stadiums, create cultural districts and develop urban retail malls to boost their image. And from my focus groups and interviews, I knew that people value lifestyle amenities very highly in the choice of locations.

But my research was pointing me toward a different bundle of amenities. I was finding that the Creative Class preferred a more active, informal, street-level variant of amenities. In their studies of Chicago, the sociologists Richard Lloyd and Terry Clark captured the new role of lifestyle amenities by calling cities "entertainment machines."[23] In a detailed statistical study, Edward Glaeser and his collaborators found considerable support for this view, which they referred to as a shift from the producer to the "consumer city," concluding that: "The future of most cities depends on their being desirable places for consumers to live. As consumers become richer and firms become mobile, location choices are based as much on their advantages for workers as on their advantages for firms."[24] An April 2000 story in *The Economist* under the provocative title "The Geography of Cool" pointed out that cities which had long been centers of culture and fashion (read: artistic and cultural creativity), from New York to Berlin, had also emerged as leading centers for attracting talented people and generating certain new technology-intensive industries.[25]

Working with Gary Gates and my graduate student team, I undertook a series of analyses to try to test this view. I began by looking closely at things like climate, professional sports, outdoor recreation and cultural assets of various sorts. In particular, I wanted to distinguish between the smaller-scale, street-level amenities and the traditional big-ticket attractions like professional sports teams, museums, the symphony, opera, ballet and other things that cities typically promote to lure people and firms and cement their major league status. This early research, outlined in my 2000 report *Competing in the Age of Talent,* found that certain types of cultural amenities are better than others for attracting talented people and generating high-tech industries.[26] Most significantly, I found little evidence that big-ticket attractions were very effective at this. Much better were the small things, the things my focus groups had mentioned—vibrant street life, readily available outdoor recreation and a cutting-edge music scene. Austin, for instance, where I had been traveling to consult with the mayor, Chamber of Commerce and high-tech companies, managed to be a highly ranked location for both talent and high-tech companies despite having no major league sports and few world-class cultural institutions of the traditional high-brow variety; instead, it boasted a dynamic music scene and active outdoor recreation. A measure of city nightlife dubbed the Coolness Index was for instance reasonably associated with a city's ability to attract talented people and high-tech industries.

Still, I yearned for more systematic proof. The typical measures of lifestyle amenities associated with *Places Rated Almanac* or *Money Magazine* essentially capture an older way of life, an older bundle of amenities. These measures are also nonscientific, inconsistent and unreliable, compiled as they are from lists of cultural institutions, art galleries and sports venues. And for many of the things I wanted to measure and assess—such as a city's music scene or street life—reliable statistics were simply unavailable.

The Bohemian Index

Working with my Carnegie Mellon team, I developed a new measure called the *Bohemian Index,* which measures the number of writers, designers, musicians, actors and directors, painters and sculptors, photographers and dancers. The Bohemian Index is an improvement over traditional measures of a region's cultural amenities because it directly counts the producers of the amenities, using reliable census data. In addition to the large regions listed in Table 14.4, smaller communities like Boulder and Fort Collins, Sarasota, Santa Barbara and Madison rank rather highly when all regions are taken into account.

The Bohemian Index turns out to be an amazingly strong predictor of everything from a region's high-technology base to its overall population and employment growth (see Table 14.4).[27] Five of the top ten and twelve of the top twenty Bohemian Index regions number among the nation's top twenty high-technology regions. Eleven of the top twenty Bohemian Index regions number among the top twenty most innovative regions.[28] The Bohemian Index is also a strong predictor of both regional employment and population growth. A region's Bohemian concentration in 1990

TABLE 14.4   The Bohemian Index and High-Tech Industry

High-Tech Index Rank	Region	Bohemian Index Rank
1	San Francisco	5
2	Boston	4
3	Seattle	7
4	Los Angeles	10
5	Washington, D.C.	13
6	Dallas	15
7	Atlanta	12
8	Phoenix	23
9	Chicago	26
10	Portland	6
40	Buffalo	46
41	Oklahoma City	47
42	Las Vegas	9
43	Grand Rapids	31
44	Providence	17
45	New Orleans	41
46	Louisville	33
47	Jacksonville	49
48	Memphis	40
49	Detroit	24

NOTE: Rank based on the forty-nine regions with over 1 million in population.

predicts both its high-tech industry concentration and its employment and population growth between 1990 and 2000. This provides strong support for the view that places with a flourishing artistic and cultural environment are the ones that generate creative economic outcomes and overall economic growth.

Diversity in the Broadest Sense

As another test of my theory that diversity attracts Creative Capital and stimulates high-tech growth, Gates and I combined our various indices into a broader measure we dubbed the Composite Diversity Index (or CDI).[29] The CDI adds together three diversity measures—the Gay Index, the Melting Pot Index and the Bohemian Index. We ranked regions on each indicator and summed the rankings.

TABLE 14.5   Technology and Diversity

High-Tech Index Rank	Region	Composite Diversity Index Rank
1	San Francisco	1
2	Boston	4
3	Seattle	8
4	Los Angeles	2
5	Washington, D.C.	7
6	Dallas	14
7	Atlanta	13
8	Phoenix	18
9	Chicago	15
10	Portland	16
40	Buffalo	48
41	Oklahoma City	39
42	Las Vegas	26
43	Grand Rapids	36
44	Providence	11
45	New Orleans	27
46	Louisville	49
47	Jacksonville	41
48	Memphis	44
49	Detroit	28

NOTE: Rank based on the forty-nine regions with over 1 million in population.

The results again support the basic notion that diversity and creativity work together to power innovation and economic growth. Five of the top ten regions on the CDI are also among the top ten high-tech regions: San Francisco, Boston, Seattle, Los Angeles and Washington, D.C. (see Table 14.5). The statistical correlation between the High-Tech Index and the CDI rankings is also quite high.[30] Even more compelling, the CDI strongly predicts high-tech growth. When we estimate the effect of the CDI on high-tech growth and factor in the percentage of college graduates in the region, population, and measures of culture, recreation, and climate, the CDI continues to have a positive and significant effect on high-tech growth from 1990 to 1998.

But there is a gaping hole in this picture. The diversity picture does not include African-Americans and other nonwhites. As noted earlier, my sta-

tistical research identifies a troubling negative statistical correlation between concentrations of high-tech firms and the percentage of the nonwhite population—a finding that is particularly disturbing in light of our
findings on other dimensions of diversity. It appears that the Creative
Economy does little to ameliorate the traditional divide between the white
and nonwhite segments of the population. It may even make it worse.

Creativity, Innovation and Economic Growth

To further test the Creative Capital theory, Gary Gates and I undertook a
series of statistical analyses of the sources of both employment growth
and population growth during the 1990s. We developed a series of models
to take into account the independent effects of factors like high-tech industry, talent, diversity and creativity. We broke the more than 200 U.S.
metropolitan regions for which complete data are available into four
groups based on their size, ranging from the largest cities (those with an
average population of 2.2 million) to the smallest (average population of
250,000). This is what we found.

- *Population growth:* Diversity and creativity combine to drive
  population growth. Neither high-technology industry nor human
  capital plays the key role. Rather, the three strongest predictors of
  population growth between 1990 and 2000 are the Bohemian Index,
  the Melting Pot Index and the CDI.
- *Employment growth:* Creativity is the key factor powering
  employment growth. As with population growth, neither high-tech
  industry nor talent appears to play a significant role. The main
  predictor of employment growth is the Bohemian Index.
- *Large regions:* Creativity and diversity work together to drive both
  population growth and employment growth in large cities. The
  Bohemian Index and the CDI are the only significant predictors of
  population and employment growth in regions with an average
  population of 2.2 million. Thus these regions should develop
  strategies to bolster their openness to diversity and invest their
  resources in the development of vibrant local artistic and cultural
  communities.
- *Small and medium-size regions:* Immigration is more important to
  the growth of small and medium-size regions. The Melting Pot Index

is the only consistent predictor of these regions' population growth. Smaller regions may benefit more from strategies that make them more open and attractive to immigrants.

Finally, with one of my advanced doctoral students, Sam Youl Lee, I conducted a more advanced statistical analysis of the creative capital theory. We looked systematically at the effects of creativity and diversity on innovation (measured as patents per capita), controlling for other factors like industry mix and human capital. The findings of this analysis also support the creative capital theory. We found that innovation is strongly associated with specialized creative capital (measured by the Bohemian Index and numbers of scientists and engineers) and diversity (the Gay Index). [31]

Resolving Zipf's Law

One of the great remaining puzzles of urban economics and regional analysis revolves around Zipf's Law.[32] Named for its creator, George Zipf, it is also referred to as the "rank-size rule." Zipf's Law says that the distribution of virtually all cities within a nation follows a simple "power law": the basic idea being that the second largest city is roughly half the size of the largest; the third, roughly one-third the size; and so on. According to detailed empirical studies, Zipf's Law accurately describes the real size distribution of U.S. cities over the past century and for all the other advanced industrial nations as well. Plotted on a logarithmic graph, populations of cities in fact form a nearly perfect line with a descending slope.

Try as they might, economists and social scientists failed to develop plausible explanations for why Zipf's Law should hold. In their book *The Spatial Economy*, the economists Masahisa Fujita, Paul Krugman and Anthony Venables write: "Attempts to match economic theory with the data usually face the problem that the theory is excessively neat . . . whereas the real world throws up complicated and messy outcomes. When it comes to the size distribution of cities, however, the problem we face is that the data offer a stunningly neat picture, one that is hard to reproduce in any plausible (or even implausible) theoretical model." After devoting more than eight pages and scads of sophisticated formulas to this problem, they conclude: "At this point we have no resolution of the striking regularity in city size distributions. We must acknowledge that it poses a real intellectual challenge to our understanding of cities. . . . [N]obody has come up with a plausible story about the process that generates the rank size rule."[33] That is until now.

The remarkable computer models built by Robert Axtell shed new light on the underlying size distribution of cities. Axtell, a former Carnegie Mellon student, is a member of the Brookings Institution's Center for Social and Economic Dynamics, a frequent visitor to the Santa Fe Institute and a leader in the field of agent-based modeling. Along with his Brookings colleague Josh Epstein, he has done pioneering work on artificial societies and developed models of the process of firm formation. Axtell is part computer scientist, part economist and part physicist. He and his peers build high-level computer programs to evaluate how people or organizations—which they refer to as "agents"—behave. Taking my creative capital theory as his point of departure, Axtell built a model of how cities form, based on three key principles:

- Creative agents cluster around other creative agents, reinforcing each other's productivity.
- Creative agents then come together to form larger economic units or firms.
- These firms then locate in cities where they grow and develop. Cities in turn grow and develop as locations for creative agents and firms.

With these three principles at the core of his program, Axtell let the computer run thousands of iterations of his model. Although it is difficult to explain, the following picture forms on the screen as the model runs. As agents begin combining into firms and firms choose locations, cities start to develop. Some grow, others decline, still others stagnate. Over thousands of these runs, a discernible pattern for the size distribution of cities comes clearly into view. The model generates a hierarchical distribution of cities that conforms almost perfectly to Zipf's Law and matches the real size distribution of U.S. cities.[34] The model thus reinforces the fundamental notion that what matters to economic growth in cities is the ability to attract creative people.

Taken together, these findings are powerful evidence that creativity and diversity work together to attract talent, generate high-tech industries and spur regional growth. Measures of diversity and creativity like the CDI and the Bohemian Index explain regional growth more reliably than conventional measures like high-tech industry or even the level of human capital. Creative capital is even more important to regional growth than human capital or high-tech industry, since both of these things are shaped by it. There is much to gain economically from being an open, inclusive and diverse community. To succeed and prosper economically, regions need to offer the 3T's of economic development. If they fail to do so, they will fall farther behind.

CHAPTER 15

From Social Capital to Creative Capital

City air makes men free. (*Stadtluft macht frei.*)
—*old German adage*

By any accounting, Robert Putnam is a gifted scholar. I greatly admire his willingness to climb down from the ivory tower to address pressing social issues and stimulate informed public debate. In his widely read book *Bowling Alone,* he makes a compelling argument that many aspects of community life declined precipitously over the last half of the twentieth century.[1] Putnam gets his title from his finding that from 1980 to 1993, league bowling declined by 40 percent, while the number of individual bowlers rose by 10 percent. This, he argues, is just one indicator of a broader and more disturbing trend. Across the nation, people are less inclined to be part of civic groups: Voter turnout is down, so is church attendance and union membership, and worst of all, people are less and less inclined to volunteer. All of this stems from what Putnam sees as a long-term decline in social capital.

By this, he means that people have become increasingly disconnected from one another and from their communities. The decline is evident in everything from the loosening bonds between family, friends and neighbors to declining participation in organizations of all sorts—churches, neighborhood organizations, political parties and recreational leagues. Through painstakingly detailed empirical research, he documents the decline in social capital in civic and social life. Putnam finds a broad shift from doing culture to watching culture—from participating in recreational leagues to watching big league sports on TV, from playing music at home to listening to CDs and watching MTV.

Although its origins lie in the nineteenth-century classics of sociology, particularly Emile Durkheim's *Suicide,* Putnam's concept of social capital draws from the more recent work of two sociologists, Pierre Bourdieu and James Coleman.[2] Bourdieu used the term social capital to explain the advantages and opportunities that accrue to people through their membership in groups, while Coleman used it to refer to the advantages that social ties afford individuals. For Putnam, social capital essentially means reciprocity. If you do something for someone, they are more likely to do something for you. To some degree, it hinges on mutual respect, trust and civic-mindedness. Declining social capital means that society becomes less trustful and less civic-minded. Putnam believes a healthy, civic-minded community is essential to prosperity.

The looming social capital deficit is thus rattling many aspects of our society, weakening our neighborhoods, affecting our health, making us less happy, damaging our educational system, threatening the well-being of our children, eroding our democracy and threatening the very sources of our prosperity. Putnam singles out four factors as the main culprits in our growing civic malaise and disconnectedness. First, longer working hours and increasing pressures of time and money mean we have less time to spend with one another. Second, rampant suburban sprawl has left us farther apart from family and friends and made it harder to get to activities. Third, television and other electronic mass media take up more of our time, leaving less of it for more active pursuits and volunteer efforts. Fourth and most important, according to Putnam, is the "generational shift" from the "civic-minded generation of World War II" to subsequent "me-oriented" generations.

Much of his account initially resonated with me. I grew up in just the sort of community whose decline Putnam laments, a tightly knit Italian-American community surrounded by relatives and friends. My father belonged to the Italian-American Club; he was the manager of my Little League team, and my mother was a den mother for my Cub Scout troop. My brother and I played in our own rock band made up of friends from our Catholic school, frequently entertaining neighborhood kids in the basement of our family home. Pittsburgh, where I now live, is filled with strong ethnic neighborhoods and community pride of the sort Putnam describes, and this strong sense of community helped to keep the region intact in the wake of the near total collapse of the region's steel industry and other heavy industries.

But as much as I would have liked to buy into Putnam's thesis, my own research led me to strikingly different conclusions. The people in my focus groups and interviews rarely wished for the kinds of community connectedness Putnam talks about. If anything, they were trying to get away from those kinds of environments. Sure, they wanted community, but not to the extent that they were inhibited from living their own life and being themselves. They did not want friends and neighbors peering over the fence into their lives. Rather, they desired what I have come to call *quasi-anonymity*. In the terms of modern sociology, these people prefer weak ties to strong.

This leads me to an even more basic observation. The kinds of communities that we desire and that generate economic prosperity are very different from those of the past. Social structures that were important in earlier years now work against prosperity. Traditional notions of what it means to be a close, cohesive community and society tend to inhibit economic growth and innovation. Where strong ties among people were once important, weak ties are now more effective. Where old social structures were once nurturing, now they are restricting. Communities that once attracted people now repel them. Our evolving communities and emerging society are marked by a greater diversity of friendships, more individualistic pursuits and weaker ties within the community. People want diversity, low entry barriers and the ability to be themselves. This is also what the statistics seem to bear out.

All of this raises deep questions that run to the very core of community and society. The life we think of as uniquely American—close families and friends, tight neighborhoods, civic clubs, vibrant electoral politics, strong faith-based institutions and a reliance on civic leadership—is giving way to something new. What's more, the very life that Putnam wants to bring back is no longer a source of economic growth, rising populations, technological innovation and higher incomes. The ways that communities create economic growth have been transformed.

Social Capital Dilemmas

Putnam's argument is not without its holes, as his critics have pointed out. The jury is still out on whether social capital is actually declining. A number of commentaries suggest that Putnam finds the answers he looks for. In a trenchant review of Putnam's work, Nicholas Lemann argues that his results are an artifact of the kinds of organizations he observes.[3] Putnam is right in one sense, Lemann suggests: Participation has fallen off in old-style organizations like bowling leagues and Elks Lodges. But new-style organizations continue to come on the scene—two prime examples being

U.S. Youth Soccer memberships for children, up from 127,000 to more than 2.4 million in two decades, and rapidly increasing membership in environmental organizations, the latter of which Putnam himself notes.

The economists Dora Costa and Matthew Kahn identify a similar pattern in their detailed study of trends in social capital between 1952 and 1998.[4] Using much the same data as Putnam, they looked closely at these trends in the community as well as at home. Costa and Hahn examined how frequently people participated in voluntary organizations, visited friends and relatives, and entertained at home. Wherever possible, they used the same basic data and measures as Putnam, supplementing this with improved data sources where needed. They concluded that the decline of social capital in American life has been dramatically overstated. They found evidence of a small decline in volunteering, a slightly larger but still not very significant drop in group membership, and virtually no decline in evenings spent at home with friends and relatives. The only area where they observed a decline comparable to what Putnam had identified was for visiting friends and relatives.

Costa and Hahn then turned their attention to the reasons for these changes. Contrary to Putnam's generational-shift argument, they found little evidence of differences between generations once education and income were taken into account. Virtually all of the decline in social capital at home (visiting friends and relatives) could be explained by the increasing rate of women's participation in the labor force. And the very slight decline in community social capital was due to the combination of income inequality and growing ethnic diversity.

To my mind, Putnam and his collaborators are on perhaps their shakiest ground with their recent research on ethnic diversity. This work, done under the auspices of Harvard University's Saguaro Seminar on Civic Engagement, suggests that places with high levels of ethnic diversity suffer from lower levels of participation and community connectedness, slow rates of economic growth and high levels of income inequality. This, according to Putnam, stems from a lack of trust both between different ethnic and racial groups and within them as well. In January 2002, while Putnam was presenting this work to the Canadian government, the *Ottawa Citizen* quoted him as saying: "The bottom line is that there are special challenges that are posed to building social capital by ethnic diversity." *The Social Capital Community Benchmark Study* produced as a result of the Saguaro Seminar puts it this way:

The problem of inequality in access to social capital is, it turns out, greatly exacerbated in ethnically diverse communities. More than size or wealth or education, it is ethnic diversity that distinguishes communities in which differences in community involvement are greatest. In ethnically diverse places like Los Angeles, Houston, or Yakima, Washington, college graduates are four to five times more likely to be politically involved than their fellow residents that did not get past high school. In ethnically less diverse places, like Montana or New Hampshire, the class gaps are less than half that large. In terms of civic activity, there is not much difference between a high-tech executive in Houston and a high-tech executive in Nashua, New Hampshire, but there is a substantial difference between an auto mechanic in Houston and an auto mechanic in Nashua.[5]

A related study of social capital in Silicon Valley comes to a similar conclusion, finding that members of ethnic groups are less likely to participate in politics or in civic affairs than their white counterparts.[6]

There is much to criticize here, but let me start by saying this line of thinking badly confuses cause and effect. In their zeal to attribute virtually all problems to the "social capital gap," these studies neglect obvious alternative explanations. For instance, many ethnically diverse communities are full of people working hard to gain a foothold in a new country, which leaves them little free time for civic affairs. Language or cultural barriers may further limit their ability to participate. They are also more likely to be excluded from or perceive that they are excluded from traditional avenues of political and civic participation. Perhaps many of them do not even hold U.S. citizenship or permanent resident status. Moreover, these studies simply assume that the social capital deficit somehow dooms ethnically diverse communities to slow growth. Yet, as the last chapter has shown, ethnic diversity as measured by the Melting Pot Index is positively associated with high-tech industry and population growth.

Some of Putnam's critics suggest that the very concept of social capital has become a tautology. As the sociologists Alejandro Portes and Patricia Landout write in their comprehensive review of social capital theory: "If your town is 'civic' it does civic things; if it is 'uncivic,' it does not."[7] Furthermore, social capital can and often does cut both ways. While it can reinforce belonging and community, it can just as easily shut out newcomers, raise barriers to entry and retard innovation. Adam Smith long ago noted this dilemma in his *Wealth of Nations,* lashing out at merchants who formed tightly knit cliques for precisely such reasons: "People of the same trade seldom meet together, even for merriment and diversion, but the conversation ends in a conspiracy against the public."[8] Mancur Olson later applied much the same thinking to show how tightly knit communities can insulate themselves from outside pressure and sow the seeds of their own demise.[9] Or as Portes and Landout put it: "The same strong ties that help members of a group often enable it to exclude outsiders."

The exclusionary side of social capital remains with us today. I hear about it all the time in my interviews and focus groups in older, tightly knit communities—places like Wilkes-Barre or Fargo or even Pittsburgh, where people say they find it hard to be themselves and do things outside the norm. In a recent newspaper interview Putnam said: "If you map social capital in the United States by where it is high and where it is low— like a weather map—there is one high in America, which is centered somewhere over Minneapolis-St. Paul. Minnesotans go bowling together. They have friends over to the house. They play cards, join groups, and belong to civic institutions."[10] But as the newspaper points out, the Twin Cities region works far better for insiders than it does for outsiders. "It will be six years in October and we still feel like we're newcomers," the paper quotes Emmett Carson, an African-American transplant from New Jersey who heads the Minneapolis Foundation. "In other communities," Carson continues, "co-workers and other people say, Hey why don't you come over? Let me take you to my church, my barber, my hairdresser. You got a problem with your car? Let me introduce you to my mechanic." People are much less likely, he says, to extend such invitations in Minneapolis. In fact, my own visits to and consulting work in Minneapolis shows me that regional leaders are working hard to open up the community and encourage lower barriers to entry and greater diversity.

High levels of social capital can also dampen the entrepreneurial spirit, as Portes and Landout write:

> In the Andean highlands of Ecuador, many successful businessmen are Protestant (or "Evangelical," as they are known locally) rather than Catholic. The reason is not that the Protestant ethic spurred them to greater achievement or that they found Evangelical doctrine to be more compatible with their own beliefs. Rather, by shifting religions, these entrepreneurs removed themselves from the host of obligations for male family heads associated with the Catholic Church. The Evangelical convert becomes, in a sense, a "stranger" in his own community, which insulates him from demands for

support from others on the strength of Catholic norms. For these men, social capital comes at too high a cost.[11]

Places with dense ties and high levels of traditional social capital provide advantages to insiders and thus promote stability, whereas places with looser networks and weaker ties are more open to newcomers and thus promote novel combinations of resources and ideas.[12] Now let's take a more detailed look at how these two types of communities fit into the broader scheme of technological innovation and economic growth.

Testing the Theories

Robert Cushing is a retired University of Texas sociologist and statistician who grew interested in these trends in social and community life during conversations with his son, a Creative Class member in California. For some time, he has been probing the relationships between social capital, diversity and innovation. He has also undertaken to systematically test the three major theories of regional growth: social capital, human capital and creative capital. His findings are startling. In a nutshell, Cushing finds that social capital theory provides little explanation for regional innovation and growth. Both the human capital and creative capital theories are much better at accounting for such growth. Furthermore, he finds that Creative Communities and social capital communities are moving in opposite directions. Creative Communities are centers of diversity, innovation and economic growth; social capital communities are not.

A dedicated empirical researcher with a serious nose for detail, Cushing went to great pains to replicate Putnam's data sources. In one analysis, he looked at the surveys conducted by a team that, under Putnam's direction, did extensive telephone interviewing in forty cities to gauge the depth and breadth of social capital. On the basis of the data, Putnam measured thirteen different kinds of social capital and gave each region a score for attributes like "political involvement," "civic leadership," "faith-based institutions," "protest politics" and "giving and volunteering." Using Putnam's own data, Cushing found very little evidence of a decline in volunteering. Rather, he found that volunteering was up in recent years. People were more likely to engage in volunteer activity in the late 1990s than they were in the 1970s. Volunteering by men was 5.8 percent higher in the five-year period 1993–1998 than it had been in the period 1975–1980. Volunteering by women was up by 7.6 percent. A variety of statistical tests confirmed these results, but Cushing did not stop there. He then combined this information on social capital trends with independent data on high-tech industry, innovation, human capital and diversity. He added the Milken Institute's High-Tech Index, the Innovation Index and measures of talent, diversity and creativity (the Talent Index, the Gay Index and the Bohemian Index). He grouped the regions according to the Milken High-Tech Index and the Innovation Index (their ability to produce patents).*

Cushing found that regions ranked high on the Milken High-Tech Index and Innovation Index ranked low on eleven of Putnam's thirteen measures of social capital. High-tech regions scored below average on almost every measure of social capital. They had less trust, less reliance on faith-based institutions, fewer clubs, less volunteering, less interest in traditional politics and less civic leadership. The two measures of social capital in which these regions excelled were "protest politics" and "diversity of friendships." Regions low on the High-Tech Index and the Innovation Index were exactly the opposite. They scored high on eleven of the thirteen Putnam measures but below average on protest politics and diversity. Cushing then threw into the mix individual wages, income distribution, population growth, numbers of college-educated residents, and scientists and engineers. He found that the high-tech regions had higher incomes, more growth, more income inequality, and more scientists, engineers and professionals than their low-tech, but higher social capital counterparts. When Cushing compared the Gay and Bohemian Indexes to Putnam's measures of social capital in the forty regions surveyed in 2000, the same basic pattern emerged: Regions high on these two diversity indexes were low on eleven of thirteen of Putnam's categories of social capital. In Cushing's words, "conventional political involvement and social capital seem to relate negatively to technological development and higher economic growth." Using this analysis, Cushing identified four distinct types of communities. While the analysis is Cushing's, the labels are my own.

Classic Social Capital Communities—These are the places that best fit the Putnam theory, places like Bismarck, North Dakota; rural South Dakota; Baton Rouge, Louisiana; Birmingham, Alabama; and Greensboro, Charlotte and Winston-Salem, North Carolina. They score high on social

---

*I feel it is important to disclose here that although I am now collaborating with Cushing, he did the initial analysis alone without any input from me or my team, aside from access to our data.

capital and political involvement but low on diversity, innovation and high-tech industry.

Organizational Age Communities—These are older, corporate-dominated communities like Cleveland, Detroit, Grand Rapids, and Kalamazoo. They have average social capital, higher than average political involvement, low levels of diversity and low levels of innovation and high-tech industry. They score high on my Working Class Index. In my view, they represent the classic corporate centers of the organizational age.

Nerdistans—These are fast-growing regions like Silicon Valley, San Diego, Phoenix, Atlanta, Los Angeles and Houston—lauded by some as models of rapid economic growth but seen by others as plagued with sprawl, pollution and congestion. These regions have lots of high-tech industry, above average diversity, low social capital and low political involvement.

Creative Centers—These large urban centers, such as San Francisco, Seattle, Boston, Chicago, Denver and Boulder, have high levels of innovation and high-tech industry and very high levels of diversity, but lower than average levels of social capital and moderate levels of political involvement. These cities score high on my Creativity Index and are repeatedly identified in my focus groups and interviews as desirable places to live and work. That's why I see them as representing the new creative mainstream.

In the winter of 2001, Cushing extended his analysis to include more than three decades of data for one hundred regions. Again he based his analysis on Putnam's own data sources: the thirty-year time series collected by DDB Worldwide, the advertising firm, on activities such as churchgoing, participation in clubs and committees, volunteer activity and entertaining people at home. He used these data to group the regions into high and low social capital communities, and found that social capital had little to do with regional economic growth. The high social capital communities showed a strong preference for "social isolation" and "security and stability" and grew the least—their defining attribute being a "close the gates" mentality, according to Cushing. The low social capital communities had the highest rates of diversity and population growth.

Finally, Cushing undertook a systematic comparison of the effect of the three theories—social capital, human capital and creative capital—on regional economic growth. He built statistical models to determine the effect of these factors on population growth (a well-accepted measure of regional growth) between 1990 and 2000. To do so, he included separate measures of education and human capital; occupation, wages and hours

worked; poverty and income inequality; innovation and high-tech industry; and creativity and diversity for the period 1970–1990.

Again his results were striking. He found no evidence that social capital
leads to regional economic growth; in fact the effects were negative. Both
the human capital and creative capital models performed much better, according to his analysis. Turning first to the human capital approach, he
found that while it did a good job of accounting for regional growth, "the
interpretation is not as straightforward as the human capital approach
might presume." Using creative occupations, bohemians, the Milken High-
Tech Index and innovations as indicators of creative capital, he found that
the creative capital theory produced formidable results, with the predictive
power of the Bohemian and Innovation Indexes being particularly high.
He concluded: "[The] creative capital model generates equally impressive
results as the human capital model and perhaps better."[13]

The World of Weak Ties

The key to understanding these changes lies in the idea of *weak ties*. Putnam and other social capital theorists favor "strong ties." These are the
kinds of relationships we tend to have with family members, close friends
and longtime neighbors or coworkers. They tend to be ties of long dura-
tion, marked by trust and reciprocity in multiple areas of life. When you
have strong ties with someone, you are likely to know one another's personal affairs and do things like trade visits, run errands and do favors for
one another. Practically all of us have at least a few such relationships. According to sociologists who study networks, most people have and can
manage between five and ten strong-tie relationships. Their advantages
are obvious. You have friends you can confide in, a neighbor who watches
your house while you're away, perhaps the uncle who gets you a job.

But weak ties are often more important. The modern theory of the
"strength of weak ties" comes from the sociologist Mark Granovetter's classic research on how people find jobs.[14] Granovetter found that weak ties
matter more to people than strong ones in finding work. Other research on
social networks has shown that weak ties are the key mechanism for mobilizing resources, ideas and information, whether for finding a job, solving a
problem, launching a new product or establishing a new enterprise. A key
reason that weak ties are important is that we can manage many more of
them. Strong ties, by their nature, consume much more of our time and energy. Weak ties require less investment and we can use them more oppor-

tunistically. Weak ties are critical to the creative environment of a city or region because they allow for rapid entry of new people and rapid absorption of new ideas and are thus critical to the creative process.[15]

I am not advocating that we adopt lives composed entirely of weak ties. That would be a lonely and shallow life indeed, and it is the very fate that Putnam fears we all face. But most Creative Class people that I've met and studied do not aspire to such a life and don't seem to be falling into it. Most maintain a core of strong ties. They have significant others; they have close friends; they call mom. But their lives are not dominated or dictated by strong ties to the extent that many lives were in the past. In a classic social capital community, a relatively small and dense network of strong ties would dominate every aspect of your life, from its day-to-day content to its long-term trajectory. You would hang out mostly with people you knew very well and who would shape your career, tastes and personal life according to their values. Life in modern communities is driven more often and in more aspects by a much larger number of loose ties. Interestingly, people seem to prefer it this way. Weak ties allow us to mobilize more resources and more possibilities for ourselves and others, and expose us to novel ideas that are the source of creativity.

Once again, let us return to Jane Jacobs. More than a decade before Bourdieu or Coleman and several decades before Putnam, she used the very phrase "social capital" in her classic *The Death and Life of Great American Cities*. She used it to describe how communities use networks of weak ties—coexisting with, but not constrained by, certain kinds of strong ties—to channel diversity and creativity, and even achieve stability in the process.

> To be sure, a good city neighborhood can absorb newcomers into itself, both newcomers by choice and immigrants settling by expediency, and it can protect a reasonable amount of the transient population too. But these increments or displacements have to be gradual. If self-government in the place is to work, underlying any float of population must be a continuity of people who have forged neighborhood networks. These networks are a city's irreplaceable *social capital* [italics added].. . . Some observers of city life, noting that strong city neighborhoods are so frequently ethnic communities—especially communities of Italians, Poles, Jews, or Irish—have speculated that a cohesive ethnic base is required for a city neighborhood that works as a social unit. In effect, this is to say that only hyphenated-Americans are capable of local self-government in big cities. I think this is absurd.

In the first place, ethnically cohesive communities are not always as naturally cohesive as they may look to outsiders. . . . Today many streets in these old ethnic communities have assimilated into their neighborhoods a fantastic ethnic variety from almost the whole world. They have also assimilated a great sprinkling of middle-class professionals and their families. . . . Some of the streets that functioned best in the Lower East Side . . . were loosely called "Jewish," but contained . . . individuals of more than forty differing ethnic origins.

In the second place, whenever ethnically cohesive neighborhoods develop, they possess another quality besides ethnic identity. They contain those who stay put. . . . Here is a seeming paradox: To maintain in a neighborhood sufficient people who stay put, a city must have the very fluidity and mobility of use. . . . Over intervals of time, many people change their jobs and the locations of their jobs, shift or enlarge their outside friendships and interests, change their family sizes, change their incomes up or down, even change many of their tastes. In short they live, rather than just exist. If they live in diversified, rather than monotonous districts. . . and if they like the place, they can stay put despite [these] changes. . . .

A city's collection of opportunities of all kinds, and the fluidity with which those opportunities and choices can be used, is an asset—not a detriment—for encouraging city-neighborhood stability.[16]

The role of such weak ties in the creative ferment of the city is not new. The shift from small homogeneous communities of strong ties to larger, more heterogeneous communities of weak ties is a basic fact of modern life, identified a century ago by the giants of modern social theory—Max Weber, George Simmel and Emile Durkheim.[17] Writing in the 1930s, the influential German critical theorist Walter Benjamin quoted from a police report written in 1798 lamenting the fact that surveillance has become impossible because "each individual, unknown to all the others, hides in the crowd and blushes before the eyes of no one."[18] In his musings on nineteenth-century Parisian life, Baudelaire portrayed a city of passing encounters, fragmentary exchanges, strangers and crowds where people could find relief from their "inner subjective demons." While Baudelaire disliked many aspects of the city—the factories, the merchants and the crowds—he "loved its freedom and its opportunities for anonymity and curious observation."[19] This aspect of city life was reflected in the *flaneur*—a citizen who is quasi-anonymous and free to enjoy the diversity of the city's experience.

Carolyn Ware identified loose ties as a fundamental feature of creative life in Greenwich Village during the 1920s.[20] "Here congregated those for whom the traditional pattern in which they grew up had become so empty or distorted that they could not continue a part of it and submit to the social controls which it imposed," writes Ware.

> Many who were drawn to the Village came to seek escape from their community, their families, or themselves. Others who did not altogether repudiate the background from which they had come sought to reconcile new conditions with whatever remained of their traditional ways. In this effort they had to struggle without the support of a well-established community to sanction their efforts, or clear standards of behavior to guide them.[21]

Later, in a section of the book devoted to the bohemian and artistic communities she calls the "Villagers," she adds:

> All types of Villagers were intensely individualistic in both their social relations and their point of view. Their social contacts were confined to more or less purposeful relations with those who had common interests. Independent of virtually all institutions and scorning the joining habit, taking full advantage of both the selectiveness and anonymity the city offered, they avoided the usual casual contacts with family, friends, neighbors, or members of the same economic or social class and the relations growing out of institutional connections. Instead, they maintained individual ties with friends scattered all over the city.[22]

Ware concludes that "the members of the groups did not remain constant but the types endured, represented by some old and some new individuals from year to year."[23]

Writing in the early decades of the twentieth century, Robert Park, the pioneering University of Chicago urban sociologist, noted the functional importance of loose ties and anonymous lifestyles in giving rise to what he called the "mobilization of the individual man."[24] Great cities, wrote Park,

> have always been melting pots of races and of cultures. Out of the vivid and subtle interactions of which they have been the centers, there have come the newer breeds and the newer social types. They have multiplied the opportunities for the individual man for contact and association with his fellows,

but they have made these contacts and associations more transitory and less stable.[25]

Park went on to point out the importance of these structures to the creative environment of the city:

This makes it possible for individuals to pass quickly and easily from one moral milieu to another, and encourages the fascinating but dangerous experiment of living at the same time in several different contiguous, but otherwise widely separated worlds. All of this tends to give city life a dangerous and adventitious character; it tends to complicate social relations and to produce new and divergent individual types. It introduces, at the same time, an element of chance and adventure which adds to the stimulus of city life and gives it, for young and fresh nerves, a peculiar attractiveness. The lure of great cities is perhaps a consequence of stimulations which act directly upon the reflexes.[26]

Park concludes by contrasting the stasis of the small, tightly knit community with the dynamism of the city:

The attraction of the metropolis is due in part, however, to the fact that in the long run every individual finds somewhere among the varied manifestations of city life the sort of environment in which he expands and feels at ease; finds, in short, the moral climate in which his particular nature obtains the stimulations that bring his innate dispositions to full and free expression. . . . In a small community, it is the normal man, the man without eccentricity or genius, who seems most likely to succeed. The small community often tolerates eccentricity. The city, on the contrary rewards it. Neither the criminal, the defective, nor the genius has the same opportunity to develop his innate disposition in a small town that he invariably finds in the big city.[27]

The desire for such quasi-anonymous communities is not limited to urban enclaves. William Whyte identified it as a primary motivator behind the great migration of the middle-class professionals out of closely knit urban neighborhoods to the more transient suburbs in the 1950s. For Whyte, suburbia was a new kind of community—the preferred home of the new, upwardly mobile "transients" who could build the lives they desired unencumbered by close family and ethnic group ties.[28]

In fact, the movement from communities of strong ties to communities of weak ties is an important long-run trend in modern life. It is given further impetus by the rise of creativity as an economic force and the massive geographic sorting of the Creative Class.

New Divides

These trends point toward deep and troubling divides in American society. I fear we may well be splitting into two distinct societies with different institutions, different economies, different incomes, ethnic and racial makeups, social organizations, religious orientations and politics. One is creative and diverse—a cosmopolitan admixture of high-tech people, bohemians, scientists and engineers, the media and the professions. The other is a more close-knit, church-based, older civic society of working people and rural dwellers. The former is ascendant and likely to dominate the nation's economic future. Not only are these places richer, faster growing and more technologically savvy, they are also attracting people. The reason is simple: These places are open and easy to enter. They are where people can most easily find opportunity, build support structures and be themselves. And they also provide the habitat that is conducive to creativity in its many varied forms.

This change cuts both ways. While it is positive that people can more easily live the lives they want on the terms they desire, I think many would agree that the ability to up and leave at virtually a moment's notice suggests a breakdown of serious belonging. I have a hard time promoting places like Silicon Valley that fit the mold of the classic high-tech, low social capital community, full of excessively individualistic people uninterested in politics, community or virtually anything outside their own lives. A shift to this kind of community concerns me.

But neither do I think it is desirable—or even possible—to bring back the kind of community we used to have. It just doesn't fit the way people live and work in the Creative Economy. What is really needed, and what growing numbers want, is a new model. More and more people in my interviews and focus groups are leaving places like Silicon Valley to build what they envision as real lives in real places. They yearn for some balance between being themselves and having some sort of community, not the old-style community Putnam romanticizes, but a new and more accepting kind. I think that places like Chicago, Seattle or Minneapolis, which score high on the Creativity Index and also possess a richness of history and a reasonably strong sense of community—have the potential to combine in-novation and economic growth with authentic community and a better way of life. Outside the United States, cities like Dublin and Toronto are able to balance openness and tolerance against a strong sense of commu-nity. The real issue is how well we understand the driving forces at work in our society today and use them to build the more cohesive and equally open and tolerant communities we desire.

CHAPTER 16

Building the Creative Community

H ow do you build a truly Creative Community—one that can survive and prosper in this emerging age? The key can no longer be found in the usual
strategies. Recruiting more companies won't do it; neither will trying
to become the next Silicon Valley. The rise of the Creative Economy has altered the rules of the economic development game. Companies were the
force behind the old game and cities measured their status by the number
of corporate headquarters they were home to. Even today many cities,
states and regions continue to use financial incentives—some of them obscenely extravagant—in their efforts to lure companies.

But while companies remain important, they no longer call all the shots.
As we have seen, companies increasingly go, and are started, where talented and creative people are. Robert Nunn, the CEO of ADD Semiconductor, told the *Wall Street Journal* the "key element of building a
technology business is attracting the right people to the company. It's a
combination of experience, skill set, raw intelligence, and energy. The
most important thing is to be somewhere where you have a pool of people
to draw that."[1]

The bottom line is that cities need a *people climate* even more than they
need a business climate. This means supporting creativity across the
board—in all of its various facets and dimensions—and building a community that is attractive to creative people, not just to high-tech companies. As former Seattle mayor Paul Schell once said, success lies in
"creating a place where the creative experience can flourish."[2] Instead of
subsidizing companies, stadiums and retail centers, communities need to
be open to diversity and invest in the kinds of lifestyle options and amenities people really want. In fact you cannot be a thriving high-tech center if
you don't do this.

Beyond Nerdistan

When they are not trying to lure firms, many cities around the country seek to emulate the Silicon Valley model of high-tech economic development. City after city has tried to turn itself into a clone of the Valley by creating R&D parks, office complexes, technology incubators and the like, all on a quintessentially suburban model. Ross DeVol of the Milken Institute has compiled a list of the hundreds of communities that call themselves a "Silicon Somewhere."

This is essentially betting the future on an economic development model from the past. Though successful in its day, this model misunderstands the changing role of creativity in spurring innovation and economic growth. In fact the heyday of the high-tech nerdistan may be ending. Many of these places have fallen victim to serious problems and some may be reaching their limits to sustainable growth. The comfort and security of places like Silicon Valley have gradually given way to sprawl, pollution and paralyzing traffic jams. As we have seen, my focus groups and statistical research tell me that Creative Class people increasingly prefer authenticity to this sort of generica. As a high-technology executive told the *Wall Street Journal* in October 2001, "I really didn't want to live in San Jose. Every time I went up there, the concrete jungle got me down."[3] His company eventually settled on a more urban Southern California location in downtown Pasadena close to the Cal Tech campus.

Places like Phoenix are well aware of the limits of the model and are trying to create concentrated populations and lifestyle amenities in their downtowns. As one of Phoenix's leading business journalists told me, "Our lack of old buildings and authentic urban neighborhoods puts us at a huge disadvantage in attracting top talent." Commenting on the low-wage factory and office jobs that dominate its sprawling suburbs, he added: "We are like Pittsburgh or St. Louis fifty years ago, but without the world-class universities."[4] Joel Kotkin finds that the lack of lifestyle amenities is causing significant problems in attracting top creative people to places like the North Carolina Research Triangle. He quotes a major real estate developer as saying, "We got into the mindset of the 1960s and 1970s. We segregated all our uses and this contributed to the sprawl here." Adds a second, "Ask anyone where a downtown is and nobody can tell you. There's not much of a sense of place here. . . . The people I am selling space to are screaming about cultural issues." The Research Triangle lacks the "hip" urban lifestyle found in places like San Francisco, Seattle, New York and Chicago, laments a University of North Carolina researcher: "In Raleigh-Durham, we can always visit the hog farms."[5] Kotkin finds similar problems in Southern California's Orange County. "There isn't that buzz that it's cool and innovative," is the way the Milken Institute's DeVol explains it.[6]

In reality, as Kotkin points out in his book *The New Geography,* there are at least three kinds of high-tech communities. First are the classic nerdistans from Silicon Valley proper and the Research Triangle to northern Virginia. Then there are what David Brooks calls "latte towns" or what Kotkin terms the "valhallas," more rural places with plentiful outdoor amenities, such as Boulder, Colorado. Finally, there are the older urban centers whose rebirth has been fueled in part by a combination of creativity and lifestyle amenities: New York's SoHo, San Francisco's SoMa and Mission districts and Seattle's Pioneer Square, just to name a few.

Leading Creative Centers, however, provide all three options. The San Francisco Bay Area consists of a classic nerdistan (Silicon Valley), several valhallas (from the Napa Valley and Marin County south to Santa Cruz), and a creative urban center. The greater Boston area contains the Route 128 suburban complex, Cambridge, where Harvard and MIT are located, and the Back Bay, Beacon Hill and the North End. Seattle has suburban Bellevue and Redmond, beautiful mountains and country, and a series of revitalized urban neighborhoods. The Denver region combines the university and lifestyle assets of Boulder with abundant skiing and the urban character of its LoDo district. Austin includes traditional nerdistan developments to the north, lifestyle centers for cycling and outdoor activities, and a revitalizing university/downtown community centered on vibrant Sixth Street, the warehouse district and the music scene. In the Creative Age, as we have seen, options are what matter.

Back to the City

Virtually all commentators on urban America over the past fifty years had agreed on one thing: Cities had lost much of their historic economic function and were in an irreversible decline. As George Gilder once put it: "Big cities are leftover baggage from the industrial era."[7] Both companies and people were moving away from the city into the new suburban enclaves and what Joel Garreau aptly dubbed "Edge Cities."[8] But urban centers have long been crucibles for innovation and creativity. Now they are coming back. Their turnaround is driven in large measure by the attitudes and location choices of the Creative Class.

During the 1970s and 1980s when I was in college and graduate school, my professors argued that cities' technological and organizational changes had made them irrelevant as economic bases. The rise of large-scale mass production, they said, had brought about a shift in the kinds of spaces required for modern manufacturing. While early manufacturing could be accommodated in multistory buildings of the sort found in many older neighborhoods—such as in New York's SoHo or Flatiron districts—these kinds of buildings and these kinds of neighborhoods were made obsolete by the shift to large-scale factories in greenfield locations. Manufacturing was moving to giant horizontal factories in the suburbs, the Sunbelt or abroad that offered the advantages of mass production and economies of scale. People were following suit, leaving for bigger homes on bigger lots in the suburbs. Government policies helped fuel this shift by encouraging home ownership and constructing extensive freeway systems.

City leaders tried to stanch the trend by buttressing the one economic activity left in cities: building taller and denser central business districts, often increasingly filled with government or nonprofit activities. Others simply decided that some neighborhoods were beyond salvation and bulldozed them in the name of "urban renewal." The replacement of once bustling mixed-use neighborhoods with office buildings created the familiar skyscraper ghost towns—filled with workers by day but empty and dangerous at night, as the middle-class workers climbed into their cars and drove to their lives in the suburbs, leaving only the underclass in the city.

I saw these changes played out vividly in my own life. I was born in 1957 in Newark, New Jersey, the city that became the poster child for urban decay. But Newark in my youth was a wonderland for a little boy, the kind of place Philip Roth has so eloquently written about—a bustling mix of industries with a prosperous downtown and thriving multiethnic neighborhoods. I would sometimes visit my mother in the downtown office building of the *Newark Star Ledger* where she worked. On weekends, our extended family would gather at my grandmother's home in the predominantly Italian-American North Newark neighborhood and on warm nights we'd take in the professional bicycle races in Branch Brook Park. During holiday seasons, we shopped in the retail district at department stores like Bamberger's. And among the times I recall most fondly were Saturdays with my father. On some of these, he took me to Newark Public

Library, turning me loose in the stacks, where I would eventually devour volume upon volume on urban America.

Then, almost all at once, everything changed. I vividly recall one Saturday drive with my father through downtown Newark in the summer of 1967, when I was ten. The once bustling streets were barricaded, buildings in flames. Everywhere I could see police, National Guardsmen and armored vehicles brought in to quell the riots. My mother's office building in downtown Newark was transformed into a barbed-wire fortress. In subsequent years I witnessed the rise and fall of the once grand factory where my father had worked for many years, Victory Optical, which provided solid livelihoods for ethnic families in Newark and surrounding communities. For many people who grew up as I did, the decline of manufacturing and of America's great urban centers signaled the end of this country's golden age.

But the past decade has seen a dramatic turnaround in the fortunes of urban America. In the face of expert pessimism, cities are back. The 2000 Census documents the dramatic resurgence of cities from New York City to Oakland, California—the latter ranked as one of *Forbes* magazine's top twenty places for high-tech business in 2000, and among the top twenty on the Milken High-Tech Index as well.[9] Even less established places have bounced back. Jersey City, which ranked sixth on the 2000 Gay Index, grew by 5 percent. My birthplace of Newark at least stopped losing people: It has even seen the rise of a new performing arts center, downtown restaurants and a local arts scene. At the June 2000 meeting of the United States Conference of Mayors, the *New York Times* reported that "The mayors complained about too many high-skilled jobs, and not enough people to fill them; too many well-off people moving back to the city, and not enough houses for all of them, driving up prices for everyone else; and too much demand for parks and serenity, and not enough open space to offer the new city dwellers appalled by sprawl."[10]

Several forces have combined to bring people and economic activity back to urban areas. First, crime is down and cities are safer. In New York City, couples now stroll city blocks where even the hardiest urban dweller once feared to tread. Cities are cleaner. People no longer are subjected to the soot, smoke and garbage of industrial cities of the past. In Pittsburgh, people picnic in urban parks, rollerbladers and cyclists whiz along trails where trains used to roll, and water-skiers jet down the once toxic rivers.

Second, cities have become the prime location for the creative lifestyle and the new amenities that go with it. We have already seen the role that

lifestyle amenities play in attracting people and stimulating regional economic growth. In a study for the Fannie Mae Foundation and the Brookings Institution, Rebecca Sohmer and Robert Lang examined the trend of
people moving downtown in some twenty-one large American cities.[11]
Gary Gates and I compared their back-to-the-city findings to our indicators of creativity and diversity. We found that downtown revitalization is
associated with the same lifestyle factors that appeal to the Creative Class.
The Gay Index, for instance, is strongly associated with percent change in
downtown population; and both the Gay Index and the Bohemian Index
correlate with the share of a region's population living downtown. The
Composite Diversity Index is the best predictor of both the percent
change in downtown population and the percent of a region's population
living downtown.[12] We also found that thriving downtowns are associated
with vibrant high-tech industries. The Milken High-Tech Index, for instance, is positively correlated with the share of a region's population living downtown.

Third, cities are benefiting from powerful demographic shifts. With
fewer people living as married couples and more staying single longer, urban areas serve as lifestyle centers and as mating markets for single people.
Cities have also benefited from their historic role as ports of entry. Like
most cities, New York lost native-born Americans in the last census, but it
more than made up for the loss by adding nearly a million new immigrants. As we have seen, my research documents the striking statistical
correlation between ethnic diversity and high-tech industry. Immigrants,
seen not long ago as mainly a burden on city services, turn out to be one
of the keys to economic growth.

Fourth, cities have reemerged as centers of creativity and incubators of
innovation. High-tech companies and other creative endeavors continue
to sprout in urban neighborhoods that were once written off, in cities
from New York to Chicago and Boston. The 2000 *State of the Cities Report*
by the U.S. Department of Housing and Urban Development found that
cities have become centers for high-tech job growth. High-tech jobs made
up almost 10 percent of all jobs in central cities according to the report,
nearly identical to the percentage found in the suburbs. Furthermore,
high-tech job growth in cities increased by 26.7 percent between 1992 and
1997, more than three times their overall increase.[13]

Seattle illustrates the trend. Nearly half of all high-tech jobs in Seattle
are located in the city versus 35 percent in the suburbs, according to research by Paul Sommers and Daniel Carlson of the University of Washing-

ton.[14] Almost a third of all high-tech companies and jobs in the region are in the central business district, Pioneer Square and Belltown, even though Microsoft and its tens of thousands of employees are located outside the city in the suburban hamlet of Redmond. Amazon.com put its new headquarters in an abandoned hospital on the outskirts of downtown. Real Networks occupies the waterfront pier where MTV's Real World was filmed. Microsoft founder Paul Allen has acquired and restored whole districts of old industrial buildings for his new "wireless world" complex of enterprises. One of the city's leading real estate firms, Martin Smith Real Estate, has created an "urban technology campus" of buildings in and around downtown. In their study of these shifts, Sommers and Carlson found that many high-tech companies prefer the urban environment for its "vertical character, specialty shops, street life, entertainment and proximity to a great mixture of businesses and cultural activities." This is a great benefit for small companies who do not have to offer the internal amenities like restaurants or health clubs that larger companies do when they are available in the immediate neighborhood. People thrive on the thick labor markets, job opportunities and amenities there. Microsoft even runs a round-the-clock bus to take its employees who live in and around downtown Seattle to its suburban headquarters.

Fifth, the current round of urban revitalization is giving rise to serious tensions between established neighborhood residents and newer, more affluent people moving in. In an increasing number of cities, the scales have tipped from revitalization to rampant gentrification and displacement.[15] Some of these places have become unaffordable for any but the most affluent. In February 2000, the New York Times reported that even employed people making $50,0000 a year could not find affordable housing in Silicon Valley, where the average housing price was more than $410,000, and the average monthly rent for a two-bedroom apartment was $1,700.[16] More than a third of the estimated 20,000 homeless people in Santa Clara County (the heart of Silicon Valley) had full-time jobs. At the height of the technology boom, the Valley's No. 22 bus became known as "the rolling hotel" because a growing number of workers had nowhere else to sleep.[17] In their 2000 book The Hollow City, Rebecca Solnit and Susan Schwartzenberg argued that rising rents were undermining San Francisco's unique advantage as a creative center by driving out artists, musicians, small shopkeepers and people with children. "When the new economy arrived in San Francisco," they write, "it began to lay waste to the city's existing culture."[18]

San Francisco has long been a trend-setting city, and the conflict that emerged there in the summer of 2000 may be a powerful portent of things to come. That summer a powerful anti–high-tech development coalition emerged in the city's SoMa and Mission districts and quickly spread city-wide. The group that brought together artists, club owners and neighborhood residents conducted more than three dozen rallies and protests in the weeks leading up to the November 7th election, including one where a group of demonstrators smashed a computer with a baseball bat outside City Hall. In a protracted battle that ultimately came to be known as the "SoMa Wars," the coalition collected more than 30,000 signatures across the city to successfully place "Proposition L" on the ballot—a measure to ban high-tech development and other forms of gentrification from SoMa, the Mission and other largely residential neighborhoods. The measure was ultimately defeated by less than 1 percent of the vote.[19] While the technology downturn of the last few years relieved some of this pressure on urban housing markets, gentrification in major urban centers continues to threaten the diversity and creativity that have driven these cities' innovation and growth in the first place. As these pressures continue to build, the prospect of a new set of "place wars" threatens to overshadow the development and politics of leading cities across the nation.

Finally, in one of the most ironic twists in recent memory, both sprawling cities and traditional suburbs are seeking to emulate elements of urban life. Cities like Atlanta, Los Angeles, Phoenix and San Jose have all undertaken major efforts to increase density in and around their urban centers, develop downtown housing and redevelop their downtown cores. San Diego has embarked on an ambitious $2.5 billion "City of Villages" initiative to generate more compact, community-oriented development by rebuilding its older neighborhoods as pedestrian-friendly centers, where homes are close to shops, parks and public transit.[20] Under the plan, neighborhoods would get upgraded services and facilities such as parks, libraries and underground utility lines in exchange for higher-density housing development. The San Diego plan also seeks to reduce traffic congestion and sprawl by inducing people to shop and work either a short walk or bus ride from where they live. The reason: The city that ranks third on my Creativity Index wants to continue to attract creative people and is running out of buildable space. Smaller cities like Chapel Hill, North Carolina, have developed urban corridors and street-level amenities and generated thriving music scenes. In the late 1990s, Orange County, California, launched the "Eclectic Orange Festival," a six-week festival of

cutting-edge culture, music, art and performance, to counter its staid culturally conservative image.

Furthermore, many formerly buttoned-down suburbs have sought to
recreate some of the urban-style amenities that members of the Creative
Class desire by developing pedestrian-friendly town centers filled with
coffee shops, sidewalk cafes, designer merchants and renovated office lofts.
The new urbanist architect Andres Duany has worked with developers to
create new suburbs that are denser and more pedestrian-friendly and that
have town centers. My friend Don Carter of UDA Architects has worked
with cities and suburbs around the country to remake their town centers
and neighborhoods into more authentic places, and also with major corporations to transform their surplus industrial land into mixed-use new
urbanist communities.

These examples illustrate not only how far the cities have come back,
but how truly pervasive the demand for quality of place has become. Now
even the suburbs are trying to emulate aspects of the quality of place associated with larger urban centers. And they are doing so for hard-nosed
economic reasons—to attract the talented people and thus the companies
that power growth in today's economy.

The University as Creative Hub

The presence of a major research university is a huge advantage in the
Creative Economy. The Boston high-tech miracle is due in large measure
to MIT. Silicon Valley is unthinkable without Stanford University, its long-
time creative hub. Many of the places that score high on my Creativity In-
dex are home to major research universities. This includes large Creative
Centers like the San Francisco Bay Area, Austin, Boston, San Diego and the
North Carolina Research Triangle, and classic college towns like Madison,
Wisconsin; Burlington, Vermont; Boulder, Colorado; and Ann Arbor,
Michigan. But it also includes smaller regions that are not typically
thought of as leading high-tech or innovative centers, such as Gainesville,
Florida; Albany and Binghamton, New York; Little Rock, Arkansas; Birmingham, Alabama; Lafayette, Indiana; East Lansing, Michigan; and perhaps most strikingly Allentown, Pennsylvania—the region once lamented
as the center of industrial decline in the famous Billy Joel song, but where
universities like Lehigh and Lafayette have now positioned it for success in
the Creative Age. In my view, the presence of a major research university is
a basic infrastructure component of the Creative Economy—more impor-

tant than the canals, railroads and freeway systems of past epochs—and a huge potential source of competitive advantage.

The potential of the university as an engine for regional economic development has captured the fancy of business leaders, policy makers and academics—and it has led them astray. A theory of sorts has been handed down that assumes a linear pathway from university research to commercial innovation to an ever-expanding network of newly formed companies. This is a naive and mechanistic view of the university's contribution to economic development.

While the university is a key institution of the Creative Economy, what's not so widely understood is the multifaceted role that it plays. It is not there merely to crank out research projects that can be spun off into companies. To be an effective contributor to regional growth, the university must play three interrelated roles that reflect the 3T's of creative places—technology, talent and tolerance.

- *Technology:* Universities are centers for cutting-edge research in fields from software to biotechnology and important sources of new technologies and spin-off companies.
- *Talent:* Universities are amazingly effective talent attractors, and their effect is truly magnetic. By attracting eminent researchers and scientists, universities in turn attract graduate students, generate spin-off companies and encourage other companies to locate nearby in a cycle of self-reinforcing growth.
- *Tolerance:* Universities also help to create a progressive, open and tolerant people climate that helps attract and retain members of the Creative Class. Many college towns from Austin, Texas to Iowa City, Iowa have always been places where gays and other "outsiders" in those parts of the country could find a home.

In doing these things, universities help to establish the broader quality of place of the communities in which they are located.

But a university cannot do this alone. The surrounding community must have the capacity to absorb and exploit the innovation and technologies that the university generates, and also help put in place the broader lifestyle amenities and quality of place sought by Creative Class people. The university is thus a necessary but insufficient condition for generating high-tech firms and growth. The economist Michael Fogarty has found a consistent pattern in the flow of patented information from universities. Intellectual property migrates from universities in older industrial regions such as Detroit and Cleveland to high-technology regions such as the greater Boston area, the San Francisco Bay Area and New York metropolitan area. Fogarty finds that although new knowledge is generated in many places, relatively few can absorb and apply those ideas. To turn intellectual property into economic wealth, Creative Communities surrounding the universities must be able to absorb and utilize it within a social structure of creativity.

The university is only one part of this social structure. It is up to communities to put the other pieces in place: both the economic infrastructure and the quality of place to retain the talent the university has attracted. Stanford did not turn the Silicon Valley area into a high-tech powerhouse on its own; regional business leaders and venture capitalists built the local infrastructure that this kind of economy needed. Palo Alto, bordering Stanford University, functions as its hub in providing office space for startup companies, venture capitalists and high-technology service providers, as well as a wide range of amenities. The same is true in Boston. The once rundown Kendall Square area around MIT has been refurbished and renovated. Its once abandoned factories and warehouses are now home to startup companies, venture capital funds, restaurants, microbreweries, cafes and hotels. More recently, regional leaders in Austin undertook aggressive measures to create not only incubator facilities and venture capital but outdoor amenities and the quality of place that creative people demand. University and regional leaders in cities like Philadelphia, Providence and even New Haven are actively trying to generate such quality of place in and around their universities.[21]

Building a People Climate

As I tell city and regional leaders around the country, the key to success today lies in developing a world-class *people climate*. While it certainly remains important to have a solid business climate, having an effective people climate is even more essential. By this I mean a general strategy aimed at attracting and retaining people—especially, but not limited to, creative people. This entails remaining open to diversity and actively working to cultivate it, and investing in the lifestyle amenities that people really want and use often, as opposed to using financial incentives to attract companies, build professional sports stadiums or develop retail complexes. The benefits of this kind of strategy are obvious. Whereas companies—or sports teams for that matter—that get financial incentives can pull up and leave at virtually a moment's notice, investments in amenities like urban parks, for example, last for generations. Other amenities—like bike lanes or off-road trails for running, cycling, rollerblading or just walking your dog—benefit a wide swath of the population.

There is no one-size-fits-all model for a successful people climate. As we have seen, the members of the Creative Class are diverse across the dimensions of age, ethnicity and race, marital status and sexual preference. An effective people climate needs to emphasize openness and diversity, and to help reinforce low barriers to entry. Thus, it cannot be restrictive or monolithic. Truly Creative Communities appeal to many different groups.

I have yet to find an American community whose leaders and citizens have sat down and written out an explicit strategy for building a people climate. Most communities, however, do have a de facto one. If you ask most community leaders what kinds of people they'd most want to attract, they'd likely say successful married couples in their thirties and forties—people with good middle-to upper-income jobs and stable family lives. And in fact this is what many communities (particularly suburban ones) actually do by emphasizing services like good school systems, parks with plenty of amenities for children and strict (read: exclusionary) zoning for single-family housing. I certainly think it is important for cities and communities to be good for children and families, and am fully supportive of better schools and parks. But as we have seen, less than a quarter of all American households consist of traditional nuclear families. Communities that want to be economically competitive need a truly open and inclusive people climate, which can appeal to the diverse groups of people that make up both the Creative Class and American society writ large.

I have already shown the importance of attracting immigrants and bohemians and of being a place that is open to all kinds of diversity, including gays. In Chapter 14, we saw that openness to immigration is particularly important for smaller cities and regions, while the ability to attract so-called bohemians is key for larger cities and regions. What I would simply add here is that for cities and regions to attract these groups they need to develop the kinds of people climates that appeal to them and meet their needs.

Furthermore, one group that has been neglected by most communities, at least until recently, is young people. Young workers have typically been thought of as transients who contribute little to a city's bottom line. But in the Creative Age, they matter for two reasons. First, they are workhorses:

They are able to work longer and harder, and are more prone to take risks, precisely because they are young and childless. In rapidly changing industries, it's often the recent graduates who have the most up-to-date skills. This is why so many leading companies from Microsoft to Goldman Sachs and McKinsey aggressively target them in their recruiting strategies.

Second, people are staying single longer. As we have already seen, the average age of marriage for both men and women has risen some five years over the past generation. College-educated people postpone marriage longer than the national averages. Among this group, one of the fastest-growing categories is the never-been-married. In December 2001, *The Economist* coined the phrase the "Bridget Jones Economy" to reflect the importance of young singles in the resurgence of large cities across the United States and in Europe. To prosper in the Creative Age, regions have to offer a people climate that satisfies this group's social interests and lifestyle needs, as well as addressing those of other groups.

Some commentators have objected to some of my findings, and thus my economic advice, saying that they are overly oriented toward younger Creative Class people, like the Austin-bound student we saw a few chapters back. These people, my critics argue, represent only a small part of the nation's skilled workforce. Of course a spiky-haired college senior would prefer a place like Austin, which has lots of other talented young people and where many of the amenities and nightlife activities are geared to the young. But is making one's city into a playland for single twenty-somethings really a formula for economic success? Does it produce a community that is socially viable in the long run? These critics point to the fact that leading creative cities like San Francisco and Seattle have very few children.[22] And they often ask questions like: Aren't these young, single college grads eventually going to grow up, get married and develop more mature preferences? Doesn't it make more sense for cities to focus on good school systems and safe streets, which appeal to the middle-aged people who hold positions of influence and really make our economy run? I reply that of course it's important to have a people climate that is valued by older people and married couples. A successful city needs a range of options to suit all kinds of people. But an environment attractive to young Creative Class people *must* be part of the mix.

Furthermore, it is clear to me that a people climate oriented to young people is also attractive to the Creative Class more broadly. Creative Class people do not lose their lifestyle preferences as they age. They don't stop bicycling or running, for instance, just because they have children. When they put their children in child seats or jogging strollers, amenities like traffic-free bike paths become more important than ever. They also continue to value diversity and tolerance. The middle-aged and older people I speak with may no longer hang in nightspots until 4 A.M., but they enjoy stimulating, dynamic places with high levels of cultural interplay. And if they have children, that's the kind of environment they want them to grow up in. Some things that benefit young people are even supported by those old enough to be their grandparents. When a colleague of mine spoke to a group of senior citizens in Pittsburgh in the winter of 2000 about the importance of lifestyle amenities like bike paths, he got a fascinating response. The seniors liked the idea a lot, because the bike lanes would keep the cyclists off the sidewalk, where the seniors were sometimes frightened by them and even knocked down.

A woman from Minneapolis that I interviewed put the age issue in perspective. She originally came to Minneapolis as a young single because of the lifestyle it offered. She liked being able to engage in active outdoor recreation with other young singles in the city's fabulous park system and being able to walk from her house to the local nightspots. She never thought it would be a good place to have a family and raise children. But when she got married and had children, she was more than pleasantly surprised to find that many of the same lifestyle amenities she enjoyed while she was single—the parks and walkable neighborhoods—were even more attractive to her as a married person and new parent.

Furthermore, communities that appeal to diverse groups also can be very attractive to traditional middle-income families. Of course many Creative Class people with families are ethnically diverse and many others prefer that their children grow up in diverse environments. But it can go even deeper. In the summer of 2001, there was a big hubbub in Pittsburgh over a list of America's twenty-five most "child-friendly cities." The commotion was over the fact that Pittsburgh, which has always seen itself as a family town, was ranked thirteenth. Of the twelve cities that ranked above it, all ranked in the top twenty on the Creativity Index—and all but two in the top twenty on the Gay Index.

While some might see this as a contradiction (How can gay cities be family-friendly?), for me the connection is simple. Cities that offer high-quality lifestyle amenities to some groups are likely to view quality of place in general as being very important. It's analogous to companies adopting innovative customer-oriented business practices: The best companies tend

TABLE 16.1   Child-Friendly Cities Are Also Leading Creativity and Gay Regions

Rank	Region	Child-Friendly Score	Creativity Index	Gay Index Rank
1	Portland, OR	A+	16	20
2	Seattle	A+	5	8
3	Minneapolis	A	10	31
4	New York	A	9	14
5	San Francisco	A	1	1
6	Boston	A–	3	22
7	Denver	A–	13	18
8	Fort Worth[a]	B+	10	9
9	Houston	B+	7	10
10	San Diego	B+	3	3
11	Silicon Valley[b]	B	1	1
12	Dallas	B	10	9
13	Pittsburgh	B	36	48
14	St. Louis	B	31	45
15	Cleveland	B	30	43
16	Chicago	B	15	26
17	Philadelphia	B	17	33
18	Phoenix	C+	19	16
19	Los Angeles	C	12	4
20	Miami	C	29	2
21	Tampa	C	26	19
22	Washington, D.C.	C	8	13
23	Baltimore[c]	C–	8	13
24	Detroit	C–	39	46
25	Atlanta	C–	13	7

NOTE: Rankings for Creativity Index and Gay Index are out of forty-nine regions over 1 million in population.
[a]Part of region; Dallas region.
[b]San Francisco region.
[c]Washington, D.C., region.
SOURCE: Child-friendly score is from Zero Population Growth.

to get it right across the board. The best cities, like the best companies, do many things well, offering something for everybody. So now let's take a look at what some cities are doing right and what others may be doing wrong.

The Creative City: Some Examples

A host of places around the world are emerging as models of the Creative Community. In most cases, this is not the result of conscious planning but is the organic product of converging strategies. In the past several years, I have worked as consultant to many cities that are trying to become Creative Communities. Time and space preclude me from discussing all of these varied permutations and efforts, so for now let's take a closer look at two of the most successful: Austin, Texas, and Dublin, Ireland. Despite their very obvious differences, both cities do all 3T's of economic development: They have vibrant cultural and music scenes alongside rapidly growing high-tech industrial sectors. And both work hard to provide the broad creative ecosystem in which all forms of creativity can take root and thrive.

Austin City Limits

Two decades ago, Austin was not on anybody's list of high-tech places, but today it ranks second on my Creativity Index, sixth in innovation and seventh on the Creative Class. What happened? Austin worked hard to develop all 3T's of its economic development strategy and build the kind of habitat required to compete and win in the Creative Age.

It started with the first T, technology. During the 1980s and 1990s, Austin went to great lengths to bolster its technology base. It began as many places do by recruiting branches of firms from other places—IBM, Intel and Motorola to name a few.[23] The city's leadership made benchmarking visits to leading high-tech regions both to learn from their best practices and to pay visits to companies they wanted to attract. Austin also was selected as the home of two major research consortia, MCC (the Microelectronics and Computer Technology Corporation) and SEMATECH (Semiconductor Manufacturing Technology), both of them supported by the federal government and leading firms in those fields. But the effort did not stop there. Under the leadership of fabled entrepreneur George Kozmetsky and others, the region built a thriving entrepreneurial climate. It also invested heavily in the second T, talent, largely by building up the University of Texas and attracting hundreds of millions of dollars in federal and state research dollars. These efforts paid off handsomely when University of Texas undergraduate Michael Dell left school to launch the personal-computer company that bears his name.

The Austin story would not be complete without the third T, tolerance, and the fabled Austin lifestyle. Ask the average person the following question: What is the first thing you think about when you hear Austin? Most people don't answer Dell, Trilogy or any other high-tech company. Many of them mention *Austin City Limits,* a reference to the live music broadcast on public TV, or perhaps the South-by-Southwest Film and Music Festival. Alongside efforts to develop technology and tolerance, the region has also made considerable investments in its lifestyle and music scene—right down to the clubs and bars of Sixth Street. The city's downtown running trail features a bronze sculpture of a famous regional figure—the late guitarist Stevie Ray Vaughn. When one high-tech company, Vignette, expanded into a new facility in downtown Austin, a part of its deal was to establish a $1 million fund to support the local music scene.[24]

Austin is indeed an open, tolerant city where many different types of people can fit in. After a speech in Austin in the spring of 2000, a group of business and political leaders invited me to join them for "Hippie Hour" at a local club. Delighted, I replied that I was certainly ready for "Happy Hour." "It's not Happy Hour," they corrected me, "we said Hippie Hour." We ended up at the Continental Club, a ramshackle old place on South Congress Street, hanging out with a crowd of hippies, musicians, Latinos, politicians and high-tech business types—a veritable cauldron of creativity where all could let their hair down and be themselves.

Austin defines itself in contrast to the Silicon Valley-style nerdistan. Former mayor Kirk Watson was a driving force behind a powerful and progressive strategy that aims to capitalize on the convergence of technology, talent and tolerance. When we met for lunch in a downtown Austin restaurant in the spring of 2000, Watson summed it up this way: "Austin has benefited from a convergence between technology and our laid-back, progressive, creative, lifestyle and music scene. The key is that we continue to preserve the lifestyle and diversity, which enables us to lure companies and people from places like Silicon Valley." He went on to say that Austin sees itself as a wholly creative place, as opposed to just a "high-tech city"—one that has worked hard to build the kind of habitat to which creative people of all types are attracted. A key aspect of the region's development strategy is to preserve its unique cultural assets and diversity and to avoid being overwhelmed by the problems that Silicon Valley has encountered: Many people in fact have migrated to Austin to escape the Valley. Reelected in the late 1990s to a second term with a record-breaking 84 percent of the vote, Watson focused his attention on seeing that technology-based development did not destroy the cultural, lifestyle and diversity features that fueled such growth in the first place. He worked hard to ensure that traditional ethnic neighborhoods can maintain their viability and that cultural venues do not get displaced. The city's leadership and its people continue to try to create a place that blends the ability to be yourself—whoever that may be—with being part of a supportive community that is open to and tolerant of difference and equally accommodating to all forms of creativity.

Van Morrison, U2 and High-Tech

Perhaps the best example of the mix of strategies required to build a Creative Community can be found across the Atlantic Ocean in Dublin.[25] Ireland itself is an international high-tech success story envied across Europe and around the world. Less than two decades ago, Ireland had a tired economy suffering from double-digit unemployment, stagnant incomes and a brain drain of its best and brightest. Today the Irish economy is the fastest growing in the OECD, boasting a roaring technology industry and productivity levels among the highest in Europe. It is the largest exporter of packaged software in the world, having outpaced the United States in 2001. Irish companies such as Iona Technologies, SmartForce and Riverdeep are players on the global stage.

How did they do it? The Irish Miracle was premised upon the 3 T's of economic development. Under the savvy leadership of the Industrial Development Authority, the nation worked aggressively to recruit leading high-tech companies through a policy of "industrialization by invitation." Financial and tax-related incentives helped recruit high-tech giants including IBM, Lotus, Intel, Microsoft, Dell, Gateway and Oracle, who were also lured by the thick talent pool emerging from the country's world-class universities. Not content to simply recruit high-tech from abroad, the Irish government formed a body known as Enterprise Ireland to support entrepreneurship and venture capital and foster the indigenous high-tech industry. Today the Irish software industry is made up of some 900 firms, employing over 30,000 people.

By investing in its higher education system, Ireland simultaneously bolstered its ability to both generate and attract top talent. Since the 1960s, the Irish government has supported the formation of technical skills in electronics and computer-related disciplines through a system of regional technical colleges. Today, 60 percent of Ireland's university students major in engineering, science or business studies.

These more traditional economic development efforts would not have worked if Ireland did not buttress them with a major lifestyle effort. Long a conservative nation, Ireland built upon its legacy of culture, art and music to become a center for bohemian energy and an eclectic milieu of scenes, lifestyles and people. Today the streets team with a mixture of people from button-downed businessmen to geeky software developers, edgy black-garbed artists and bohemian musicians. In a remarkable fusion of history and progressiveness, Ireland has turned cities like Dublin into lifestyle centers for dynamic creative people and those who want to be around such amenities.

The first step revolved around attracting creative talent. The basic idea of recruiting technology companies and entrepreneurs was extended to the artistic and cultural creative scene of actors, writers and musicians. By offering tax breaks to culturally creative people and a high-quality place to live and work, the country has not only retained its growing legion of native celebrities, such as U2, Van Morrison and Liam Neeson, but also plays host—and home—to many international stars such as Andrew Lloyd Weber.

The second step revolved around building true quality of place grounded in history and authenticity. Dublin began by restoring its Temple Bar district, painstakingly revitalizing the same pubs where James Joyce, Bram Stoker and Samuel Beckett might have once had a pint. In the mid-1990s, Ireland used $25 million in European Union tourism funds to transform Temple Bar into an authentic cultural district. As the *New York Times* reported in October 2000, "Planners were determined not to turn the neighborhood into a Euro-Disney of faux-Georgian architecture, but to encourage innovative design."[26] In the early 1990s, Temple Bar Properties, a government-funded agency, hired a young team of innovative Dublin architects to draw up guidelines for revitalization of the thirty-six-square-block area once slated to become a city transportation depot. Temple Bar now teems with pubs, restaurants, cafes and more than a thousand units of residential housing. Today the district is hipper and more energetic than ever before. Music pulsates through the cobblestone streets from the small, eclectic bars and restaurants located along its winding roads. This winning combination of preserving the old while incorporating the new has made Temple Bar, U2, authentic Indian cuisine and Guinness as famous as the Blarney stone and the Book of Kells. It is now extending this approach to other districts throughout the city. A couple of years ago, I accompanied Pennsylvania Governor Tom Ridge and a cadre of business and political leaders on a trade mission to Ireland. When I arrived at the prim and proper Shelbourne hotel in Dublin, I was awestruck by the sight of the legendary Rolling Stone, Ron Wood, outfitted in leather rock-star regalia with a pint of Guinness in hand. "Mr. Wood lives in Dublin and typically hosts his private parties at our hotel," whispered one of the hotel's discreetly courteous staff, as they whisked me to my room.

This clever and forward-looking strategy of leveraging authentic cultural assets to attract people and spur economic revitalization is a far cry from the generic "mall" approach of chain stores, chain restaurants and chain bars that so many second-class cities waste millions of dollars seeking to pursue. The strategy has paid off. Today, some 53 percent of new immigrants are returning Irish, and 40 percent of the country's population is now under 30 years old.

Regions across the United States and the world have much to learn from the Irish Experience. By investing in the 3 T's simultaneously, Ireland was able to transform itself from an economic and technology laggard to a veritable growth machine in a very short period of time. Cities and regions need to recognize the importance of incorporating all three facets of the new economic model: technology, talent and tolerance. Without all of these factors working together, communities will be unable to become true Creative Communities and achieve the economic growth and quality of life their citizens deserve.

Why Some Places Get Trapped

I have heard countless people across the country use the same phrase to describe the inability of their city's leadership to adapt to the demands of the Creative Age: "They just don't get it." It is not that these cities do not want to grow or encourage high-tech industries. In most cases, their leaders are doing everything they think they can to spur innovation and high-tech growth. But most of the time, they either can't or won't do the things required to create an environment or habitat that is attractive to the Creative Class. They pay lip service to the need to attract talent, but continue to pour resources into underwriting big-box retailers, subsidizing downtown malls, recruiting call centers and squandering precious taxpayer dollars on extravagant stadium complexes. Or they try to create facsimiles of neighborhoods or retail districts, replacing the old and authentic with the new and generic—and in doing so drive the resident Creative Class away.

At a time when genuine political will seems difficult to muster for virtually anything, city after city across the country can generate the political capital to underwrite hundreds of millions of dollars of investment in professional sports stadiums. The ostensible economic goal of these facilities is one to which they are sublimely irrelevant. The most recent studies show that stadiums do not generate economic wealth and actually reduce local incomes.[27] And ponder, for a moment, the opportunity costs of these facilities. Imagine what could be accomplished if the hundreds of millions of dollars were spent on university research or other things that actually generate economic wealth—or even on more fine-grained neighborhood improvements and lifestyle amenities that attract and retain talented people. Not once during any of my focus groups and interviews did any member of the Creative Class mention professional sports as playing a role of any sort in their choice of where to live and work. Why are most civic leaders unable even to imagine devoting those kinds of resources or political will to pursue the things that really matter to their economic future or to people?

The answer is simple. These cities are trapped by their past. The economist Mancur Olson long ago noted that the decline of nations and regions is a product of an organizational and cultural hardening of the arteries that he called "institutional sclerosis."[28] Places that grow and prosper in one era, he argued, find it difficult, oftentimes impossible, to adopt new organizational and cultural patterns regardless of how beneficial they might be. Consequently, innovation and growth shift to new places, which can adapt to and harness these shifts for their benefit. This phenomenon, he contends, is how the United States surpassed England as the world's great economic power. It also accounts for the midcentury shift in economic activity from the old industrial cities to newer cities in the South and West. Olson's analysis presciently identified why so many cities remain trapped in the culture and attitudes of the bygone organizational age. Cities like Detroit, Cleveland and Pittsburgh were the stars of that age. The cultural and attitudinal norms that drove their success became so powerful that they have prevented the new norms and attitudes of the Creative Age from becoming generally accepted. This process stamped out much of the creative impulse, causing talented and creative people to seek out more congenial and challenging places. Their departure, in turn, removed much of the impetus for change.

In traveling to cities for my speaking engagements, I have come up with a handy metric to distinguish those cities that are part of the Creative Age from those that are not. If city leaders tell me to wear whatever I want, take me to a casually contemporary café or restaurant for dinner, and most important encourage me to talk openly about the role of diversity and gays, I am confident their city will be able to attract the Creative Class and prosper in this emerging era. If on the other hand they ask me to "please wear a business suit and a tie," take me to a private club for dinner, and ask me to "play down the stuff about bohemians and gays," I can be reasonably sure they will have a hard time making it.

Pittsburgh: The Base Case

I could use many places as examples of cultural inertia. But I think it best not to pick on someone else's town. Besides, my adopted home of Pittsburgh has inspired the research that led to this book—in a sense it is my Park Forest (the community immortalized in Whyte's *The Organization Man*), and I know it more intimately than any other place.

Despite having many of the assets required to compete and prosper in the Creative Age, Pittsburgh has found it difficult to make the necessary cultural and attitudinal changes. Trapped between a large Working Class and a traditional corporate leadership that retains a strong commitment to organization-man values, it has struggled to generate an environment and culture that appeals to the Creative Class. The members of that class, sandwiched between these two value systems, find it difficult to validate their identities in the city and so frequently move away.

I moved to Pittsburgh in 1987, recruited to be part of Carnegie Mellon's contribution to the region's economic revitalization effort, and it has been my home ever since. I immediately fell in love with the city. It reminded me of the place where I grew up, with its urban working-class feel, wonderful industrial age architecture and close-knit ethnic neighborhoods. The region had been a key driver of industrial growth in the United States, and despite its image as a steel town it was a center for innovation in a wide range of industries. As a remarkable dissertation by the former Carnegie Mellon history student Mark Samber documents, Pittsburgh at the turn of the twentieth century was an integrated high-tech industrial complex— the Silicon Valley of its day.[29] Pittsburgh financiers and entrepreneurs largely spawned the American steel industry, the aluminum industry (with Alcoa) and the modern electrical industry (with Westinghouse, whose alternating-current method of electric generation came to be the industry standard). The Mellons played the role of early venture capitalists, investing both financial and managerial resources in a wide array of technology-based high-growth companies. The region was also home to the nation's first applied research and development center, the Mellon Institute, which became a model for subsequent technology-based economic development efforts across the country, including those in Boston during the 1940s and 1950s. As late as the 1950s, the region was a world-class center for industrial R&D, with major laboratories associated with Westinghouse, U.S. Steel, Alcoa, PPG, Gulf and some forty other corporations.[30]

Pittsburgh was also home to cultural and media innovations like the nation's first major regular exhibit of contemporary art (the Carnegie International, started in 1896 and still held every four years), the first all-movie theater (J. P. Harris's Nickelodeon), one of the first two commercial radio stations in the country (KDKA, still broadcasting today) and one of the nation's original public television stations (WQED, also still broadcasting). Today, the city is home to world-class universities and tremendous research capabilities in core areas of the high-tech age, and home to a huge number of students. It has all the amenities that count in the most-livable rankings, plus plenty of potential outdoor recreation facilities: abundant urban parks and greenspace, rolling hills and three rivers. Yet the region has failed to turn these assets into a vibrant high-tech economic base and continues to lose people, ranking among the slowest-growing regions in the country over the past several decades.

What's the problem? With such a legacy and such assets, why hasn't the region been able to turn things around? Much of my research has examined this question, and much of my community activity over the past decade has been devoted to various revitalization efforts. The root of the problem is not simply economic, nor is it as many believe linked to the community's image as an aging Rustbelt city. The problem is fundamentally one of culture and attitudes. Pittsburgh people lovingly say the city is slow to follow national trends, or as the mayor often jokingly says: "Why do you want to be in Pittsburgh when the world ends? Because Pittsburgh is always ten years behind everywhere else." A successful product of the industrial and organizational age, Pittsburgh is struggling to make the cultural transition to the Creative Age. It thus exemplifies a fundamental problem that faces many other cities too. Trapped in the culture of a bygone era, it has great difficulty opening up the social space in which members of the Creative Class can validate their identities.

Consider that Pittsburgh, for many years, was the poster child for corporate America. It was a headquarters city as recently as the 1960s and 1970s, hosting the main offices of as many as twenty Fortune 500 firms—more than any other city but New York and Chicago. Over time, these large organizations literally stamped out a once glorious innovative and entrepreneurial spirit, replacing it with a conformist organizational age ethos. The following account from the late 1970s captures the change quite nicely.

The Duquesne Club [is] the exclusive gathering place of Pittsburgh's mightiest corporate leaders. The top men from U.S. Steel, Alcoa, Gulf Oil, Westinghouse and the city's other industrial giants have been coming to the club's stately dining rooms and paneled lounges since before the turn of the century. An old waiter there was talking recently about how the club has changed over the years. . . . "The men who belonged to the club in the old days were the creators," he said. "They created all these companies and all this wealth. They had an *aura* about them. When Mr. Mellon showed up at the club, all the employees would come running from the kitchen and the back rooms. They'd whisper, 'Where's Mr. Mellon? I want to get a look at Mr. Mellon.' The men we have today are maintainers, caretakers of the wealth," the old waiter went on. "They're not the same. They're more informal, friendlier maybe, a little more pleasant. . . . But," he concluded sadly, "it's just not the same."[31]

Writing in 1961 at the completion of the Pittsburgh Economic Study, the noted regional economist Benjamin Chinitz—then a professor at the University of Pittsburgh—had this to say:

My feeling is that you do not breed as many entrepreneurs per capita in families allied with steel. . . . The son of a salaried executive is less likely to be sensitive to opportunities wholly unrelated to his father's field than the son of an independent entrepreneur. . . . There is an aura of second-class citizenship attached to the small businessman in an environment dominated by big business. It manifests itself in the kinds of social clubs he can belong to, the residential areas he will comfortably fit into, the business organizations he can join, and so forth.[32]

Things have changed little in the decades since. The Duquesne Club continues to be the favored haunt of Pittsburgh's corporate class. Entrepreneurship, while on the upswing, continues to lag far behind trends in other regions and the nation as a whole.

While the corporate elite formed a sort of entitled aristocracy congregating in the same private clubs, the city's political leadership remained beholden to the increasingly aged—but still numerous and always voting—members of the old Working Class. Vast numbers of people at every level of the workforce, from factory hands and secretaries to engineers and scientists, worked for big companies. Just about everyone was somewhere on a corporate ladder. It seemed natural: It was what there was to do in life. Moreover, after the great influx of Europeans crested in the early 1900s, there was virtually no subsequent immigration. The city prided itself on ethnic diversity but defined it as having a Polish Falcons hall next to a Slovak-American Social Club, down the street from a Catholic church and a Presbyterian church. The city's culture was firmly divided into highbrow—the symphony, the museum, the stuff they made you learn about in school—and lowbrow, the Penguins and the Steelers. The corporations and the foundations funded the high culture, renovating buildings for the symphony, opera, ballet and theater.

The CEOs of the big firms also were the leadership of the nonprofit Allegheny Conference on Community Development, which in terms of urban development functioned almost as a de facto government alongside the elected one. Over the years, the Allegheny Conference spearheaded some of the nation's most massive experiments in urban renewal. Some of these, particularly in the Conference's glorious early days, were forward-looking and progressive, for instance, pioneering efforts at smoke and flood control, early initiatives to privatize key cultural institutions and transforming the city's once blighted industrial area at the downtown "Point" of the three rivers into a spectacular urban park. But others reflected the worst of slash and burn urban renewal. Often done under the auspices of the Urban Redevelopment Authority, the mayor's office and other public agencies, these experiments replaced neighborhood business districts with bland mall-style developments encircled by multilane traffic loops. Neighborhood groups have devoted great effort in recent years to countering the disastrous impacts of these mega-projects, actively working to put their communities back the way they were before public bulldozers tore them apart.

This, then, was the state of affairs that prevailed when I arrived in 1987 and that still lingers today—a culture, I might add, that remains more Babbitt than Bobo. The region's large creative community was fractured and balkanized into distinct enclaves: technological innovators here, entrepreneurs there, high cultural denizens on the one side and street-scene mavens on the other.

How much room is there, in this picture, for the rise of a unified and self-aware Creative Class? Not a lot. Compounding this, Pittsburgh's demographics resemble the ends of a barbell: the very old and the very young. The region suffers from a "missing middle" of thirty- and forty-somethings. In the economic devastation of the early 1980s, the region lost much of its up-and-coming Creative Class and failed to attract replacements. Without these people, Pittsburgh has lacked the energy, influence, attitudes and the all-important disposable income that have spurred change in other cities and regions. As one of my students put it, "Pittsburgh's problem is it doesn't have the ex-hippies that became yuppies in places like San Francisco and Seattle."[33] Translation: few influential middle-aged creative types in the Paul Allen mold. The region is split between an older population with organizational age values and a younger population with neither the influence nor the income yet to change this value system. It's not just that the city lacks the vibrancy and transformative energy that comes from committed forward-looking people who are willing to embrace new ideas and take risks. In fact, such efforts have bubbled up over the past several years. Rather, the region's command-and-control power structure continues to ignore and squelch these emerging Creative Class efforts, thus limiting their impact and damping their transformative energy.

The region's business and political leadership is not attuned to the demands of this new class. In the late 1990s, these leaders expended virtually all of their political capital, and much of the regular kind, on a billion-dollar-plus spending package for two new sports stadiums and a convention center, even after their initial proposals were soundly rejected in a popular vote. Many of them continue to think the key to success is building a corporate-centered downtown, even as company headquarters pack up and move elsewhere. They pay little attention to the region's impressive repository of historic industrial age architecture—a compelling attraction to people in the Creative Class. Both within the city and in nearby towns they continue to promote slash and burn redevelopment strategies, replacing the region's authentic architecture with generica of the sort found in suburban strip malls, even though creative people tell them that the authenticity of its neighborhoods is what attracted them here in the first place.

In the mid-1990s, large developers with the financial backing of key regional development agencies tore down virtually all of the historic Homestead Steel Works in the name of "brownfield redevelopment," making way for a giant waterfront mall that features islands of big-box retail stores amid yawning acres of parking lots. One of my Carnegie Mellon colleagues has devoted his life to saving Homestead's main street from a similar fate at the hands of a big-box retailer. When another colleague presented slides of the Homestead waterfront's "transformation" to a national group of historians and geographers, the audience let out a giant, collective gasp.

In the late 1990s, Pittsburgh's mayor and his close advisors unveiled their "Fifth and Forbes plan" to raze several blocks in the center of downtown and replace them with an urban mega-mall complete with a Nordstrom's, multiplex cinema and chain nightspots like a Hard Rock Café and a Planet Hollywood. The National Trust for Historic Preservation called the plan perhaps the worst example of urban renewal of the past forty years. The *New York Times* singled it out as "redevelopment gone too far." Creative Class people (including the Ground Zero folks mentioned earlier) were aghast, and along with historic preservationists they vigorously protested the plan, which derailed itself when the business deals behind it came apart.

Even though regional leaders tout the universities as the key to a high-tech future, the Oakland neighborhood where Carnegie Mellon and the University of Pittsburgh are located is far from a creative community on a par with those around other major universities—certainly not a draw for the Creative Class. Yet its economic importance to the region cannot be underestimated. This neighborhood is by itself the third largest employment center in the entire state of Pennsylvania, with tens of thousands of Creative Class employees and more than 35,000 students. Many of the region's fastest-growing companies and some of its bigger employers are spin-off companies from the universities, and the two biggest company-recruitment wins in recent years, the Rand Corporation and the disk-drive maker Seagate, located major facilities in Pittsburgh expressly to be close to the universities.

Despite its strategic importance, the Oakland neighborhood—which houses many historic buildings, including the Carnegie Museums and Library, and borders a wonderful urban park that was once a leading example of the City Beautiful movement—has been neglected, and a number of its historic buildings have been torn down to make way for institutional expansion. It has no movie theater, few upscale retailers and little of the typical amenities found in university districts elsewhere. A major music venue has been razed, another has been turned into a private garage for the car collection of a descendant of one of Pittsburgh's early industrial leaders, and others have simply closed their doors. Much of the residential space is substandard student housing for which slumlords charge exorbitant rents. Countless students I have spoken to say the university neighborhood is "a hole" from which they cannot wait to escape. Upon hearing that a local vagrant exposed himself to one of my top female students sitting at a university bus stop, a longtime neighborhood leader said: "Tell her to grow up and get used to urban living." Thus it should come as little surprise that college students choose to leave when they graduate.

In early 2002, the city's corporate and institutional leadership, working once again with the Allegheny Conference, unveiled its plan to revitalize the area, in part by building a suburban-style research campus between the universities. It did so with little input from students, the high-tech businesses located in the neighborhood, or the city's first-rate architectural and urban design communities. But forces have emerged recently to challenge this effort and to channel it in directions where it will benefit less affluent neighborhood residents as well as making it more attractive to students and members of the Creative Class. Only time will tell how this latest urban redevelopment effort will pan out.

City leaders continue to promote Pittsburgh as a place that is good for families (in itself a fine thing), seemingly unaware of the demographic changes that have made young people, singles, new immigrants and gays critical to the emerging social fabric. The facts speak for themselves. While the region does fairly well on the first T, technology, it ranks 113th overall on the Melting Pot Index (39th among forty-nine large regions), 141st on the Gay Index (46th out of the large regions) and 103rd on the Bohemian Index (44th among large regions). At the end of a talk I gave to the Pittsburgh Young President's Organization, one CEO raised his hand. "Excuse me, Professor," he said, "but I would not hire anyone who would come to work with tattoos, earrings and pajamas." Save for my response, his comment went unchallenged by his peers, including numerous CEOs of high-tech companies where virtually anything goes.

While the perception may be worse than the reality, the people in focus groups I have conducted feel that Pittsburgh is not open to minority groups, new immigrants or gays. Young women feel there are substantial barriers to their advancement. According to focus groups and interviews conducted by Elizabeth Currid, one of my graduate students, foreign-born students from the University of Pittsburgh report being subject to discrimination and say there "is nothing in Pittsburgh for them." Even though most of these students were enthusiastic about remaining in the United States, only one out of several dozen said she was seriously considering Pittsburgh as a place to live and work. After attending a baseball game in our new Pirates stadium, one of my Asian-born doctoral students told me he did not see one Asian face and only a few African-American ones, adding that he had "never seen so many white people in one place" in his life.

Talented members of racial and ethnic minorities as well as professional women express their desire to leave the city at a rate far greater than their white male counterparts. So do creative people from all walks of life. Case in point: "Dieselboy," aka Damian Higgins, who at age twenty-eight is one of the foremost drum and bass DJs in the world. He is a Pittsburgh native who paid his dues in the city, but then left for Philadelphia and its more dynamic dance-music scene. Thus, he joined "DJ Sine" and "Producer 1.8.7," aka Jordana Lasense, a popular dance-music producer whose releases have topped the electronic music charts, in exiting the city. Not to mention pop-culture idol Christina Aguilera, who got her start singing the national anthem at Steeler games. If audio identity is important to a city, Pittsburghers are certainly producing it, but not enough of them in Pittsburgh.

Is there hope for Pittsburgh? Of course there is. First, although the region's economy is not dynamic, neither is it the basket case it could easily have become. Figures such as overall employment rates and average per capita income compare favorably to national averages—quite an achievement for a region that lost more than 150,000 jobs in steel and heavy industry, along with several major corporate headquarters, in the manufacturing downturn of recent decades. The region absorbed the impact partly by attrition and partly by shifting to service-based industries such as education, high-tech and health care. Today the largest nongovernment employer within the city limits is not a steel or manufacturing company, but the University of Pittsburgh. Credit is due, as well, to the local high-tech sector. Though it is not one of the nation's foremost, it has grown enough to help keep the region from falling into an economic black hole, and elements of a social structure of creativity have begun to form. Twenty years ago there were no significant venture capital firms in the area; now there are many, and thriving high-tech firms like FreeMarkets and many others continue to be formed and make their mark.

There are signs of life in the social and cultural milieu as well. The region's immigrant population has begun to tick upward, fed by students and professors at the universities and employees in the medical and technology sectors. Major suburbs to the east of the city now have Hindu temples and a growing Indian-American population. The area's gay community, while not large, has become more active and visible: Pittsburgh's increasing status in the gay world is reflected in the fact that it is the "location" for Showtime's *Queer as Folk* TV series.

Many of Pittsburgh's Creative Class have proven to be relentless cultural builders. The Andy Warhol Museum and the Mattress Factory, a museum/workspace devoted to large-scale installation art, have achieved worldwide recognition. Two nonprofit art groups started as grassroots efforts over thirty years ago, Pittsburgh Filmmakers and the Manchester Craftsmen's Guild, have grown into broad-based community assets and are nationally known. Smaller visual-arts collectives like the Brew House (which originated as a squatter-artist project) have thrived, as have a multitude of small theater companies. Street-level culture has a growing foothold in Pittsburgh, too, as main street corridors in several older Working Class districts have been transformed. Along Carson Street on the South Side—a former steel-mill neighborhood once famous for having a polka named after it—galleries, theaters and cafés have sprung up amid the older stores and bars; and as one local wit has observed, this is now a place where "blue-hairs of both types converge." Similar street-level scenes are evolving elsewhere, perhaps most notably along Penn Avenue in Garfield—long one of the city's poorest neighborhoods, and predominately black. An old industrial building has been transformed into housing for "artists-in-cities," where artists receive subsidized living/work space. Community development leaders are now striving to extend these successful redevelopment efforts to include a creative economic component. One, dubbed "Cool Space Locator," works to identify space in revitalizing urban neighborhoods for high-tech companies.

Still, in Pittsburgh, as elsewhere, deep social divides remain. The edgy street-level venues in Garfield and the new upscale development on the South Side do little to address the desperate plight of a large economic underclass. And while growing numbers of Creative Class types infiltrate and gentrify low-income urban areas, huge numbers of people in all classes continue to segregate themselves distinctly into different places—and different ways of life—along income and racial lines. The 1999 State of the

Region report issued by the University Center for Social and Urban Research (UCSUR) at the University of Pittsburgh found Pittsburgh increasingly balkanized along racial and income lines. For instance, African-Americans were heavily concentrated in certain urban neighborhoods, while newer suburbs were predominantly white. Black children were three and a half times more likely to die in infancy, and over half were growing up below the poverty line.[34]

In the midst of all of this, the Creative Class is gradually beginning to make its presence felt. While Pittsburgh has a reasonably large Creative Class—some 325,000 people, making it 22nd among large regions and 53rd among all regions—in the past its ranks have been highly fragmented into separate "high-tech," "professional," "artistic" and "cultural" groups. My local focus groups highlighted this lack of connectivity time and time again. But over the past several years, connections have started to be built and things have begun to come together.

Groups like the Ground Zero collective have added to the vitality with cultural events aimed at building diversity and spurring community revitalization. The group is perhaps the first Pittsburgh effort to blur the old distinctions between different kinds of creative people and transcend the outdated bourgeois-bohemian split. While the founders of previous art groups were often classic bohemian types who interacted with the business community mainly by turning to it for foundation grants or private donations, the Ground Zero people are self-aware members of the Creative Class who see the need for fundamental change. Their members are drawn from the spectrum of the Creative Class and include architects and urban designers; product designers, software engineers and other professionals; as well as musicians, artists, performers and the like. The interpenetration of artistic, technological and economic creativity is thus growing more evident.

Political leaders are in some cases open to new models of development. Pittsburgh mayor Tom Murphy has been an ardent promoter of biking and foot trails, among other things, and Alleghany County executive Jim Roddey at one point convened a New Idea Factory to gather broad input on development strategies. The city's absolutely first-rate architecture and urban design community has become much more vocal about the need to preserve historic buildings, invest in neighborhoods and institute tough design standards. It would be very hard today (dare I say nearly impossible) to knock down historic buildings and dismember vibrant urban neighborhoods as was done in the past. As these new groups and efforts reach critical mass, the norms and attitudes that have long prevailed in the city are being challenged.

For what it's worth, I'll put my money—and a lot of my effort—into Pittsburgh making it. It's more than my Park Forest; as I sometimes like to say, it's my *base case.* If Pittsburgh, with all of its assets and its emerging human creativity, somehow can't make it in the Creative Age, I fear the future does not bode well for other older industrial communities and established cities. But for my city to flourish both culturally and economically, the members of its Creative Class will have to grow up and shoulder even more responsibility, by building a compelling vision of the future and by taking on established interests. And this is not just the case in Pittsburgh, but in communities across the United States and the world.

CHAPTER 17

The Creative Class Grows Up

History is not over.
—*Carlos Fuentes*

Class is a dirty word in America. Many commentators and political leaders like to pretend it doesn't exist and are quick to condemn anyone who even talks about class differences or uses the phrase "class consciousness." But for the Creative Class and society as a whole, a little more class awareness would be a healthy thing. It would help us to see more clearly who we are and how we stand in relation to others, and help us plan for the future more systematically.

Sweeping periods of transformation—like the one we are going through today—have always been marked by new economic classes growing and taking center stage. When the people in those classes were able to pull together as a class, they did great things. They helped their societies navigate the difficult transition into a new age, at times improving the conditions for all. The early bourgeoisie of Western Europe led the movement away from monarchy and the old feudal order. The Working Class in the late 1800s and early 1900s led efforts to win better wages and working conditions for huge numbers of people.

The members of the Creative Class today need to see that their economic function makes them the natural—indeed the only possible—leaders of twenty-first-century society. But being newly emergent, the Creative Class does not yet have the awareness of itself, *as a class,* that is needed. For the most part, Creative Class people persist in defining themselves by their differences: They are engineers or artists, boomers or X-ers, liberals or conservatives, urbanites or suburbanites. Or they think only of number one. Members of the Creative Class have been widely criticized as uninvolved and me-oriented. The journalist Paulina Borsook coined an apt term with the title of her book *Cyberselfish*—a critical study of the techno-libertarian culture of Silicon Valley, where many are deeply absorbed in their own lives and see little need for civic engagement.[1] Vast numbers of Creative Class people are concerned mainly with building their résumés, building their bodies and acquiring the status kit of our age: a stylishly renovated home with a Sub-Zero refrigerator, Viking stove and an SUV in the drive. They naively assume that if they take care of their own business, the rest of the world will take care of itself and continue to provide the environment they need to prosper. Time and again, I find such people complaining that traditional forms of organized politics or organized anything "aren't for us." This is understandable. The old forms are relics of the past age; they often leave much to be desired. But here's the catch: Unless we design *new* forms of civic involvement appropriate to our times, we will be left with a substantial void in our society and politics that will ultimately limit our ability to achieve the economic growth and rising living standards we desire.

Granted, not all members of the Creative Class are uninvolved. Many work on political campaigns, volunteer to help the disadvantaged, devote their time to environmental initiatives and so forth. Some have even taken time off from lucrative careers to work full-time on issues they deem important. But these are isolated efforts dealing largely with individual issues and causes—too diffuse to address the core issues we face as a society entering the Creative Age.

It's now time for the Creative Class to grow up. We must evolve from an amorphous group of self-directed, albeit high-achieving, individuals into a more cohesive, more responsible group. We must recognize that despite our differences, we share certain interests and concerns. Recent events make this ever more imperative. The bursting of the NASDAQ bubble and the subsequent recession were early signs that it wouldn't be clear sailing all the way to Utopia. The grisly events of September 11 drove this message home even more powerfully. Every era, every generation has its defining experience. Perhaps the terrorist attack of that day and the consequences shaped in its aftermath will be ours.

In the wake of the attack, I found myself thinking back to the world of my parents. The people of my parents' age have been called "the greatest generation" for responding, often magnificently, in times of crisis and ferment. They answered the call. My generation and my class have been answering no call but our own. We haven't taken seriously—or haven't taken seriously enough—the obligations of leadership that come with our position as the norm-setting class.

I realize I am putting a lot on the line. Not only am I informing creative people everywhere that they are now members of a new class, I am telling them to develop a corresponding class-awareness and begin to act on it. Yet I feel this presumption is justified. Creative workers already constitute a de facto class by virtue of their dominant economic role and function. This new class is also defined in part by its members' insistence on defining themselves. This is a fine and healthy thing to do—but any concept of personal identity requires a well-defined notion of how one relates to others: what one's obligations are to other people, and what one expects of them. Call it relational identity. Many people in the Creative Class, I fear, do not have any well-evolved sense of this.

The challenge before the Creative Class is a tall order. There are great obstacles in its way—perhaps the largest being the panoply of existing interests and entrenched groups. As Mancur Olson noted in his classic book *The Logic of Collective Action,* those who organize around discrete goals with sustained effort have a great advantage over those who have strong interests but are diffuse and disorganized.[2] To put it more bluntly, the stuff that gets done has organization behind it. This fact somehow seems to escape the many rugged and perhaps romantic individualists of the Creative Class. To take just one example: Many Creative Class people bemoan trends like suburban sprawl and mindless urban renewal. But these are the products of well-organized groups—developers, contractors, building-trade unions and politicians—eager to enrich themselves or to erect tangible monuments to their efforts. Countering such well-ensconced interests with their institutional power bases takes a lot more than firing off an angry letter to the editor or signing a petition.

To be effective, the Creative Class may ultimately have to invent new forms of collective action. I doubt that its members could ever form a unionlike organization (an "American Federation of Creative Workers") or a traditional political party (a "Creative Workers Party")—or that such entities would be effective. The members of the Creative Class are too disparate to be herded together in such fashion. What is required instead is a shared vision that can motivate the specific actions we choose to take. This vision must reflect the very principles of the Creative Age: that creativity is the fundamental source of economic growth, and that it is an essential part of everyone's humanity that needs to be cultivated. Such a shared vision can provide a guiding path for any new groups that form and also imbue new direction into our existing institutions and governing bodies.

The Creative Class, in my view, has three fundamental issues to address: (1) investing in creativity to ensure long-run economic growth, (2) overcoming the class divides that weaken our social fabric and threaten economic well-being, and (3) building new forms of social cohesion in a world defined by increasing diversity and beset by growing fragmentation. We can meet them only by ensuring that the creativity of the many is tapped and that the benefits of the Creative Age are extended to everyone.

Investing in Creativity

Virtually every citizen has a stake in the nation's long-term economic strength. The United States has thrived thus far by acting systematically to become the world's leading Creative Economy. For instance, we have invested heavily in research and development, maintained a strong university system, committed strongly to free expression and remained open and attractive to the world's best and most creative minds.

As a result, our economy—like all advanced economies—continues to restructure away from manufacturing and services toward higher-value-added creative sectors. The recession of 2000–2001 only seems to have accelerated this shift. According to a November 2001 report by the Employment Policy Foundation, job loss over the twelve-month period ending in September 2001 was heavily concentrated in manufacturing, which lost some 1.2 million jobs. Meanwhile, industries and jobs dominated by the Creative Class actually expanded, as 636,000 new jobs were created in managerial, technical and professional fields.[3] Long-term competitiveness lies in both increasing the creative component of manufacturing industries and continuing the shift to higher-value creative sectors.

But if we're already on the right track and taking the global lead in creativity, why worry? Because history tells us that such leads can be easily lost. As Joel Mokyr and others have shown, creativity does not enact or sustain itself; it needs to be cultivated. And if we do not keep finding more robust ways of doing this, others will.[4] Unlike traditional factors of production such as land or capital, creativity cannot be passed down from generation to generation. It has to be constantly fermented and reproduced in the firms, places and societies that use it. Furthermore, we are playing on a constantly changing field. The game of economic development isn't static: Other players see the value of cultivating creativity. Writing in 1993, Paul Romer made this forecast:

> We do not know what the next major idea about how to support ideas will be. Nor do we know where it will emerge. There are, however, two safe predictions. First, the country that takes the lead in the twenty-first century will be the one that implements an innovation that supports the production of commercially relevant ideas in the private sector. Second, new meta-ideas of this kind will be found. Only a failure of imagination, the same one that leads the man on the street to suppose that everything has already been invented, leads us to believe that all of the relevant institutions have been designed and that all of the policy levers have been found.[5]

The most crucial policy decision in my view is where we choose to invest. In the past, firms as well as governments tended to make large-scale investments in physical capital—new machines, factories, canals, roads, airports and other forms of physical infrastructure. These investments paid off in terms of increased efficiency and also generated demand and pervasive multiplier effects. Writing during the Great Depression, John Maynard Keynes argued that systematic investment of *any* sort can pay off powerfully. To drive home his point, he said only half-jokingly:

> If the Treasury were to fill old bottles with bank notes, bury them at suitable depths in disused coal mines which are then filled up with town rubbish, and leave them to private enterprise on the well-tried principles of *laissez faire* to dig them up again . . . there need be no more unemployment and, with the help of the repercussions, the real income of the community and its capital wealth also would probably become a great deal greater than it actually is.[6]

We can of course do much better than this. To do so, we need to shift both public and private funds away from investments in physical capital, toward investment in creative capital. The members of the Creative Class invest heavily in cultivating and nurturing their own creativity, recognizing what labor economists have long known: Investments in their education and skill development are the most effective and highest-return investment they can make. It is in their own and society's interest to ensure that companies, regions and the nation do the same. Research and development spending by government and industry for instance is among the highest-returning investments of any—and perhaps one of the only true investments the federal government makes. But as a nation, our total investments in R&D amount to less than 3 percent of our Gross Domestic Product, a fraction of our spending on housing, infrastructure and other physical capital.

At the regional level, the trend is even worse. States and regions across the country continue to pour countless billions into sports stadiums, convention centers, tourism-and-entertainment centers and other projects of dubious economic value. The payback would be far greater if these regions channeled only a fraction of such funds into creative capital, for example, by supporting new biotechnology and software research or by investing in the arts and cultural creativity broadly. Such investments generate substantial and ongoing returns by attracting top scientific, technical and creative talent, generating spin-off companies and attracting firms from other places. By adding to the stock of creative capital, they increase wealth and incomes substantially and generate jobs for people across the classes. As far as the stadiums are concerned, they'd be better off putting the money in a passbook savings account: Such spending actually reduces net local wealth and income.[7]

Given that creativity has emerged as the single most important source of economic growth, the best route to continued prosperity is by investing in our stock of creativity in *all* its forms, across the board. This entails more than just pumping up R&D spending or improving education, though both are important. It requires increasing investments in the multidimensional and varied forms of creativity—arts, music, culture, design and related fields—because all are linked and flourish together. It also means investing in the related infrastructures and communities that attract creative people from around the world and that broadly foment creativity.

Overcoming Class Divides

America is far from a unified society. Many commentators have noted the widening income gaps and growing stratification that define our social life. As this book has shown, our society is divided along class lines—divides that are being etched ever more deeply into the American economic landscape as a result of growing geographic segmentation. In every region across the country, cities and suburbs are increasingly balkanized into communities of haves and have-nots. The places where Creative Class people congregate offer their residents far more resources for getting ahead—from better schools to social connections. Worse yet, such divides are growing more pervasive as the classes sort themselves into different regions. The "winner-take-all" society described by Robert Frank and Philip Cooke is being replicated on a mammoth geographic scale: Either your region is a growing Creative Class Center or a laggard with large concentrations of the Working or Service Classes.[8]

The worsening divides in our society are not merely a problem of social equity; they are *economically inefficient* for the nation as a whole. If tapping human creativity is the key to economic success, then having large numbers of Working and Service Class people who don't do much creative work is tantamount to wasting a resource. We've been able to get away with it thus far, but sooner or later it will catch up with us—just as failure to tap the creativity of workers on the factory floor caught up with U.S. industrial corporations several decades ago, when Japanese firms using the methods of the creative factory overtook them. If these growing social divides are not addressed and allowed to persist, they will eventually limit our long-run economic growth and development.

Members of the Creative Class thus have an economic interest as well as a moral imperative to reduce class divides, not just through charity or government transfer payments but by tapping the creativity of the many and thus ensuring that all are integrated into the Creative Economy. The motive of human dignity is here aligned with economic motives. Employing millions of people merely to do rote work like pushing brooms, stacking boxes or stuffing circuit boards is a monstrous waste of human capabilities. Someday it may be seen to be as retrograde, both ethically and economically, as compelling humans to pick cotton on a plantation.

The Creative Class can start by offering those in the other classes a tangible vision of ways to improve their own positions, either by becoming part of the Creative Economy or by coexisting with it. The members of this new class need to work hard to ensure that our borders, both physical and cultural, remain open and that we do not waver on our commitments to diversity. They also need to commit themselves to ensuring access to full opportunity and unfettered social mobility for all, clearly acknowledging that obstacles and barriers are not only morally problematic but economically counterproductive.

As an example of how such thinking might be applied, consider the persistent problem of the so-called economic underclass. On this issue, like many issues, we're often caught up in a polarized debate that misses the essential point. Conservatives criticize the so-called "welfare state" for in-

creasing rather than alleviating poverty and insist that we cut welfare benefits and essentially force people to work, albeit mainly in low-end jobs.[9]
Liberals counter that people have little incentive to take such jobs because
they pay so little—barely enough to support an individual, let alone a family—and thus the solution is to raise the minimum wage or institute a
mandatory living wage. They also bemoan the loss of "good" manufacturing jobs that formerly afforded access to middle-income status to the less
skilled and the less educated.[10] But the economic reality, however sad, is
that most of those manufacturing jobs are gone for good. And the essential
point that's missed is this: The low-end jobs pay poorly because they are not
creative jobs. Moreover it makes no economic sense to push people into
make-work jobs that create little economic value. What makes far more
sense is to have as few of these jobs as possible, and to redirect the people
toward more creative work that adds value, pays well and is rewarding.

There is a great deal of creative potential going untapped in so-called
underclass communities. For instance, one of the poorest ghettos in Pittsburgh, the Hill District, has spawned a host of creative talents: the jazz
musicians Kenny Clarke, Stanley Turrentine and George Benson, the
Pulitzer Prize–winning playwright August Wilson and many others. DJs
and musicians in this neighborhood and others like it are busy defining
the cutting edge of electronic music—the blending of artistic and technical creativity. I sometimes like to ask my students: "Where does the music
you listen to come from?" Much of it, they eventually conclude, comes
originally from disadvantaged communities.

In the working-class community where I grew up, I saw firsthand the incredible talent and creativity of regular working people who were among
the brightest and hardest-working people I have ever come across. But I
also saw how their talents were stymied by established economic organizations and social structures. Their advice stays with me to this day: "Get an
education, get ahead, and get out." I can only imagine how much more
difficult it is for creative people growing up in truly disadvantaged neighborhoods. While it may be an extreme case, the author Barbara Ehrenreich, who spent part of a year cleaning houses and waiting tables, created
far less value working these jobs than she did using her creativity to write a
book about her experiences.[11] Not everyone can or should be a musician
or a DJ, an author or a playwright, a software developer or a product designer—but surely there are many people in such neighborhoods whose
talents can be cultivated for more creative ends than flipping burgers, assembling widgets or being a security guard.

Some people find the very notion of the Creative Class elitist. But the existence of a large and growing new class of highly paid creative workers is not the problem; rather, I submit, it is a healthy sign. What is elitist— and inequitable, inefficient and even dangerous—is the persistence of a social order in which some people are considered natural creators, while others exist to serve them, carry out their ideas and tend to their personal needs. Keeping creativity as the province of a select few is the real prescription for trouble of all sorts, from injustice to inefficiency. The good news is that creativity has been spreading broadly across our society and will continue to do so. New forms of organization that are more conducive to creativity have been evolving and taking root, from the no-collar workplace and the creative factory to emerging Creative Communities around the country. The task ahead is to build on these efforts, carrying them forward into all spheres of society. And to do so will require new forms of social cohesion in line with the new realities of our age.

Building Social Cohesion

Many have noted the general decline in social cohesion in our society. They bemoan the breakdown of the nuclear family, the decline of core institutions like churches and civic groups and a host of other signs that they say mark the end of civil society.

While such concerns are serious and legitimate, they are not necessarily harbingers of disaster. Social disruption is quite natural in periods of economic transformation. History shows that the biggest mistake is to try to forestall change or reverse it. When the nature of the economy has changed, old institutions stop working. People and social groups can't relate to each other as they once did because their economic roles are different. The strong social capital communities that Robert Putnam and his many followers advocate won't pass muster, because people work differently today and desire very different kinds of lives.[12]

One thing, however, is certain: We cannot hope to sustain a strong Creative Economy in a fractured and incoherent society. Thus our economic and social challenges are inextricably intertwined. As we have seen, diverse and open communities have compelling competitive advantages in stimulating creativity, generating innovations and increasing wealth and economic growth. The key is to create new mechanisms for building social cohesion in an era defined by diversity, high rates of mobility, weak ties and contingent commitments. Here again, we have mostly been looking in the wrong place. Groups like the Rotary Club and bowling leagues provide ways to build and measure a certain kind of social cohesion but they are not the thing itself. And what we need to build today is very different from what worked when I was growing up in the 1960s.

Strong communities, not any institutions within them, are the key to social cohesion. As group attachments break down, the community itself must be the social matrix that holds us together, much as it is now the economic matrix that matches people to opportunities and companies to people. With everything else in flux—companies, careers, even families— our communities are often the only real constants in the social equation. Being geographically rooted, they are social units that persist. Each of us lives in one, even if only temporarily. And with communities playing this central role, it behooves us to make each as strong and cohesive as it can be—while also, paradoxically, accommodating the mobility and change that define so much of our lives.

As Jane Jacobs noted long ago, communities generate social stability by mixing more permanent residents with people who come and go.[13] Those who stay for extended periods provide the continuity, while newcomers provide the diversity and interplay that generate the creative mix. In to- day's era—with more people moving more often—it is imperative for any community to attract talented people to begin with. As I've noted, Cre- ative Class people especially are very selective, and shy away from places that do not reflect their values or allow them to validate who they are. But bringing people in is only the first step. Harnessing the talents of those who want to contribute to civic life, while they are there, is another. Al- though they may stay for only a few years, many have a lot to offer. If it takes several years for them to be accepted or connected, their potential may well be lost. Thus communities need to make it easier for people of all sorts to become involved. They essentially need to complement low barri- ers to entry with low barriers to effective participation.

Communities can no longer attract and retain people simply by offering a high-paying job, an affordable place to live and a fast way to get between the two. People are more likely to personally commit to selecting and main- taining a community if it is a diverse, desirable, authentic and cohesive place to live and work. In Toronto, a thriving multidimensional Creative Center, Creative Class people from all walks of life live side-by-side with new immigrants (who are roughly half of the city's population) and less af- fluent groups with whom their children share the same schools. But true intermixing of this nature is very hard to find in the United States.

Affluent Creative Class people who move into racially, ethnically or economically diverse neighborhoods cannot simply assume that their presence automatically "revitalizes" these places. For many Working Class and Service Class residents, it doesn't. Instead, all it usually does is raise their rents and perhaps create more low-end service jobs for waiters, housecleaners and the like. While the classes may be living in close physical proximity, they do not intermix in any meaningful way. They might as well be occupying separate universes. Such neighborhoods and communities must become proving grounds for the idea that people of all types and backgrounds can truly live and work together. It needs to happen at the community level and spread from there across the nation as a whole if we are to achieve the social cohesion and economic vitality on which long-run prosperity depends.

Creativity to What End?

By now it should be clear that just triggering creativity in great salvos won't automatically solve our problems. Creativity is not an unmitigated good but a human capacity that can be applied toward many different ends. The scientific and technical creativity of the last century gave us wonderful new inventions, but also terrible new weapons. Massive, centralized experiments in new forms of economic and social life led to fiascos like the Soviet Union, while here in the United States, free-market creativity has turned out a great deal that is trivial, vulgar and wasteful.

Why, then, should promoting creativity everywhere be a main theme of our policies and our lives? Why not focus on promoting some attribute that seems to be more universally positive and beneficial—say, spiritual growth, or civility? Wouldn't that, over the long run, make us better people who can more wisely direct the creative impulse that flows so naturally? My answer is that of course, we should cultivate both of those virtues. But neither of them is an economic force that increases the resources with which we may do good in the world. Creativity is.

We must carefully consider the ends to which we direct our creativity. It is a precious asset not to be squandered trivially, and a powerful force to be harnessed and directed with careful consideration of all its possible consequences. Which brings us back to the question posed at the very outset of this book: What do we *really* want? What kind of life—and what kind of society—do we want to bequeath to coming generations?

This is not something we can leave to the vagaries of chance, to the decisions of political leaders or even to the most forward-looking public policy. Nor is it a question that the Creative Class can any longer afford to ignore—unaware of its considerable power or even its own existence. To purposefully address it we must harness all of our intelligence, our energy and most important our awareness. The task of building a truly creative society is not a game of solitaire. This game, we play as a team.

APPENDIX

Where the Numbers Come From

In retrospect, I probably could have written this book using no statistics at all. The main story that I've tried to convey here is an intensely human one that transcends numbers. It is a story about how and why we live and work as we do. Many of my arguments could have been made as convincingly just by telling stories from my field notes and letting my human subjects and observations speak for themselves.

But numbers are important for several reasons. They show the relative magnitude of various trends and effects. They can confirm (or fail to confirm) key concepts and theories as well as the initial findings of more exploratory field work. They tell you whether the inferences you make are well grounded or off the mark. And sometimes, good hard statistical analysis can do more than confirm what you already largely know: It can point you toward connections or conclusions you would not otherwise have seen.

None of these benefits accrue, however, unless the numbers themselves are sound and carefully derived. Thus I want to take some time here to explain how my research team and I arrived at the key statistics about the Creative Class and the other classes, as well as for the various regional indicators used in this book.

Counting the Classes

Estimating the size of the various classes was not easy. Nor was it easy to get a handle on the changing composition of our class structure over time. The historical data are messy and hard to compare. The existing occupational categories do not necessarily align themselves along class lines, and regional figures are often not strictly comparable to national ones. Here is how my research team and I tackled the issues.

Occupations and Classes

Since the classes are defined on the basis of occupation, we used occupational data to determine their composition. The best source for this kind of data is the

U.S. Bureau of Labor Statistics, and we used several of their datasets. A big issue here, as anyone who has looked through the BLS or Census workforce data can attest, is that the basic categories tend to change frequently.

The most current system of occupational classifications was introduced by the U.S. government in 1998. This, the 1998 Standard Occupation Classification (SOC) System, is the most up-to-date system available and is compatible with the new North America Industrial Classification System or NAICS. This system is a good bit more detailed than previous classification systems, including hundreds of occupations and tens of thousands of job titles. It contains many new occupations, such as those in information technology fields, and more fine-grained classifications for traditional occupations.

Defining the Classes

The major occupational categories included in the definitions of the major classes are as follows.

Creative Class: The Creative Class has two major sub-components: a Super-Creative Core and creative professionals.

Super-Creative Core
- Computer and mathematical occupations
- Architecture and engineering occupations
- Life, physical, and social science occupations
- Education, training, and library occupations
- Arts, design, entertainment, sports, and media occupations

Creative Professionals
- Management occupations
- Business and financial operations occupations
- Legal occupations
- Healthcare practitioners and technical occupations
- High-end sales and sales management

Working Class:

- Construction and extraction occupations
- Installation, maintenance, and repair occupations
- Production occupations
- Transportation and material moving occupations

Service Class: The Service Class is composed of the following major occupational categories:

- Health care support occupations
- Food preparation and food-service-related occupations
- Building and grounds cleaning and maintenance occupations
- Personal care and service occupations
- Low-end sales and related occupations
- Office and administrative support occupations
- Community and social services occupations
- Protective service occupations

Agriculture:

- Farming, fishing, and forestry occupations

Major Data Sources

The data for the historical and regional analyses come from three major sources.

Current (1999) Data and Regional Comparisons

The data for 1999 and for the regional comparisons are from the U.S. Bureau of Labor Statistics, Occupational Employment Survey (OES) for 1999. These are based on the 1998 Standard Occupational Classification System and were taken from the BLS website. These data provide the most detailed occupational breakdown currently available. They also allow for analysis at the regional or metropolitan-area level. We compared the OES data to the current BLS *Employment and Earnings* data and found them to be quite similar (see Appendix Table 1).

Historical Estimates

The historical estimates are from two sources. The data for the period 1900–1960 are from the U.S. Bureau of the Census, *Historical Statistics of the United States, Colonial Times to 1970* (1976). *The Historical Statistics* (Series D 233-682) reports the occupations of "economically active" (employed) people for ten-year periods from 1900 to 1970 and is based on payroll records from employers reported to the BLS. These data are adjusted according to 1970 benchmarks, using the 1950, 1960 and 1970 "standard occupation classification (SOC)" systems. The figures for 1970–1991 are from the U.S. Bureau of Labor Statistics, *Employment and Earnings* as reported in the U.S. Bureau of the Census, *Statistical Abstract of the United States* for various years. These are based on data collected in the U.S. Bureau of the Census, *Current Population Survey* (CPS) that reports the "experienced civilian labor force, by sex and occupation."

APPENDIX TABLE 1   Counting the Classes, 1999

Share	Employees (OES data)	Percent Share	Employees (Emp. & Earnings data)	Percent Share
Creative Class	38,278,110	30.0%	38,453,000	28.8%
Super-Creative Core	14,932,420	11.7	14,133,000	10.6
Other Creative Class	23,345,690	18.3	24,320,000	18.2
Working Class	33,238,810	26.1	32,760,000	24.5
Service Class	55,293,720	43.4	58,837,000	44.1
Agriculture	463,360	0.4	3,426,000	2.6
Total	127,274,000		133,488,000	

NOTE: The 1999 *Employment and Earnings* data add to slightly less than the total because some occupations are not listed. The OES data omits agricultural workers, so only those in agriculturally related employment are included.

SOURCES: U.S. Bureau of the Census, *Statistical Abstract of the United States: 2000,* Washington, D.C., 2000, Table 669; U.S. Bureau of Labor Statistics, Occupation and Employment Statistics, 1999, available on-line.

Historical Comparability and Matching

My team and I have worked to ensure the comparability of the different data sources. It should come as little surprise that there are significant differences in the way occupations have been classified over the course of a century. For instance, the figures for 1970 and earlier used adjusted versions of the 1970 classification system, whereas those for 1980 and 1991 use the 1980 system, which the BLS notes is "radically different from the 1970 census system"(as cited in *Labor Force, Employment, and Earnings,* 1992, p. 379). The 1999 (as well as the regional) data is based on the 1998 classification system, which according to the BLS is also "not directly comparable with earlier years" (from the BLS/OES website FAQ).

Furthermore the ultimate sources of the data also differ over time. The *Historical Statistics* are based on employer payroll records, so only employed people are included. These data do not include self-employed people, owners and partners in unincorporated firms, household workers and unpaid family workers. While these data do cover only non-agricultural establishments, workers in agricultural, forestry or fishing occupations who work for non-agricultural establishments are included. *Employment and Earnings* data are from the Current Population Survey and include self-employed people, owners and partners in unincorporated firms, household workers and unpaid family workers.

To account for these differences, my team and I scrutinized the occupational-level data in order to reconcile them to the baseline 1998 classification system. Both the *Historical Statistics* and *Employment and Earnings* data were examined and matched against the detailed occupational categories. The matching was done along two lines. Whenever possible, major categories were matched to one another. For example, the Service Class includes "clerical and kindred workers" from the *Historical Statistics,* "clerical and kindred workers" from the 1970 and 1980 *Employment and Earnings,* and "administrative support, including clerical" from the 1991 and 1999 *Employment and Earnings.* In other cases, where the fit was less obvious, we examined and matched individual occupational categories. For example, the Super-Creative Core includes "engineers, technical" from the *Historical Statistics,* "engineers" from the 1970 and 1980 *Employment and Earnings,* and "engineers" from the 1991 and 1999 *Employment and Earnings.* In all cases, we were conservative in allocating occupations to the Creative Class. For instance, while sales professionals are included in the government definition of "professional and technical workers," we included only high-end sales professionals in the Creative Class. For 1970 and afterward, we included only executive-level managers (i.e., "Executive, administrative, and managerial") in our accounting, while the remaining management occupations were included in the Service Class.

Every occupation listed in the *Historical Statistics* and *Employment and Earnings* was matched to the 1998 baseline classifications. The figures were then totaled to give a consistent count of the number of people within each occupational category and class across all years and data sources. Two members of my research team and I verified all matching. Appendix Table 2 summarizes the historical estimates for the major classes.

Comparing Regions

Regional comparison is a big part of this book. The regional data are based on the 1999 BLS OES data that provide detail at the regional level. My team and I used these data to identify the class composition of more than 200 "metropolitan statistical areas" (MSAs) across the United States. Appendix Table 3 compares the regional totals to the national ones. According to these data, 81 percent of the workforce is located in MSAs, 103 million of 127 million total workers. Of this figure, approximately 1.5 million employees that work in MSAs are not counted because of disclosure restrictions. The figures for each of the major classes conform to this trend, with between 78 and 82 percent of their members located in MSAs. Not surprisingly, a considerably lower share of agricultural workers are located in MSAs.

Regional Indicators

The regional analysis in this book is also based on a series of technical indicators, many of which my team and I developed in the course of this project. The following provides brief descriptions.

APPENDIX TABLE 2   Historical Estimates for Various Classes, 1990-1999

	Creative Class	Super-Creative Core	Working Class	Service Class	Agriculture	Total Workforce
1900	2,900	709	10,402	4,839	10,889	29,030
	10.0%	2.4%	35.8%	16.7%	37.5%	
1910	4,130	1,021	14,234	7,388	11,536	37,291
	11.1%	2.7%	38.2%	19.8%	30.9%	
1920	4,945	1,279	16,974	8,885	11,396	42,206
	11.7%	3.0%	40.2%	21.1%	27.0%	
1930	6,789	1,847	19,272	12,290	10,333	48,686
	13.9%	3.8%	39.6%	25.2%	21.2%	
1940	7,326	2,059	20,596	14,796	9,020	51,742
	14.2%	4.0%	39.8%	28.6%	17.4%	
1950	9,767	2,584	24,265	17,973	6,994	58,999
	16.6%	4.4%	41.1%	30.5%	11.9%	
1960	12,187	3,680	25,617	22,614	4,134	67,990
	17.9%	5.4%	37.7%	33.3%	6.1%	
1970	15,724	6,007	28,616	30,955	2,450	79,802
	19.8%	7.5%	35.9%	38.8%	3.1%	
1980	18,215	7,963	30,779	44,938	2,703	97,270
	18.7%	8.2%	31.7%	46.2%	2.8%	
1991	29,670	10,691	30,334	53,391	3,459	116,877
	25.4%	9.2%	26.0%	45.7%	3.0%	
1999	38,278	14,932	33,238	55,293	463	127,274
	30.1%	11.7%	26.1%	43.4%	0.4%	

NOTE: All data are in thousands. The top number in each row is the total number of workers in the class, while the bottom line is the percent share of the total. Percentages may not add to 100 due to unreported occupations.

SOURCES: For 1900–1960, U.S. Bureau of the Census, *Historical Statistics of the United States, Colonial Times* to 1970, Series D 233–682, New York: Basic Books, 1976. For 1970–1990, U.S. Bureau of the Census, *Statistical Abstract of the United States.* Washington, D.C., various years, Table Nos. 602, 675, and 629. For 1999, U.S. Bureau of Labor Statistics, Occupation and Employment Statistics, 1999, available on-line.

High-Tech Index: The basic measure for high-technology industry, the High-Tech Index, is a widely used measure developed by Ross DeVol and his colleagues at the Milken Institute. The measure was initially presented in the Milken Institute study *America's High Tech Economy,* and the Milken Institute researchers graciously made the data available for the period 1978–2000. The High-Tech Index ranks metropolitan areas based on a combination of two factors: (1) its high-tech industrial output as a percentage of total U.S. high-tech industrial output; and (2)

Appendix Table 3   Regional versus National Data for the Major Classes, 1999

Class	National Total	Percent Share	MSA Total	Percent Share	MSA Share of Total
Creative Class	38,278,110	30.0%	31,388,880	30.2%	82.0%
Super-Creative Core	14,932,420	11.7	11,752,240	11.3	78.7
Working Class	33,238,810	26.1	26,072,640	25.1	78.4
Service Class	55,293,720	43.4	45,920,660	44.3	83.0
Agriculture	463,360	0.36	272,440	0.26	58.7
Total	127,274,000		103,654, 560		81.4

NOTE: MSA refers to Metropolitan Statistical Area.

SOURCE: U.S. Bureau of Labor Statistics, Occupation and Employment Statistics, 1999, available on-line.

the percentage of the region's own total economic output that comes from high-tech industries compared to the nationwide percentage. According to the Milken Institute researchers, the former favors large metropolitan areas, while the second favors smaller regions with large technology sectors. By combining them, the High-Tech Index creates a less biased measure.

Innovation Index: The Innovation Index is a measure of patented innovations per capita. It covers the calendar year 1999 and is based on data from the U.S. Patent and Trademark Office.

Gay Index: This index is based on research by Gary Gates, now at the Urban Institute in Washington, D.C., along with Dan Black, Seth Sanders, and Lowell Taylor. The Gay Index is essentially a measure of the over- or under-representation of coupled gay people in a region relative to the United States as a whole. The fraction of all such U.S. gay people who live in a given metropolitan area is divided by the fraction of the total U.S. population who live in that area. The resulting number is a ratio: a value over 1.0 says that a region has a greater-than-average share of gay couples, while a value below 1.0 suggests that gays are under-represented. The Gay Index has been calculated for major metro areas across the United States in 1990 and 2000, and is based on the decennial U.S. Census.

Bohemian Index: Calculated in the same fashion as the Gay Index, the Bohemian Index is a measure of artistically creative people. It includes authors, designers, musicians, composers, actors, directors, painters, sculptors, artist printmakers, photographers, dancers, artists, and performers. It is based on the 1990 U.S. Decennial Census Public Use Microdata Sample.

Talent Index: This is a measure of the human capital in a region, based on a region's share of people with a bachelor's degree and above. It is based on the 1990 U.S. Decennial Census Public Use Microdata Sample.

Melting Pot Index: This index measures the relative percentage of foreign-born people in a region. It is also based on the 1990 U.S. Decennial Census Public Use Microdata Sample.

Composite Diversity Index: This composite measure combines the Gay Index, Bohemian Index and Melting Pot Index.

Creativity Index: This a composite measure that is based on four indices for the most current year available: the Innovation Index (1999), High-Tech Index (2000), Gay Index (2000) and the Creative Class (1999)

APPENDIX TABLE 4 Class Structure for Small and Medium-Sized Regions, 1999

Rank[a]	Region	Overall Rank[b]	Creative Class Share	Employment	Super-Creative Core Share	Employment	Working Class Share	Employment	Service Class Share	Employment	Total Employment
					Regions with 500,000 to 1 million people						
1	Albany, NY	15	33.70%	149,250	15.20%	67,540	18.50%	82,000	47.80%	211,730	443,250
2	Albuquerque, NM	26	32.20%	104,150	12.80%	41,250	21.50%	69,580	46.20%	149,300	323,150
3	Columbia, SC	33	31.90%	87,350	10.90%	29,820	20.90%	57,160	47.10%	129,000	273,860
4	Omaha, NE-IA	43	30.80%	121,700	11.50%	45,430	22.90%	90,260	46.30%	182,540	394,500
5	Little Rock, AR	44	30.80%	93,890	8.40%	25,620	24.50%	74,640	44.80%	136,510	305,040
6	Birmingham, AL	47	30.70%	141,190	9.50%	43,860	28.80%	132,570	40.40%	186,040	460,070
7	Baton Rouge, LA	48	30.70%	90,910	12.60%	37,480	25.90%	76,760	43.30%	128,530	296,530
8	Richmond, VA	56	30.10%	160,270	10.60%	56,310	25.90%	137,430	44.00%	233,880	531,580
9	Dayton, OH	59	30.10%	131,680	12.10%	52,830	29.10%	127,580	40.80%	178,650	438,110
10	Colorado Springs, CO	60	29.90%	66,430	14.20%	31,400	21.50%	47,770	48.50%	107,530	221,880
11	Harrisburg, PA	62	29.80%	101,040	10.70%	36,150	25.60%	86,800	44.60%	151,400	339,240
12	Syracuse, NY	63	29.80%	108,200	13.50%	49,090	25.10%	91,410	45.10%	163,870	363,480
13	Charleston, SC	64	29.70%	68,350	10.90%	25,080	25.40%	58,480	44.70%	102,910	229,990
14	Springfield, MA	65	29.70%	74,070	11.90%	29,560	25.80%	64,330	44.50%	110,880	249,280
15	Allentown, PA	88	28.70%	72,630	9.20%	23,280	28.10%	70,940	43.20%	109,180	252,840
16	Tulsa, OK	90	28.70%	112,700	9.20%	36,040	29.30%	114,920	42.00%	164,790	392,500
17	Tucson, AZ	96	28.40%	89,680	11.70%	36,910	20.60%	64,920	50.80%	160,480	315,710
18	Bakersfield, CA	115	27.80%	58,410	12.60%	26,370	23.70%	49,690	36.00%	75,710	210,030
19	McAllen, TX	117	27.80%	41,000	13.20%	19,440	23.50%	34,640	46.30%	68,310	147,570

(continues)

APPENDIX TABLE 4 (*continued*)

Rank^a	Region	Overall Rank^b	Creative Class Share	Creative Class Employment	Super-Creative Core Share	Super-Creative Core Employment	Working Class Share	Working Class Employment	Service Class Share	Service Class Employment	Total Employment
20	Mobile, AL	126	27.40%	59,200	8.40%	18,170	30.20%	65,410	42.30%	91,570	216,400
21	Honolulu, HI	130	27.20%	101,800	10.10%	37,880	19.00%	71,100	53.70%	200,670	373,990
22	Toledo, OH	132	27.10%	85,300	8.50%	26,820	29.40%	92,270	43.40%	136,440	314,290
23	El Paso, TX	134	27.00%	65,250	11.60%	28,140	31.00%	75,040	41.90%	101,280	241,690
24	Knoxville, TN	140	26.70%	81,570	7.90%	24,130	29.30%	89,350	44.00%	134,120	305,090
25	Wichita, KS	145	26.60%	73,470	10.30%	28,300	32.30%	89,080	41.00%	113,050	275,800
26	Fort Wayne, IN	171	25.40%	67,420	9.00%	23,900	38.20%	101,370	36.30%	96,410	265,610
27	Fresno, CA	176	25.10%	83,050	10.00%	33,030	20.70%	68,380	42.50%	140,490	330,450
28	Scranton, PA	186	24.70%	65,760	8.20%	21,780	32.00%	85,100	43.20%	114,940	265,800
29	Greenville, SC	193	24.50%	119,090	8.70%	42,420	39.50%	191,710	35.90%	174,350	485,500
30	Sarasota, FL	199	24.10%	62,530	6.60%	17,100	24.40%	63,160	51.50%	133,480	259,170
31	Stockton, CA	200	24.10%	41,300	9.40%	16,150	27.80%	47,670	43.60%	74,770	171,310
32	Youngstown, OH	203	23.80%	57,010	8.10%	19,370	34.90%	83,560	41.20%	98,610	239,180
	Regions with 250,000 to 500,000 people										
1	Melbourne, FL	8	35.5%	57,920	16.3%	26,640	21.0%	34,320	43.5%	70,950	163,250
2	Huntsville, AL	9	35.3%	60,380	17.4%	29,660	27.0%	46,070	37.6%	64,310	170,870
3	Boise City, ID	11	35.2%	75,940	14.4%	30,940	24.1%	51,890	40.5%	87,230	215,530
4	Lansing, MI	13	34.3%	68,450	16.5%	32,920	18.7%	37,230	46.9%	93,590	199,560
5	Provo, UT	18	33.0%	44,620	15.9%	21,470	22.4%	30,270	44.2%	59,890	135,370
6	Madison, WI	19	32.8%	74,500	12.7%	28,880	22.5%	51,220	44.6%	101,370	227,330
7	Jackson, MS	21	32.5%	73,290	10.6%	23,840	22.6%	50,880	44.7%	100,700	225,240
8	Des Moines, IA	31	32.1%	96,550	9.4%	28,360	20.6%	61,890	47.1%	141,520	300,720
9	Pensacola, FL	35	31.5%	46,480	11.0%	16,200	23.5%	34,650	44.8%	66,180	147,570

10	Tallahassee, FL	37	31.3%	39,400	13.9%	17,540	15.6%	19,630	53.1%	66,900	126,040
11	Montgomery, AL	38	31.2%	44,190	9.7%	13,770	21.4%	30,320	47.4%	67,030	141,540
12	Binghamton, NY	45	30.8%	36,770	15.9%	19,040	21.4%	25,530	47.8%	57,110	119,560
13	Spokane, WA	54	30.2%	53,540	11.0%	19,520	26.1%	46,260	43.6%	77,250	177,180
14	Corpus Christi, TX	58	30.1%	47,580	12.0%	19,020	23.0%	36,340	46.9%	73,990	157,910
15	Lincoln, NE	66	29.7%	41,410	9.9%	13,750	25.4%	35,470	44.9%	62,530	139,410
16	Macon, GA	81	29.0%	44,800	10.2%	15,690	22.3%	34,410	48.8%	75,360	154,570
17	Fayetteville, NC	82	29.0%	29,330	10.9%	11,060	20.9%	21,150	50.1%	50,770	101,290
18	Charleston, WV	98	28.4%	36,410	9.2%	11,860	26.3%	33,780	45.3%	58,160	128,350
19	Santa Barbara, CA	100	28.3%	44,750	12.5%	19,760	17.3%	27,310	50.2%	79,320	157,880
20	Huntington, WV	102	28.3%	29,460	8.3%	8,620	24.3%	25,320	47.3%	49,250	104,100
21	Fort Collins, CO	103	28.2%	31,140	12.4%	13,700	23.9%	26,390	47.7%	52,590	110,260
22	South Bend, IN	105	28.2%	33,720	10.8%	12,900	30.6%	36,610	41.2%	49,210	119,540
23	New London, CT–RI	107	28.1%	29,160	12.2%	12,640	22.1%	22,960	49.6%	51,530	103,810
24	Utica–Rome, NY	113	27.9%	35,440	13.1%	16,680	19.6%	24,880	52.6%	66,870	127,230
25	Brownsville, TX	114	27.8%	26,820	13.3%	12,770	22.6%	21,790	49.4%	47,630	96,370
26	Beaumont, TX	116	27.8%	42,070	10.6%	16,080	29.9%	45,300	42.3%	64,030	151,400
27	Eugene, OR	131	27.2%	34,950	10.0%	12,910	27.8%	35,810	44.3%	56,930	128,610
28	Lexington, KY	133	27.0%	68,900	10.4%	26,500	28.3%	72,200	43.7%	111,370	254,950
29	Anchorage, AK	135	27.0%	30,690	6.4%	7,330	23.4%	26,590	49.7%	56,540	113,820
30	Daytona Beach, FL	136	27.0%	39,370	9.8%	14,270	20.3%	29,690	52.5%	76,700	146,070
31	Erie, PA	143	26.7%	31,210	9.1%	10,660	29.2%	34,150	44.1%	51,630	117,040
32	Augusta, GA–SC	144	26.7%	48,550	9.8%	17,930	25.8%	46,890	47.4%	86,340	182,070
33	Chattanooga, TN–GA	146	26.6%	54,340	8.5%	17,280	30.9%	63,080	42.3%	86,430	204,180
34	Fort Pierce, FL	147	26.6%	25,250	8.4%	7,990	17.9%	16,970	53.4%	50,690	94,970
35	Peoria, IL	148	26.6%	44,420	8.2%	13,640	25.3%	42,340	47.9%	80,060	167,150
36	Fort Myers, FL	151	26.4%	42,330	7.6%	12,220	21.5%	34,450	52.0%	83,310	160,090

(continues)

APPENDIX TABLE 4 — (continued)

Rank[a]	Region	Overall Rank[b]	Creative Class		Super-Creative Core		Working Class		Service Class		Total Employment
			Share	Employment	Share	Employment	Share	Employment	Share	Employment	
37	Rockford, IL	153	26.4%	44,270	8.6%	14,430	32.4%	54,350	41.1%	68,930	167,550
38	Canton, OH	154	26.4%	42,630	8.7%	14,040	31.3%	50,500	42.3%	68,380	161,510
39	Springfield, MO	156	26.4%	38,360	7.6%	11,000	28.1%	40,890	45.4%	66,120	145,520
40	Biloxi, MS	161	26.1%	37,330	10.8%	15,480	29.8%	42,600	44.2%	63,250	143,180
41	Savannah, GA	163	26.0%	35,110	8.5%	11,490	21.3%	28,700	52.7%	71,110	135,020
42	Evansville, IN–KY	174	25.3%	35,100	8.1%	11,280	33.1%	45,920	41.6%	57,770	138,900
43	Columbus, GA–AL	178	25.1%	30,180	9.7%	11,660	26.9%	32,360	48.0%	57,800	120,400
44	Davenport, IA–IL	180	25.0%	44,680	7.8%	14,000	26.9%	47,970	48.0%	85,660	178,540
45	Kalamazoo, MI	182	25.0%	52,080	9.8%	20,460	33.3%	69,370	41.7%	86,930	208,520
46	Appleton, WI	185	24.7%	45,320	9.1%	16,650	35.5%	65,020	39.6%	72,620	183,170
47	Killeen, TX	189	24.6%	21,660	12.9%	11,330	21.9%	19,260	53.5%	47,120	88,040
48	Saginaw, MI	194	24.5%	38,160	9.2%	14,340	29.8%	46,460	45.6%	70,980	155,780
49	Johnson City, TN–VA	195	24.5%	42,460	8.8%	15,290	34.9%	60,440	40.6%	70,330	173,400
50	Modesto, CA	198	24.2%	36,290	9.1%	13,720	27.8%	41,730	41.1%	61,740	150,160
51	Reading, PA	206	23.7%	37,080	8.0%	12,590	36.1%	56,590	40.1%	62,800	156,610
52	Visalia, CA	222	22.9%	25,770	9.8%	10,970	22.5%	25,350	36.6%	41,200	112,420
53	Lancaster, PA	226	22.7%	47,510	7.2%	14,990	34.5%	72,120	42.5%	88,960	209,130
54	York, PA	232	22.3%	34,970	7.2%	11,290	39.3%	61,500	38.3%	59,950	156,500
55	Shreveport, LA	234	22.1%	32,560	2.1%	3,120	26.1%	38,420	51.7%	76,150	147,410
56	Reno, NV	240	21.2%	35,990	5.8%	9,860	26.0%	44,070	52.8%	89,590	169,650
57	Lafayette, LA	242	21.1%	30,320	2.5%	3,570	32.6%	46,880	46.0%	66,230	143,870
58	Fayetteville, AR	243	21.1%	30,820	7.6%	11,060	37.2%	54,480	41.7%	61,020	146,320
59	Lakeland, FL	245	20.9%	33,280	4.6%	7,240	32.5%	51,690	45.0%	71,600	159,020
60	Salinas, CA	247	20.6%	29,950	8.0%	11,570	17.7%	25,670	46.3%	67,210	145,270

61	Hickory, NC	19.4%	35,870	6.0%	11,140	47.2%	87,310	33.2%	61,370	184,810
62	Naples, FL	19.1%	15,890	2.1%	1,740	23.7%	19,710	57.3%	47,690	83,290
63	Ocala, FL	16.4%	9,620	3.7%	2,150	31.9%	18,730	50.9%	29,820	58,630

Regions with less than 250,000 people

1	Bloomington, IL	39.9%	32,240	13.3%	10,750	18.1%	14,600	42.1%	34,010	80,850
2	Gainesville, FL	39.2%	44,990	20.9%	24,020	13.5%	15,460	47.1%	54,100	114,750
3	Bryan, TX	38.4%	25,840	22.1%	14,890	14.9%	10,030	46.6%	31,410	67,360
4	Santa Fe, NM	35.3%	20,810	12.5%	7,390	17.8%	10,480	46.9%	27,670	58,960
5	Springfield, IL	32.5%	30,320	11.9%	11,140	16.9%	15,770	50.6%	47,290	93,380
6	Portland, ME	32.2%	47,480	10.8%	15,870	20.2%	29,780	47.6%	70,280	147,540
7	Lafayette, IN	31.4%	23,480	15.7%	11,710	27.0%	20,140	41.6%	31,080	74,700
8	Sherman, TX	31.1%	11,780	11.6%	4,370	28.1%	10,640	40.7%	15,410	37,830
9	Monroe, LA	31.0%	19,350	8.4%	5,240	24.2%	15,090	44.7%	27,850	62,320
10	Las Cruces, NM	30.4%	14,280	16.4%	7,720	20.8%	9,750	45.5%	21,360	46,970
11	Charlottesville, VA	30.3%	18,950	14.7%	9,160	23.4%	14,610	46.2%	28,880	62,490
12	Muncie, IN	30.3%	14,830	10.1%	4,930	25.4%	12,410	44.3%	21,690	48,930
13	Cedar Rapids, IA	29.8%	33,910	11.3%	12,920	27.1%	30,810	43.0%	48,930	113,850
14	Bangor, ME	29.7%	14,110	8.9%	4,220	18.7%	8,910	51.4%	24,430	47,540
15	Tyler, TX	29.3%	21,780	8.7%	6,490	24.4%	18,130	45.6%	33,940	74,440
16	Dover, DE	29.2%	11,770	11.1%	4,470	21.4%	8,620	49.3%	19,860	40,250
17	La Crosse, WI–MN	29.2%	17,890	11.1%	6,800	21.9%	13,390	48.8%	29,910	61,240
18	Wilmington, NC	29.2%	30,290	9.8%	10,160	22.4%	23,290	48.3%	50,150	103,830
19	Richland, WA	29.1%	18,200	14.2%	8,890	23.8%	14,920	46.1%	28,860	62,560
20	San Angelo, TX	28.8%	10,740	10.1%	3,780	19.2%	7,150	51.8%	19,320	37,310
21	Great Falls, MT	28.8%	9,160	7.6%	2,410	20.4%	6,500	50.5%	16,080	31,830
22	Wheeling, WV–OH	28.7%	15,550	5.3%	2,840	21.6%	11,660	49.7%	26,880	54,090

(continues)

APPENDIX TABLE 4 (continued)

Rank^a	Region	Overall Rank^b	Creative Class Share	Creative Class Employment	Super-Creative Core Share	Super-Creative Core Employment	Working Class Share	Working Class Employment	Service Class Share	Service Class Employment	Total Employment
23	Bismarck, ND	89	28.7%	14,350	10.5%	5,230	18.7%	9,340	52.6%	26,280	49,970
24	Eau Claire, WI	91	28.7%	19,680	8.4%	5,750	24.1%	16,550	47.2%	32,450	68,680
25	Asheville, NC	93	28.5%	29,420	8.5%	8,730	25.9%	26,720	45.5%	46,930	103,100
26	Topeka, KS	94	28.4%	24,210	3.5%	2,940	25.0%	21,250	46.6%	39,710	85,170
27	Redding, CA	95	28.4%	15,300	13.0%	7,010	23.8%	12,830	47.7%	25,700	53,830
28	Chico, CA	101	28.3%	18,350	11.0%	7,100	17.6%	11,410	52.3%	33,900	64,760
29	Duluth, MN–WI	104	28.2%	28,230	10.3%	10,280	24.1%	24,140	47.4%	47,380	100,050
30	Lawrence, KS	106	28.2%	9,730	10.5%	3,640	22.1%	7,630	49.7%	17,160	34,520
31	Lewiston, ME	109	28.0%	11,250	7.7%	3,080	25.8%	10,370	46.0%	18,470	40,120
32	Iowa City, IA	110	28.0%	14,520	8.7%	4,510	18.2%	9,440	53.7%	27,870	51,870
33	Columbia, MO	112	27.9%	15,770	3.2%	1,820	19.3%	10,920	52.8%	29,900	56,590
34	Fargo, ND–MN	118	27.7%	25,710	7.8%	7,270	24.3%	22,500	48.0%	44,540	92,750
35	Amarillo, TX	121	27.5%	24,280	9.1%	8,060	23.7%	20,890	48.7%	42,960	88,260
36	State College, PA	124	27.4%	10,310	10.1%	3,810	28.8%	10,840	43.6%	16,380	37,590
37	Altoona, PA	125	27.4%	13,540	8.5%	4,220	29.5%	14,550	43.1%	21,280	49,370
38	Longview, TX	127	27.3%	22,930	9.9%	8,310	28.7%	24,100	43.8%	36,730	83,910
39	Florence, SC	129	27.3%	14,210	5.4%	2,830	29.5%	15,380	43.2%	22,540	52,130
40	Abilene, TX	137	26.9%	13,000	7.99%	3,810	20.3%	9,820	52.6%	25,430	48,370
41	Billings, MT	138	26.8%	17,670	7.7%	5,070	23.8%	15,730	49.4%	32,620	66,020
42	Rocky Mount, NC	141	26.7%	14,680	7.5%	4,140	28.8%	15,820	44.2%	24,270	54,910
43	Sumter, SC	142	26.7%	9,120	12.2%	4,150	34.6%	11,810	38.7%	13,210	34,140
44	Tuscaloosa, AL	149	26.5%	17,900	9.8%	6,650	28.3%	19,110	44.9%	30,340	67,600
45	Cheyenne, WY	152	26.4%	7,630	5.0%	1,430	23.9%	6,890	49.7%	14,350	28,870
46	Fort Walton Beach, FL	155	26.4%	15,060	8.4%	4,800	24.6%	14,020	48.9%	27,890	57,090
47	Yuba City, CA	157	26.2%	7,420	11.2%	3,180	24.7%	6,970	49.1%	13,880	28,270

48	Roanoke, VA	26.2%	34,170	9.8%	12,710	31.0%	40,420	42.7%	55,650	130,280
49	Green Bay, WI	26.2%	35,120	9.7%	13,050	31.8%	42,650	42.0%	56,270	134,040
50	Odessa, TX	26.1%	24,370	7.4%	6,890	29.1%	27,150	44.6%	41,620	93,250
51	Janesville, WI	26.0%	14,160	10.0%	5,460	29.1%	15,840	44.9%	24,440	54,440
52	Wichita Falls, TX	25.8%	12,690	8.4%	4,110	21.9%	10,770	52.2%	25,640	49,100
53	Rochester, MN	25.8%	14,170	12.3%	6,730	24.1%	13,220	50.1%	27,500	54,920
54	Burlington, VT	25.7%	24,740	12.2%	11,690	25.3%	24,340	48.6%	46,750	96,100
55	Texarkana, AR	25.7%	11,420	7.6%	3,360	25.3%	11,240	48.6%	21,580	44,400
56	Williamsport, PA	25.7%	10,350	8.4%	3,370	27.8%	11,170	46.5%	18,700	40,250
57	Mansfield, OH	25.6%	18,190	8.3%	5,940	33.7%	23,990	40.7%	28,960	71,140
58	Pittsfield, MA	25.5%	8,470	10.5%	3,480	22.9%	7,610	51.6%	17,160	33,240
59	San Luis Obispo, CA	25.3%	23,960	9.0%	8,550	17.2%	16,300	55.4%	52,450	94,590
60	Champaign, IL	25.3%	17,790	4.3%	3,030	26.1%	18,330	48.3%	33,990	70,310
61	Dubuque, IA	25.2%	11,640	7.4%	3,430	28.0%	12,930	46.5%	21,490	46,230
62	Parkersburg, WV–OH	25.1%	14,660	4.8%	2,820	31.5%	18,370	43.5%	25,380	58,410
63	Johnstown, PA	25.0%	20,070	7.6%	6,080	27.7%	22,220	47.2%	37,880	80,170
64	Dothan, AL	25.0%	15,950	6.9%	4,380	33.3%	21,250	41.7%	26,660	63,860
65	Gadsden, AL	25.0%	7,560	6.1%	1,850	27.5%	8,330	47.2%	14,290	30,270
66	Rapid City, SD	24.7%	11,890	7.6%	3,630	19.3%	9,280	55.7%	26,790	48,060
67	Lima, OH	24.7%	16,050	7.2%	4,670	31.4%	20,430	43.9%	28,510	64,990
68	Pine Bluff, AR	24.6%	5,870	10.6%	2,540	31.2%	7,450	44.2%	10,550	23,870
69	Wausau, WI	24.6%	14,600	7.8%	4,610	35.1%	20,870	40.3%	23,970	59,440
70	Sharon, PA	24.5%	10,610	7.5%	3,240	30.7%	13,280	44.7%	19,330	43,220
71	Decatur, AL	24.5%	13,650	9.1%	5,070	40.9%	22,800	34.5%	19,260	55,780
72	Casper, WY	24.0%	6,090	5.6%	1,420	34.7%	8,810	41.3%	10,480	25,380
73	Alexandria, LA	24.0%	10,840	2.0%	910	22.5%	10,160	53.4%	24,130	45,220
74	Yakima, WA	23.8%	17,150	9.5%	6,840	27.9%	20,110	48.3%	34,800	72,060

(continues)

APPENDIX TABLE 4 (continued)

Rank[a]	Region	Overall Rank[b]	Creative Class Share	Creative Class Employment	Super-Creative Core Share	Super-Creative Core Employment	Working Class Share	Working Class Employment	Service Class Share	Service Class Employment	Total Employment
75	Jamestown, NY	205	23.7%	13,060	11.3%	6,240	29.7%	16,380	46.0%	25,370	55,120
76	Glens Falls, NY	207	23.6%	11,150	11.1%	5,260	22.3%	10,540	53.7%	25,340	47,200
77	Waco, TX	208	23.5%	20,620	8.9%	7,840	31.2%	27,370	45.2%	39,640	87,630
78	Goldsboro, NC	209	23.5%	8,160	8.0%	2,790	27.5%	9,550	48.7%	16,900	34,700
79	Elmira, NY	210	23.5%	9,480	9.8%	3,960	28.3%	11,420	48.2%	19,420	40,320
80	Bellingham, WA	211	23.5%	14,130	11.1%	6,690	26.6%	15,990	49.6%	29,820	60,120
81	Sioux Falls, SD	212	23.5%	24,250	6.3%	6,550	22.8%	23,560	53.5%	55,250	103,220
82	Punta Gorda, FL	213	23.5%	6,040	1.2%	300	21.0%	5,400	55.5%	14,280	25,720
83	Albany, GA	214	23.4%	11,890	9.6%	4,900	28.3%	14,390	48.1%	24,460	50,840
84	Kokomo, IN	215	23.3%	10,050	7.6%	3,290	37.0%	15,960	39.8%	17,170	43,180
85	Anniston, AL	216	23.2%	10,230	8.0%	3,530	33.7%	14,860	43.0%	18,980	44,100
86	Waterloo, IA	217	23.1%	15,850	11.1%	7,620	30.4%	20,880	46.4%	31,860	68,590
87	Sioux City, IA–NE	218	23.1%	13,900	6.3%	3,820	33.1%	19,910	43.6%	26,260	60,210
88	Merced, CA	219	23.1%	12,790	12.1%	6,680	27.5%	15,240	41.4%	22,950	55,420
89	Lake Charles, LA	220	23.1%	17,470	4.3%	3,280	31.4%	23,770	45.3%	34,280	75,730
90	Terre Haute, IN	221	23.0%	12,570	6.3%	3,470	29.7%	16,280	47.2%	25,850	54,740
91	Pueblo, CO	223	22.9%	11,040	2.3%	1,100	20.9%	10,070	56.2%	27,080	48,190
92	St. Cloud, MN	224	22.9%	17,600	9.4%	7,270	27.1%	20,870	49.9%	38,400	77,000
93	Florence, AL	225	22.8%	11,290	7.9%	3,910	33.3%	16,510	43.4%	21,480	49,550
94	Clarksville, TN–KY	227	22.7%	11,080	7.6%	3,700	26.1%	12,760	51.2%	24,980	48,820
95	Steubenville, OH–WV	228	22.7%	9,880	6.9%	3,000	38.0%	16,550	39.2%	17,100	43,580
96	Jackson, MI	229	22.6%	11,070	9.9%	4,830	35.3%	17,250	42.1%	20,590	48,910
97	St. Joseph, MO	230	22.6%	8,130	9.2%	3,300	25.0%	8,980	52.4%	18,830	35,940
98	Barnstable, MA	231	22.4%	12,580	9.1%	5,130	15.9%	8,930	61.7%	34,620	56,130
99	Joplin, MO	233	22.3%	15,230	7.5%	5,140	34.9%	23,900	42.6%	29,120	68,420

100	Cumberland, MD–WV	235	21.9%	5,720	1.7%	450	23.7%	6,190	54.4%	14,190	26,100
101	Benton Harbor, MI	236	21.8%	11,770	10.4%	5,590	29.9%	16,130	48.2%	26,010	53,980
102	Athens, GA	237	21.7%	12,570	2.4%	1,370	24.2%	14,010	54.2%	31,410	57,990
103	Enid, OK	238	21.6%	3,970	1.5%	270	29.8%	5,480	48.6%	8,940	18,390
104	Grand Forks, ND–MN	239	21.4%	7,840	10.6%	3,880	21.6%	7,920	56.7%	20,800	36,710
105	Greenville, NC	241	21.2%	11,260	9.3%	4,950	24.8%	13,170	54.1%	28,750	53,180
106	Panama City, FL	244	21.0%	9,430	2.1%	960	19.4%	8,700	59.5%	26,720	44,900
107	Owensboro, KY	246	20.8%	6,630	2.2%	690	28.9%	9,210	50.1%	15,950	31,830
108	Sheboygan, WI	248	20.6%	9,120	7.9%	3,480	39.6%	17,540	39.8%	17,650	44,310
109	Fort Smith, AR–OK	249	20.6%	18,920	6.1%	5,640	40.9%	37,640	38.5%	35,430	92,030
110	Danville, VA	250	20.3%	7,480	7.8%	2,870	37.8%	13,920	41.6%	15,320	36,790
111	Medford, OR	251	20.1%	12,540	7.5%	4,650	25.9%	16,150	53.5%	33,370	62,350
112	Myrtle Beach, SC	252	19.5%	16,280	2.7%	2,250	24.5%	20,410	55.7%	46,400	83,340
113	Laredo, TX	255	18.7%	9,790	2.7%	1,420	26.8%	14,020	54.5%	28,540	52,350
114	Jacksonville, NC	256	18.5%	5,640	1.2%	380	20.1%	6,140	61.0%	18,590	30,500
115	Decatur, IL	258	18.4%	7,390	1.6%	660	24.3%	9,750	57.3%	22,960	40,100
116	Lawton, OK	259	18.2%	6,150	1.0%	340	32.9%	11,140	48.9%	16,550	33,840
117	Bloomington, IN	260	18.1%	7,220	4.7%	1,880	33.8%	13,530	48.1%	19,250	40,000
118	Lynchburg, VA	261	18.0%	14,600	4.0%	3,210	36.6%	29,690	45.1%	36,660	81,230
119	Lubbock, TX	262	17.9%	15,860	2.9%	2,570	23.9%	21,180	57.6%	50,920	88,440
120	Elkhart, IN	263	17.7%	21,830	4.8%	5,960	55.8%	68,940	26.5%	32,700	123,470
121	Yuma, AZ	265	16.0%	6,930	8.7%	3,750	23.7%	10,250	39.6%	17,110	43,190
122	Houma, LA	266	15.0%	9,720	1.2%	780	43.7%	28,260	40.7%	26,360	64,690
123	Jackson, TN	267	14.8%	5,590	1.6%	620	36.4%	13,730	48.8%	18,400	37,720
124	Victoria, TX	268	14.2%	3,590	1.6%	410	31.4%	7,940	54.4%	13,780	25,310

NOTE: In some cases, the names of Standard Metropolitan Statistical Areas have been shortened to reflect their core city.

[a] Rank among regions in the given size class.
[b] Overall Rank is for all 268 regions for which data are available.

APPENDIX TABLE 5 Creativity Index for Small and Medium-Size Regions, 1999

Rank[a]	Region	Creativity Index	Rank				
			Overall[b]	Creative Class	High Tech	Innovation	Diversity
		Regions with 500,000–1 million people					
1	Albuquerque, NM	965	8	26	9	62	14
2	Albany, NY	932	17	15	68	21	39
3	Tucson, AZ	853	31	96	18	60	49
4	Allentown–Bethlehem, PA	801	39	88	75	24	90
5	Dayton, OH	766	46	59	49	51	149
6	Colorado Springs, CO	756	48	60	39	20	199
7	Harrisburg, PA	751	50	62	44	97	122
8	Little Rock, AR	740	53	44	59	155	80
9	Birmingham, AL	722	60	47	47	187	74
10	Tulsa, OK	721	61	90	55	104	108
11	Columbia, SC	719	62	33	90	145	88
12	Richmond, VA	711	66	56	67	144	97
13	Baton Rouge, LA	696	72	48	112	80	139
14	Charleston, SC	663	85	64	129	160	58
15	Knoxville, TN	650	89	140	111	74	103
16	Syracuse, NY	645	91	63	93	93	185
17	Omaha, NE–IA	637	97	43	37	186	174
18	Wichita, KS	619	101	145	32	113	161
19	Toledo, OH	611	103	132	116	43	178
20	Sarasota–Bradenton, FL	600	107	199	144	100	33
21	Mobile, AL	594	109	126	123	148	87
22	Greenville, SC	593	110	193	86	81	125

23	Honolulu, HI	580	111	130	83	230	54
24	Springfield, MA	577	112	65	156	149	130
25	Fort Wayne, IN	569	113	171	92	67	173
26	Bakersfield, CA	531	131	115	117	198	112
27	Fresno, CA	516	138	176	121	236	27
28	El Paso, TX	464	156	134	133	238	106
29	Stockton–Lodi, CA	459	158	200	153	207	56
30	McAllen, TX	451	164	117	179	265	66
31	Scranton–Wilkes-Barre, PA	400	191	186	119	162	212
32	Youngstown, OH	253	239	203	189	174	258

Regions with 250,000 to 500,000 people

1	Madison, WI	925	20	19	82	14	38
2	Des Moines, IA	862	27	31	27	65	91
3	Santa Barbara, CA	856	28	100	63	19	36
4	Melbourne, FL	855	29	8	45	37	133
5	Boise City, ID	854	30	11	23	1	187
6	Huntsville, AL	799	40	9	38	69	163
7	Lansing–East Lansing, MI	739	54	13	128	109	86
8	Binghamton, NY	731	59	45	56	9	234
9	Lexington, KY	717	63	133	118	41	68
10	New London–Norwich, CT–RI	715	64	107	69	49	135
11	South Bend, IN	693	74	105	30	88	158
12	Jackson, MS	691	75	21	66	205	96
13	Fort Collins, CO	689	76	103	73	7	205
14	Tallahassee, FL	675	80	37	97	142	123
15	Provo, UT	674	81	18	64	57	264

(continues)

APPENDIX TABLE 5 (continued)

Rank[a]	Region	Creativity Index	Overall[b]	Creative Class	High Tech	Innovation	Diversity
				Rank			
16	Eugene, OR	672	82	131	85	116	69
17	Kalamazoo–Battle Creek, MI	653	87	182	36	68	138
18	Charleston, WV	653	87	98	109	120	94
19	Lincoln, NE	645	91	66	78	89	198
20	Anchorage, AK	640	94	135	98	169	35
21	Spokane, WA	637	97	54	81	163	142
22	Pensacola, FL	615	102	35	154	182	89
23	Reno, NV	610	104	240	126	77	22
24	Rockford, IL	602	106	153	77	47	196
25	Fort Myers–Cape Coral, FL	598	108	151	141	158	28
26	Corpus Christi, TX	563	116	58	131	222	100
27	Appleton–Oshkosh–Neenah, WI	560	118	185	157	15	156
28	Montgomery, AL	555	120	38	139	227	117
29	Salinas, CA	544	125	247	132	140	13
30	Utica, NY	528	133	113	149	101	186
31	Brownsville, TX	522	135	114	106	257	77
32	Fort Pierce–Port St. Lucie, FL	519	136	147	221	133	57
33	Lancaster, PA	517	137	226	84	59	193
34	Chattanooga, TN–GA	513	139	146	151	161	104
35	Peoria, IL	507	141	148	178	18	223
36	Daytona Beach, FL	506	142	136	152	202	79
37	Saginaw, MI	497	145	194	127	16	245
38	Reading, PA	491	147	206	140	48	189
39	Johnson City–Kingsport–Bristol, TN–VA	490	148	195	145	71	176

40	Augusta–Aiken, GA–SC	474	151	144	136	189	132
41	Evansville–Henderson, IN–KY	471	154	174	158	105	167
42	Macon, GA	458	159	81	165	201	171
43	Erie, PA	458	159	143	176	72	227
44	Savannah, GA	456	161	163	183	237	37
45	Naples, FL	434	170	254	216	143	29
46	Canton, OH	433	171	154	175	70	244
47	Springfield, MO	430	173	156	134	190	166
48	Lafayette, LA	423	175	242	164	136	111
49	Modesto, CA	420	178	198	193	194	72
50	Davenport–Moline–Rock Island, IA–IL	407	185	180	180	96	214
51	Biloxi, MS	406	186	161	159	231	121
52	Huntington–Ashland, WV–KY–OH	405	187	102	219	206	144
53	Columbus, GA–AL	397	192	178	113	253	136
54	Hickory, NC	393	193	253	174	130	127
55	Lakeland–Winter Haven, FL	385	196	245	195	219	32
56	Beaumont, TX	372	198	116	148	228	207
57	Fayetteville, AR	366	200	243	207	176	82
58	York, PA	360	202	232	192	92	201
59	Fayetteville, NC	309	220	82	238	254	194
60	Killeen, TX	302	223	189	173	210	202
61	Visalia, CA	289	227	222	248	251	65
62	Ocala, FL	263	237	264	229	217	101
63	Shreveport, LA	233	247	234	137	250	220

Regions with less than 250,000 people

1	Santa Fe, NM	907	23	10	130	26	3
2	Gainesville, FL	827	34	2	170	30	48

(continues)

APPENDIX TABLE 5 (continued)

Rank[a]	Region	Creativity Index	Rank				
			Overall[b]	Creative Class	High Tech	Innovation	Diversity
3	Portland, ME	813	36	28	89	134	12
4	Burlington, VT	809	37	166	54	3	44
5	Lafayette, IN	758	47	36	96	33	152
6	Cedar Rapids, IA	745	51	61	21	10	238
7	Sherman, TX	732	58	39	107	98	102
8	Richland, WA	700	69	80	58	75	168
9	Iowa City, IA	695	73	110	167	28	75
10	State College, PA	683	77	124	124	25	120
11	Asheville, NC	682	78	93	177	117	6
12	Wilmington, NC	678	79	78	114	107	99
13	Lawrence, KS	663	85	106	162	84	62
14	Barnstable–Yarmouth, MA	646	90	231	125	31	43
15	Rochester, MN	642	93	165	22	2	243
16	Charlottesville, VA	638	96	51	163	78	145
17	Bryan–College Station, TX	630	99	3	161	53	229
18	San Luis Obispo, CA	566	114	172	110	90	143
19	Longview, TX	565	115	127	150	125	109
20	Springfield, IL	557	119	23	169	199	129
21	Greenville, NC	554	122	241	29	166	85
22	Eau Claire, WI	551	123	91	160	58	219
23	Athens, GA	550	124	237	199	82	7
24	Las Cruces, NM	543	126	49	198	203	84
25	Albany, GA	541	127	214	52	239	30
26	Roanoke, VA	539	128	158	108	132	140

27	Williamsport, PA	536	129	168	94	99	184
28	Elmira, NY	534	130	210	138	22	172
29	Columbia, MO	526	134	112	211	111	118
30	Dover, DE	512	140	75	213	152	124
31	Amarillo, TX	505	143	121	122	224	107
32	Benton Harbor, MI	498	144	236	101	91	151
33	Fort Walton Beach, FL	493	146	155	135	139	154
34	Champaign–Urbana, IL	490	148	173	182	61	169
35	Bloomington, IL	484	150	1	194	159	236
36	Kokomo, IN	474	151	215	190	17	182
37	Monroe, LA	474	151	41	120	246	190
38	Tyler, TX	468	155	74	186	191	155
39	Bloomington, IN	461	157	260	222	94	40
40	Fargo–Moorhead, ND–MN	453	162	118	171	129	204
41	Lubbock, TX	452	163	262	33	167	164
42	Duluth–Superior, MN–WI	451	164	104	115	156	249
43	La Crosse, WI–MN	451	164	77	191	95	260
44	Elkhart, IN	448	167	263	103	66	197
45	Green Bay, WI	443	168	159	197	112	165
46	Lynchburg, VA	436	169	261	79	83	215
47	Glens Falls, NY	431	172	207	105	122	206
48	Abilene, TX	430	173	137	210	247	50
49	Topeka, KS	422	176	94	166	188	209
50	Chico, CA	421	177	101	142	218	191
51	San Angelo, TX	418	179	85	99	255	217
52	Muncie, IN	416	180	52	252	262	95
53	Redding, CA	412	181	95	225	175	170

(continues)

APPENDIX TABLE 5 (continued)

Rank[a]	Region	Creativity Index	Rank				
			Overall[b]	Creative Class	High Tech	Innovation	Diversity
54	Lewiston, ME	412	181	109	242	259	55
55	Decatur, IL	412	181	258	12	157	235
56	Pittsfield, MA	410	184	170	218	64	216
57	Bellingham, WA	404	188	211	185	118	160
58	Altoona, PA	404	188	125	188	181	177
59	Mansfield, OH	401	190	169	102	184	221
60	Dothan, AL	393	193	181	206	204	92
61	Rocky Mount, NC	389	195	141	88	240	218
62	Johnstown, PA	375	197	179	104	192	226
63	Parkersburg–Marietta, WV–OH	368	199	177	187	121	224
64	Medford, OR	365	201	251	196	209	53
65	Panama City, FL	358	203	244	220	106	147
66	Florence, SC	356	204	129	261	123	208
67	Myrtle Beach, SC	344	205	252	200	215	64
68	Bangor, ME	343	206	67	234	233	200
69	Decatur, AL	340	207	196	247	185	105
70	Jackson, MI	333	208	229	266	114	131
71	Punta Gorda, FL	332	209	213	233	153	146
72	Casper, WY	332	210	201	265	165	114
73	Houma, LA	331	211	266	224	137	116
74	Waco, TX	325	212	208	143	245	159
75	Merced, CA	325	212	219	232	232	67
76	Alexandria, LA	324	214	202	243	226	81
77	Jackson, TN	321	215	267	235	110	137

78	Janesville–Beloit, WI	318	216	162	256	86	253
79	Terre Haute, IN	314	217	221	146	154	242
80	Bismarck, ND	312	218	89	205	212	257
81	Lake Charles, LA	311	219	220	215	183	148
82	Goldsboro, NC	308	221	209	228	234	98
83	Wheeling, WV–OH	305	222	87	239	197	246
84	Sioux Falls, SD	297	224	212	168	147	254
85	Billings, MT	295	225	138	155	241	247
86	Sumter, SC	294	226	142	201	256	179
87	Waterloo–Cedar Falls, IA	281	228	217	181	146	251
88	Yuba City, CA	276	229	157	212	243	192
89	Great Falls, MT	275	230	86	240	229	248
90	St. Joseph, MO	274	231	230	214	177	181
91	Fort Smith, AR–OK	274	231	249	184	213	157
92	Sheboygan, WI	274	231	248	236	63	256
93	Odessa, TX	273	234	160	208	211	225
94	Laredo, TX	268.5	235	255	227	268	63
95	Anniston, AL	267	236	216	257	261	76
96	Tuscaloosa, AL	254	238	149	253	244	175
97	Sharon, PA	253	239	192	249	115	267
98	Florence, AL	249	241	225	237	179	180
99	Cheyenne, WY	241	242	152	172	258	252
100	Dubuque, IA	241	242	175	241	151	268
101	Yakima, WA	241	242	204	226	221	183
102	Jamestown, NY	235	245	205	230	196	211
103	Texarkana, TX, AR	235	245	167	204	249	222
104	Sioux City, IA–NE	229	248	218	259	127	241

(continues)

APPENDIX TABLE 5 (continued)

Rank[a]	Region	Creativity Index	Overall[b]	Creative Class	High Tech	Innovation	Diversity
					Rank		
105	Wichita Falls, TX	223	249	164	203	225	261
106	Lima, OH	222	250	188	217	193	255
107	Yuma, AZ	215	251	265	209	260	126
108	Wausau, WI	191	252	191	263	195	239
109	Gadsden, AL	187.5	253	183	246	267	188
110	Joplin, MO	183	254	233	231	170	259
111	Rapid City, SD	182	255	187	223	220	265
112	St. Cloud, MN	182	255	224	202	208	262
113	Steubenville–Weirton, OH–WV	174	257	228	268	172	237
114	Pueblo, CO	168	258	223	254	216	213
115	Grand Forks, ND–MN	154	259	239	244	173	266
116	Pine Bluff, AR	135	260	190	255	263	233
117	Clarksville–Hopkinsville, TN–KY	115	261	227	258	248	231
118	Danville, VA	114	262	250	267	242	203
119	Victoria, TX	113	263	268	250	214	232
120	Lawton, OK	107	264	259	245	235	230
121	Jacksonville, NC	105	265	256	260	266	195
122	Owensboro, KY	91	266	246	251	223	263
123	Cumberland, MD–WV	83	267	235	262	264	228
124	Enid, OK	73	268	238	264	252	250

NOTE: In some cases, the names of Standard Metropolitan Statistical Areas have been shortened to reflect their core city.

[a] Rank is for regions of a given size class.

[b] Overall Rank is based on all 268 regions for which data are available.

NOTES

Chapter 1

1. For a careful empirical comparison of technological change at the turn of the twentieth century versus modern times, see Robert Gordon, "Does the New Economy Measure Up to the Great Inventions of the Past?" Cambridge, Mass.: National Bureau of Economic Research, Working Paper No. 7833, August 2000. His answer is a resounding no. The great majority of the technological inventions in the National Academy of Engineering's "Greatest Engineering Accomplishments of the 20th Century" occurred prior to 1950. Only two of the top ten occurred after World War II (semiconductor electronics, no. 5, and computers, no. 8), while the Internet, the subject of so much New Economy hype, ranks thirteenth. See www.greatachievements.org.

2. Among the most popular, indeed classic works in this vein, see Sinclair Lewis, *Main Street*. New York: Harcourt, Brace and Company, 1920; and *Babbitt*. New York: Harcourt, Brace and World, 1922; William H. Whyte, Jr., *The Organization Man*. New York: Simon and Schuster, 1956; David Riesman, *The Lonely Crowd: A Study of the Changing American Character*. New Haven: Yale University Press, 1950; C. Wright Mills, *White Collar: The American Middle Classes*. New York: Oxford University Press, 1951; John Kenneth Galbraith, *The New Industrial State*. New York: Houghton-Mifflin, 1967. Also see Anthony Sampson, *Company Man: The Rise and Fall of Corporate Life*. New York: Times Books, 1995.

3. There are many statements of the free agent view, but the most notable is Daniel Pink, *Free Agent Nation: How America's New Independent Workers Are Transforming the Way We Live*. New York: Warner Books, 2001.

4. Again there are many statements of this view, but for a contemporary one see Kevin Kelly, *New Rules for the New Economy: 10 Radical Strategies for a Connected World*. New York: Viking, 1998.

5. Fiorina preceded me in speaking to the Annual Meeting of the National Governors Association in Washington, D.C., in winter 2000, where she made these remarks.

6. Jacobs's work is the classic statement of these themes. See Jane Jacobs, *The Death and Life of Great American Cities*. New York: Random House, 1961; *The Economy of Cities*. New York: Random House, 1969; *Cities and the Wealth of Nations*. New York: Random House, 1984.

7. Personal interview by author, Ottawa, Canada, September 2001.

8. On this point see Manuel Castells, *The Power of Identity: The Information Age: Economy, Society, and Culture, Volume I*. Oxford: Blackwell Publishers Ltd., 1997.

9. The classic statement here is that of Karl Marx in both *Capital* and *The Communist Manifesto* among his many other works.

10. Daniel Bell, *The Coming of Post-Industrial Society*. New York: Basic Books, 1973.

11. "The Changing American Family." *New York Times,* May 15, 2001.

12. The concept of the "nerdistan" is Joel Kotkin's, see *The New Geography: How the Digital Revolution Is Reshaping the American Landscape.* New York: Random House, 2000.

13. David Brooks, *Bobos in Paradise: The New Upper Class and How They Got There.* New York: Simon and Schuster, 2001.

14. Kelly, *New Rules for the New Economy;* George Gilder, *Telecosm: How Infinite Bandwidth Will Revolutionize Our World.* New York: The Free Press, 2000; *Microcosm: The Quantum Revolution in Economics and Technology.* New York: Simon and Schuster, 1989. Also see William J. Mitchell, *City of Bits: Space, Place and the Infobahn.* Cambridge: MIT Press, 1995.

15. Pink, *Free Agent Nation.*

16. The number of books touting the advantages of the virtual world is astounding; see, for example, Don Tapscott, *The Digital Economy: Promise and Peril in the Age of Networked Intelligence.* New York: McGraw Hill, 1996; and Diane Coyle, *The Weightless World: Strategies for Managing in a Digital Economy.* Cambridge: MIT Press, 1997.

17. Jeremy Rifkin, *The End of Work: The Decline of the Global Labor Force and the Dawn of the Post-Market Era.* New York: Putnam, 1995.

18. Richard Sennett, *The Corrosion of Character: The Personal Consequences of Work in the New Capitalism.* New York: W.W. Norton, 1998.

19. Jill Andresky Fraser, *White-Collar Sweatshop: The Deterioration of Work and Its Rewards in Corporate America.* New York: W.W. Norton, 2001. Of course the classic statement of the overwork thesis is Juliet Schor, *The Overworked American.* New York: Basic Books, 1991.

20. Tom Frank, *One Market Under God: Extreme Capitalism, Market Populism, and the End of Economic Development.* New York: Doubleday, 2001; and *The Conquest of Cool: Business Culture, Counterculture, and the Rise of Hip Consumerism.* Chicago: University of Chicago Press, 1997.

21. Robert Putnam, *Bowling Alone: The Collapse and Revival of American Community.* New York: Simon and Schuster, 2000.

22. See Paul David, "Understanding Digital Technology's Evolution and the Path of Measured Productivity Growth: Present and Future in the Mirror of the Past," in Eric Brynolfsson and Brian Kahin (eds.), *Understanding the Digital Economy.* Cambridge: MIT Press, 2001.

Chapter 2

1. See Paul Romer, "Economic Growth," in *The Fortune Encyclopedia of Economics,* David R. Henderson (ed.). New York: Time Warner Books, 1993, p. 9; "Ideas and Things." *The Economist,* September 11, 1993, p. 33; "Beyond the Knowledge Worker." *Worldlink,* January-February 1995, also available at his website. The classic statement is Romer, "Endogenous Technical Change." *Journal of Political Economy,* 98(5), 1990, pp. 71–102.

2. Many writers have chronicled the rise of the industrial/organizational age, but among the most important contributions is Alfred Chandler, *The Visible Hand: The Managerial Revolution in American Business.* Cambridge: Belknap Press of Harvard University, 1977. Also see Michael Piore and Charles Sabel, *The Second Industrial Divide: Possibilities for Prosperity.* New York: Basic Books, 1984.

3. Joseph Schumpeter, *Capitalism, Socialism and Democracy.* New York: Harper & Row, first edition 1942, second (revised) edition 1947, third and final author's revision 1950; quotes are from Harper Torchbooks edition of the latter, 1975, pp. 132–134.

4. Personal interview, summer 2000.

5. George Gilder, *Telecosm: How Infinite Bandwidth Will Revolutionize Our World*. New York: The Free Press, 2000.

6. Gilder, *Telecosm*, p. 256.

7. Gilder, *Telecosm*, p. 262.

8. Gilder, *Telecosm*, p. 263.

9. Gilder, *Telecosm*, pp. 263–264.

10. Gilder, *Telecosm*, pp. 259, 261.

11. Gilder, *Telecosm*, pp. 248, 252.

12. The classic statement is, of course, from E. F. Schumacher, *Small Is Beautiful: Economics as if People Mattered*. Point Roberts, Wash.: Hartley & Marks Publishers, 1998.

13. "Too Much Corporate Power?" *Business Week* (cover story), September 11, 2000, pp. 144–158.

14. There is a vast and highly contentious literature on the effects of big versus small firms on everything from innovation to job generation. On these matters I find myself in agreement with my colleague Ashish Arora, who says that both big and small firms play distinct roles in what he terms "the division of innovative labor." See Ashish Arora, Andrea Fosfuri and Alphonso Gambardella, *Markets for Technology*. Cambridge: MIT Press, 2002.

15. See Daniel Pink, *Free Agent Nation: How America's New Independent Workers Are Transforming the Way We Live*. New York: Warner Books, 2001.

16. For a succinct statement see Pink, *Free Agent Nation*, pp. 24–29, "The Hollywood Organizational Model." This perspective builds off a much richer set of academic studies; see, for instance, Michael Storper, "The Transition to Flexible Specialization in the U.S. Film Industry: External Economies, the Division of Labor, and Crossing Industrial Divides." *Cambridge Journal of Economics*, 13, 1989; Michael Storper and Susan Christopherson, "The Effects of Flexible Specialization on Industrial Politics and the Labor Market: The Motion Picture Industry." *Industrial and Labor Relations Review*, April 1989.

17. James Surowiecki, "Hollywood's Star System, at a Cubicle Near You." The Financial Page, *The New Yorker*, May 28, 2001, p. 58.

18. See Richard Florida and Martin Kenney, *The Breakthrough Illusion*. New York: Basic Books, 1990, for an early statement of this thesis.

19. See, for example, Arthur Koestler, *The Act of Creation*. London: Hutchinson and Co., 1964; Margaret Boden, *The Creative Mind: Myths and Mechanisms*. New York: Basic Books, 1990; Robert J. Sternberg (ed.), *Handbook of Creativity*. New York: Cambridge University Press, 1999; Dean Keith Simonton, *Origins of Genius: Darwinian Perspectives on Creativity*. New York: Oxford University Press, 1999; Carl R. Rogers, "Toward a Theory of Creativity." Chapter 19 in his *On Becoming a Person: A Therapist's View of Psychotherapy*. Boston: Houghton Mifflin and Co., 1961; Douglas Hofstader, *Godel, Escher, Bach: An Eternal Golden Braid*. New York: Basic Books, 1979; Silvano Arieti, *Creativity: The Magic Synthesis*. New York: Basic Books, 1976.

20. See Antonio Preti and Paolo Miotto, "The Contribution of Psychiatry to the Study of Creativity: Implications for AI Research," www.comapp.dcu.ie/~tonyv/MIND/antonio. html, p. 2. Also see F. Barron and D. M. Harrington, "Creativity, Intelligence and Personality." *Annual Review of Psychology*, 32, 1981, pp. 439–476; D. W. McKinnon, "The Nature and Nurture of Creative Talent." *American Psychologist*, 17, 1962, pp. 484–494; M. Dellas and E. L. Gaier, "Identification of Creativity in Individuals." *Psychological Bulletin*, 73, 1970, pp. 55–73.

21. See Boden, *The Creative Mind*; Arieti, *Creativity: The Magic Synthesis*; and S. A. Mednick, "The Associative Basis of the Creative Process." *Psychological Review*, 69, 1968, pp. 220–232.

22. Boden, *The Creative Mind*, p. 255. Also see Thomas Kuhn, *The Structure of Scientific Revolutions*. Chicago: University of Chicago Press, 1962.

23. Schumpeter, *Capitalism, Socialism and Democracy*, p. 84.

24. Joel Mokyr, *The Lever of Riches: Technological Creativity and Economic Progress*. New York: Oxford University Press, 1990. Schumpeter initially advanced this distinction in his article "The Creative Response in Economic History." *Journal of Economic History*, 7, 1947, 149–159.

25. Boden, *The Creative Mind*, p. 245.

26. Boden, *The Creative Mind*, pp. 255–256.

27. The "four steps of the creative process" are generally credited to Graham Wallas, *The Art of Thought*. New York: Harcourt Brace & World, 1926.

28. Simonton, *Origins of Genius*.

29. As quoted in Boden, *The Creative Mind*, p. 254.

30. Boden, *The Creative Mind*, pp. 254–255.

31. Wesley Cohen and Daniel Levinthal, "Fortune Favors the Prepared Firm." *Management Science*, February 1994, pp. 227–251.

32. Anthony Storr, *Churchill's Black Dog, Kafka's Mice: And Other Phenomena of the Human Mind*. New York: Grove Press, 1988, p. 103.

33. Teresa M. Amabile, *Creativity in Context*, Boulder, CO: Westview Press, 1996, p. 15. Originally published as *The Social Psychology of Creativity*, 1983.

34. Cited in Thomas P. Hughes, *American Genesis: A Century of Invention and Technological Enthusiasm*. New York: Viking, 1989, p. 29.

35. Simonton, *Origins of Genius*, pp. 206–212.

36. Mokyr, *The Lever of Riches*, p. 16; this warning is reprised in Epilogue, p. 301.

37. Paul Romer, "Ideas and Things." *The Economist*, September 11, 1993, on-line version, p. 2.

38. *Ibid.*, p. 2.

39. A comprehensive review of the new growth theory is presented in Joseph Cortwright, *New Growth Theory, Technology and Learning: A Practitioner's Guide to Theories for the Knowledge Based Economy*. Report prepared for the U.S. Economic Development Administration, Washington, D.C., 2000.

40. Lawrence Lessing, *The Future of Ideas*. New York: Random House, 2001.

41. There are many studies of the new role of knowledge and intelligence in the factory, see, for example, Shoshana Zuboff, *In the Age of the Smart Machine: The Future of Work and Power*. New York: Perseus, 1989; Dorothy Leonard-Barton, *Wellsprings of Knowledge: Building and Sustaining the Sources of Innovation*. Boston: Harvard Business School Press, 1995; James Womack, Daniel Jones and Daniel Roos, *The Machine That Changed the World*. New York: Rawson/Macmillan, 1990; Michael Dertouzos, Richard Lester and Robert Solow, *Made in America: Regaining the Productive Edge*. Cambridge: MIT Press, 1989; Richard Lester, *The Productive Edge: How U.S. Industries Are Pointing the Way to a New Era of Economic Growth*. New York: W.W. Norton, 1998.

42. On Japanese transplant factories, see Martin Kenney and Richard Florida, *Beyond Mass Production: The Japanese System and Its Transfer to the United States*. New York: Oxford University Press, 1993. On environmental innovation, see Richard Florida and Derek Davison, "Gaining from Green: Environmental Management Systems Inside and Outside the Factory." *California Management Review*, 43(3), Spring 2001, pp. 64–84; and Richard Florida, "Lean and Green: The Move to Environmentally-Conscious Manufacturing." *California Management Review* 39(1), Fall 1996, pp. 80–105.

43. Field research visit and personal interviews by author.

44. Zuboff, *In the Age of the Smart Machine*; also see Joanne Gordon, "The Hands-on, Logged-on Worker." *Forbes*, October 30, 2000, pp. 136–142.

45. Personal interview by author, November 1990.

46. Adam Smith, *The Wealth of Nations*, 1776, entire text on-line at The Adam Smith Institute, www.adamsmith.org.uk. Quote is from Book Five, Chapter 1, Part 3, Article II.

47. John Seely Brown and Paul Duguid, *The Social Life of Information*. Boston: Harvard Business School Press, 2000.

48. William H. Whyte, Jr., *The Organization Man*. New York: Simon and Schuster, 1956.

49. Jane Jacobs, *The Death and Life of Great American Cities*. New York: Random House, 1961.

50. Interview by James Kunstler, September 6, 2000, Toronto, Canada, for *Metropolis Magazine*, March 2001. Available on-line at www.kunstler.com/mags_jacobs1.htm.

Chapter 3

1. Peter Drucker, *Post-Capitalist Society*. New York: Harper Business, 1993, quote is from p. 8; also "Beyond the Information Revolution." *The Atlantic Monthly*, October 1999, 284(4), pp. 47–57; "The Next Society." *The Economist*, November 1, 2001 (*Economist Survey*), pp. 1–20. Fritz Machlup is often credited with the term from his 1962 book, *The Production and Distribution of Knowledge in the United States*. Princeton: Princeton University Press, 1962. There are many others who have written on the knowledge economy; see, for example: Ikujiro Nonaka and Hiroetaka Takeuchi, *The Knowledge Creating Company: How Japanese Companies Create the Dynamics of Innovation*. New York: Oxford University Press, 1995; Alan Burton Jones, *Knowledge Capitalism: Business, Work and Learning in the New Economy*. Oxford: Oxford University Press, 1999. Steven Brint provides a comprehensive review of this entire field in his article, "Professionals and the Knowledge Economy: Rethinking the Theory of the Postindustrial Society." *Current Sociology*, July 2001, 49(1), pp. 101–132.

2. The R&D figures are from the National Science Foundation, Division of Science Resources, "National Patterns of R&D Resources, 2000 Update," 2001, at www.nsf.gov/sbe/srs/nsf01309/start.htm.

3. Patent data are from the U.S. Patent and Trademark Office.

4. The exact figures are as follows. There were 55.2 scientists and engineers per 100,000 people in 1900. This rose to 410.5 in 1950 and to 1821.1 in 1999. The historical data on scientists and engineers are from U.S. Bureau of the Census, *Historical Statistics of the United States from Colonial Times to the Present*. New York: Basic Books, 1976; and U.S. Bureau of the Census, *2000 Statistical Abstract of the United States*. Washington, D.C.: U.S. Government Printing Office, 2001.

5. The exact figures for bohemians are as follows. There were 266.8 bohemians per 100,000 people in 1900, 344.1 in 1950, and 899.9 in 1999. Historical data on bohemians are from *Historical Statistics of the United States* and the *2000 Statistical Abstract*.

6. "The Creative Economy." *Business Week* (Special Double Issue: *The 21st Century Corporation*), *Business Week Online*, August 28, 2000, pp. 1–5. www.businessweek.com/2000/00_35/b3696002.htm.

7. John Howkins, *The Creative Economy*. New York: Allen Lane, The Penguin Press, 2001. There is also an interesting report, *The Creative Economy Initiative*, by the New England Council, June 2000, which uses the term "creative economy." But the New England Council report limits its definition of the creative economy to artistic and cultural fields.

8. Others have written on the intellectual capital economy; see, for example, Thomas A. Stewart, *Intellectual Capital: The New Wealth of Organizations.* New York: Doubleday/Currency, 1997; and Leif Edvinsson and Michael S. Malone, *Intellectual Capital: Realizing Your Company's True Value by Knowing Its Hidden Brainpower.* New York: HarperCollins, 1997.

9. Paul Romer, "Economic Growth," in *The Fortune Encyclopedia of Economics,* David R. Henderson (ed.). New York: Time Warner Books, 1993, p. 33.

10. Venture capital data are from Venture Economics, at www.ventureeconomics.com/vec/stats.

11. Richard Florida and Martin Kenney, *The Breakthrough Illusion.* New York: Basic Books, 1990.

12. An overview of this history is provided in Richard Florida and Mark Samber, "Capital and Creative Destruction: Venture Capital, Technological Change, and Economic Development," in Trevor Barnes and Meric Gertler (eds.), *The New Industrial Geography: Regions, Regulation and Institutions.* London: Routledge, 1999, pp. 265–291.

13. The literature on the modern-day venture capital industry is vast. See Paul Gompers and Josh Lerner, *The Venture Capital Cycle.* Cambridge: MIT Press, 1999; and "The Venture Capital Revolution." *Journal of Economic Perspectives,* 15(2), Spring 2001, pp. 145–168. Also see William Bygrave and Jeffry Timmons, *Venture Capital at the Crossroads.* Boston: Harvard Business School Press, 1990; Thomas Doerflinger and Jack Rivkin, *Risk and Reward: Venture Capital and the Making of America's Great Industries.* New York: Random House, 1987; John W. Wilson, *The New Venturers: Inside the High-Stakes World of Venture Capital.* Reading, Mass.: Addison-Wesley Publishing Company, 1985; Richard Florida and Martin Kenney, "Venture Capital-Financed Innovation in the USA." *Research Policy,* 17, 1988, pp. 119–137.

14. Joseph Schumpeter, *Capitalism, Socialism, and Democracy.* New York: Harper & Row, 1942, p. 69.

15. Robert Dalzell, *Enterprising Elite: The Boston Associates and the World They Made.* Cambridge: Harvard University Press, 1987; Naomi Lamoreaux, *Insider Lending: Banks, Personal Connections, and Economic Development in Industrial New England.* Cambridge, England: Cambridge University Press, NBER Series on Long Term Factors in Economic Development, 1996.

16. See Richard Florida and Mark Samber, "Capital and Creative Destruction," in Barnes and Gertler (eds.), *The New Industrial Geography,* pp. 265–291; and Samber, *Networks of Capital: Creating and Maintaining a Regional Industrial Economy in Pittsburgh, 1865–1919.* Pittsburgh: Carnegie Mellon University, Department of History, doctoral dissertation, 1995.

17. On the history of ARD, see Patrick Liles, *Sustaining the Venture Capital Firm.* Cambridge: Harvard University, Management Analysis Center, 1977. An excellent history of early forms of venture capital is provided in Martha Louise Reiner, *The Transformation of Venture Capital: A History of Venture Capital Organizations in the United States.* Berkeley: University of California, Graduate School of Business Administration, doctoral dissertation, July 1989. For a broader discussion of the links between MIT and early venture capital in Boston, see Stuart Leslie, *The Cold War and American Science.* New York: Columbia University Press, 1992.

18. On Silicon Valley, see Annalee Saxenian, *Regional Advantage: Culture and Competition in Silicon Valley and Route 128.* Cambridge: Harvard University Press, 1994; Martin Kenney (ed.), *Understanding Silicon Valley: Anatomy of an Entrepreneurial Region.* Stanford: Stanford University Press, 2000, pp. 98–123; Michael Malone, *The Big Score.* New

York: Doubleday, 1985; Paul Frieberger and Michael Swaine, *Fire in the Valley: The Making of the Personal Computer*. Berkeley: Osborne-McGraw Hill, 1984; Dirk Hanson, *The New Alchemists: Silicon Valley and the Microelectronics Revolution*. Boston: Little Brown, 1982. For a historical perspective, see Leslie, *The Cold War and American Science*; Arthur Norberg, "The Origins of the Electronics Industry on the Pacific Coast," *Proceedings of the Institute of Electrical and Electronics Engineers*, 64(9), September 1976, pp. 1314–1322; Timothy Sturgeon, "Origins of Silicon Valley: The Development of the Electronics Industry in the San Francisco Bay Area," unpublished Master's thesis, Department of City and Regional Planning, University of California at Berkeley, 1992. For antidote to the booster-ish quality that is typical of much of the writing on Silicon Valley, see Dennis Hayes, *Behind the Silicon Curtain*. Montreal: Black Rose Books, 1990.

19. Florida and Kenney, *The Breakthrough Illusion*, and Martin Kenney and Richard Florida, "Venture Capital in Silicon Valley: Fuelling New Firm Formation," in Martin Kenney (ed.), *Understanding Silicon Valley: Anatomy of an Entrepreneurial Region*. Stanford: Stanford University Press, 2000, pp. 98–123.

20. See Richard Florida and Martin Kenney, "Venture Capital, High-Technology and Regional Development." *Regional Studies*, 22(1), 1988, pp. 33–48.

21. Gompers and Lerner, *The Venture Capital Cycle*; William Sahlman and Howard Stevenson, "Capital Market Myopia." *Journal of Business Venturing*, 1, 1997, pp. 7–30.

22. For example, George Gilder, *Microcosm: The Quantum Revolution in Economics and Technology*. New York: Simon and Schuster, 1989.

23. The literature on Japanese industrial capitalism is vast. See James Abbeglen, *The Japanese Factory*. Cambridge: MIT Press, 1958; Robert Cole, *Japanese Blue Collar*. Berkeley: University of California Press, 1971; Ronald Dore, *Japanese Factory, British Factory*. Berkeley: University of California Press, 1973; and especially Andrew Gordon, *The Evolution of Labor Relations in Japan: Heavy Industry, 1853–1955*. Cambridge: Harvard University Press, 1985. Martin Kenney and I examined the evolution of the Japanese manufacturing system and its transfer to the United States in our book *Beyond Mass Production*. New York: Oxford University Press, 1993.

24. Taiichi Ohno, *Toyota Production System* (English translation). Portland: Productivity Press, 1988, p. 54. Original Japanese edition, Tokyo: Diamond, Inc., 1978.

25. Akio Morita, *Made in Japan*. New York: Penguin, 1986, p. 165.

26. Timothy Sturgeon, "Modular Production Networks: A New American Model of Industrial Organization." *Industrial and Corporate Change*, 11(4), 2002.

27. Personal interview by author, 1986.

28. This was part of a large-scale project on The Globalization of the Automotive Industry funded by the Alfred P. Sloan Foundation. See Richard Florida and Timothy Sturgeon, *Globalization and Jobs in the Automotive Industry. Final Report to the Alfred P. Sloan Foundation, 1999*; also available as an MIT: International Motor Vehicle Program Monograph, Center for Technology, Policy, and Industrial Development, 2002.

29. Charles Fine, *Clockspeed: Winning Industry Control in the Age of Temporary Advantage*. New York: Perseus Books, 1998.

30. See, for example, Joel Mokyr, *The Lever of Riches: Technological Creativity and Economic Progress*. New York: Oxford University Press, 1990; David Landes, *The Unbound Prometheus: Technological Change and Industrial Development in Western Europe from 1750 to the Present*. Cambridge: Cambridge University Press, 1969; Nathan Rosenberg and L. E. Birdzell, Jr., *How the West Grew Rich: The Economic Transformation of the Industrial World*. New York: Basic Books, 1986; Jared Diamond. *Guns, Germs, and Steel: The Fates of Human Societies*. New York: W.W. Norton and Company, 1997.

31. See Fernand Braudel, *The Structures of Everyday Life: The Limits of the Possible. Volume I of Civilization and Capitalism, 15th–18th Century.* Berkeley: University of California Press, 1992.

32. See Mokyr, *The Lever of Riches*; Landes, *The Unbound Prometheus*; and Rosenberg and Birdzell, *How the West Grew Rich.*

33. See Braudel, *The Structures of Everyday Life.*

34. See Mokyr, *The Lever of Riches*; Landes, *The Unbound Prometheus*; Rosenberg and Birdzell, *How the West Grew Rich.*

35. Mokyr, *The Lever of Riches,* p. 68.

36. Marc Demarest, "The Firm and the Guild: On the Future of Knowledge Work and Information Technology," April 1995, available on-line at www.heva.net/demarest/marc/ethiccmp2.html, p. 8.

37. See Mokyr, *The Lever of Riches*; Landes, *The Unbound Prometheus;* and Rosenberg and Birdzell, *How the West Grew Rich.*

38. Demarest, "The Firm and the Guild," p. 9.

39. See David Hounshell, *From the American System to Mass Production.* Baltimore: Johns Hopkins University Press, 1984.

40. See Alfred Chandler, *The Visible Hand: The Managerial Revolution in American Business.* Cambridge: Belknap Press of Harvard University, 1977.

41. See E. P. Thompson, "Time, Work-Discipline, and Industrial Capitalism." *Past and Present,* 88, 1967; David Landes, *Revolution in Time: Clocks and the Making of the Modern World.* Cambridge: Harvard University Press, 1983.

42. There are a huge number of works on early industrial cities, but for a thorough discussion see Peter Hall, *Cities in Civilization.* New York: Fromm International Publishing, 2001.

43. See Michael Piore and Charles Sabel, *The Second Industrial Divide: Possibilities for Prosperity.* New York: Basic Books, 1984; Oliver Williamson, *The Economic Institutions of Capitalism.* New York: The Free Press, 1985.

44. There is an enormous literature on the history of the research and development laboratory. Superb overviews can be found in David Hounshell, "Edison and the Pure Science Ideal in 19th Century America." *Science,* 207(4431), February 8, 1988; Margaret Graham, "Industrial Research in the Age of Big Science." *Research on Technological Innovation, Management and Policy,* 2, 1985; Michael Dennis, "Accounting for Research: New Histories of Corporate Laboratories and the Social History of American Science." *Social Studies of Science,* 17, 1987, pp. 479–518; David Mowery and Nathan Rosenberg, *Technology and the Pursuit of Economic Growth.* Cambridge: Cambridge University Press, 1989.

45. On the rise of the research university, see Roger Geiger, *To Advance Knowledge: The Growth of American Research Universities, 1900–1940.* New York: Oxford University Press, 1986; Geiger, *Research and Relevant Knowledge.* New York: Oxford University Press, 1993.

46. On taylorism, see Daniel Nelson, *Managers and Workers.* Madison: University of Wisconsin Press, 1975; Nelson, *Frederick W. Taylor and the Rise of Scientific Management.* Madison: University of Wisconsin Press, 1980. On fordism, see Michel Aglietta, *A Theory of Capitalist Regulation: The U.S. Experience.* London: New Left Books, 1979; also see William Lazonick, *Competitive Advantage on the Shop Floor.* Cambridge: Harvard University Press, 1990; Lazonick, *Business Organization and the Myth of the Market Economy.* New York: Cambridge University Press, 1991.

47. William H. Whyte, Jr., *The Organization Man.* New York: Simon and Schuster, 1956; David Reisman, *The Lonely Crowd: A Study of the Changing American Character.* New Haven: Yale University Press, 1961; C. Wright Mills, *White Collar: The American Middle*

Classes. New York: Oxford University Press, 1951; Richard Yates, *Revolutionary Road.* Boston: Little, Brown and Co., 1961.

48. See Douglas Smith and Robert Alexander, *Fumbling the Future: How Xerox Invented then Ignored the First Personal Computer.* New York: William Morrow and Company, 1988.

49. See Florida and Kenney, *The Breakthrough Illusion.*

Chapter 4

1. See Daniel Bell, *The Coming of Post-Industrial Society.* New York: Basic Books, 1973; Peter Drucker, *The Age of Discontinuity.* New York: HarperCollins, 1969; Drucker, *Post-Capitalist Society.* New York: Harper Business, 1995; Fritz Machlup, *The Production and Distribution of Knowledge in the United States.* Princeton: Princeton University Press, 1962.

2. See, for example, Erik Olin Wright, *Classes.* London: Verso, 1990; *Class Counts.* Cambridge, England: Cambridge University Press, 1996; *Class Crisis and the State.* London: Verso, paperback reissue, 1996.

3. Robert Reich, *The Work of Nations.* New York: Alfred A. Knopf, 1991.

4. Paul Fussell, *Class: A Guide Through the American Status System.* New York: Summit, 1983.

5. Steven Barley, *The New World of Work.* London: British North American Committee, 1996.

6. Barbara Ehrenreich, *Nickel and Dimed: On Not Getting By in America.* New York: Henry Holt & Company, 2001.

7. As cited in Bill Bishop, "As City Booms, Poor Get Poorer." *Austin American-Statesman,* January 2, 2000.

8. Barley, *The New World of Work,* p. 7.

9. Steven Brint, "Professionals and the Knowledge Economy: Rethinking the Theory of the Postindustrial Society." *Current Sociology,* 49(1), July 2001, pp. 101–132.

10. See Ronald Inglehart, "Globalization and Postmodern Values." *The Washington Quarterly,* 23(1), Winter 2000, pp. 215–228; *The Silent Revolution: Changing Values and Political Styles in Advanced Industrial Society.* Princeton: Princeton University Press, 1977; *Culture Shift in Advanced Industrial Society.* Princeton: Princeton University Press, 1990; *Modernization and Postmodernization: Cultural, Economic and Political Change in Forty-Three Societies.* Princeton: Princeton University Press, 1997; and "Culture and Democracy," in Lawrence Harrison and Samuel Huntington (eds.), *Culture Matters: How Values Shape Human Progress.* New York: Basic Books, 2000, pp. 80–97.

11. Paul H. Ray and Sherry Ruth Anderson, *The Cultural Creatives: How 50 Million People Are Changing the World.* New York: Harmony Books, 2000. See introductory chapter, pp. 7–42, especially the "Values and Beliefs" charts, pp. 28–29. Inglehart is cited in the Preface, p. xii.

12. Inglehart, "Globalization and Postmodern Values," p. 225.

13. Inglehart, "Culture and Democracy," p. 84.

14. Robert Fogel, *The Fourth Great Awakening and the Future of Egalitarianism.* Chicago: University of Chicago Press, 2000, p. 191.

Chapter 5

1. Peter Drucker, "Beyond the Information Revolution." *The Atlantic Monthly,* 284, October 4, 1999, pp. 47–57, quote from p. 57.

2. This e-mail was forwarded to me by one of my students in spring 2001.

3. William C. Taylor, "Eric Raymond on Work." *Fast Company,* November 1999, p. 200. Also see Eric Raymond, *The Cathedral and the Bazaar: Musings on Linux and Open Source by an Accidental Revolutionary.* Sebastopol, Calif.: O'Reilly and Associates, Inc., 1999.

4. *Information Week,* Annual Salary Survey, 2000 and 2001.

5. Personal interview by author, summer 2000.

6. Personal interview by author, winter 2000.

7. Personal interview by author, spring 2000.

8. Richard Lloyd, "Digital Bohemia: New Media Enterprises in Chicago's Wicker Park Neighborhood." Paper presented at the annual conference of the American Sociological Association, August 2001.

9. Laurie Levesque, "A Qualitative Study of Organizational Roles in High Tech Start-up Firms." Paper presented at the Annual Conference of the Academy of Management, Toronto, 2000; *Role Creation Processes in Start-up Firms.* Pittsburgh: Carnegie Mellon University, Graduate School of Industrial Administration, doctoral dissertation, 2001; "Creating New Roles: Understanding Employee Behavior in High Tech Start-ups." Paper presented at the Annual Conference of the Academy of Management, Washington, D.C., 2001.

10. Raymond, *The Cathedral and the Bazaar.*

11. See Robert Merton, "Priorities in Scientific Discovery: A Chapter in the Sociology of Science." *American Sociological Review,* 22(6), 1957, pp. 635–659; and *The Sociology of Science.* Chicago: University of Chicago Press, 1973.

12. See Partha Dasgupta and Paul David, "Information Disclosure and the Economics of Science and Technology," in G. Feiwel (ed.), *Arrow and the Ascent of Modern Economic Theory.* New York: New York University Press, 1987; and "Toward a New Economics of Science." *Research Policy,* 23(3), May 1994, pp. 487–521. Also see Paula Stephan, "The Economics of Science." *Journal of Economic Literature,* 34, 1996, pp. 1199–1235.

13. Scott Stern, "Do Scientists Pay to Be Scientists?" Cambridge, Mass.: National Bureau of Economic Research, Working Paper 7410, October 1999. Also see Michelle Gittleman and Bruce Kogut, "Why Do Firms Do Research (By Their Own Scientists?): Science, Scientists and Innovation Among US Biotechnology Firms." Paper presented at the Annual Conference of the Academy of Management, Toronto, 2000; and "Does Good Science Lead to Valuable Knowledge: Biotechnology Firms and the Evolutionary Logic of Citation Patterns." Philadelphia: Wharton School, University of Pennsylvania, Jones Center, Working Paper 2001–04, 2001.

14. Though neither are scientific surveys, they do highlight the importance of location. The Zogby survey findings are reported in "U.S. Workers Face Care Dilemma: Love It or Leave It? National Survey Finds," PR Newswire Association Inc., February 12, 2001. The second survey, cited by the *Wall Street Journal,* is based on a sample of 970 job seekers by CareerEngine.com in summer 2001, see Kemba Dunham, "The Jungle: Focus on Pay, Recruitment and Getting Ahead." *Wall Street Journal,* July 3, 2001.

15. Elizabeth Chambers, Mark Foulon, Helen Handfield-Jones, Steven Hanklin and Edward Michaels, "The War for Talent." *The McKinsey Quarterly,* 3, 1998, pp. 44–57.

16. *The Towers Perrin Talent Report: New Realities in Today's Workplace.* New York: Towers Perrin, 2001.

17. Robert Fogel, *The Fourth Great Awakening and the Future of Egalitarianism.* Chicago: University of Chicago Press, 2000.

Chapter 6

1. Personal interviews and communication by author, 2000–2001.

2. Richard Florida and Martin Kenney, *The Breakthrough Illusion*. New York: Basic Books, 1990.

3. *Information Week* Annual Salary Survey, 2000–2001, as analyzed by the author.

4. *The Towers Perrin Talent Report: New Realities in Today's Workplace*. New York: Towers Perrin, 2001.

5. "The End of the Job." *Fortune* (cover story), September 19, 1994.

6. Alan Burton Jones, *Knowledge Capitalism: Business, Work and Learning in the New Economy*. Oxford: Oxford University Press, 1999, p. 48.

7. Daniel Pink, *Free Agent Nation: How America's New Independent Workers Are Transforming the Way We Live*. New York: Warner Books, 2001.

8. Mickey Butts, "Let Freedom Ring" (a review of Dan Pink's *Free Agent Nation*). *The Industry Standard*, April 30, 2001, p. 77.

9. Rosemary Batt, Susan Christopherson, Ned Rightor and Danielle Van Jaarsveld, *Net Working: Work Patterns and Workforce Policies for the New Media Industry*. Washington, D.C.: Economic Policy Institute, 2001.

10. Rob Walker, "Personal Days" (a review of *Free Agent Nation*). *New York Times*, Book Review, April 29, 2001.

11. Jeffrey Pfeffer as cited in a review of Pink's book, "Not Holding a Job Is the New Work System." *New York Times*, May 27, 2001. Also see Pfeffer, "Fighting the War for Talent Is Hazardous to Your Organization's Health." *Organizational Dynamics*, 29(4), Spring 2001, pp. 248–259.

12. Jeremy Rifkin, *The End of Work: The Decline of the Global Labor Force and the Dawn of the Post-Market Era*. New York: Putnam, 1995; Stanley Aronowitz and Wil DeFazio, *The Jobless Future: Sci-Tech and the Dogma of Work*. Minneapolis: University of Minnesota Press, 1994.

13. Jill Andresky Fraser, *White-Collar Sweatshop: The Deterioration of Work and Its Rewards in Corporate America*. New York: W.W. Norton, 2001.

14. Richard Sennett, *The Corrosion of Character: The Personal Consequences of Work in the New Capitalism*. New York: W.W. Norton, 1998.

15. Joanne Ciulla, *The Working Life: The Promise and Betrayal of Modern Work*. New York: Times Books, 2000, p. 232.

16. Ciulla, *The Working Life*, p. 230.

17. On-line dialogue on *Fast Company*'s magazine website, see www.fastcompany.com.

18. Personal communication with the author, winter 2001.

19. Gideon Kunda, Stephen R. Barley and James A. Evans, "Why Do Contractors Contract? The Experience of Highly Skilled Technical Professionals in a Contingent Labor Market." *Industrial and Labor Relations Review*, 2001.

20. Stephen Barley, *The New World of Work*. London: British North American Committee, 1996. Lawrence Friedman argues that virtually all major economic and social institutions are moving to a horizontal structure; see his *The Horizontal Society*. New Haven: Yale University Press, 1999.

21. Batt et al., *Net Working*.

22. Job Satisfaction Survey, conducted by Lucent Technologies, February 2001, on 262 "network professionals," available at www.lucentservices.com/knowledge/surveys/01jobs/.

23. Louis Uchitelle, "As Job Cuts Spread, Tears Replace Anger." *New York Times*, August 5, 2001, on-line edition, pp. 6–7.

Chapter 7

1. Michelle Conlin, "Job Security, No. Tall Latte, Yes." *Business Week,* April 2, 2001, pp. 62–63.

2. Alastair Gordon, "As Work and Life Blur, Office Furniture Goes 24/7." *New York Times,* September 2, 2001, section 3, p. 10.

3. Terry Pristin, "The Suits Loosen Up, a Bit Uneasily." *New York Times,* April 6, 2000.

4. Jane Eisner, "Changing Work Culture Must Be Well-Fashioned." *Philadelphia Inquirer,* February 11, 2001, on-line edition, pp. 1–2.

5. "Banana Republic Storms the Office." *Business Week,* September 11, 2000.

6. See, for example, Scott Omellanuk, "Survival Strategies for the Casual Office." *Wall Street Journal,* June 23, 2000.

7. Stephanie Armour, "Companies Rethink Casual Clothes." *USA Today,* June 27, 2000.

8. Pristin, "The Suits Loosen Up."

9. Peter Waldman, "Hot-Button Issue: Getting Lawyers to Ditch Their Suits." *Wall Street Journal,* March 19, 1999.

10. Personal interview by author, spring 2001.

11. "Geek Chic." *Wall Street Journal,* September 7, 2000.

12. Personal communication, winter 2001.

13. These figures are drawn from Lonnie Golden, "Flexible Work Schedules: What Are We Trading Off to Get Them?" *Monthly Labor Review,* March 2001, pp. 50–67.

14. See Phillip Rones, Randy Ilg and Jennifer Gardner, "Trends in Hours of Work Since the Mid–1970s." *Monthly Labor Review,* April 1997, pp. 3–14.

15. See Malcolm Gladwell, "Designs for Working: Why Your Bosses Want to Turn Your Office into Greenwich Village." *New Yorker,* December 8, 2000, pp. 60–70; and Jeffrey Huang, "Future Space: A New Blueprint for Business Architecture." *Harvard Business Review,* April 2001, pp. 149–157.

16. Personal communication, summer 2001.

17. See Jane Jacobs, *The Death and Life of Great American Cities.* New York: Random House, 1961; quote is from the Modern Library Edition, p. 245.

18. Thomas Allen, *Managing the Flow of Technology.* Cambridge: MIT Press, 1977.

19. See Claudia Deutsch, "New Economy: IBM and Steelcase Lay Out Their Vision of the Office of the Future." *New York Times,* January 14, 2001, p. C4.

20. Gordon, "As Work and Life Blur."

21. Gladwell, "Designs for Working," pp. 60–70.

22. Gladwell, "Designs for Working," p. 62.

23. Gladwell, "Designs for Working," pp. 64–65.

24. Gladwell, "Designs for Working," p. 62.

25. Motoka Rich, "Shut Up So We Can Do Our Jobs!" *Wall Street Journal,* posted on the *Hollywood Sentinel* on-line, September 30, 2001.

26. Personal communication, spring 2000.

Chapter 8

1. Personal interview by author, fall 2001.

2. As quoted in "Danger: Toxic Company." *Fast Company,* November 19, 1998, p. 152.

3. Jill Andresky Fraser, *White-Collar Sweatshop: The Deterioration of Work and Its Rewards in Corporate America.* New York: W.W. Norton, 2001.

4. Arlie Russell Hochschild, *The Time Bind: When Work Becomes Home and Home Becomes Work.* New York: Henry Holt & Company, 2000.

5. David Thielen, "Ultimate Management Secrets from Former Microsoft Superstar." Boardroom, Inc., www.bottomlinesecrets.com, 2001. Also see *The 12 Simple Secrets of Microsoft Management.* New York: McGraw Hill Professional Publishing, 1999; www.12 simplesecrets.com. Also see Richard Selby and Michael Cusumano, *Microsoft Secrets: How the World's Most Powerful Software Company Creates Technology, Shapes Markets and Manages People.* New York: The Free Press, 1999.

6. As quoted in Christine Canabou, "The Sun Sets on the Bohemian Workplace." *Fast Company,* August 2001, www.fastcompany.com/learning/bookshel/ross.html, p. 2; David Brooks, *Bobos in Paradise: The New Upper Class and How They Got There.* New York: Simon and Schuster, 2001.

7. Timothy Butler and James Waldroop, "Job Sculpting: The Art of Retaining Your Best People." *Harvard Business Review,* September-October 1999, pp. 144–152.

8. See Peter Drucker, "Management's New Paradigm." *Forbes,* 7, October 5, 1998, pp. 152–177.

9. Jack Beatty, "Cannibalistic Capitalism." *Atlantic Unbound/Atlantic online,* June 7, 2001, www.theatlantic.com/unbound/polipro/pp.2001-06-07.htm, pp. 1–2.

10. *Fast Company* on-line dialogue, www.fastcompany.com.

11. Lydia Saad, "American Workers Generally Satisfied, but Indicate Their Jobs Leave Much To Be Desired." *Gallup News Service,* September 3, 1999, www.gallup.com/poll/releases/pr990903.asp.

12. Michelle Conlin, "Job Security, No. Tall Latte, Yes." *Business Week,* April 2, 2001, p. 63.

13. William H. Whyte, Jr., *The Organization Man.* New York: Simon and Schuster, 1956.

14. Denise Rousseau, "The Idiosyncratic Deal: Flexibility Versus Fairness?" *Organizational Dynamics,* 29(4), Spring 2001, pp. 260–273; "The Boundaryless Human Resource Function: Building Agency and Community in the New Economic Era." *Organizational Dynamics,* 27(4), Spring 1999, pp. 6–18; and *Idiosyncratic Employment Arrangements: When Workers Bargain for Themselves.* Armonk, N.Y.: W.E. Sharpe, 2002.

15. My discussion of open source software development draws heavily from the conversations and insights of my colleagues at the Software Center at Carnegie Mellon, particularly Mary Shaw, Ashish Arora, Timothy Halloran, Guillermo Dabos and Orna Raz. The literature on open source development is abundant, but see, for example, Eric Raymond, *The Cathedral and the Bazaar: Musings on Linux and Open Source by an Accidental Revolutionary.* Sebastopol, Calif.: O'Reilly and Associates, Inc., 1999; Pekka Himanen, with Linus Torvalds and Manuel Castells, *The Hacker Ethic: And the Sprit of the Information Age.* New York: Random House, 2001; Karim Lakhani and Eric Von Hippel, "How Open Source Software Works: Free User-to-User Assistance." Cambridge: MIT, Sloan School of Management, Working Paper No. 4117, May 2000.

16. Josh Lerner and Jean Triole, "The Simple Economics of Open Source Software." Boston: Harvard Business School Working Paper No. 00-059, and National Bureau of Economic Research Working Paper No. 7600, December 2000.

17. "John Seely Brown Interview," by Michael Schrage, *Wired,* August 2000. Also see John Seely Brown and Paul Duguid, *The Social Life of Information.* Boston: Harvard Business School Press, 2001.

18. Whyte, *The Organization Man,* p. 446.

19. See Richard Florida, "Science, Reputation and Organization." Pittsburgh: Carnegie Mellon University, unpublished working paper, January 2000. Also see Scott Stern, "Do

Scientists Pay To Be Scientists?" Cambridge: National Bureau of Economic Research, Working Paper No. 7410, October 1999. Also see Michelle Gittleman and Bruce Kogut, "Why Do Firms Do Research (By Their Own Scientists?): Science, Scientists and Innovation Among US Biotechnology Firms." Paper presented at the annual conference of the Academy of Management, Toronto, August 2000; and "Does Good Science Lead to Valuable Knowledge: Biotechnology Firms and the Evolutionary Logic of Citation Patterns." Philadelphia: Wharton School, University of Pennsylvania, Jones Center, Working Paper No. 2001-04, 2001.

20. See Paul Freiberger and Michael Swaine, *Fire in the Valley: The Making of the Personal Computer.* Berkeley: Osborne/McGraw Hill, 1984. Chapter 11, "The Big Morph," develops these themes in more detail.

21. Richard Lloyd, "Digital Bohemia: New Media Enterprises in Chicago's Wicker Park Neighborhood." Paper presented at the annual conference of the American Sociological Association, August 2001.

22. Conlin, "Job Security, No," p. 62.

23. The best expression of this may be the runaway bestseller *The Cluetrain Manifesto,* subtitled *The End of Business as Usual,* by Rick Levine, Christopher Locke, Doc Searls and David Weinberger. Cambridge: Perseus Books, 2000.

24. As quoted in Christine Canabou, "The Sun Sets on the Bohemian Workplace." *Fast Company,* August 2001, www.fastcompany.com/learning/bookshelf/ross.html, p. 3.

25. Quote from "Danger: Toxic Company." *Fast Company,* November 19, 1998, p. 152; but also see Jeffrey Pfeffer, *The Human Equation: Building Profits by Putting People First.* Boston: Harvard Business School Press, 1998.

26. Personal interviews by and communication with the author, 1999–2000.

27. Personal interviews by author, spring 2001.

Chapter 9

1. Juliet Schor, *The Overworked American.* New York: Basic Books, 1991.

2. The classic statements are E. P. Thompson, "Time, Work-Discipline, and Industrial Capitalism." *Past and Present,* 88, 1967; David Landes, *Revolution in Time: Clocks and the Making of the Modern World.* Cambridge: Harvard University Press, 1983; Sebastian De Grazia, *Of Time, Work and Leisure.* New York: Twentieth Century Fund, 1962. Also see Stephen Jay Gould, *Time's Arrow, Time's Cycle: Myth and Metaphor in the Discovery of Geological Time.* Cambridge: Harvard University Press, 1987; Stephen Hawking, *A Brief History of Time: From the Big Bang to Black Holes.* New York: Bantam Books, 1988; Robert Levine, *A Geography of Time.* New York: Basic Books, 1997; J. David Lewis and Andrew Wiegert, "The Structure and Meanings of Social Time." *Social Forces,* 60(2), December 1981; Frank Dubinskas (ed.), *Making Time: Ethnographies of High-Tech Organizations.* Philadelphia: Temple University Press, 1988. Joanne Ciulla, *The Working Life: The Promise and Betrayal of Modern Work,* New York: Times Books, 2000, provides a very good overview of these concepts, as does John Robinson and Geoffrey Godbey, *Time for Life: The Surprising Ways Americans Use Their Time,* 2nd edition. University Park: The Pennsylvania State University Press, 1999.

3. Ciulla, *The Working Life,* p. 174.

4. See Steven Greenhouse, "Report Shows Americans Have More 'Labor Days.'" *New York Times,* September 1, 2001, on-line edition, pp. 1–2. The ILO study is available at www.ilo.org.

5. Robinson and Godbey point to many flaws in Schor's overworking thesis. According to the authors, Schor misuses the time diary data in a variety of problematic ways that leave her findings questionable. They write that Schor's results "are *not* [italics in original] supported by diary data. In constructing her arguments, Schor uses our time-diary data for 1975, and then mixes those data with time-estimate data. . . . She does not use our 1965 time-diary data—the major benchmark year for our analysis—because rural residents (who don't differ that much from urban Americans in their uses of time) were excluded and because of other sampling issues (which we have handled by poststratification and weighting). She also does not take into account our time-diary data and published articles from the 1985 study, relying instead on regression estimates from 1975 data on housework that do not reflect the surprising changes in actual diary housework times we have found since 1965. Finally, Schor averages government data both on work hours and on work-weeks that show increased hours of work that were not evident to earlier analysts of these data." They note that like "many analysts" Schor uses the findings of a 1988 Harris Poll that Americans' work hours had increased as free time declined by 30 percent since 1972. They then quote the "more careful research of Hamilton" as pointing out that the real difference was that the "question wording" had changed in the Harris Poll: "There was no dramatic increase in work between 1973 and 1985, nor was there a dramatic decrease in leisure. . . . The Harris workweek 'finding' appears to reflect changes in the methods used rather than any real change. The same conclusion appears justified with regard to his finding about free time." Godbey and Robinson quote Hamilton on p. 50. See R. Hamilton, "Work and Leisure: On the Reporting of Poll Results." *Public Opinion Quarterly,* 55, 1991, pp. 347–356; the quote is from pp. 354–355. For Schor's response, see Juliet Schor, "Civic Engagement and Working Hours: Do Americans Really Have More Free Time Than Ever Before?" Paper presented at the Conference on Civic Engagement in American Democracy, Portland, Maine, September 26–28, 1997, available at www.silicon.com/rdb/swt/putok.htm.

6. Robinson and Godbey, *Time for Life,* Chapter 22, "A 1990s Update: Trends Since 1985," pp. 325–338.

7. Robinson and Godbey, *Time for Life,* pp. 338–340.

8. See Phillip Rones, Randy Ilg and Jennifer Gardner, "Trends in Hours of Work Since the Mid-1970s." *Monthly Labor Review,* April 1997, pp. 3–14.

9. Robinson and Godbey, *Time for Life,* p. xvi.

10. Leslie Perlow, *Finding Time: How Corporations, Individuals, and Families Can Benefit from New Work Practices.* Ithaca: Cornell University Press, 1997.

11. Rosabeth Kanter, *Men and Women of the Corporation.* New York: Basic Books, 1977, as cited in Perlow, "Boundary Control: The Social Ordering of Work and Family Time in a High-Tech Corporation." *Administrative Science Quarterly,* 43, 1998, p. 330.

12. Robinson and Godbey, *Time for Life,* p. 25.

13. Robinson and Godbey, *Time for Life,* Chapter 16, "Perceptions of Time Pressure," pp. 229–240.

14. Robinson and Godbey, *Time for Life,* pp. 233–238.

15. Paul Romer, "Time: It Really Is Money." *Information Week,* September 11, 2001; found at www.informationweek.com/803/romer.htm, May 2001. The classic economic perspective on time is Gary Becker, "A Theory of the Allocation of Time." *Economic Journal,* 75, 1965, pp. 493–517. Also see Stephan Linder, *The Harried Leisure Class.* New York: Columbia University Press, 1970.

16. Brad Templeton's home page, under "Bill Gates Wealth Index," www.templetons. com/brad/billg.html, December 2001.

17. Trilogy home page, www.trilogy.com. Quote was found under "Life at Trilogy" on

November 1, 2000. Interestingly, when this portion of the site was rechecked in December 2001, the quote had disappeared.

18. As cited in Rick Marin, "Is This the Face of a Midlife Crisis?" *New York Times,* June 25, 2001.

19. See, for example, Alexandra Robbins and Abby Wilner, *The Quarterlife Crisis: The Unique Challenges of Life in Your Twenties.* New York: Jeremey P. Tarcher/Putnam, 2001; also see Marin, "Is This the Face of a Midlife Crisis?"

20. Robinson and Godbey, *Time for Life,* p. 44.

Chapter 10

1. Janelle Brown, "A Poster Child for Internet Idiocy." Salon.com, August 1, 2001: salon. com/tech/feature/2000/08/01/dotcomguy/print.html.

2. Joseph Pine III and James H. Gilmore, *The Experience Economy: Work Is Theatre and Every Business a Stage.* Boston: Harvard Business School Press, 1999, pp. 2, 11.

3. C. Campbell, *The Romantic Ethic and the Spirit of Modern Consumerism.* Oxford: Blackwell, 1987; and "The Sociology of Consumption," in D. Miller (ed.), *Acknowledging Consumption: A Review of New Studies.* London: Routledge, 1996, pp. 96–126.

4. Ben Malbon, *Clubbing: Dancing, Ecstasy, and Vitality.* London: Routledge, 1999, p. 33.

5. Carl Rogers, "Toward a Theory of Creativity," in *On Becoming a Person: A Therapist's View of Psychotherapy.* Boston: Houghton Mifflin, 1961, p. 348.

6. Rogers, "Toward a Theory of Creativity," pp. 352–354.

7. Thorstein Veblen, *The Theory of the Leisure Class.* New York: New American Library, 1959; orig. 1899.

8. Gary Cross, *The All-Consuming Century: Why Commercialism Won in Modern America.* New York: Columbia University Press, 2000.

9. As quoted in James Atlas, "Cashing Out Young." *Vanity Fair,* December 1999, p. 216.

10. Clair Brown, *American Standards of Living, 1918–1988.* Oxford: Blackwell Publishers, 1994, p. 3. Interestingly, Brown continues: "The material richness of life brought with it new concerns, however. People now worried about consuming too many calories as well as too much fat or salt. Having sufficient space to store clothes and consumer goods became a problem. Finding time to buy and maintain all the goods the family wanted to consume became one more demand in a society already feeling the stress of work and family commitments."

11. Robert Fogel, *The Fourth Great Awakening and the Future of Egalitarianism.* Chicago: University of Chicago Press, 2000, p. 191. Alan Wolfe provides a thoughtful review of recent works on consumption in "Undialectical Materialism: America Consumed by Consumption." *The New Republic,* October 23, 2000, pp. 29–35.

12. Andy Sheehan, *Chasing the Hawk.* New York: Delacorte, 2001.

13. Cited in Joan Raymond, "Happy Trails: America's Affinity for the Great Outdoors." *American Demographics,* August 2000, on-line version, pp. 1–4.

14. Cited in Raymond, "Happy Trails."

15. As cited in Bear Stearns, *America at Leisure: How Do Americans Spend Their Leisure Time?* New York: Bear Stearns, June 2001.

16. Bear Stearns, *America at Leisure,* p. 33.

17. John Robinson and Geoffrey Godbey, *Time for Life: The Surprising Ways Americans Use Time,* 2nd edition. University Park: The Pennsylvania State University Press, 1999.

18. *The Lifestyle Market Analyst* is compiled by Equifax and based on the responses to

15.3 million consumer information questionnaires that are weighted and stratified based on demographic information from the U.S. Census and Claritas. It rates activities for various demographic and income groups, as well as geographic regions, based on a Lifestyle Index: An index value of 100 is the national average, thus an index value over 100 exceeds the national average, while a value less than 100 is below the national average. More than half of all survey respondents own a CD player (69.6 percent), personal computer (53.8 percent), cell phone (53.7 percent), listen to records (51.9 percent) and donate to charitable causes (51.2 percent). More than 40 percent (41.6 percent) engage in exercise and physical fitness. Thomas Link, a graduate student at Carnegie Mellon University, assisted with the analysis of these data.

19. Personal interviews by author, winter 2000.

20. Personal interview by author, spring 2000.

21. See Bear Stearns, *America at Leisure.*

22. Paul Fussell, *Class: A Guide Through the American Status System.* New York: Summit, 1983, p. 115.

23. See *Men's Fitness,* January 2001; see also Nanci Hemlich, "Blame the Cheesesteak: Unfit Philly Wins Flab Crown." *USA Today,* December 7, 1999 (on-line version).

24. These correlations should not be taken as scientifically valid proof of causality of any sort, but simply to suggest that a relationship may exist. The Spearman correlations are as follows: the Creativity Index (0.47), Talent Index/BA and above (0.43), high-tech industry (0.32), patents (0.37), Bohemian Index (0.53), and Gay Index (0.48). All are significant at the 0.01 level. Sam Lee assisted with this analysis.

25. Cesar Graña, *Bohemian Versus Bourgeois.* New York: Basic Books, 1964, p. 74.

26. Graña, *Bohemian Versus Bourgeois,* p. 149.

27. There is a large literature on street scenes but see, for example, Nicholas Fyfe (ed.), *Images of the Street: Planning, Identity and Control in Public Space.* New York: Routledge, 1998; Tracy Skelton and Gil Valentine (eds.), *Cool Spaces: Geographies of Youth Cultures.* New York Routledge, 1998. Also see Janine Lopiano-Misdom and Joane DeLuca, *Street Trends: How Today's Alternative Youth Cultures Are Creating Tomorrow's Mainstream Markets.* New York: HarperBusiness, 1997.

28. Malbon, *Clubbing,* p. 174.

29. This section draws heavily from interviews and focus groups conducted by the author between 1999 and 2001. For an excellent overview of the role of street scenes in cities, see Richard Lloyd and Terry Nichols Clark, "The City as an Entertainment Machine," in Kevin Fox Gotham (ed.), *Critical Perspectives on Urban Redevelopment. Research in Urban Sociology,* Vol. 6. Oxford: JAI Press/Elsevier, 2001, pp. 357–378.

30. See Tom Frank, *One Market Under God: Extreme Capitalism, Market Populism, and the End of Economic Development.* New York: Doubleday, 2001; and *The Conquest of Cool: Business Culture, Counterculture, and the Rise of Hip Consumerism.* Chicago: University of Chicago Press, 1997.

31. Malbon, *Clubbing,* p. 55.

32. Kara Swisher, "How Kitchen Fixes Can Add Up Fast." *Wall Street Journal,* August 7, 2001.

Chapter 11

1. Max Weber, *The Protestant Ethic and the Spirit of Capitalism.* London: Routledge, 1992 (orig. 1921).

2. See, for instance, Romans 13: "Let every person be subject to the governing authori-

ties; for there is no authority except from God, and those authorities that exist have been instituted by God," etc.; or Titus 2 and 3, in which slaves must give their masters "satisfaction in every respect" and "show complete and perfect fidelity," while all are "subject to rulers" and "ready for every good work." Quotes from the Holy Bible, New Revised Standard Version. Nashville: Thomas Nelson, Inc., 1990, New Testament, pp. 162, 214–215.

3. Cesar Graña, *Bohemian Versus Bourgeois.* New York: Basic Books, 1964; also expanded and reissued as *Modernity and Its Discontents: French Society and the French Man of Letters in the Nineteenth Century.* New York: Harper Torchbooks, 1967.

4. Georg Lukas, *History and Class Consciousness.* Cambridge: MIT Press, 1971 (Rodney Livingstone, translator); Antonio Gramsci, *Prison Notebooks; Selections.* Geoffrey N. Smith International Publishers Company, 1971 (Quintin Hoare, translator).

5. Graña, *Modernity and Its Discontents,* p. 169.

6. Graña of course has Paris covered. On Greenwich Village, see Carolyn Ware's classic study, *Greenwich Village, 1920–1930.* Berkeley: University of California Press, 1963 (orig. 1935).

7. Graña, *Modernity and Its Discontents,* p. 208.

8. Graña, *Modernity and Its Discontents,* p. 131.

9. Graña, *Modernity and Its Discontents,* pp. 132–133.

10. Jackson Lears, "The Golden Age." *The New Republic,* August 21, 2000 (on-line edition).

11. Daniel Bell, *The Coming of Post-Industrial Society.* New York: Basic Books, 1973.

12. Daniel Bell, *The Cultural Contradictions of Capitalism.* New York: Basic Books, 1976, p. 13.

13. The classic source work on narcissism in our society is Christopher Lasch, *The Culture of Narcissism: American Life in an Age of Diminishing Expectations.* New York: W.W. Norton, 1979.

14. Bell, *The Cultural Contradictions of Capitalism,* pp. xxvi–xxvii.

15. Bell, *The Cultural Contradictions of Capitalism,* pp. xxiv–xxv.

16. Bell, *The Cultural Contradictions of Capitalism,* pp. 21–22.

17. David Brooks, *Bobos in Paradise: The New Upper Class and How They Got There.* New York: Simon and Schuster, 2001.

18. This quote is from the dust jacket of *Bobos in Paradise.*

19. David Brooks, "The Organization Kid." *The Atlantic Monthly,* 287(4), April 2001, pp. 40–54.

20. Brooks, "The Organization Kid," p. 54.

21. For a full-scale conservative appraisal of the sixties, see Roger Kimball, *The Long March: How the Culture Revolution Changed America.* San Francisco: Encounter Books, 2000.

22. There is a huge literature on subcultures, see, for instance, Dick Hebidge, *Subculture: The Meaning of Style.* London: Methuen, 1979; Ken Gelder and Sarah Thornton (eds.), *The Subcultures Reader.* London: Routledge, 1997.

23. Tom Frank, *One Market Under God: Extreme Capitalism, Market Populism, and the End of Economic Development.* New York: Doubleday, 2001; and *The Conquest of Cool: Business Culture, Counterculture, and the Rise of Hip Consumerism.* Chicago: University of Chicago Press, 1997. Also see Kalle Lasn, *Culture Jam: The Uncooling of America.* New York: Eagle Brook/William and Morrow, 1999.

24. The dean of American popular music writing and criticism is Greil Marcus; see his *Mystery Train: Images of America in Rock 'n' Roll Music.* New York: Penguin, 1975; *Lipstick Traces; A Secret History of the Twentieth Century.* Cambridge: Harvard University Press,

1989; *Double Trouble: Bill Clinton and Elvis Presley in a Land of No Alternatives.* New York: Henry Holt and Company, 2000.

25. John Seabrook, *Nobrow: The Culture of Marketing, the Marketing of Culture.* New York: Alfred Knopf, 2000.

26. Paul Freiberger and Michael Swaine, *Fire in the Valley: The Making of the Personal Computer.* Berkeley: Osborne/McGraw Hill, 1984, pp. 17–18.

27. On the Homebrew Club, see Freiberger and Swaine, *Fire in the Valley,* p. 104. Also see John Markoff, "A Strange Brew's Buzz Lingers in Silicon Valley." *New York Times,* March 26, 2000.

28. Personal interview by author and Martin Kenney, March 1987.

29. See Kevin Gray, "Paul Allen: Revenge of the Nerd." *Details,* October 2000, pp. 256–263; Sam Howe Verhovek, "He's Turning Seattle into His Kind of Town." *New York Times* (on-line version), May 17, 2000; Neil Strauss, "Making a Museum out of Music." *New York Times,* June 26, 2000.

30. Jimi Hendrix, "If 6 Was 9," 1967.

31. See Harvey Blume, "Geek Studies." *The Atlantic Unbound,* July 13, 2000; "Two Geeks on Their Way to Byzantium: An Interview with Richard Powers." *The Atlantic Unbound,* June 28, 2000; Scott Stossel, "Soul of the New Economy." *The Atlantic Unbound,* June 8, 2000. All available on-line at www.theatlantic.com.

32. Jon Katz, *Geeks: How Two Lost Boys Rode the Internet out of Idaho.* New York: Villard, 2000.

33. Personal interviews by author, 1999–2001.

34. Visit and personal interview by author, fall 2001.

Chapter 12

1. Adjusted for the costs of living differences, the average salary for an IT worker in Austin was $65,310 compared to $47,173 in San Francisco in 2001 (based on salary data from the *Information Week* Salary Survey adjusted for cost-of-living).

2. Kevin Kelly, *New Rules for the New Economy.* 1998, pp. 94–95.

3. Some classic statements include: Robert Park, E. Burgess and R. McKenzie, *The City.* Chicago: University of Chicago Press, 1925; Jane Jacobs, *The Death and Life of Great American Cities.* New York: Random House, 1961; *The Economy of Cities.* New York: Random House, 1969; *Cities and the Wealth of Nations.* New York: Random House, 1984; Wilbur Thompson, *A Preface to Urban Economics.* Baltimore: The Johns Hopkins University Press, 1965; Edwin Ullman, "Regional Development and the Geography of Concentration." *Papers and Proceedings of the Regional Science Association,* 4, 1958, pp. 179–198.

4. See Michael Porter, "Clusters and the New Economics of Competition." *Harvard Business Review,* November-December 1998; "Location, Clusters, and Company Strategy," in Gordon Clark, Meric Gertler and Maryann Feldman (eds.), *Oxford Handbook of Economic Geography.* Oxford: Oxford University Press, 2000; "Location, Competition and Economic Development: Local Clusters in a Global Economy." *Economic Development Quarterly,* 14(1), February 2000, pp. 15–34.

5. The literature on agglomeration economies is vast, for a recent review see Maryann Feldman, "Location and Innovation: The New Economic Geography of Innovation, Spillovers, and Agglomeration," in Clark, Gertler and Feldman (eds.), *The Oxford Handbook of Economic Geography,* pp. 373–394; Adam Jaffe, "Real Effects of Academic Research." *American Economic Review,* 79(5), 1989; David Audretsch and Maryann Feldman, "R&D

Spillovers and the Geography of Innovation and Production." *American Economic Review,* 86(3), 1996; David Audretsch, "Agglomeration and the Location of Innovative Activity." *Oxford Review of Economic Policy,* 14(2), 1998, pp. 18–30.

6. Robert Putnam, *Bowling Alone: The Collapse and Revival of American Community.* New York: Simon and Schuster, 2000.

7. Joel Kotkin, "The New Geography of Wealth." *Reis.com, Techscapes,* December 2001; available on-line at www.reis.com/learning/insights_techscapes_art.cfm?art=1.

8. See Jacobs, *Cities and the Wealth of Nations.*

9. Robert Lucas, Jr., "On the Mechanics of Economic Development." *Journal of Monetary Economics,* 22, 1988, pp. 38–39.

10. See Edward Glaeser, "Are Cities Dying?" *Journal of Economic Perspectives,* 12, 1998, pp. 139–160. The human capital literature has grown large; other important contributions include: Glaeser, "The New Economics of Urban and Regional Growth," in Clark, Gertler and Feldman (eds.), *The Oxford Handbook of Economic Geography,* pp. 83–98; James E. Rauch, "Productivity Gains from Geographic Concentrations of Human Capital: Evidence from Cities." *Journal of Urban Economics,* 34, 1993, pp. 380–400; Curtis Simon, "Human Capital and Metropolitan Employment Growth." *Journal of Urban Economics,* 43, 1998, pp. 223–243; Curtis Simon and Clark Nardinelli, "The Talk of the Town: Human Capital, Information and the Growth of English Cities, 1861–1961." *Explorations in Economic History,* 33(3), 1996, pp. 384–413. A comprehensive review is provided by Vijay K. Mathur, "Human Capital-Based Strategy for Regional Economic Development." *Economic Development Quarterly,* 13(3), 1999, pp. 203–216.

11. Spencer Glendon, "Urban Life Cycles." Cambridge: Harvard University, Department of Economics, unpublished working paper, November 1998.

12. Patricia Beeson, personal communication with author, winter 2000.

13. See Richard Lloyd and Terry Nichols Clark, "The City as an Entertainment Machine," in Kevin Fox Gotham (ed.), *Critical Perspectives on Urban Redevelopment. Research in Urban Sociology,* Vol. 6. Oxford: JAI Press/Elsevier, 2001, pp. 357–378.

14. Erica Coslor, "Work Hard, Play Hard: The Role of Nightlife in Creating Dynamic Cities." Pittsburgh: Heinz School of Public Policy and Management, Carnegie Mellon University, unpublished paper, December 2001.

15. Ray Oldenburg, *The Great Good Place: Cafes, Coffee Shops, Bars, Hair Salons and Other Hangouts at the Heart of a Community.* New York: Marlowe and Company, 1989.

16. Personal interview by author, spring 2001.

17. Bonnie Menes Kahn, *Cosmopolitan Culture: The Gilt Edged Dream of a Tolerant City.* New York: Simon and Schuster, 1987.

18. Personal interview by author, winter 2001.

19. I am indebted to Lenn Kano, a former Carnegie Mellon student for this term.

20. Simon Frith, *Performing Rites: On the Value of Popular Music.* Oxford: Oxford University Press, 1996, p. 273, italics in original.

21. Manuel Castells, *The Power of Identity: The Information Age: Economy, Society, and Culture,* Volume I. Oxford: Blackwell Publishers, 1997.

22. Richard Lloyd, "Digital Bohemia: New Media Enterprises in Chicago's Wicker Park." Paper presented at the annual conference of the American Sociological Association, August 2001, p. 8.

Chapter 13

1. See the Appendix for a complete discussion of regional data sources. Kevin Stolarick, Sam Lee and Brian Knudsen assisted with this analysis.

2. See Terry Clark (ed.), *Trees and Real Violins: Building Post-Industrial Chicago: An Oral History and Global Interpretation of a Half-Century of Chicago Politics, from Mayor Daley I to Mayor Daley II.* University of Chicago, Department of Sociology, draft manuscript, 2001. In a section entitled "Yuppies: A Chicago Ethnic Group," Clark writes: "The city started from a different position than places like Washington, D.C. For instance, the term 'yuppie' (young urban professional) was popularized by a Chicago journalist to label 'outsiders' treated with hostility by a blue-collar Chicago bar crowd. 'I overheard it in a New York bar/restaurant in 1983. I used it in a column, and people soon started using the word. *Newsweek*, in a cover story, gave me credit for it. I overheard it, thought it was funny, used it in a column, and it took off from there.' . . . The same 'yuppies' would not have appeared so much as 'outsiders' in say Washington, D.C., or Berkeley, where there were fewer blue-collar bars with strong local traditions, and citizens were more educated. Chicago's specifics, in this case its strong tradition of ethnic turf and neighborhood politics, have led social issues to be redefined so as to be understandable using traditional categories. By labeling young persons who walk their dogs, read the *Wall Street Journal*, and drive fancy sports cars as an alien ethnic group, they can be treated in ways that make sense in terms of the past rules of the game. That is, smirked at if they pass your street corner, or not served in your neighborhood bar. Initially. But by 2000, Chicago was teeming with 'those people,' and resistance was disappearing."

3. The correlation coefficient between Creative Class and Working Class regions is –0.52; and for Creative Class and Service Class regions it is –0.21. Both are significant.

4. Data on per capita student populations are from *Greater Philadelphia's Knowledge Economy: Leveraging the Region's College and Universities in the New Economy.* Philadelphia: Pennsylvania Economy Leagues, Fall 2000.

5. Susan McElroy, Leon Andrews and Sheila Washington, *African Americans Choosing Allegheny County: Factors That Influence Their Decisions.* Pittsburgh: report to the Pittsburgh Foundation, October 1999.

6. Elizabeth Currid, *The Urban Elixir: Immigrants and the Growth of Cities.* Pittsburgh: Report to Grant Makers of Western Pennsylvania, June 2001.

7. The correlation between the Creative Class and innovation is 0.34, high-tech industry is 0.38, and talent is 0.64; all are significant. The correlation between it and employment growth (0.03) is significant.

8. The correlations between the Working Class and various factors are: innovation (–0.10), high-tech industry (–0.16), talent (–0.45), employment growth (–0.15) and population growth, all are negative and significant (–0.18). The correlations between the Service Class and factors are: innovation (–0.15), high-tech (–0.09), talent (0.07), employment growth (0.15) and population growth (0.11). Significance is mixed.

Chapter 14

1. See Robert Lucas, Jr., "On the Mechanics of Economic Development." *Journal of Monetary Economics*, 22, 1988, pp. 1–42; Edward Glaeser, "Are Cities Dying?" *Journal of Economic Perspectives*, 12, 1998, pp. 139–160. The human capital literature has grown large; other important contributions include: Glaeser, "The New Economics of Urban and Regional Growth," in Gordon Clark, Meric Gertler and Maryann Feldman (eds.), *The Oxford Handbook of Economic Geography.* Oxford: Oxford University Press, pp. 83–98; James E. Rauch, "Productivity Gains from Geographic Concentrations of Human Capital: Evidence from Cities." *Journal of Urban Economics*, 34, 1993, pp. 380–400; Curtis Simon, "Human Capital and Metropolitan Employment Growth." *Journal of Urban Economics*, 43, 1998, pp. 223–243;

Curtis Simon and Clark Nardinelli, "The Talk of the Town: Human Capital, Information and the Growth of English Cities, 1861–1961." *Explorations in Economic History,* 33(3), 1996, pp. 384–413; Edward Glaeser, Jose Scheinkman and Andrei Shliefer, "Economic Growth in a Cross Section of Cities." *Journal of Monetary Economics,* 36, 1995, pp. 117–143. A comprehensive review is provided by Vijay K. Mathur, "Human Capital-Based Strategy for Regional Economic Development." *Economic Development Quarterly,* 13(3), 1999, pp. 203–216.

2. John M. Quigley, "Urban Diversity and Economic Growth." *Journal of Economic Perspectives,* 12(2), Spring 1998, pp. 127–138.

3. See Jane Jacobs, *The Death and Life of Great American Cities.* New York: Random House, 1961; *The Economy of Cities.* New York: Random House, 1969; *Cities and the Wealth of Nations.* New York: Random House, 1984. Also see A. E. Andersson, "Creativity and Regional Development." *Papers of the Regional Science Association,* 56, 1985, pp. 5–20; Pierre Desrochers, "Diversity, Human Creativity, and Technological Innovation." *Growth and Change,* 32, 2001.

4. The correlation between the Talent Index and the Creative Class is 0.64, which is understandable since these occupations require high levels of education. The correlation between the Talent Index and the Working Class is –0.45. Both are significant. The point of these correlations is not that talent is more associated with certain kinds of occupations, which should be obvious, but to again stress the geographic sorting of American regions by occupation, human capital and other factors. Fifteen of the top twenty Talent regions number among the top twenty high-tech regions, while fourteen of the top twenty Talent regions rank among the top twenty most innovative regions. The statistical correlations between these two factors are again uniformly high and significant. The Pearson correlation between the Milken High-Tech Index and the Talent Index is 0.4; the Spearman rank order correlation is 0.61. The Pearson correlation between innovation and population with a college degree is 0.45; the Spearman correlation is 0.55.

5. Pascal G. Zachary, *The Global Me, New Cosmopolitans and the Competitive Edge: Picking Globalism's Winners and Losers.* New York: Perseus Books Group, PublicAffairs, 2000.

6. Steven Greenhouse, "Foreign Workers at Highest Level in Seven Decades." *New York Times,* September 4, 2000.

7. William Frey and Ross DeVol, "America's Demography in the New Century: Aging Baby Boomers and New Immigrants as Major Players." Milken Institute, March, 2000; William Frey, "The New Demographics: Race, Space, Boomer Aging." *The Brookings Review,* 18(3), Summer 2000, pp. 18–21.

8. Eric Schmitt, "Most Cities in U.S. Expanded Rapidly over the Past Decade." *New York Times,* May 7, 2001.

9. Bruce Lambert, "Forty Percent in New York City Are Foreign-Born, Study Finds." *New York Times,* July 24, 2000.

10. Annalee Saxenian, *Silicon Valley's New Immigrant Entrepreneurs.* Berkeley: Public Policy Institute of California, 1999.

11. See the following: Pam Belluck, "Short of People, Iowa Seeks to be Ellis Island of Midwest." *New York Times,* August 28, 2000; Monica Rhor, "A Philadelphia Plan Seeks Replacement People." *Philadelphia Inquirer,* May 17, 2001; Martha Moore, "Wanted: Immigrants Needed in Pittsburgh." *USA Today,* May 3, 2001.

12. The correlation between the Melting Pot Index and High-Tech Index is (0.10) and significant. For patents it is 0.007 and insignificant. The correlation with population growth is 0.28 and significant, while for employment growth it is 0.04 and insignificant.

13. The correlation between the Creative Class and the Melting Pot Index (0.10) is as insignificant as that between Talent and the Melting Pot Index (0.08).

14. Daniel Black, Gary Gates, Seth Sanders and Lowell Taylor, "Demographics of the

Gay and Lesbian Population in the United States: Evidence from Available Systematic Data Sources." *Demography,* 37(2), May 2000, pp. 139–154.

15. Bill Bishop, "Technology and Tolerance: Austin Hallmarks." *Austin American-Statesman,* June 25, 2000.

16. Several cautions must be noted regarding the census data and gays and lesbians. The data measure only individuals in same-sex unmarried partner relationships. As such, these figures do not take into account nonpartnered gays. In addition, Black and his collaborators note that the 1990 census only captured approximately 35 percent of all gay/lesbian partnerships in 1990. See Black et al., "Demographics of the Gay and Lesbian Population."

17. The Pearson correlation between the 1990 Gay Index and the High-Tech Index is 0.57, and it is 0.48 using the 2000 Gay Index. Both are significant at the 0.001 level. The Pearson correlation between the 1990 Gay Index and technological growth is 0.17, and it is 0.16 using the 2000 Gay Index. Again, both are significant at the 0.001 level. The results were similar when we ran the analysis using the Progressive Policy Institute's New Economy Index for the 46 regions for which we could match the data.

18. The growth index measures change in high-tech output within metropolitan areas from 1990 to 1998 relative to national change in output during the same period.

19. The only qualitative difference was that the Pearson correlation between percent college graduates and the High-Tech Index was slightly higher than the same correlation with the Gay Index. However, the Spearman rank order correlation with the High-Tech Index was higher for the Gay Index.

20. The correlation between the Gay Index and Creative Class regions was 0.40 in 1990 and 0.27 in 2000 (both significant), while the correlation between Working Class Centers and the Gay Index was –0.30 in 1990 and –0.26 in 2000.

21. Paul Gottlieb, *Amenity-Oriented Firm Location.* Princeton University, The Woodrow Wilson School, unpublished doctoral dissertation, January 1994; "Residential Amenities, Firm Location and Economic Development." *Urban Studies,* 32, 1995, pp. 1413–1436.

22. Dora Costa and Matthew Kahn, "Power Couples: Changes in the Locational Choice of the College Educated, 1940–1990." Cambridge: National Bureau of Economic Research, Working Paper No. 7109, May 1999.

23. See Richard Lloyd and Terry Nichols Clark, "The City as an Entertainment Machine," in Kevin Fox Gotham (ed.), *Critical Perspectives on Urban Redevelopment. Research in Urban Sociology,* Vol. 6. Oxford: JAI Press/Elsevier, 2001, pp. 357–378.

24. Edward L. Glaeser, Jed Kolko and Albert Saiz, "Consumer City." Cambridge: National Bureau of Economic Research, Working Paper No. 7790, July 2000.

25. "The Geography of Cool." *The Economist,* April 15, 2000, p. 91. Also see William Boston, "Berlin Becomes Magnet for Net Startups." *Wall Street Journal,* February 29, 2000; Sally McGrane, "Go To: Berlin." *Wired,* November 2000. Both articles report that Berlin has been successful at both generating and attracting high-tech companies because of its lifestyle offerings.

26. See Richard Florida, *Competing in the Age of Talent: Quality of Place and the New Economy.* Report to the Richard King Mellon Foundation, Pittsburgh, January 2000; "The Economic Geography of Talent. "Annals of the Association of American Geographers, 2002, forthcoming; "Bohemia and Economic Geography." *Journal of Economic Geography,* 2, 2002, pp.55–71. All are also available on my Web site at www.heinz.cmu.edu/~florida/.

27. Bohemians are positively correlated with high-tech industry (0.38), with population growth (0.28) and with employment growth (0.23). All are significant at the 0.001 level.

28. Alone, the Bohemian Index can explain nearly 38 percent of the variation in high-tech concentration. Together, the Bohemian Index and the Talent Index account for nearly 60 percent of the high-tech concentration measure.

29. One question raised by this strong connection between gays and high technology is the extent to which gays and lesbians are overrepresented in the industry. If gays and lesbians make up large fractions of this industry, then it could be that the location of high-technology firms brings about a larger concentration of gays in a region. To look at this, Gates and I analyzed 1990 census data to assess the extent to which gays and lesbians are overrepresented in some high-technology fields and industries. Gay men are about 1.3 times more likely to be scientists and engineers than the population in general. Lesbians are as likely as the rest of the population to be in these occupations. If the gay men and lesbians are combined, the result shows that they are 1.2 times more likely than the population to be scientists and engineers. We also examined those employed in the computer and data processing services industry: Gay men are 2.3 times and lesbians are 1.3 times more likely than the population to be employed in this industry. Together, gays and lesbians are 1.9 times more likely than the population to be employed in the computer services industry. While some of the correlation between gays and high technology might result from their overrepresentation in the industry, it seems difficult to explain how their overrepresentation would predict growth. To do so would be to suggest that gays and lesbians are somehow on the average more productive or entrepreneurial than their heterosexual counterparts.

30. The correlation coefficient between CDI and high-tech industry is 0.475. The Spearman rank order correlation between the Milken Tech-Pole and CDI is 0.63.

31. See Richard Florida and Sam Youl Lee, "Innovation, Human Capital, and Diversity." Paper presented at the annual conference of the Association of Public Policy and Management, Washington, D.C., November 2001.

32. George Zipf, *Human Behavior and the Principle of Least Effort.* New York: Addison–Wesley, 1949. Later the Nobel Prize winner Herbert Simon elaborated on Zipf's early findings; see Herbert Simon, "On a Class of Skew Distribution Functions." *Biometrika,* 42, 1955, pp. 425–440.

33. Masahisa Fujita, Paul Krugman and Anthony J. Venables, *The Spatial Economy: Cities, Regions and International Trade.* Cambridge: MIT Press, 1999, pp. 216–225.

34. Robert Axtell and Richard Florida, "Emergent Cities: A Microeconomic Explanation." Washington, D.C.: Brookings Institution, April 2001.

Chapter 15

1. Robert Putnam, *Bowling Alone: The Collapse and Revival of American Community.* New York: Simon and Schuster, 2000. Also see "The Prosperous Community." *The American Prospect,* Spring 1993; and "The Strange Disappearance of Civic America." *The American Prospect,* Winter 1996.

2. Emile Durkheim, *Suicide: A Study in Sociology (1897)*; Pierre Bourdieu, "The Forms of Capital" (1983), in John Richardson, ed., *Handbook of Theory and Research for the Sociology of Education.* New York: Greenwood Press, 1986, pp.241–258; George Hohmans, *Social Behavior: Its Elementary Forms.* New York: Harcourt Brace and World, 1961; James Coleman, "Social Capital in the Creation of Human Capital." *American Journal of Sociology,* 94, 1988, pp. S95–S120; Coleman, *The Foundations of Social Theory.* Cambridge: Harvard University Press, 1990; Ronald S. Burt, *Structural Holes: The Social Structure of Competition.* Cambridge: Harvard University Press, 1992; "The Contingent Value of Social Capital." *Administrative Science Quarterly,* 42, 1997, pp. 339–365. For a broad review of the concept, see Michael Woolcock, "Social Capital and Economic Development: Toward a Theoretical Synthesis and Policy Framework." *Theory and Society,* 27, 1998, pp. 151–208; and Alejandro

Portes, "Social Capital: Its Origins and Applications in Modern Sociology." *Annual Review of Sociology,* 22, 1998, pp. 1–24.

3. Nicholas Lemann, "Kicking in Groups." *The Atlantic Monthly,* April 1996; also available on-line at www/theatlanticmonthly.com/issues/96apr/kicking/kicking.htm.

4. Dora Costa and Matthew Kahn, "Understanding the Decline in Social Capital, 1952–1998." Cambridge: National Bureau of Economic Research, Working Paper No. 8295, 2001.

5. *Social Capital Community Benchmark Survey: Executive Summary,* prepared by the Saguaro Seminar: Civic Engagement Project in America. Cambridge: John F. Kennedy School of Government, Harvard University, 2001, p. 7.

6. James Koch, Ross Miller, Kim Wallesh and Elizabeth Brown, *Building Community: Social Connections and Civic Involvement in Silicon Valley, Preliminary Findings Report.* Santa Clara, Calif.: Santa Clara University and Collaborative Economics, February 2001.

7. Alejandro Portes and Patricia Landout, "Unsolved Mysteries: The Tocqueville Files II." *The American Prospect,* 7, May 26, 1996; also available on-line at www.prospect.org/print-friendly/print/V726/26-cnt-2.html, p. 4.

8. Adam Smith, *An Inquiry into the Nature and Causes of the Wealth of Nations.* Edinburgh: 1776, Book One, Chapter X, Part 2, entire text on-line at The Adam Smith Institute, www.adamsmith.org.uk.

9. Mancur Olson, *The Rise and Decline of Nations: Economic Growth, Stagflation, and Social Rigidities.* New Haven: Yale University Press, 1986; *The Logic of Collective Action: Public Goods and the Theory of Groups.* Cambridge: Harvard University Press, 1971.

10. Kay Miller, "Breaking in Is Hard To Do." *Minneapolis Star Tribune,* October 4, 2000.

11. Portes and Landout, "Unsolved Mysteries," p. 4.

12. Sometimes, I think, Putnam's social capital world bears a bit of similarity to the fictional town of Zenith in of Sinclair Lewis's *Babbitt*—a conformist world where clubs and voluntary organizations were less the product of civic-mindedness and more about getting ahead and securing status. Writes Lewis: "Of a decent man in Zenith it was required that he should belong to one, or preferably two or three, of the numerous lodges and prosperity-boosting lunch-clubs; to the Rotarians, the Kiwanis, or the Boosters; to the Oddfellows, Moose, Masons, Red Men, Woodmen, Owls, Eagles, Maccabees, Knights of Pythias, Knights of Columbus, and other secret orders characterized by a high degree of heartiness, sound morals and reverence to the Constitution." Sinclair Lewis, *Babbitt.* New York: Harcourt, Brace and World, 1922.

13. See Robert Cushing, "Creative Capital, Diversity and Urban Growth." Unpublished manuscript, Austin, Texas, December 2001.

14. See Mark Granovetter, *Getting a Job: A Study of Contacts and Careers.* Cambridge: Harvard University Press, 1974; "Economic Action and Social Structure: The Problem of Embeddedness." *American Journal of Sociology,* 91(3), November 1884, pp. 481–510; "The Nature of Economic Relationships," in Richard Swedberg (ed.), *Explorations in Economic Sociology.* New York: Russell Sage Foundation, pp. 3–41; "A Theoretical Agenda for Economic Sociology," in Mauro Guillen, Randall Collins, Paula England and Marshall Meyer (eds.), *New Directions in Sociology.* New York: Russell Sage Foundation, 2002. Also see Peter Marsden and Karen Campbell, "Measuring Tie Strength." *Social Forces,* 63(2), December 1984, pp. 482–501.

15. See Brian Uzzi, "Social Structure and Competition in Interfirm Networks: The Paradox of Embeddedness." *Administrative Science Quarterly,* 42, 1997, pp. 35–67, for an exposition of the ways that social ties affect innovation and risk taking.

16. Jane Jacobs, *The Death and Life of Great American Cities.* New York: Random House, 1961; quote as in the 1993 Modern Library edition, p. 180–182.

17. Their contributions are succinctly outlined in the classic article by Louis Wirth, "Urbanism as a Way of Life." *American Journal of Sociology,* 44, July 1, 1938, pp. 1–24.

18. Walter Benjamin, *The Arcades Project.* Cambridge: Harvard University Press, 2000, translated by Howard Eiland and Kevin McLaughlin.

19. Cesar Graña, *Bohemian and Bourgeois.* New York: Basic Books, 1964, pp. 135–136; also expanded and reissued as *Modernity and Its Discontents: French Society and the French Man of Letters in the Nineteenth Century.* New York: Harper Torchbooks, 1967.

20. See Carolyn Ware, *Greenwich Village, 1920–1930.* Berkeley: University of California Press, 1963 (orig. 1935).

21. Ware, *Greenwich Village, 1920–1930,* p. 5.

22. Ware, *Greenwich Village, 1920–1930,* p. 237.

23. Ware, *Greenwich Village, 1920–1930,* p. 238.

24. Robert Park, E. Burgess and R. McKenzie, *The City.* Chicago: University of Chicago Press, 1925.

25. Park, Burgess and McKenzie, *The City,* p. 40.

26. Park, Burgess and McKenzie, *The City,* p. 40.

27. Park, Burgess and McKenzie, *The City,* p. 41.

28. William H. Whyte, Jr., *The Organization Man.* New York: Simon and Schuster, 1956.

Chapter 16

1. Peter Loftus, "Location, Location, Location." *Wall Street Journal,* October 15, 2001, p. R14.

2. As quoted in Scott Kitsner, "Seattle Reboots Its Future." *Fast Company*, May 2001, p. 44.

3. Uri Cummings as quoted in Loftus, "Location, Location, Location," p. R14.

4. Personal communication, Fall 2001.

5. Joel Kotkin, "The High-Tech South Part II: Raleigh Durham—The South's Answer to Silicon Valley?" Reis.com, January 10, 2001.

6. Edmund Sanders and P. J. Huffstutter, "Dreams of High-Tech Glory Passing Orange County By." *Los Angeles Times,* July 9, 2000; Joel Kotkin, "Orange County: The Fate of a Post-Suburban Paradise." LaJolla, Calif.: LaJolla Institute, October 2000; available at www.lajollainstitute.org.

7. George Gilder, *Microcosm: The Quantum Revolution in Economics and Technology.* New York: Touchstone, 1990.

8. Joel Garreau, *Edge City: Life on the New Frontier.* New York: Doubleday & Company, 1991.

9. On Oakland's turnaround, see Joel Kotkin, "Grass-Roots Business: The City by the Bay? To Them, It's Oakland." *New York Times,* February 18, 2001.

10. Timothy Egan, "Urban Mayors Share the (Not Unwelcome) Burden of Coping with Prosperity," *New York Times,* June 13, 2000.

11. Rebecca R. Sohmer and Robert E. Lang, "Downtown Rebound." Washington, D.C.: Fannie Mae Foundation and Brookings Institution Center on Urban and Metropolitan Policy Center Note, May 2001.

12. The Sohmer and Lang data set covers only a small sample of cities, and Gates and I could only match twenty-one cities to our data. We ran the analyses for two measures of downtown growth: percent change in downtown population and change in percent of the population living downtown. The correlation between the CDI and percent downtown population is 0.52 and for change in downtown share is 0.46. The Gay Index is correlated

with percent downtown population at 0.48 and change in downtown share at 0.39. The Bohemian Index is correlated with percent downtown at 0.54 and change in downtown share at 0.35. The Milken High-Tech Index is correlated with percent downtown at 0.50 and downtown share at 0.30. All are statistically significant.

13. *The State of the Cities 2000.* Washington, D.C.: U.S. Department of Housing and Urban Development, June 2000. High-tech jobs made up 9.2 percent of all city jobs compared to 9.3 percent for the suburbs. Suburbs experienced a faster rate of high-tech job growth: 34.7 versus 26.7 percent for cities.

14. Paul Sommers and Daniel Carlson, "The New Society in Metropolitan Seattle: High Tech Firm Location Decisions Within the Metropolitan Landscape." Washington, D.C.: Brookings Institution, May 2000.

15. On gentrification see Neil Smith, *The New Urban Frontier: Gentrification and the Revanchist City.* London: Routledge, 1996.

16. Evelyn Nieves, "Many in Silicon Valley Cannot Afford Housing Even at $50,000 a Year." *New York Times,* February 20, 2000. Also see John Riter, "Priced Out of Silicon Valley." *USA Today,* May 18, 2000; "The California Housing Market: Squeezed Out." *The Economist,* July 22, 2000.

17. Nieves, "Many in Silicon Valley."

18. Rebecca Solnit and Susan Schwartzenberg, *Hollow City: The Siege of San Francisco and the Crisis of American Urbanism.* New York: Verso, 2000. On San Francisco's history, also see Richard Walker, "Landscape and City Life: Four Ecologies of Residence in the San Francisco Bay Area." *Ecumene,* 2(1), 1995, pp. 33–64.

19. See Bill Hayes, "Artists vs. Dotcoms: Fighting San Francisco's Gold Rush." *New York Times,* December 14, 2000. Also see the detailed coverage in the *San Francisco Gate* at www.sfgate.com.

20. See Lori Weisberg and Susan Gembrowski, "Planners Say It Takes Villages to Grow a City." *San Diego Union Tribune,* January 6, 2002.

21. I have been involved in consulting efforts in each of these cities.

22. Between 1990 and 2000, San Francisco was the only U.S. city to lose children while adding population. Over this period, the city lost 4,100 children, as the share of the city's population under eighteen years of age dropped from 16.1 percent to 14.5 percent. Nearly a quarter of San Franciscans are between twenty-five and thirty-four, an age group that grew 14 percent during the 1990s.

23. This section draws from personal interviews conducted by the author between 1992 and 2001, particularly ongoing conversations with Mayor Kirk Watson and reporter Bill Bishop of the *Austin American-Statesman.* See Bob Walker's story in the October 2000 issue of *Money Magazine,* pp. 109–114; and the insightful reporting of Bishop and his colleagues: Dylan Rivera and Bill Bishop, "High-Tech Companies Leading the Charge Downtown." *Austin American-Statesman,* March 3, 2000; Bishop, "What Is Austin Becoming?" *Austin American–Statesman,* May 9, 2000; Bishop, "Austin Wants to Be Austin: Austin Doesn't Want to Be Silicon Valley." *Austin American-Statesmen,* February 26, 2000.

24. Kirk Ladendorf and Leah Quinn, "Vignette Seeks New Digs Because It Digs Downtown." *Austin American-Statesman,* August 29, 2000.

25. My discussion of Ireland draws heavily from conversations with Anita Sands, a former Carnegie Mellon graduate student who is now my colleague in the Software Center. See Anita Sands, *Ireland and the 3Ts: Technology, Talent and Tolerance.* Pittsburgh: Carnegie Mellon, Heinz School of Public Policy and Management, unpublished paper, December 2001. Also see "From Backwater to Boomtown: Dublin Is a Magnet for Technology and Young People." *New York Times,* October 31, 2000.

26. Florence Williams, "Dublin: Now Fair and Worldly." *New York Times*, October 12, 2000.

27. See John Seigfried and Andrew Zimbalist, "The Economics of Sports Facilities and Their Communities." *Journal of Economic Perspectives*, 14(3), Summer 2000, pp. 95–114.

28. Mancur Olson, *The Rise and Decline of Nations: Economic Growth, Stagflation, and Social Rigidities*. New Haven: Yale University Press, 1986; *The Logic of Collective Action: Public Goods and the Theory of Groups*. Cambridge: Harvard University Press, 1971; "Big Bills Left on the Sidewalk: Why Some Nations Are Rich, and Others Poor." *Journal of Economic Perspectives*, 10(2), 1996, pp. 2–24; also see Jonathan Rauch, *Demosclerosis: The Silent Killer of American Government*. New York: Crown Publishing Group, 1994.

29. Mark Samber, *Networks of Capital: Creating and Maintaining a Regional Industrial Economy in Pittsburgh, 1865–1919*. Pittsburgh: Carnegie Mellon University, Department of History, doctoral dissertation, 1995.

30. See Edward Wiedlein, "Pittsburgh as Research Center." *Journal of Engineering Education*, 49(8), April 1959, pp. 661–664. Wiedlein was a former president of the Mellon Institute.

31. Mike Vargo, "Up Against the Future." *Pennsylvania Illustrated*, February 1980, pp. 26–27.

32. Benjamin Chinitz, "Contrasts in Agglomeration: New York and Pittsburgh." *The American Economic Review*, 51(2), May 1961, pp. 279–289; quote is from pp. 284–285.

33. Personal interview by author, Fall 2001.

34. Ralph Bangs et al., *State of the Region Report: Economic, Demographic and Social Conditions in Southwestern Pennsylvania*. Pittsburgh: University of Pittsburgh, University Center for Urban and Social Research, 1999.

Chapter 17

1. Paulina Borsook, *Cyberselfish: A Critical Romp Through the Terribly Libertarian Culture of High Tech*. New York: Perseus Books/PublicAffairs, 2000.

2. Mancur Olson, *The Logic of Collective Action: Public Goods and the Theory of Groups*. Cambridge: Harvard University Press, 1965.

3. Employment Policy Foundation, "Changing U.S. Economy Places Emphasis on Education and Skills." Washington, D.C.: Employment Policy Foundation, September 2001.

4. Joel Mokyr, *The Lever of Riches: Technological Creativity and Economic Progress*. New York: Oxford University Press, 1990.

5. Paul Romer, "Economic Growth," in David R. Henderson (ed.), *The Fortune Encyclopedia of Economics*. New York: Time Warner Books, 1993.

6. Keynes quote from the economist Brad DeLong's web page at http://econ161.berkeley.edu/Economists/keynes.html.

7. A review of these studies is provided in John Seigfried and Andrew Zimbalist, "The Economics of Sports Facilities and Their Communities." *Journal of Economic Perspectives*, 14(3), Summer 2000, pp. 95–114.

8. Robert Frank and Philip Cook, *The Winner-Take-All-Society*. New York: Martin Kessler Books at The Free Press, 1995.

9. Charles Murray, *Losing Ground: American Social Policy, 1950–1980*. New York: Basic Books, 1984.

10. William Julius Wilson, *The Truly Disadvantaged: The Inner City, the Underclass and*

Public Policy. Chicago: University of Chicago Press, 1989; and *When Work Disappears: The World of the New Urban Poor.* New York: Alfred A. Knopf, 1996.

11. Barbara Ehrenreich, *Nickel and Dimed: On Not Getting By in America.* New York: Henry Holt & Company, 2001.

12. Robert Putnam, *Bowling Alone: The Collapse and Revival of American Community.* New York: Simon and Schuster, 2000.

13. See Jane Jacobs, *The Death and Life of Great American Cities.* New York: Random House, 1961.

ACKNOWLEDGMENTS

Like any creative project, this book is the product of extensive and fruitful collaboration. It has benefited enormously from the efforts of a top-flight research team. Gary Gates of the Urban Institute developed the Gay Index and collaborated on much of the regional analysis. Kevin Stolarick of Carnegie Mellon collaborated on the initial definition and analysis of the Creative Class and the changing American class structure, as well as on the analysis of the *Information Week* Salary Survey data. Two doctoral students at Carnegie Mellon's Heinz School helped immensely with the statistical analysis: Sam Youl Lee was integrally involved in the regional data analysis, while Brian Knudsen developed historical statistics on the classes and participated in the regional analysis. Elizabeth Currid, a graduate student at Carnegie Mellon, worked closely with me preparing an initial outline and early draft of this book. Each of them has my personal thanks for the energy, hard work and intelligence they contributed to this project.

Bill Frucht, my editor at Basic Books, supported this effort in innumerable ways, working closely with me on its core ideas, scope and structure, as well as providing a deft hand in tightening and improving the writing. Mike Vargo, an accomplished journalist and gifted writer, worked side-by-side with me for more than a year on the writing, structure, concepts and overall approach to this book. They have been partners in this enterprise: Mere words cannot express my appreciation for their commitment, intelligence and tireless effort.

My agent Susan Schulman believed in this project from the outset, was a constant source of energy, ideas and encouragement, and worked astutely to find just the right editor and publisher. I thank Bill Morris for introducing me to Susan. I am grateful to the team affiliated with Basic Books for their commitment to the book, especially John Donatich, Jamie Brickhouse, Matty Goldberg, John Hughes, Elizabeth Maguire, Christine Marra, Vanessa Mobley, Joanna Pinkser and Elizabeth Tzetzo.

Diane O'Toole supported many aspects of this project, providing insightful comments as well as scheduling interviews, proofreading drafts and producing tables, charts and text.

Several others worked diligently on the project. At Carnegie Mellon, Derek Davison assisted with the research reported in Competing in the Age of Talent; Anita Sands prepared a major study of Dublin; Erica Coslor conducted a study of nightlife; Guillermo Dabos provided insights on the management of creative work; Matt Cline and Ji Yoon Woong assisted with various aspects of data collection and analysis; Irene Tinagli assisted with research on Europe; Sophie Forbes, Sarah Gross, Thomas Link, Beth Newman and Nicole Tichon assisted with aspects of the project. Matt Fleckenstein and Yvonne Campos of Campos Research Associates conducted some of the early focus groups. I thank them all. A special debt of gratitude goes to the people who took time from their busy schedules to participate in field research, personal interviews and focus groups.

Two people have conducted independent research to test the propositions advanced in this book. Robert Axtell of the Brookings Institution developed an ingenious adaptive agent model of city formation based on the basic notion of the clustering of talented and creative people. Robert Cushing of the University of Texas at Austin developed statistical tests of my theory against other leading theories of regional growth.

Projects as extensive as this one require generous and patient funders and I have been fortunate to have them. The Alfred P. Sloan Foundation has generously supported my work over the past decade. The Heinz Endowments and Richard King Mellon Foundation supported my initial research on lifestyle amenities and regional growth. The Pennsylvania Technology Investment Authority and other sponsors provided additional support through the Software Center at Carnegie Mellon University.

Carnegie Mellon provided the immediate social structure of creativity for this project; a uniquely stimulating environment in which to develop and test ideas. My colleagues across campus encourage sharp thinking through a rare combination of collegiality and critical intelligence. I would especially like to thank Ashish Arora, Wesley Cohen, Jeffrey Hunker, Mark Kamlet, David Hounshell, David Lewis, Susan McElroy, Denise Rousseau, Katherine Shaw, Mary Shaw and Joel Tarr. I also benefited from a two-year sabbatical at Harvard's Kennedy School of Government and at MIT, during which I began developing the initial ideas for this book. My colleagues at *Information Week*, especially Bob Evans, Brian Gillooly and Rusty Weston, have always been supportive, and I thank them for allowing me access to their survey data.

I also appreciate and have drawn upon the insights and work of many others along the way—especially Lewis Branscomb, Harvey Brooks, Michael Camp, Gordon Clark, Terry Clark, Hirsh Cohen, Meric Gertler, Gary Gerreffi, Paul Gottlieb, Martin Kenney, Terry Lumish, Frank Mayadas, Heather Munroe-Blum, Gail Pesyna, Patricia Thornton, Richard Walker and David Wolfe.

Many professional associates and friends in Pittsburgh have not only influenced my thinking but helped make this a more stimulating place to live and work. In particular, I'd like to thank: Deb Baron, David Black, Ellsworth Brown, Melisa Crawford, Christy Cunningham, Caren Glotfelty, Court Gould, Scott Izzo,

Bob Hurley, Max King, Andre Heinz, Jeffrey Lewis, Mandara Meyers, Lou Musante, Tom Sokolowski, Kyra Straussman and Mike Watson.

Special thanks are due Bill Bishop, Donald Carter, Michelle Gittleman, Andrew Haupt and Anne-Marie Lubenau for reading and commenting on various parts of the book.

My interactions with insightful professionals at organizations like the International Downtown Association, International Economic Development Council, National Governors Association and National League of Cities, to name just a few, have contributed a great deal to this work. During the course of this project, I have also been invited to many cities and regions to speak, consult or conduct research. I extend my personal thanks to my hosts and audiences in Austin, Boise, Baltimore, Bellevue, Grand Rapids, Houston, Kansas City, Memphis, Milwaukee, Minneapolis, New Haven, New York, Ottawa, Quebec City, Philadelphia, Phoenix, Providence, Toronto and many others. Appreciation is due to the outstanding business leaders, political officials and economic development professionals I have come to know during this project. While it is impossible to name them all, I am especially grateful to Kip Bergstrom, Dave Feehan, Sam Katz, Tim McNulty, Tom Ridge, Bill Scranton, John Thomasian, Kirk Watson, Rick Weddle and Robert Yaro.

My brother, Robert, and sister-in-law, Virginia Daut, talented writers themselves, offered ideas and comments on this project. On my visits to their home in Hoboken, they afforded me the incomparable joy of watching their two children, my niece, Sophia, and nephew, Luca, come into this world and grow.

Finally, I would like to express my special thanks to Elizabeth Taaffe for her intelligence and insight as well as her unswerving support throughout this entire process.

INDEX

All statistics are for the United States unless indicated otherwise.

African-Americans: high-tech firms and, 80; Pittsburgh, 313

Agriculture, 57–59, 329; employment and earnings estimates, 330(table); farming workforce percentages, 332(table); metropolitan vs. national data, 333(table)

Allegheny Conference on Community Development (Pittsburgh), 307, 310

Allen, Paul, 206, 208

Allen, Thomas, 124–125

Amabile, Teresa, 34

Amazon.com, 289

America: Creative Class population, 9; free agent infrastructure, 107; heroes in literature, 207; material life of the working class, 170, 371(n10); the New Economy and the September 11 tragedy, 12. *See also* Society; United States

American Compensation Association, 97

American Moderns (Stansell), 195

American Research and Development (ARD), 50

Americans' Use of Time Project, 146; free time, 172; housewives, 151

Anderson, Ruth, 81

Architecture, older buildings, 123–124

Aronowitz, Stanley, 108

Arora, Ashish, 355 (n14)

Art: appearance as, 179–180; vs. mass marketing of alternative culture, 201. *See also* Bohemians

Artists: computers and, 209; front-loaded careers, 155; performance, 156–159, 176–177

Atlantic Monthly, The, 134, 199

Austin, 72, 217, 285, 298–300

Austin 360 Summit, 190–191

Authenticity: community value and, 228, 230–231; vs. mass marketing, 187

Automotive industry: emergence of the assembly line and, 63–64; global suppliers and, 54–55

Axtell, Robert, 265

Banana Republic, 118

Barley, Stephen, 70, 72, 113–114

Barney's, 119

Batt, Rosemary, 107, 114

Baudelaire, Charles, 179–180, 193, 278

Bear Stearns, 175

Beatty, Jack, 134

Beauty, 194; and animated intellectual suspension, 195

Beeson, Patricia, 222

Bell, Daniel, 196–197

Bell Labs, 139

Bicycling, 173–174, 181–182

Bill Gates Wealth Index, 151–152

Black, Dan, 255

Blacks: high-tech firms and, 80; Pittsburgh, 313

Blake, William, 193

Blick, Julie, 170

Bobos (bourgeoisie-bohemian), 210; children of, 199; restaurants and, 198

Bobos in Paradise (Brooks), 13, 197,199

Boden, Margaret, 31, 32–33, 33–34

387